THE AESTHETICS OF DARKNESS

HELLENISTICA GRONINGANA

1. **M.A. Harder, R.F. Regtuit, G.C. Wakker,** *Callimachus*, 1993.
2. **M.A. Harder, R.F. Regtuit, G.C. Wakker,** *Theocritus*, 1996.
3. **M.A. Harder, R.F. Regtuit, G.C. Wakker,** *Genre in Hellenistic Poetry*, 1998.
4. **M.A. Harder, R.F. Regtuit, G.C. Wakker,** *Apollonius Rhodius*, 2000.
5. **L. Rossi,** *The Epigrams Ascribed to Theocritus: A Method of Approach*, 2001.
6. **M.A. Harder, R.F. Regtuit, G.C. Wakker,** *Hellenistic Epigrams*, 2002.
7. **M.A. Harder, R.F. Regtuit, G.C. Wakker,** *Callimachus II*, 2004.
8. **G. Berkowitz,** *Semi-Public Narration in Apollonius' Argonautica*, 2004.
9. **A. Ambühl,** *Kinder und junge Helden. Innovative Aspekte des Umgangs mit der literarischen Tradition bei Kallimachos*, 2005.
10. **J.S. Bruss,** *Hidden Presences. Monuments, Gravesites, and Corpses in Greek Funerary Epigram*, 2005.
11. **M.A. Harder, R.F. Regtuit, G.C. Wakker,** *Beyond the Canon*, 2006.
12. **É. Prioux,** *Regards alexandrins. Histoire et théorie des arts dans l'épigramme hellénistique*, 2007.
13. **M.A. Tueller,** *Look Who's Talking: Innovations in Voice and Identity in Hellenistic Epigram*, 2008.
14. **E. Sistakou,** *Reconstructing the Epic. Cross-Readings of the Trojan Myth in Hellenistic Poetry*, 2008.
15. **M.A. Harder, R.F. Regtuit, G.C. Wakker,** *Nature and Science in Hellenistic Poetry*, 2009.
16. **M.A. Harder, R.F. Regtuit, G.C. Wakker,** *Gods and Religion in Hellenistic Poetry*, 2009.

HELLENISTICA GRONINGANA 17

THE AESTHETICS OF DARKNESS

A STUDY OF HELLENISTIC ROMANTICISM IN APOLLONIUS, LYCOPHRON AND NICANDER

Evina SISTAKOU

PEETERS

LEUVEN – PARIS – WALPOLE, MA

2012

A catalogue record for this book is available from the Library of Congress.

© 2012 – Peeters – Bondgenotenlaan 153 – B-3000 Leuven – Belgium

ISBN 978-90-429-2654-7
D/2012/0602/124

To Antonios Rengakos
teacher and friend

TABLE OF CONTENTS

ACKNOWLEDGEMENTS

The first time I ever attempted to read Lycophron's *Alexandra*, Gothic aesthetics flashed through my mind; the *Argonautica* of Apollonius Rhodius had already fascinated me with its dark story, characters and settings; and I have always been wondering why Nicander chose to write on such an appalling subject matter as snakes and poisons, until I realized that the aesthetic effect was much more powerful than any actual 'meaning' in his poetry. It occurred to me that these poets, along with Euphorion, Moschus and Parthenius, strike an un-Callimachean tone. *Could we probably gain an insight into their aesthetics by reviewing them in the light of European Romanticism?*

Annette Harder warmly embraced this 'Romantic' reading of Hellenistic poetry in our discussions during the Groningen Workshops. And, upon the completion of *The Aesthetics of Darkness*, she welcomed (for a second time) the publication of my study in the *Hellenistica Groningana* series. I am truly grateful for both.

Teachers, colleagues and friends contributed in crucial ways to the making of this book. I owe a deep debt of gratitude to Daniel Jakob, not least because he helped me establish the theoretical framework of my study. My mentor, Michalis Kopidakis, pointed out to me some of the most fascinating parallels from Archaic and Classical literature. Richard Hunter has reviewed a great deal of the first draft, and his sharp eye rescued me from factual errors. Heartfelt thanks go to David Konstan, not only for reading through the entire manuscript but first and foremost for his incredible generosity to share his views on aesthetics with me. Yannick Durbec has substantially contributed with bibliography and critical remarks. Floris Overduin facilitated my work by sending me a copy of his dissertation on Nicandrean poetics.

I am greatly indebted to Peeters, for once more publishing my book, and especially to Remco Regtuit for helping me throughout the editorial process.

Before closing I need to express a special thanks to Antonios Rengakos who has supported and encouraged me during the last 15 years. If he deserves an extra credit on this occasion, it is for fervently believing in the idea of Hellenistic darkness in the first place. As a small token of gratitude I dedicate this book to him.

NOTE

* Greek quotations are always followed by a translation. Translations inserted in the main body of the text as quotations (i.e. without being accompanied by the Greek original) are marked as italics.

* I have used the following translations, with slight modifications, for Apollonius' *Argonautica*, Lycophron's *Alexandra* and Nicander's *Theriaca* and *Alexipharmaca*:

APOLLONIUS *Argonautica*: R. Hunter. 1998 [1993]. *Apollonius of Rhodes. Jason and the Golden Fleece*. Oxford: Oxford University Press.

LYCOPHRON *Alexandra*: A.W. Mair / G.R. Mair. 1921. *Callimachus, Hymns and Epigrams. Lycophron. Aratus*. London: Heinemann (with modifications and some alterations after G.W. Mooney. 1988 [1921]. *The* Alexandra *of Lycophron*. New Hampshire: Ayer Company, Publishers.)

NICANDER *Theriaca* and *Alexipharmaca*: A.S.F. Gow / A.F. Scholfield 1997 [1953]. *Nicander. The Poems and Poetical Fragments*. London: Bristol Classical Press.

* Unless otherwise noted, translations of brief excerpts from other Greek authors are mine.

CHARTING DARKNESS

INTRODUCTION

It lieth, gazing on the midnight sky,
Upon the cloudy mountain-peak supine;
Below, far lands are seen tremblingly;
Its horror and its beauty are divine.
Upon its lips and eyelids seems to lie
Loveliness like a shadow, from which shine,
Fiery and lurid, struggling underneath,
The agonies of anguish and of death.
Yet it is less the horror than the grace
Which turns the gazer's spirit into stone,
Whereon the lineaments of that dead face
Are graven, till the characters be grown
Into itself, and thought no more can trace;
'Tis the melodious hue of beauty thrown
Athwart the darkness and the glare of pain,
Which humanize and harmonize the strain.

Percy Shelley *On the Medusa of Leonardo da Vinci* (1819)

The blending of eroticism and horror, pleasure and pain, beauty and death, so peculiarly 'Romantic' in its essence, is the subject of the masterly treatise on 19th century European literature by Mario Praz. His 1933 book emphatically entitled *The Romantic Agony* opens with a chapter on the image of the Medusa–"this glassy-eyed, severed female head, this horrible, fascinating Medusa, that was to be the object of the dark loves of the Romantics and the Decadents throughout the whole of the century"[1]–as portrayed by Percy Shelley in his 1819 poem 'On the Medusa of Leonardo da Vinci'[2]. Praz then goes on to summarize the aesthetics behind Shelley's poem as follows: "The discovery of Horror as a source of delight and beauty ended by reacting on men's actual conception of beauty itself: the Horrid, from being a category of the Beautiful, ended by becoming one of its essential elements, and the 'beautifully horrid' passed by insensible degrees into the 'horribly

---

1. Praz (1970) 26; cf. ibid. pp. 23-52 on the idea that the horrible 'Beauty of the Medusa' epitomizes the notion of Romantic darkness. See also Wilk (2000) 200 who observes that "from the late eighteenth century until the end of the nineteenth, she [i.e. Medusa] was a frequently used symbol of the Romantics, who saw her as the Dark Lady, a manifestation of Death".

2. On Shelley's *ekphrasis* of Medusa, the questions about viewing terror as posed by the poem, along with its psychoanalytical and political implications, see Jacobs (1985), Mitchell (1994) 151-181 and Scott (1996).

beautiful'"[3]. Examples may be easily multiplied, as one thinks of Lord Byron, Mary Shelley, Edgar Allan Poe, Charles Baudelaire, Oscar Wilde, to quote only a few representatives of the Romantic agony. From this perspective, 18th and 19th century literature may be viewed as an experimentation with the potential of monstrosity, horror, death, or the *passions mauvaises*, the evil passions of man, to become the source of aesthetic pleasure. The present study is largely inspired by this and similar readings of Romantic and Decadent aesthetics, for which I have employed the notion of *darkness*–though applying it to a quite unexpected target literature, namely Hellenistic poetry. Being aware that attempting such an anachronism verges on the unacceptable, for conventional scholarship at least, I have nevertheless decided to succumb to the allure of the idea itself: that 'Romanticism', stripped off its historical context, shares certain features with the aesthetics of the Hellenistic era; that 'Hellenistic Romanticism' runs counter to Callimachus' aesthetics; that its distinguishing feature is what I have termed *darkness*; and that at least some Hellenistic authors may be read against the backdrop of this dark aesthetics. But before elaborating on the centre of this study, the notion of darkness, I will roughly sketch out its periphery, the comparison between Romantic and Hellenistic aesthetics.

Hellenistic Romanticism?

The succession of movements in European culture, such as the transition from Medieval to Renaissance aesthetics, or from Neoclassicism to Romanticism, has both a historical and an artistic aspect. One of the stereotypical conceptions of the 'Romantic', inspired by this scheme, is exactly its polarity with the 'Classical', the latter denoting a balance between opposing forces in art and aesthetics, whereas the former suggests the disturbance of this balance[4]. This polarity is multifaceted–sentimental vs. naive, imagination vs. reason, revolutionarism vs. conservativism, originally creative vs. bound by strict rules, inspiration vs. poetic craftmanship[5]. Can we project these distinctions onto ancient Greek literature?

---

3. Praz (1970) 27.

4. That this antithesis is as old as European literature itself (including Greece and Rome) is convincingly argued by Walter Pater in his 1889 essay "On Classical and Romantic" (in Gleckner/Enscoe [1962]).

5. For an overview of this somewhat 'passé' distinction, see Praz (1970) 1-22 and the collected essays of various thinkers (W. Pater, H. Grierson, T. Hulme etc.) in Gleckner/Enscoe (1962). That these antithetical notions form the basis of Romanticism, which is viewed as a general tendency towards innovation and modernity, is shown by de Paz (2000) 29-48.

Viewing ancient literary history from a modern standpoint suggests distinguishing between three main phases from its beginnings until the imperial period, namely the Archaic, the Classical and the Hellenistic. Although this periodization is historically defined (as said, from a modern standpoint), and despite the fact that within each phase there are essential differences as regards the genres, the trends, and the authors themselves, we sense that each one of them corresponds to a particular aesthetics[6]. The Hellenistic age, broadly defined as an age of artistic innovation and reaction to the literary past–even though the exact proportion of the avant-garde to the traditional in it is still open to dispute–, experienced its own revolution against the 'Classical' (and the 'Classicist', if we thus characterize the imitators of the Classical)[7]. It is well-known that, after Aristotle had introduced a retrospective view of literature in his *Poetics*, the Alexandrian scholars compiled the canons, i.e. the lists of 'Classical' authors for each literary genre, thus asserting the meta-Classical character of their epoch[8]. Given that from the early Alexandrian era, the *poetae docti* were acutely aware of their epigonality, we may argue that the Hellenistic aesthetics is a 'Romantic' reaction to canonical viz 'Classical' literature[9].

But can Romanticism be more accurately defined? Most literary critics would reply in the negative[10]. As a vague term deriving from the word *romance* (a narrative genre of Medieval provenance dealing with a story of adventure and love), *Romanticism* was initially understood as a turn towards the remote past, and, by extension, as a preference for the bizarre, the imaginary and the magical[11]. It is important to note that the Medieval and Renaissance romance evolved as a response to historical epic by emphasizing the fantastic element in storytelling on the one hand, and love on the other[12]. There are obvious analogies here with Hellenistic

6. On the stereotypes accompanying this periodization, see Hunter (2008b) 10-16.

7. The most recent claim that Hellenistic poetry has developed within the framework of past literature and that there is no "epigonal nostalgia" nor "classicising enthusiasm" in the way Hellenistic poems explored and reconstructed the literary past is found in Fantuzzi/Hunter (2004), esp. pp. vii-viii and 1-41.

8. Pfeiffer (1968) e.g. 87-104 records the various phases of this process.

9. According to an older view supported by Wimmel (1965) 63-68, it was a crisis in 4th century poetry that had led to the formation of a new Hellenistic aesthetics; cf. the critical response to this hypothesis by Henrichs (1993).

10. The *locus classicus* in scholarship is A. Lovejoy's essay "On the Discrimination of Romanticisms" (1924) who, in arguing that "the word 'Romantic' has come to mean so many things that, by itself, it means nothing", denies hypostasis to a general, unified movement of Romanticism; the contrary view of defending 'Romanticism' was taken by R. Wellek in 1949: both essays in Gleckner/Enscoe (1962).

11. See e.g. Roe (2005) and Kucich (2005).

12. The antithesis between epic and romance explains in many ways the emergence of a Romantic mood in literature: on this long-standing question, see Ker (1908).

6 THE AESTHETICS OF DARKNESS

poetics, especially if we consider its archaicizing thematics and tone, the rewriting of myth under the perspective of aitiology (a scholarly version of the penchant for folklore), and the rejection of heroic epic in favour partly of the fairytale-like and partly of the love element[13]. Apollonius of Rhodes in the *Argonautica* epitomizes these Romantic-age trends, and it is he who is considered to be among the forerunners of the ancient romance[14].

Even conceptual modes that prepared the emergence of Romanticism may *mutatis mutandis* find a parallel in Hellenistic literature. The exploration of time and space became popular during Romanticism, and spawned notions such as exoticism and primitivism; the aesthetics of folk culture came into vogue; new poetic forms evolved as a consequence of an increasing experimentality; psychological issues concerning old age and childhood and the emphasis upon femininity became central topics of literature. Hellenistic literature sets the same trends. Callimachus collects rare local myths in the *Aitia*, some of which, such as the cults of the heroes, have their roots in folk traditions of the Archaic *polis*[15]. And whereas Apollonius sets his epic within an exotic environment, Theocritus builds his idealized eutopia on the primitivism of a bucolic society[16]. Innovation in the creation of new forms, such as the idyll and the epyllion, goes hand in hand with new perspectives in content, as when gods and heroes in childhood and youth are depicted, old-aged and marginal figures come to the fore and women protagonists pave the way for gendered poetics[17].

13. For these axioms of Hellenistic scholarship, see e.g. Kambylis (1965), Reinsch-Werner (1976), Fuhrer (1992), and the more recent approaches by Fantuzzi/Hunter (2004) 42-88, Hunter (2005) and Morrison (2007); cf. Loehr (1996) for an overview of Graeco-Roman aitiology. On the significance of love in Hellenistic literature, see the thorough analysis by Rohde (1960) 12-177; eroticism as an aesthetic ideal of Alexandrianism is explored by Papanghelis (1994) 58-82.
14. The idea was first developed in the rather neglected treatise on the ancient romance by Heiserman (1977) but became a commonplace of Hellenistic scholarship only after Beye (1982) 71-76; cf. for more details below p. 48 and n. 157.
15. On the incorporation of folk elements into the *Aitia*, see Šwiderek (1952-1953). For a historical approach to the Hellenistic predilection for local myths of the past, see Scheer (2003).
16. On Theocritus' bucolic sensibility, see Bonelli (1979) 26-43; folk elements have been stressed by Horowski (1973); the connection of bucolic and/or pastoral with European Romanticism is a long-standing problem of scholarship, see e.g. Halperin (1983) and Kegel-Brinkgreve (1990). Recent approaches in Fantuzzi/Papanghelis (2006), esp. by Gutzwiller (pp. 1-23), Bernsdorff (pp. 167-207) and Fantuzzi (pp. 235-262).
17. The Hellenistic sensibility concerning childhood and youth is explored by Ambühl (2005), whereas the orientation towards old age and femininity has not received systematic attention; on Hekale as a symbol of the old-aged hero, see McNelis (2003) and Ambühl (2004); on women in Hellenistic literature, see Gutzwiller (2007) 195-199 with a short bibliographical note on p. 237.

During the Romantic period the individuality of the author, and not the limitations posed by literary forms, became central for the writing of literature. For Romantic genre theory, mostly developed in Germany by theorists such as the Schlegel brothers, the generic categories of the 'Moderns', i.e. not the Classics, are highly individualized ('every poem is a genre for itself'), open to experimentation (even science receives its own poetics) and all-encompassing (modes and moods, different varieties of sensibility and sensation, and aesthetic categories, such as the sublime and the beautiful, exist alongside the traditional forms of epic and novel)[18]. Similar developments in Hellenistic genre theory and practice hardly need any documentation[19].

As said, striving for individuality is one of the desiderata of the Romantic author; this new notion of the self resides within the development of the idea of imagination. Despite the fact that the reproduction of generic models, the existence of the mythical tradition and the pre-set conditions of composition and performance imposed strict limits upon the individuality of Greek poets of the Archaic and Classical period, Hellenistic poets introduce drastic changes as regards their identity and role[20]. The *Aitia*-Prologue best exemplifies the individuation of the poet in a series of metaphors, the most striking of which is the image of the poet as a child at play (*Ait*. fr. 1.5-6 Pf.). Further, in the second *Aitia* fragment, the notion that the poet depends upon divine inspiration collapses under the illusion of the dream, thus rendering the powerful archetype of the Muse a cultural phantom[21].

Whereas the examples of poetic individuality may easily be multiplied, Hellenistic imagination is more difficult to define. In my opinion, the handling of myth conveys more than anything the essence of Hellenistic imagination. Greek myth, a cultural phenomenon reflecting collective identities and values, has undergone radical alterations during the Hellenistic period. It is not only the collection of local, virtually

18. On a thorough analysis of (German) genre theory during Romanticism, see Rajan (2000).
19. Cf. the term *Kreuzung der Gattungen* coined by Wilhelm Kroll in the 1920s, and the recent overview of the problem by Rossi (2000). On the transformations of the genre during the Hellenistic era, see Fantuzzi/Hunter (2004) 17-26.
20. Gelzer (1993) and Parsons (1993) sketch out the changes in the poets' identities during the Hellenistic period, although they are reluctant to acknowledge a high degree of individuality in them; cf. the objections raised by Henrichs (1993). From another viewpoint, we may argue that Hellenistic scholars invented the idea of poetic imagination, rendered as poetic licence (ποιητικὴ ἐξουσία) in the Homeric scholia, see Meijering (1987) 62-67.
21. The juxtaposition of the invocation to the Muses with the literary models evoked by Callimachus is explored by Fantuzzi/Hunter (2004) 1-17.

unknown myths from the remote past of the Archaic *polis* that changed
it. Hellenistic poets gain control over the myth by exploring its suscepti-
bility to fiction by either devising minor episodes within the broader
tradition of Greek myth or inventing an entirely new mythology[22]. The
former reaches its climax with the quasi-mythological stories of Parthenius[23], the latter with the bucolic mythology of Theocritus[24]. As for the
μῦθος, the πρᾶξις articulated as a coherent plot, it becomes extinct[25]; in
some genres, such as didactic poetry, artistic imagination explores the
poeticization of any type of non-mythical, prosaic material.

   Hellenistic culture marks a break with everything 'Classical' and is, at
the same time, a creative reworking of it. Despite being limited by the
conventions of their literary system, the Hellenistic *literati* turned the
spotlight on imagination and individuality as no Greek poets had done
before. Yet, I do not suggest here that some Hellenistic poets were
Romantics *avant la lettre*. My claim is simply that numerous peculiari-
ties of Hellenistic aesthetics which are non-Classical in quality show an
affinity with some aspects of Romanticism[26]. But, does this assumption,
and especially the penchant for dark aesthetics, apply to each and every
poet active during the last three centuries BC? Definitely not. And the
most obvious exception is the leading figure of the Alexandrian avant-
garde, Callimachus.

An un-Callimachean trend

To understand how Callimachus' poetic universe is constituted, one has
to have recourse to the notion of aesthetic distance. This is particularly
true of the *Aitia*, whose novel-like narratives, anchored in the distant

---

   22. Hellenistic poets herald the liberation of the imagination (as the Romantic poets
did) on the basis of the revision of myth, see Radke (2007).
   23. Fictionality in these cases does not amount to pure invention, since these stories
derive as a rule from previous collections of myths or local histories; however, their con-
forming with stereotypical plot-types and set patterns and their novelistic features relate
them to the precursors of novel, see Lightfoot (1999) 256-263.
   24. Recognized as the first fully fictional world in literature by Payne (2007); cf.
Fantuzzi (2000) on the demythologizing of poetry in Theocritus.
   25. Callimachus' axiom of οὐχ ἓν ἄεισμα διηνεκές with all its possible manifestations in Hellenistic poetry–the catalogue form, the framing of the narrative, the lack or
discontinuity of plot–bears some similarity with the Romantic ideal of 'fragmentation' as
described in the 'Preface' to Coleridge's *Kubla Khan*, see Sistakou (2009a); on the
Romantic fascination with the fragment, see Thomas (2005).
   26. Nineteenth century scholarship viewed Alexandrian literature through a Romantic
prism, especially Erwin Rohde and Auguste Couat; for a fascinating overview of these
trends in Hellenistic scholarship, see Pfeiffer (1955).

past, in a world of heroes and gods, are either mediated by the framework, a dramatized dialogue between the Muses and the scholarly persona of the narrator (Books 1-2), or filtered through the repeated references to authoritative sources, such as gods, historians or scientists (Books 3-4)[27]. This anti-emotional stance has been thus described[28]:

> Judging by the extant fragments, the stories told in the *Aitia* offered considerable potential for the exploration of dramatic anguish and romantic yearning, and it is characteristic of Callimachus, and of the elitist tradition whose spokesman he was, that he studiously avoided this exploration. Vulgar emotions were among the 'common things' which he loathed.

Callimachus' readers are constantly made aware that the narrator, first-person, dramatized or omniscient, whether in the *Aitia*, the *Hymns* or the *Hekale*, views his literary world through the lens of the scholar and the commentator.

Part and parcel of this distanced, often ironic, perspective is the avoidance of rhetorical excess. Callimachus never carries his expression to extremes nor does he resort to expressionist style[29]. An obvious reason may be Callimachus' quest for brevity and accuracy–a plausible explanation of λεπτός if taken to denote the aesthetic quality of poetic discourse. Παχύς, the opposite of λεπτός, has been interpreted as an attack on the 'excessively ornamented, over-detailed, florid' and/or 'rough' style, mainly in reference to the poetry of Antimachus[30]. When the *Aitia*-Prologue contrasts poetic slenderness with the thunder of Zeus, it is the bombastic style and the affective experience it creates that are criticized (*Ait.* fr.1.19-20 Pf.)[31]. The closure of the *Hymn to Apollo* may be read along the same lines, if the juxtaposition of Ἀσσυρίου ποταμοῖο μέγας ῥόος with ὀλίγη λιβὰς ἄκρον ἄωτον is analyzed in terms of the antith-

---

27. Although the *Aitia* explore the entire cosmos (the human existence, the divine and the notion of time), there is a constant juxtaposition of serious with humorous tones, a play between the narrator and the characters, a sense of fragmentation and distancing; this reading of the *Aitia*, put forward by Hutchinson (2003), is best expressed by the following phrase (p. 51): "The *Aitia*, like the *Argonautica*, sweeps across the whole range of the Greek world; but its narrator is a static and intellectual figure". On the complex narrative structure of *Aitia* 1-2, see Harder (1988).
28. By Pollitt (1986) 14.
29. Fantuzzi/Hunter (2004) 44 rightly point out "the lack of obvious verbal adornment", "the spareness of style", "the sense of control", "the elimination of excess" and the "severe poetic discretion" of Callimachus' style.
30. This interpretation of παχύς is suggested by Krevans (1993) 156-160.
31. Cf. Propertius' imitation of the passage (2.1.39-40): *sed neque Phlegraeos Iovis Enceladique tumultus/ intonet angusto pectore Callimachus.* For the thunder of Zeus as a stylistic metaphor and the identification of 'Zeus' with Homer or Aeschylus (in the Aristophanic context at least), see Asper (1997) 196-198; it is seen as a metaphor of 'stylistic grandeur' by Petrovic (2006).

esis between the low quality of uncontrollable expression on the one
hand and the elegance of highly selective phrasing on the other.

To further illustrate the point that Callimacheanism should be understood, among other things, as an exercise in formalistic discipline and
well-balanced discourse[32], it is worth emphasizing the aesthetic divide
between Callimachus and, say, Apollonius by an example. The episode
in which the Argonauts are plunged into darkness while sailing the
Aegean and are eventually rescued by the epiphany of Apollo near the
island of Anaphe is treated both in the *Aitia* and Book 4 of the *Argonautica*. The comparison between the two passages highlights the distance
between Callimachean and Apollonian aesthetics. I will only quote here
the verses focusing on the moment of crisis:

Ait. fr. 250.8-11 SH and fr. 18.5-8 Pf.
*When Tiphys knew not...how to steer...Nonacrinian Callisto, unbathed in the
streams of Ocean...they were afraid...but the son of Aison, full of grief, raised
his hands to you, Hiëios, and swore many an offering to Pytho, many to Ortygia,
if you would drive the swirling darkness from the ship...* [Transl. F. Nisetich]

Arg. 4.1694-1705
*Suddenly, however, as they raced over the great expanse of the Cretan sea they
were terrified by the darkness which men call katoulas (=deadly or enshroud-
ing); no stars penetrated the deadly darkness, no beams of the moon; down
from the heavens spread a black emptiness, or it was some other gloom rising
up from the furthest depths. They had no idea whether they were moving in
Hades or over the waters. They handed over their hopes of return to the power
of the sea, helpless to control where it might lead them. Jason, however, raised
up his hands and in a loud voice called upon Phoibos, summoning him to save
them. In his despair tears flowed down; countless were the offerings he prom-
ised to provide, many at Pytho, many at Amyklai, many to Ortygia.* [Transl. R.
Hunter]

Although a minute sample (and an uncertain one, since the Callimachean
text is preserved in broken bits), it is representative in that it reflects the
intellectual vs. the emotional style[33]. Callimachus insists on scholarly
details–the mythological digression on the constellation Ursa Major, the
cult epithet of Apollo Ἰήιος and the ambivalent Homeric *glossa* ἀμιχ-
θαλόεις, to which he obviously attributes the lesser known interpretation

---

32. The essence of Callimachus' self-restraint and the way he exploits what Ezra
Pound describes as 'logopoeia' (i.e. the ironies resulting from the dynamic relation
between verbal expression, usage and poetic context) are brilliantly captured by Papanghelis (1994) 89-91.

33. This may correspond to the different generic conventions of elegy and epic, com-
pactness in narrative vs. completeness in treatment respectively, cf. Harder (2002) 218-
223.

of 'smoky'; his controlled expression becomes evident in the laconic description of both the feelings of the Argonauts and the plight they are in. Conversely, Apollonius overemphasizes darkness by alluding both to the primordial Chaos and the underground night of Hades[34], two images that combine unearthly grandeur with terror, and explicitly stresses the agony of the heroes: thus, the scene triggers the affective rather than the intellectual response of the reader[35].

As a moment of *pathos* this dark story from the Argonaut myth does not sit well within the larger context of Callimachean thematics. Callimachus is not attracted by the morbid; he expressly rejects it when he scornfully refers to the image of the crane that revels in the blood of the Pygmies in the *Aitia*-Prologue (*Ait*. fr. 1.13-14 Pf.)[36]. However, there are passages suggesting that rhetorical and thematic hyperboles may be at work in Callimachus too. An obvious example is the *Hymn to Delos*: battles between gods and struggles of natural forces are set against the backdrop of the powerful personification of geographical locations–personification being one of the vital components of the sublime[37]. But, the embedding of the plot into the hymnic frame and the intertextual play with recognizable scenes from Homer, Hesiod and tragedy, a play that often verges on parody, dulls the emotional effect of the hymn. Much more explicit is the way in which Callimachus treats the dark myth of Erysichthon as a black comedy in highlighting its repercussions for family and social environment rather than its macabre details–not to mention the deliberate elimination of the autophagy ending of the story[38].

It is not only the tone but also the subject matter that reflect Callimachean vs. Romantic aesthetics. For instance, one favourite scenario of Hellenistic poetry, the catasterism, presents ample opportunity for the

34. For thorough discussion of Apollonius' imagery, see Vian (1993) 207. Livrea (1987) 189-190 offers an interesting analysis of the passage by reference to the 'Erebos-Aspekt des Meeres' as studied by Wachsmuth.

35. Conte (2007) 49-57 may be correct when he makes a fine distinction between Apollonius' *sympatheia*, which he calls "the affective and psychological colouring typical of Alexandrian and neoteric poetry", and Virgil's *empatheia*, a feature permeating the entire narrative and enhancing its tragic pathos. We should not confuse the emotional involvement of the reader of a 'grand' epic, such as Homer or even Virgil, with the sophisticated exploitation of affect by Apollonius and other Hellenistic Romantics; on this point, see Fantuzzi/Hunter (2004) 98-104.

36. Asper (1997) 199-207.

37. In this hymn Callimachus exploits the supranormal, see Williams (1993); on the fairytale aspects of Callimachus' hymns, see Gigante Lanzara (1995). On personification and the sublime, see Knapp (1985).

38. Ovid (*Met*. 7.738-878) does not omit any of the tale's macabre details; for Ovid's rhetorical exaggeration in the treatment of Erysichthon, see Griffin (1986). On the comic elements in Callimachus' narration of the myth of Erysichthon, see McKay (1962).

poet to shed light on the dark side of metamorphosis thematics: namely
the dramatic incidents, usually unrequited love or hubristic behaviour,
which result in the transformation of the unfortunate hero(ine) into a different entity. Instead, Callimachus in the *Lock of Berenike* reverses the
natural order of the events, since the metamorphosis of the queen's lock
of hair has been materialized before the beginning of the elegy; thereupon, the scholarly narrator wittily captures (and at the same time under-
mines) the 'Romantic' soliloquy of the catasterized lock[39]. But it is not
only the distanced perspective that renders Callimachus' elegy so
restrained in its emotionality. The crucial factor is the lack of dark aspects
in the hard-luck story which, however, is dramatically narrated by the
lock–the most violent action being the cutting off of the lock from the
queen's hair with iron and steel (*Ait.* fr. 110.47-50 Pf.)! This mixture of
un-tragic subject matter and melodramatic tone, almost a parody of metamorphosis literature, stands in stark contrast with another catasterism
myth as recounted by a contemporary of Callimachus, Eratosthenes of
Cyrene, in his famous elegy *Erigone* (and in his prose collection of
Catasterisms). Although we are unable to reconstruct the elegy with any
degree of certainty, its synopsis reflects a taste for 'blood and death' thematics: after the Attic hero, and a follower of Dionysus, Ikarios, is killed
by intoxicated farmers, his daughter Erigone, upon finding her father's
dead body, hangs herself from a tree; the god punishes the Athenians by
causing mass suicides among unmarried girls; at the end, Ikarios, Erigone
and her dog Maira are transformed into stars[40]. According to the title the
emphasis of the poem must have been placed on the heroine[41].

Unfortunate heroines like Erigone are the unwritten rule in the
poetry of the Alexandrian avant-garde, but here again there is a world

---

39. On the distance between the lock and the narrator, cf. the excellent analysis by
Gutzwiller (1992), e.g. 373 "by allowing the voice of the lock to slip back and forth
between the two poles of the poet's persona and distinct character, Callimachus could
present all the Romantic and fantastic details of the catasterism while yet maintaining his
own stance of bemused scepticism".

40. On the ancient sources of the story, and their (hypothetical) interrelations, see
Rosokoki (1995) 21-24 and 47-52.

41. Also later reworkings of the episode, which most probably drew upon Eratosthenes' *Erigone*, bring the dark side of the myth to the fore. It is worth noting that Nonnus' narration of the episode in the *Dionysiaca* (47.34-264) is full of Gothic details, such
as the bleeding ghost of Ikarios which haunts Erigone's dreams (148-159), the maiden's
desperate search for her father's tomb and her lament thereon (205-228), and the elaborate
account of Erigone's suicide at the scene of the crime (229-245). Although no secure
parallels can be drawn between the lost poem of Eratosthenes and Nonnus, it is not
improbable that the latter actually found inspiration in the famous Hellenistic elegy; however, Rosokoki (1995) 64-75 is reluctant, but not wholly dismissive, to accept a very close
relation between the two.

of difference between Callimachus and other Hellenistic poets. Callimachus' sole poem dedicated to a feminine figure, the *Hekale*[42], tells the story of a woman who, motivated by her strong maternal instinct, offers hospitality to Theseus and then dies peacefully from old age. If the ancient scholion informing us that the *Hekale* was intended as a response to the μέγα ποίημα is correct (Sch. Ψ *H. Ap.* 106), then it might reflect Callimachus' dislike for certain poetic vogues of his era rather than merely his rejection of long-scale poetry. Callimachus may be reacting against the extravagance, in both content and style, of exactly this type of poetry–and its pretence at being serious and dignified. Although this line of reasoning is purely speculative, it seems that the μεγάλη γυνή, as used in the context of the *Aitia*-Prologue with reference to Mimnermus' *Nanno* (fr. 1.11-12 Pf.), suggests a kind of love poetry developed around a feminine figure with an emphasis on the sentimental and the dramatic. A supportive argument would be that the *Nanno* served as a model for Antimachus' *Lyde*, which is dismissed by Callimachus as a παχὺ γράμμα (fr. 398 Pf.)[43]. The passionate tone of both poems is admired by Posidippus in his poetological-amatory epigram (*AP.* 12.168.1) Ναννοῦς καὶ Λύδης ἐπίχει δύο... Hermesianax in his own *Leontion* attests the erotic fire of Mimnermus for Nanno (fr. 7.37 CA) and, more importantly, projects the melodramatic plot and style of the *Lyde* onto Antimachus' biography (fr. 7.41-46 CA=Antimachus test. 11 Matthews):

Λυδῆς δ᾽ Ἀντίμαχος Λυδηίδος ἐκ μὲν ἔρωτος
    πληγεὶς Πακτωλοῦ ῥεῦμ᾽ ἐπέβη ποταμοῦ·
†δαρδανη† δὲ θανοῦσαν ὑπὸ ξηρὴν θέτο γαῖαν
    †καλλίων αἴζαον διηλθεν† ἀποπρολιπὼν
ἄκρην ἐς Κολοφῶνα, γόων δ᾽ ἐνεπλήσατο βίβλους
    ἱράς, ἐκ παντὸς παυσάμενος καμάτου.

Antimachus, stricken by his love for Lyde and his Lydean passion, went to the stream of Pactolus...when she died he buried her in the dry land...leaving behind...he went to the outermost places of Colophon; and he filled the sacred books with his lamentations, at rest from all toil and trouble.

Despite the fact that details of composition and aim of the *Nanno*, the *Lyde* and the *Leontion* elude us (scholars keep wondering whether these

42. Callimachus is also attested as the author of a lost epic poem about Galatea (fr. 378-379 Pf.); however, the Nereid is not a typically dark heroine (she is only involved in an unlucky love affair with Akis who is killed by Polyphemos, see Ov. *Met.* 13.738-897) nor is it probable that Callimachus treated the myth as a love story (see Pfeiffer [1949] ad loc.).

43. Matthews (1996) 26-32 tends to believe that Callimachus criticizes *Lyde* on the basis of its epicizing, grandiose style. On Antimachus' dignity of style, see Cameron (1995) 332-337.

were the first subjective love elegies), the bigger picture which emerges is that there was a growing gulf between poets writing within a 'Romantic' framework and Callimachus' demand for aesthetic refinement[44].

To get a faint idea of what the aesthetics of this sort of love poetry was we should attempt to identify this un-Callimachean trend by a specific example. A story-pattern widely circulating in Hellenistic times was about young females who, possessed by strong passions, such as love, jealousy or revenge, were doomed to self-destruction or death[45]. The story-pattern was quite popular among early Alexandrian poetry, reached its Hellenistic climax with Parthenius' collection of *Erotika Pathemata* and came into vogue with the Roman neoterics and the Augustan poets. Female figures in love are not totally absent from Callimachus' poetry; we may recall such legendary couples as Akontios and Kydippe (*Ait*. fr. 80-83 Pf.), or Phrygius and Pieria (*Ait*. fr. 67-75 Pf.), and yet remark that they lived happily ever after; but even dramas, like the one about Leimonis who is put to death by her own father for adultery (*Ait*. fr. 94-95 Pf.), are kept at a distance, since their emotional effect is undercut by the intellectual stance of the scholarly narrator[46]. The description of female sexual obsession by poets sharing different aesthetic views is a case in point. Sickness as a result of falling in love is a hallmark of love poetry, but Callimachus and his older contemporary Theocritus differ markedly in its depiction:

Ait. fr. 75.12-19 Pf.
The evening before [...] the girl turned deathly pale, the sickness we bid go plague the mountain goats and falsely label 'sacred' came on and nearly finished her. A second time the nuptial couch was strewn, a second time the girl fell sick, a quartan fever lasting seven months. For the third time they thought to marry her: that third time a deadly chill pierced Kydippe. [Transl. F. Nisetich]

Id. 2.82-92
I saw, and madness seized me, and my hapless heart was aflame. My looks faded away. No eyes had I thereafter for that show, nor know how I came home again, but some parching fever shook me, and ten days and ten nights I lay upon my bed. Mark, Lady Moon, whence came my love.

44. This view is roughly adopted by Cameron (1995) 303-338; see e.g. how he sums up the debate (p. 306): "it was precisely the elevation, the dignity of Antimachus' style that critics singled out, some in admiration, others (notably Callimachus) in disparagement. Posidippus, another name on the Florentine list, describes him as sober (σώφρων). The *Kydippe*, with its garrulous narrator constantly interrupting himself, was anything but dignified or sober." The Alexandrian debate over λεπτότης or σεμνότης is also explored by Prioux (2007) 107-113.

45. An outline of this pattern in Lightfoot (1999) 23-29.

46. On the sophisticated manipulation of the discourse of desire by Callimachus in the elegy of Akontios and Kydippe, see Rynearson (2009).

And oftentimes my colour would turn as pale as fustic, and all my hair was fall-ing from my head, and bones alone were left of me, and skin. And to whose house did I not go, what hag's did I pass over, of those that had skill in charms? But no light matter was it, and time was flying away. [Transl. A.S.F. Gow]

The scenes are not directly comparable: in the first, it is Artemis that causes Kydippe, who has already taken an oath to marry Akontios, to become ill on the eve of her wedding to another man; in the second, Simaitha 'the Sorceress' falls ill as a consequence of experiencing love at first sight during a festival of Artemis. Their essential difference, however, lies within the perspective (objective vs. subjective perception of the pathology of love), the rhetoric (scientific vs. pictorial representation of the symptoms) and the motivation behind the plot (external vs. internal moti-vation, namely god inflicted illness vs. psychological distress). Simaitha's pathological love soon induces her to resort to magic, to the powers of darkness, Hekate and Selene, and in this respect Theocritus' archetypal heroine parallels the most dark Hellenistic female, Apollonius' Medea.

The aforementioned passages from Apollonius, Eratosthenes and The-ocritus as read against the backdrop of Callimachean poetics indicate that Callimachus, in contrast to other contemporary poets, abhors Romantic excess in subject matter, tone and style. He also abhors the aesthetics of darkness: before attempting a closer definition, we must first turn to the parameters that gave birth to darkness—namely the pursue of the sublime through fear, the fascination with ugliness and the exploitation of visual imagination, to which I will now turn my attention.

From fear to the sublime

Darkness is inconceivable without fear, and fear forms an integral part of the treatment of emotions in Greek literary theory. Already Gorgias in the *Encomium of Helen* offers a fine portrayal of the overwhelming emotions that poetry is capable of arousing in the souls of its listeners (fr. 11.9 D.-K.): ἧς τοὺς ἀκούοντας εἰσῆλθε καὶ φρίκη περίφοβος καὶ ἔλεος πολύδακρυς καὶ πόθος φιλοπενθής 'the hearers of poetry are overcome by fearful horror and tearful pity and grievous desire'. When Ion in Pla-to's dialogue describes the emotions that enhance the effectiveness of his performance, he concludes that fear is, along with pity, dominant[47]. On

---

47. Pity and fear are analyzed by Halliwell (1998) 168-184 as interconnected notions in regard to Aristotle's *Rhetoric*, with pity being the predominant emotion and fear the secondary or dependent upon it.

this account, the rhapsode has to burst into tears when narrating a sorrow-ful story, whereas a fearful or terrible narration is perceived as a hair-raising, heart-stopping experience on the part of the performer (*Ion* 535c); in both cases, the expectation is that the audience develops symptoms similar to those of the rhapsode (*Ion* 535e). The same duo of emotions is the quintessence of *katharsis* which derives from the contemplation of human suffering as experienced by the characters of tragedy in Aristotle's *Poetics* (*Poet.* 1449b). Yet, according to Aristotle, poet and audience are much more in control of their emotions in contrast to the emotive burst described by the Platonic Ion[48].

Negative feelings in poetry become, instead of a source of unconscious enchantment as Plato believes, or of ethical, emotional or cognitive expe-rience as Aristotle maintains, the vehicle for aesthetic pleasure in the trea-tise *On the Sublime* by 'Longinus'[49]. Emotion, rendered as *pathos* by 'Longinus', is a constituent of sublimity–though not indispensable to it (8.2). But 'Longinus' is primarily concerned with the effectiveness of poetry: one of the strongest emotions that may be created by sublimity is fear, and therefore the terms δεινός and φοβερός are recurrent in his treatise[50]. 'Longinus' illustrates fear by juxtaposing Homer with the anon-ymous poet of the *Arimaspean Epic* and Aratus in reference to the depic-tion of a tempest scene which sets the sailors of a ship in danger. Whereas Homer in *Il.* 15.264-268 succeeds in evoking the φοβερόν, the other two fail; it is interesting that Aratus' slenderness of style (λεπτότης) in verse 299 of the *Phainomena* ὀλίγον δὲ διὰ ξύλον ἄϊδ' ἐρύκει 'a little plank wards off Hades' seems to be the reason for this failure (10.6 πλὴν μικρὸν αὐτὸ καὶ γλαφυρὸν ἐποίησεν ἀντὶ φοβεροῦ). Images of super-natural grandeur, such as the 'Battle of the Gods' and other cosmic scenes involving terrifying natural phenomena from the *Iliad*, have a similar sub-lime impact upon the reader (9.5-8).

If the sublime according to 'Longinus' is synonymous to excess in emotion and language, then again, as in the case of Romantic aesthetics, Callimachus' slenderness stands at the opposite pole. In portraying the sublime authors in terms of anti-Callimachean metaphors, 'Longinus' often becomes a Telchinean persona. Thus, in the comparison between

48. Belfiore (1992) 181-225 offers an excellent analysis of fear and pity (sometimes in connection with shame) in the entire Aristotelian corpus; of particular relevance here is the discussion of the terms ἔκπληξις and κατάπληξις (pp. 216-222) that represent the emotional effects of poetry, primarily fear, in rhetorical and poetological theory.

49. An overview of 'Longinus' in Fuhrman (1973) 135-160 and more recently Hunter (2009).

50. On 'Longinus' and the 'low' emotions, i.e. pity, grief and fear (8.2 οἶκτοι λῦπαι φόβοι), see Innes (1995).

Demosthenes and Cicero, the former resembles a thunderbolt or a flash of lightning in the power, speed and intensity of his speech, whilst the latter a widespread conflagration (12.4, cf. 35.4): both recall Callimachus' anathema, Zeus' bombast. Another metaphor, that of water, is recurrent in 'Longinus', who eventually seems to be subverting the essence of Callimachus' closure to the *Hymn to Apollo* by expressing his admiration for the Ocean and the great rivers on the one hand, and his dislike for the lucid yet small flow of the stream on the other (35.4). These poetological metaphors would easily suit Romantic authors–yet clearly not Callimachus. But is this the case for all Hellenistic poets? 'Longinus' points out the lack of sublimity in Apollonius (and Theocritus), especially if he is to be compared with Homer (33.4.8-5.1): ἐπεί-τοιγε καὶ ἄπτωτος ὁ Ἀπολλών<ιος ἐν τοῖς> Ἀργοναύταις ποιητής, κἂν τοῖς βουκολικοῖς πλὴν ὀλίγων τῶν ἔξωθεν ὁ Θεόκριτος ἐπιτυχέστατος· ἆρ' οὖν Ὅμηρος ἂν μᾶλλον ἢ Ἀπολλώνιος ἐθέλοις γενέσθαι; 'Apollonius makes no mistakes in the *Argonautica*; Theocritus is very felicitous in the *Pastorals*, apart from a few passages not connected with the theme; but would you rather be Homer or Apollonius?' [Transl. D.A. Russell][51]. He goes on by comparing Eratosthenes' 'flawless' *Erigone* with Archilochus–once more in favour of the Archaic poet (33.5.1-5). But even if the 'polished' verses of Apollonius, Theocritus or Eratosthenes are less sublime than those of their Archaic and Classical predecessors (we should not forget that in the eyes of 'Longinus' the latter represent the Golden Age of literature), they are obviously more sublime than those of Callimachus[52]. In other words: though Callimachus' style is by definition anti-sublime and his λεπτότης synonymous to the non-grand, this has not prevented several of his contemporaries to strive for effect and sensation, for the grand and the sublime, as I will try to demonstrate while exploring darkness[53].

51. Cf. Fantuzzi/Hunter (2004) 99-100 who note that 'Longinus' denies the higher regions of sublimity to Apollonius arguing that the cosmic resonances of the *Argonautica* are less pervasive than those in e.g. Homer or Virgil.

52. On 'Longinus' as an anti-Callimachus, see Cajani (2002). That Callimachus is passed over in silence by 'Longinus' is also an indication that he could by no means be considered sublime, cf. Hunter (2008c) 547-555.

53. Differently Hunter (2009) 134-141 who views the Hellenistic poets' emphasis upon descriptive detail, naturalistic depiction and intellectualism as obstacles to the sublime: the effect of an Aratean or Apollonian passage, Hunter maintains, is that of mannerism not of sublimity. Nevertheless, a little later (pp. 141-160) Hunter argues that especially the *Argonautica* includes sublime passages, only of a lesser degree as compared to the ones in Homer or Virgil; in effect, what Apollonius does is to cut down on epic size (e.g. in the depiction of fantastic monsters like the earthborn men or Talos) not to eliminate magnitude altogether.

Now, back to fear as reworked by thinkers of the sublime. It took many centuries until 'Longinus' was rediscovered by European aesthetics. Strangely enough *On the Sublime* was translated by the defender of Neo-classicism, Nicolas Boileau, in the 17th century, but became the bible for Romantic aesthetics a hundred years later, when the sublime eventually converged with the notions of fear and darkness. The milestone in this development is the publication in 1757 of the aesthetic treatise *A Philo-sophical Enquiry into the Origin of Our Ideas of the Sublime and Beauti-ful* by the political theorist and philosopher Edmund Burke[54]. Burke departs from previous conceptions of the sublime associated with God or Nature in maintaining an affective position on its understanding (1.18):

> The passions which belong to self-preservation, turn on pain and danger; they are simply painful when their causes immediately affect us; they are delightful when we have an idea of pain and danger, without being actually in such circumstances; this delight I have not called pleasure, because it turns on pain, and because it is different enough from any idea of positive pleasure. Whatever excites this delight, I call *sublime*.

Indeed fear is dominant among human passions, and its experience through art is a source of delight: this is why, Burke argues, terms denot-ing 'astonishment or admiration' and 'terror' bear a close affinity in many languages (2.2, e.g. θάμβος, δεινός and αἰδέω in Greek or *vereor* and *stupeo* in Latin). But Burke rejects clearness in the representation of the fearful object–pain, danger or death–, since only obscurity can enhance human passions, and, in particular, the feeling of terror (2.3). Therefore, it is only through words, the words of poetry, which are capa-ble of conveying darkness, uncertainty and confusion more than any other form of art–Burke contrasts the obscurity of poetry with the 'clear-ness' of description in painting–, that the sublime can be achieved (2.4):

> The most lively and spirited verbal description I can give, raises a very obscure and imperfect *idea* of such objects; but then it is in my power to raise a stronger *emotion* by the description than I could do by the best paint-ing. This experience constantly evinces. The proper manner of conveying the *affections* of the mind from one to another, is by words. [...] So that poetry with all its obscurity, has a more general as well as a more powerful dominion over the passions than the other art. And I think there are reasons in nature why the obscure idea, when properly conveyed, should be more affecting than the clear. It is our ignorance of things that causes all our admiration, and chiefly excites our passions.

---

54. I quote Burke's text after Ashfield/de Bolla (1996). For a discussion of Burke's theory of the sublime, see Weiskel (1976) 83-106 and de Bolla (1989) 59-72; for an updated but general overview, see Shaw (2006) 48-71.

In conceptualizing the sublime, and, by extension, the aesthetics of the terrible in terms of cognition and language, Burke has introduced a new dimension into the notion of darkness in literature: more than other arts, even more than nature itself, poetic discourse can create the most powerful impressions of passions, especially fear. However, by emphasizing the importance of strong vs. clear poetic language for the creation of the sublime, Burke opts for expressionist rhetoric and affective word rather than elaborate diction. Thus, to pick up the thread of my analysis, Burke, like 'Longinus', appears to represent the un-Callimachean taste of style[55]. As I intend to show, there are Hellenistic poets apart from Callimachus that aim at creating the same sublime effect through darkness.

The discovery of ugliness

To speak of darkness presupposes recourse to ugliness, an umbrella term comprising everything that opposes beauty, that violates proportion, form, harmony–according to a well-known stereotype 'everything that is anti-Classical'[56]. Thersites, the archetype of physical and moral ugliness, makes his first appearance in the *Iliad*, whereas Greek mythology and Archaic epic abound with depictions of monsters and evil beings. But whereas for Plato the artistic representation of ugliness may lead to moral corruption, it is Aristotle who makes a clear distinction between ugliness in real life and ugliness in art. The latter may be a source of pleasure (ἡδονή) or joy (τὸ χαίρειν) for the subject that contemplates ugly images. According to Aristotle the only reason for experiencing pleasure upon confronting these images is that they are a product of artistic mimesis (*Poet.* 1448b)[57]:

> ἃ γὰρ αὐτὰ λυπηρῶς ὁρῶμεν, τούτων τὰς εἰκόνας τὰς μάλιστα ἠκριβωμένας χαίρομεν θεωροῦντες, οἶον θηρίων τε μορφὰς τῶν ἀτιμοτάτων καὶ νεκρῶν.

---

55. Burke appears as an anti-Callimachus too, when he suggests that the sublime and the beautiful are diametrically opposed concepts (e.g. in 3.27): "For sublime objects are vast in their dimensions, beautiful ones comparatively small; beauty should be smooth, and polished; the great, rugged and negligent; [...] beauty should not be obscure; the great ought to be dark and gloomy; beauty should be light and delicate; the great ought to be solid, and even massive".

56. This broad definition of ugliness, along with the Neoclassical stereotype that Greek art only depicts beauty and harmony, is owed to Eco (2007) 9-41.

57. Pleasure stemming from mimesis and cognition, in regard to this particular Aristotelian passage, is treated by Halliwell (2002) 180-193.

We take delight in viewing the most accurate possible images of objects which in themselves cause distress when we see them (e.g. the shapes of the lowest species of animal, and corpses). [Transl. M. Heath]

Ugliness was re-discovered as an aesthetic value along with beauty during the debate between the so-called 'Ancients' and 'Moderns'[58]. Though this is not a suitable place for a review of this, chiefly philosophical, debate, it is worth touching upon its crucial stages from the mid-18th to the end of the 19th century. One of the most outstanding representatives of the German Enlightenment, Gotthold Lessing published *Laokoon* (1766), a treatise on the limits of poetry and painting, as a response to Winckelmann's Neoclassical aesthetics. The comparison between the two artistic media aside, the *Laokoon* may be viewed as the first systematic account of ugliness in its various expressions in poetry and painting, and its effects, ranging from the horrible to the ridiculous. Friedrich Schlegel in his treatise *Über das Studium der griechischen Poesie* (1797) maintains that Modern poetics, as opposed to Classical, are characterized by "the total predominance of the characteristic, the individual, and the interesting", and it is from this basis that the 'Moderns', i.e. the Romantics, explored the aesthetics of ugliness. Ugliness appears to be an anathema to the Classical-oriented criticism of Schlegel–who, however, establishes a code for understanding ugliness as an aesthetic preference for the irregular and the deformed, and, from an ethical point of view, for the evil. For many decades, theorists saw ugliness as an integral part of the aesthetics of beauty, but it was the German philosopher Karl Rosenkranz who eventually defined ugliness as a distinct object of aesthetics (*Aesthetik des Hässlichen*, 1853)[59]. But already in 1827, in the 'Preface' to his play *Cromwell*, Victor Hugo paved the way for the introduction of a particular facet of ugliness, the grotesque, into Romantic art. For Hugo only this art is capable of harmonizing the everlasting contraries, the sublime and the grotesque, and therein lies its deep contrast with the Classical (§35):

58. On the redemption of ugliness during Romanticism, and its philosophical background, see the excellent overview in Eco (2007) 270-309, on which the following presentation is based.

59. This is how Eco (2007) 279 summarizes Rosenkranz' main theses: "Karl Rosenkranz [...] works out a phenomenology that ranges from the description of the *unseemly* to that of the *repugnant*, via the horrendous, the vacuous, the nauseating, the criminal, the eldritch, the demoniac, the witchlike, down to the celebration of caricature, which can transform the repugnant into the ridiculous and whose deformation becomes beautiful thanks to the *wit* that amplifies it, to the fantastic".

Let us resume, therefore, and try to prove that it is of the fruitful union of the grotesque and the sublime types that modern genius is born–so complex, so diverse in its forms, so inexhaustible in its creations; and therein directly opposed to the uniform simplicity of the genius of the ancients; let us show that that is the point from which we must set out to establish the real and radical difference between the two forms of literature.

There seems to be no evidence that philosophical or rhetorical treatises of the Hellenistic period devised individual theories about ugliness analogous to the ones developed during Romanticism. In practice, though, Hellenistic aesthetics took a fresh turn towards the grotesque, the deformed and the ugly on the one hand, and anything pertaining to human passion on the other. Although Hellenistic scholarship has long acknowledged the emergence of this new aesthetic trend, primarily in the fine arts, it has rendered it, as a rule, as a movement resembling baroque and rococo or as an idiosyncratic type of realism–though rarely as a Romantic twist[60]. But, the affinity with European movements aside, Hellenistic sculpture and art attest to an indisputable fact: that Hellenistic artists saw in the depiction of ugliness, and in what we might by extension call darkness, the potential for a non-Classical, avant garde aesthetics. In effect, the ugly and the grotesque in Hellenistic art is a thematic preference, a quality of the content rather than the form, a specific category connecting with the object of mimesis. Nevertheless, the mere fact that sculptors and painters of the Hellenistic period chose to depict ugliness, the grotesque and the pathetic demonstrates that they regarded these as highly appropriate subjects for their artistic medium: it is first and foremost in the translation of this subject matter into visual images that the dynamics of darkness became apparent[61]. Visualizing the negative aspects of *pathos*, the deformed and the ugly must have held a strong attraction for Hellenistic poets too, which they aspired to represent by means of their own art, viz by the power of words.

60. See Pollitt (1986) 111-149 on Hellenistic baroque and rococo and Zanker (1987) esp. 39-112 on pictorial realism in Hellenistic aesthetics. Fowler (1989) explores the baroque, the burlesque and the grotesque trends in Hellenistic art and literature on the one hand, and the passionate on the other.

61. Darkness was a source of delight for artists, as Fowler (1989) 188 argues: "So these poets and artists took joy in the tentacles of the octopus, the teeth of the rhinoceros, the legs of the cicada; in the vertebrae of the hunchback as well as in the folds of Aphrodite's flesh. They delighted in black street musicians, drunken old women, dying Persians and Gauls, sleeping satyrs, and dancing dwarfs. Nothing was too ugly or too sad for their attention. Their passion was for the particulars of life, and these they represented with realism and with magic".

The affect of visuality

The starting point to explain the interconnectedness between visuality
and darkness is again Aristotle's *Poetics*, and the concept of ὄψις introduced therein[62]. Aristotle maintains that the soul of tragedy resides
within the plot, the πρᾶξις, whereas its visual representation during performance may have a strong emotional effect upon the audience, but of
an inferior quality compared to fear and pity that originate from its inner
dramatic structure[63]. This is how Aristotle describes the affect of what
might be called 'the spectacle' (*Poet.* 1453b):

> ἔστιν μὲν οὖν τὸ φοβερὸν καὶ ἐλεεινὸν ἐκ τῆς ὄψεως γίγνεσθαι,
> ἔστιν δὲ καὶ ἐξ αὐτῆς τῆς συστάσεως τῶν πραγμάτων, ὅπερ ἐστὶ
> πρότερον καὶ ποιητοῦ ἀμείνονος. [...] τὸ δὲ διὰ τῆς ὄψεως τοῦτο
> παρασκευάζειν ἀτεχνότερον καὶ χορηγίας δεόμενόν ἐστιν. οἱ δὲ μὴ
> τὸ φοβερὸν διὰ τῆς ὄψεως ἀλλὰ τὸ τερατῶδες μόνον παρασκευάζον-
> τες οὐδὲν τραγῳδίᾳ κοινωνοῦσιν· οὐ γὰρ πᾶσαν δεῖ ζητεῖν ἡδονὴν
> ἀπὸ τραγῳδίας ἀλλὰ τὴν οἰκείαν.

> It is possible for the evocation of fear and pity to result from the spectacle,
> and also from the structure of the events itself. The latter is preferable and
> is the mark of a better poet. [...] Producing this effect through spectacle is
> less artistic, and is dependent on the production. Those who use spectacle
> to produce an effect which is not evocative of fear, but simply monstrous,
> have nothing to do with tragedy; one should not seek every pleasure from
> tragedy, but the one that is characteristic of it. [Transl. M. Heath]

Although Aristotle restricts his argument to theatrical performance, the
idea that 'spectacularity' evokes the monstrous (τὸ τερατῶδες) once
more shifts the emphasis from the intellectual to the sensual pleasure of
art[64]. In this respect the visual presentation of *pathos*, i.e. physical suffering of the tragic heroes, affects the audience emotionally but does not
reflect a deeper tragic structuring of plot[65]. Aristotle may not be rejecting
the value of performance *per se*–though at times he appears to consider

62. On Aristotle's notion of ὄψις, see Halliwell (1998) 66-69 and 337-343.
63. Konstan (forthcoming, Opsis) argues that ὄψις does not inspire true emotions but
'instinctive reactions' such as shock or horror, or what the Stoics label 'proto- or pre-
emotions (προπάθειαι)'.
64. The hypothesis that Aristotle is not only criticizing fourth-century productions of
tragedy but also the 'grotesqueries' of Aeschylus is an attractive one, see Halliwell (1998)
95 n. 20. Aeschylus is said to have presented monstrosities on stage, see e.g. Aristoph.
Frogs 833-834 who uses the same term as Aristotle: ἀποσεμνυνεῖται πρῶτον [i.e.
Aeschylus], ἅπερ ἑκάστοτε/ ἐν ταῖς τραγῳδίαισιν ἐτερατεύετο. Τὸ τερατῶδες is,
according to Konstan (forthcoming, Opsis), the pre-emotional counterpart of the frightening (τὸ φοβερόν).
65. Thus the presentation of human *pathos* on stage may be viewed as a dispensable
part of tragedy, see Halliwell (1998) 223 n. 30.

it an inferior category of art as compared to the poet's–, but he rather draws attention to the fact that visualization may easily slide into the sensational[66].

But visualization is not limited to the theatre; the visual may also be translated into poetry through the use of rhetorical images. The evocation of imagery is central to the composition of poetry, and Greek epic, tragedy and lyric, abound with it[67]. Under the influence of rhetoric, ἐνάργεια 'vividness' becomes the focal point of the pictorial description, which, in turn, gives way to φαντασία 'imagination'[68]. Thus, poets explore the dynamics of visual imagination by conjuring up images and thereby arousing the emotion of the reader[69]. 'Longinus' in 15.1-7 introduces φαντασία, ὄψις and εἰδωλοποιία to denote either the poetic images which capture the imagination of the audience or the actual representation of supernatural scenes onstage. As he maintains, φαντασία is one of the vital parameters of the sublime, but, whereas orators (or prose writers in general) must keep within the limits of credibility, poets are free to stretch their imagination beyond reality to amaze their audiences (15.1-2)[70]:

κᾰλεῖται μὲν γὰρ κοινῶς φαντασία πᾶν τὸ ὁπωσοῦν ἐννόημα γεννητικὸν λόγου παριστάμενον· ἤδη δ' ἐπὶ τούτων κεκράτηκε τοὔνομα ὅταν ἃ λέγεις ὑπ' ἐνθουσιασμοῦ καὶ πάθους βλέπειν δοκῇς καὶ ὑπ' ὄψιν τιθῇς τοῖς ἀκούουσιν. ὡς δ' ἕτερόν τι ἡ ῥητορικὴ φαντασία βούλεται καὶ ἕτερον ἡ παρὰ ποιηταῖς οὐκ ἂν λάθοι σε, οὐδ' ὅτι τῆς μὲν ἐν ποιήσει τέλος ἐστὶν ἔκπληξις, τῆς δ' ἐν λόγοις ἐνάργεια, ἀμφότεραι δ' ὅμως τό τε <παθητικὸν> ἐπιζητοῦσι καὶ τὸ συγκεκινημένον.

66. Cf. Halliwell (1998) 341 who points out that Aristotle "frowns on the misuse of spectacle to achieve an effect of 'the portentous' or 'the sensational' ".

67. For a theoretical approach of imagery in early Greek poetry, see Silk (1974), cf. Barlow (2008) 1-16.

68. Manieri (1998), in her analysis of the poetic image in Greek poetry, focuses on two key terms, ἐνάργεια and φαντασία; on ἐνάργεια in particular, see Zanker (1981).

69. Cf. Quint. *Inst.* 6.2.29-30 who calls these images φαντασίαι: *quas φαντασίας Graeci uocant...per quas imagines rerum absentium ita repraesentantur animo ut eas cernere oculis ac praesentes habere uideamur, has quisquis bene ceperit is erit in adfectibus potentissimus.* On the interconnection between ἐνάργεια/φαντασία and the arousal of emotions, see Webb (1997).

70. Visual imagination does not only pertain to the artist but also to his audience, which is urged to 'supplement' the details of a scene that is omitted from the image or *tableau* in question (the technical term coined by von Blanckenhagen [1975] to denote the active role assumed by the 'viewer' is "der ergänzende Betrachter"). This is how Zanker (1996) 413 describes the effect of the so-called Marsyas group on the viewer: "Here the gaze of the Silen meets that of another member of the group, the Scythian slave of Apollo whetting the knife for Marsyas' hideous execution; but the viewer is enabled to visualise the full horror of the climactic moment, all the more heightened in fact because what is presented is merely an anterior moment of horror; any subsequent stage in the fate of Marsyas can only be even more terrible. In this way the whole narrative can be filled in, and to powerful effect".

The term φαντασία is used generally for anything which in any way suggests a thought productive of speech; but the word has also come into fashion for the situation in which enthusiasm and emotion make the speaker see what he is saying and bring it visually before his audience. It will not escape you that rhetorical visualization has a different intention from that of the poets: in poetry the aim is astonishment, in oratory it is clarity. Both, however, seek emotion and excitement. [Transl. D.A. Russell]

Apart from its obvious meaning, ἔκπληξις 'surprise' has also the connotation of 'fear'[71]. Could this be the missing link between visual imagination and the aesthetics of darkness, both of which amount to the creation of the sublime? This point is further reinforced by the immediate context, as 'Longinus' (15.2) illustrates ἔκπληξις by quoting the scene from Euripides' *Orestes*, where the hero is pursued by the Erinyes, vividly illustrated as having bloody faces and serpent hair (*Or.* 255-257), a verse from *Iphigenia in Tauris* on the same motif (*IT.* 291), and then again (at 15.8) another distich from *Orestes* about the Erinyes (*Or.* 264-265). 'Longinus' chooses as a typical paradigm of visual imagination the description of the Erinyes, whose appearance and status strongly evoke Medusa, the Romantic archetype of beauty in horror[72].

What the critique of theatrical representation offered by Aristotle and the idea of visual imagination in poetry as introduced by 'Longinus' have in common is the recognition that the image has the ability to convey strong passions to the audience. My focus is on the visualization of the narrative by means of rhetoric, a device that raises a series of critical questions. Does visualization reflect the degradation of the tragic, the latter being rendered as a coherent plot structure by Aristotle, and the emergence of the sensational? Does visualization aim at enhancing visual imagination, the power by which an object is presented to the mind of the reader? And, by extension, does the stirring of visual imagination pertain to the evocation of low emotions, such as horror or passion, and may consequently be linked to the aesthetics of darkness? As will emerge during the course of this study, these questions may be answered in the affirmative; and, once more,

71. E.g. in Aeschylus *Pers.* 606 κακῶν ἔκπληξις 'terror caused by misfortunes' (*LSJ*); cf. Polybius 3.81.6 'mental disturbance, passion' and ἔκπληκτος 'terrifying' Luc. *Herm.* 18 or 'amazed, terror-stricken' Orph. *H.* 39.10 (also in *LSJ*).

72. By analogy Quintilian illustrates the φαντασίαι '*visiones*' of the orator by reference to the mental image of a murder: the speaker and the listener summon up the scene 'before their eyes', viz the agony of the victim, the sheding of his blood, his groaning and suffering (*Inst.* 6.2.31-32).

it is Romantic-age culture that provides the basis for reinforcing the point[73].

Visuality, as a self-conscious act, has held a fascination for artists and poets from the mid-18th century down to the late 19th, while the obsession with visual culture became manifest in popular forms of public entertainment such as art exhibitions, masquerades, fireworks, theatrical performances, the pleasure gardens and the like[74]. Novel modes of visualization were introduced during this period. The first responses to the question as to whether art can reproduce visuality relate to the aesthetic ideal of the *picturesque*, denoting the viewing of nature through art in accordance with Romantic sensibility. Yet, and due to the emergence of new developments in optics, the 19th century has seen an increasing emphasis on visual experimentation, as for instance through the three-dimensional perspective of the *panorama* in painting or the *diorama* in the theatre. In exploiting the potential of these devices, artists explored the boundaries between reality and illusion, the visible and the invisible, the seen and the unseen. To represent the invisible as potentially visible within a dark setting was the idea behind an innovative spectacle of 19th century mass culture, the *phantasmagoria*. Deriving from the Greek words φάντασμα and ἀγείρειν, lit. 'a gathering of ghosts', the *phantasmagoria* aims at generating a thrilling effect of fear to the audience by projecting images of ghosts, skeletons and demons in total darkness by use of a magic lantern. Within a study of darkness, the *phantasmagoria* is a cultural phenomenon of paramount importance, because it couples the illusionary potential of a highly sensational spectacle with the aesthetics of the horrible[75]. With the *phantasmagoria* the Romantic quest for the limits between reality and imagination reaches its climax and, although an extremity of pop culture, it is indicative of how the growing preoccupation with visuality inevitably gave rise to the exploitation of horror. It is no coincidence that one of the favourite subjects of the producers of phantasmagoric spectacles was the Medusa, the mythological figure that became the avatar of Romantic darkness, as said before. To thus visualize horror is the ultimate expression of the artistically beautiful.

---

73. The following overview of the relation between Romanticism and visuality is based upon the excellent monograph by Thomas (2008), see esp. the introductory chapter "Regarding Visuality-From the Picturesque to the Panorama" pp. 1-19.

74. See de Bolla (2003) for the various manifestations of mass visual culture during the 18th century.

75. On the *phantasmagoria*, see Thomas (2008) 152-176.

In light of this theoretical anachronism, Hellenistic aesthetics may also be considered as a result of the growing importance of visuality in post-Classical culture. As in the case of Romanticism, the emergence of a new visual sensibility became manifest in a host of artistic expressions and cultural phenomena of the Hellenistic age[76]. An outstanding example is the thriving of the *ekphrasis*, the descriptive digression of a work of art within a poem. Though this device is as old as the *Iliad*, it was Alexandrianism that found its most refined sensibility in poetic *ekphrases*[77]. To reconstruct an *objet d'art* by means of rhetoric was a sweeping vogue in Hellenistic times, a vogue that introduced visual discourse in both literature and art[78]. The point is best illustrated by considering the fascination with viewing on a microscopic scale in the *Lithika* or observing statues in the *Andriantopoiika* of the 'New Posidippus'. Perspectives similar to the ones introduced by the *picturesque* or the *panorama* during Romanticism may also be found in Hellenistic poetry, for instance in the eutopic idealization of nature in the stylized Theocritean bucolic and in the panoramic representation of Greece in Callimachus' *Hymn to Delos* respectively[79]. We may even infer that Ptolemaic Alexandria in particular was the metropolis of visual culture, which evolved from a combination of elements: scientific treatises such as Euclid's *Optics*, and the *Catoptrics*, on reflections in mirrors, attributed to him and to Archimedes, Herophilus' celebrated theory on the anatomy of the human eye, the flourishing of astronomical and geographical observation, the new mapping of the world were major achievements pertaining to visuality during the reign of the first Ptolemies; and, on the other hand, a preoccupation with the spectacular, with attending art exhibitions (like the *tableau* of Adonis described in Theocritus *Idyll* 15, the *locus classicus* for understanding the Alexandrian mania for spectacles), theatrical performances, religious festivals, and lavishing processions for the ruling dynasty–the Grand Procession for Ptolemy Philadelphus, according to the narration of Callixenus, being the prime example of a majestic

76. Prioux (2007) offers a valuable analysis of what she calls the *regards Alexandrins*, the history and theory of the visual in Hellenistic culture.

77. For a thorough analysis of Hellenistic *ekphrases*, see Manakidou (1993); the interrelations between Alexandrian poetry and art are explored by Webster (1964) 156-177.

78. Indispensable for the study of Hellenistic modes of viewing art is the monograph by Zanker (2004).

79. Zanker (1996) 412 n. 5 rightly points out that we should not limit visualization in Hellenistic poetry to the device of the *ekphrasis* but include in it each type of pictorial description.

spectacle set within a highly elaborate scenery (attested by Athenaeus *Deipn.* 5.25-35)[80].

The emphasis on visuality, and the development of visualization in poetry as a consequence of its growing importance, is a common thread connecting Hellenistic and Romantic culture. The paradigm of Romanticism has shown that it was the sensation of the visual that spawned the aesthetics of ugliness, horror and eventually darkness; what remains to be demonstrated is that a similar process took place during the Hellenistic era. But before thoroughly exploring the critical turn towards darkness in Hellenistic literature, it is vital to understand the notion of darkness itself.

Romantic darkness

Darkness, hardly a critical term or a distinguishable movement in literature, is mostly used by scholars to suggest certain facets of Gothic or Romantic poetics[81]. *Dark Romanticism* is a name given to a literary subgenre of 19th century American Romanticism that reacted against the Age of Enlightenment by taking a pessimistic view of nature, religion and society. It is also called *Negative Romanticism*, because it focuses on social outcasts, places emphasis on individuality and affect and, most importantly, casts doubt on cosmic order and religion in establishing a negative relationship between man and God. Lord Byron, Mary Shelley, Edgar Allan Poe, Nathaniel Hawthorne and Herman Melville are well-known representatives of this literary trend, also termed *Gothicism*[82]. Darkness also occurs in the ambiguous critical term *Dark*

80. The catalogue is largely based on the definition of *visual culture* offered by de Bolla (2003) 4 (in reference to 18th century Britain): "But I am claiming that something recognizable as precisely a *culture* based on the visual, on modalities of visualization, the production and consumption of visual matter (representations, maps, diagrams), as well as any number of mechanical objects intended for use in some form of looking, observing, surveying, spying, and so forth, all requiring and producing various modes of address, attention, or forms of understanding–that all this did come together in ways that theretofore had not resulted in a coherence or coalescence such that it became possible to identify something called *visual cutlure*".

81. Darkness, as a term pertaining primarily to Gothicism, is discussed by Cavallaro (2002) 21-26.

82. As said in the beginning of this introduction, this trend is first described by Praz (1970) in the 1930's. The term *Negative Romanticism* was coined by Peckham (1951) to denote the tendency of the Romantic individual towards isolation, despair and doubt. *Dark Romanticism* is studied in a collection of essays by Thompson (1974) as a concept supplementary to the Gothic; for its definition in contrast with *Light* or *Positive Romanticism*, see Alsen (2000) 1-9. On the close connection between *Dark Romanticism* and the Gothic from a feminist perspective, see especially Williams (1995).

Fantasy, sometimes considered to be synonymous with Gothic tales and sometimes categorized as a fantasy genre. The definition according to which *Dark Fantasy* describes a certain emotional affect horror or fantasy stories may have on their readers is quite relevant to the present analysis[83]. Darkness may also be associated with those considering corruption, pessimism and decay as the most appropriate object of art–those pursuing the dark ideal of *Decadence*. Decadence, for many a form of late or lesser Romanticism, explores the sensuous pleasure stemming from the fatal and the appalling, the 'Beauty of the Medusa' in Mario Praz' terminology, a cultural mode which, not coincidentally, has its origins in the Gothic novel and the works of Edgar Allan Poe[84].

Accordingly, and despite its limited usage and vagueness, darkness may be broadly applied as a descriptive name that embraces the grotesque, the gloomy, the morbid, the uncanny, the imaginary and the illogical, all of which are inextricably interwoven in the subject matter, the tone and the rhetoric of a literary work. Reworked as an aesthetic concept, darkness manifests itself as a fascination with the evil passions of man, an emphasis on the ugly and the monstrous, an obsession with morbidity and death, a blurring of the boundaries between reality and imagination; its effect ranges from pleasure in the representation of horror to the overwhelming sense of the sublime[85].

Since darkness is a nebulous concept and its range cannot be limited to a sole artistic movement, its study is beset with difficulties. As its precise definition eludes us, I will instead outline four key notions, through which, in my opinion at least, darkness manifests itself in culture–namely the fantastic, the Gothic, the grotesque and the uncanny. Each notion will be illustrated with examples from Archaic and Classical Greek literature which help us trace the literary predecessors of Hellenistic darkness; these notions, dominating European culture throughout the 19th and 20th centuries, will be employed as heuristic tools for the reconstruction of the aesthetics of darkness in Hellenistic poetry; it will thus be evident why the close reading of Hellenistic poetry through the lens of darkness is combined throughout the study with specific examples drawn from Romantic and Decadent literature of the modern era.

---

83. The term is thoroughly discussed by Wolfe (1986). For a collection of essays on the *Dark Fantastic*, a broader concept denoting "the various aspects of the darker side of the human condition as expressed by and explored in a wide variety of fantastic fiction and art" (p. xiii), see Sullivan (1997).

84. An overview of the various definitions of Decadence in Weir (1995) 1-22.

85. For an analysis of darkness from the viewpoint of horror, terror and fear, see Cavallaro (2002) 1-17.

The fantastic mode

No two scholars are unanimous as regards the definition and the scope of, even the labelling apropriate to, *the fantastic*[86]. Mastering the terminology is the first task of the researcher. 'The fantastic' and 'fantasy' are used interchangeably to denote the broad category of a genre or any literary work where the supernatural, the eerie and the imaginary, in one word the anti-realistic, are thematized. The fantastic mode comprises numerous subcategories, such as myth, legend, folklore, allegory, fairytale, horror fiction, science fiction, science fantasy, Gothic fiction, magical realism, utopia and many more[87].

To define the fantastic presupposes to address the archetypal question about the nature of artistic imitation and its relation to reality[88]. Fantasy has been initially interpreted as a tendency towards the irrational and the absurd. Socrates, at the beginning of *Phaedrus*, seeks to rationalize the story of Boreas and Orithyia by testing its plausibility; however, Socrates maintains, one is less successful, when attempting to explain other modes of storytelling (*Phaedr.* 229d-e):

ἐγὼ δέ, ὦ Φαῖδρε, ἄλλως μὲν τὰ τοιαῦτα χαρίεντα ἡγοῦμαι, λίαν δὲ δεινοῦ καὶ ἐπιπόνου καὶ οὐ πάνυ εὐτυχοῦς ἀνδρός, κατ᾽ ἄλλο μὲν οὐδέν, ὅτι δ᾽ αὐτῷ ἀνάγκη μετὰ τοῦτο τὸ τῶν Ἱπποκενταύρων εἶδος ἐπανορθοῦσθαι, καὶ αὖθις τὸ τῆς Χιμαίρας, καὶ ἐπιρρεῖ δὲ ὄχλος τοιούτων Γοργόνων καὶ Πηγάσων καὶ ἄλλων ἀμηχάνων πλήθη τε καὶ ἀτοπίαι τερατολόγων τινῶν φύσεων· αἷς εἴ τις ἀπιστῶν προσβιβᾷ κατὰ τὸ εἰκὸς ἕκαστον, ἅτε ἀγροίκῳ τινὶ σοφίᾳ χρώμενος, πολλῆς αὐτῷ σχολῆς δεήσει.

86. A listing of the various definitions of the fantastic offered by the American critic Gary Wolfe (in Sandner [2004] 271-273) is indicative of the problem; cf. the discussion of the diverse theories of fantasy by Hume (1984) 5-28. The theory of the fantastic includes the structural analysis of Todorov (1975). Matthews (2002) concentrates on English and American exemplars of the fantastic; he also provides a comprehensive guide to the related bibliography (pp. 166-196). For an anthology of the critical approaches to the fantastic from antiquity until today, see Sandner (2004)–a truly valuable tool. For a useful introduction that bridges its modern conception with Greek antiquity, see Baumbach/Hömke (2006) 1-71.

87. A theoretical approach to 'fantasy' as mode, genre or formula in Attebery (1992) 1-17.

88. The famous *locus* for the definition of mimesis is Plato's *Republic* Book 10, where Socrates illustrates the relation between reality and poetry by the analogy of the mirror (e.g. *Rp.* 596d-e). Abrams (1971) studies the bipolar distinction between mimesis and the Romantic ideal of imagination under the telling title *The Mirror and the Lamp*; on fantasy, along with mimesis, as the twin impulses behind literary creation, see Hume (1984). On artistic mimesis as an imperfect representation of reality, see Halliwell (2002), esp. 37-71 (in Plato) and 151-176 (in Aristotle); for a comprehensive review of the concept of 'mimesis', see Potolsky (2006).

Now I quite acknowledge that these allegories [i.e. the story of Orithyia and Boreas] are very nice, but he is not to be envied who has to invent them; much labour and ingenuity will be required of him; and when he has once begun, he must go on and rehabilitate Hippocentaurs and Chimeras dire. Gorgons and winged steeds flow in apace, and numberless other inconceivable and portentous natures. And if he is sceptical about them, and would fain reduce them one after another to the rules of probability, this sort of crude philosophy will take up a great deal of time. [Transl. B. Jowett]

A sense that there are different degrees of probability in myth seems to underlie Socrates' criticism. Thus, through Socrates, Plato does not reject myth in its entirety but in particular the unlikely and the fantastic part of it–the one pertaining to monster narratives which is not susceptible to logical reasoning[89]. More closely related to modern conceptions of the fantastic is the Homeric scholion on *Iliad* 14.342-351, a comment on the episode where Zeus makes love to Hera being clad in a golden cloud, which suggests a tripartite distinction of the poetic modes (τρόποι): the mimetic of truth or the realistic (ὁ μιμητικὸς τοῦ ἀληθοῦς), the imaginary but convincing (ὁ κατὰ φαντασίαν τῆς ἀληθείας) and the one that goes beyond reality and may be identified with pure fantasy (ὁ καθ' ὑπέρθεσιν τῆς ἀληθείας καὶ φαντασίαν). The latter includes not only the miraculous scene of Zeus and Hera's lovemaking but anything pertaining to the incredible and the monstrous, such as the presentation of the Cyclopes and the Laistrygonians[90]. Other instances of the extraordinary, especially with regard to gods, are considered as τερατεία 'portentous monstrosity' by the Homeric scholia; the effect achieved by the employment of monstrosities in each case is described as ἔκπληξις[91].

Ancient references to the fantastic are sporadic, and, in defining the fantastic as the incredible and the impossible in terms of reality, fail to

89. The idea that mythical monsters, or anything transcending the boundaries of nature, are the task of the poet is suggested by Philip Sydney in his *Apology for Poetry* (1595): "Only the poet, disdaining to be tied to any such subjection, lifted up with the vigour of his own invention, doth grow in effect into another nature, in making things either better than Nature bringeth forth, or, quite anew, forms such as never were in Nature, as the Heroes, Demigods, Cyclopes, Chimeras, Furies, and such like".

90. For a discussion of the passage, see Meijering (1987) 68-69; cf. Richardson (2006) 184-187 on the distinction between fictional and factual narrative by the Homeric scholia.

91. Two examples suffice to illustrate the nature of τερατεία: the bloody mist shed by Zeus after the death of Sarpedon (Sch. *Il.* 16.459 ἁρμόδιος ἡ τερατεία) and the gathering of the winds into Zephyr's hall to share his banquet as a parallel to the representation of Aeolus' winds in the *Odyssey* (Sch. *Il.* 23.229 τετεράτευται τὰ περὶ τοῦ Αἰόλου). The fantastic as an element indispensable to the action of the divine in epic is discussed by Feeney (1991) 51-53.

bring its many and various aspects into relief. Although the fantastic is manifest in all types of literature from its very beginnings, its theoretical framework has fully developed only late, from the early 18th century, running counter to the dominance of Classical theories of imitation[92]. The British essayist Joseph Addison was the first to regard the fantastic as a separate literary genre and, more interestingly, foundational to the discourse of the sublime[93]. His definition of the fantastic as the entirely imaginary strongly evokes the passage from *Phaedrus*–but now the 'monsters' are contextualized into Medieval folkore myth (*The Spectator* n. 419, published in 1712):

> There is a kind of writing wherein the poet quite loses sight of nature and entertains his reader's imagination with the characters and actions of such persons as have many of them no existence but what he bestows on them. Such are Fairies, Witches, Magicians, Demons, and departed Spirits. This Mr. Dryden calls "the fairy way of writing", which is, indeed, more difficult than any other that depends on the poet's fancy...

The liberation of artistic imagination during the 18th and 19th century resulted into the Romantic boom of fantastic literature–and vice versa[94]. The fantastic turn took various shapes in the course of the 19th century, such as the fascination with the Gothic novel, the collecting and publishing of ballads and folktales, the establishment of children's literature, the defense of the fairytale, the emergence of horror fiction. Medievalism and Gothic primitivism were the dominant trends of the fantastic in early Romantic literature and a nostalgic return to the past through the re-writing of ancient fantasies came to the fore. The fantastic was moreover regarded as an artistic response to scientific progress and the triumph of reason[95]: the supernatural, considered from the very beginning to be the core of the fantastic, demands from the reader what Coleridge called "the willing suspension of

---

92. For an outline of the so-called 'mimetic' theories, see Abrams (1971) 8-14.

93. That fantastic literature functions, according to Addison, as a discourse of the sublime is argued by Sandner (2004) 316-325; cf. the views of Walter Scott on the association between the supernatural and the sublime (in Sandner [2004] 51-55).

94. Cf. the distinction between imagination and fancy as proposed by Samuel Taylor Coleridge (in Sandner [2004] 37-40).

95. In fact, we may distinguish between a primary and a secondary employment of the fantastic in the history of literature: the first is inherent in ancient cultures (Egypt, Babylonia, China, India, Persia, Greece and Rome) and regarded as part of the real; the second marks a conscious return to the primary fantastic as a reaction to an Age of Reason. On this reading of the fantastic, see Matthews (2002) 1-5 and Sandner (2004) 6-11 and esp. p. 11 n. 2 for bibliography on the history of the supernatural beliefs and the secularization of imagination during the 18th century.

disbelief"[96]. Thus, the departure from reality into the realm of the supernatural, which questions the dominance of logic, science and, in literature, of realism, has created the modern fantastic that is, by definition, a 'sceptical literature'[97].

Modern theorists of the genre tackle the question 'what is the fantastic' from entirely new perspectives. Northrop Frye, in his influential monograph *The Anatomy of Criticism* (1957), interprets fantasy in terms of archetypal patterns. Drawing upon the anthropological study of cult by James Frazer and Carl Jung's psychological archetypes, Frye views fantasy as the core of a romance with a quest structure where the hero engages in a series of marvellous events and struggles against enemies with supernatural forces[98]. Tzvetan Todorov in his 1970 monograph on the fantastic narrows its definition by labelling the hesitation experienced by the reader when confronting the intrusion of the supernatural element into the real world as the quintessence of the fantastic. For Todorov the fantastic inhabits the interspace between the real and the imaginary, and its neighbouring genres are the uncanny and the marvellous respectively[99]. As a consequence Todorov excludes from the fantastic an array of works which either deal with dreams and illusions within a reality framework or are set within an entirely imaginary domain, a fantastic storyworld. Unlike Todorov, Colin Manlove in the introduction to his *Modern Fantasy* (1975) broadens the generic category of fantasy by classifying as such "a fiction evoking wonder and containing a substantial and irreducible element of the supernatural with which the mortal characters in the story or the readers become on at least partly familiar terms". For Manlove the supernatural presupposes the existence of an impossible world, wholly other to the empirically known, from which the sense of mystery and wonder derives. An important criterion in his understanding of fantasy is the conception of time: fantasy is a retrospective mode in that it draws on the past for nourishment–the Medieval and/or Christian world order–and it is a contemplation of what is old and lost that lies in the core of the genre[100].

---

96. In his *Biographia Literaria* (ch. 14) Coleridge explains how he directed his literary efforts to "persons and characters supernatural, or at least romantic–yet so as to transfer from our inward nature, a human interest and a semblance of truth sufficient to procure for these shadows of imagination that willing suspension of disbelief for the moment, which constitutes poetic faith".

97. Sandner (2004) 6: "Fantastic literature is a necessarily sceptical literature, appearing after primary belief in the supernatural has waned". On the polarity between fantasy and realism, see Hume (1984) 29-51.

98. See Sandner (2004) 108-115.

99. Todorov (1975) 24-40.

100. On Manlove's introduction, see Sandner (2004) 156-166.

Charting the theories of the fantastic is a daunting task, and only peripheral to the present study. The vexed issue is if modern aspects on, and paradigms of, the fantastic may shed new light on the interpretation of Greek literature[101]. If we take as a point of departure the restricted definition of fantasy by Todorov, then myth seems to be an impediment to classifying any kind of Greek poetry as fantasy; "myth is the natural enemy of fantasy", practically because the characters inhabiting a mythical world and their audience cannot experience the hesitation whether what they perceive is real or not–the central premise in Todorov's theory[102]. On the contrary, the all-encompassing definition by John Clute provides a more useful basis for discussing ancient fantasy: "A fantasy text is a self-coherent narrative. When set in this world, it tells a story which is impossible in the world as we perceive it; when set in an otherworld, that otherworld will be impossible, though stories set there may be possible in its terms"[103]. All types of ancient fantasy fiction, i.e. fantasies of travel beyond the known world and stories of the supernatural, look back to the *Odyssey*. But, although the *Odyssey* is set entirely into the world of myth, i.e. it is 'mythological' in the modern sense of the word, only the part of the *Apologoi* which comprises the fairytale adventures of Odysseus deserves to be called a 'fantasy' proper; the rest of the epic, the narration about the Homecoming Husband is almost 'realistic' in design and tone–or 'mimetic', in the ancient sense of the term[104]. Evaluated in terms of the abovementioned definition, the *Odyssey* can only be labelled as fantasy when set in the 'otherworld' of the Great Wanderings, whereas there is no genuine supernatural element within the world of the Ithaca-plot, the equivalent of 'this world'; thus, the *Odyssey* may be divided into two self-coherent narratives, the former of which is fantastic/fictional and the latter realistic/mimetic. The Great Wanderings of Odysseus have often invited comparison with the story-cycle of Sinbad the Sailor and the geography of the *Odyssey* has been

---

101. Baumbach (2006) attempts to write a 'history' of the precursors to the literary fantastic in antiquity, by tracing the development of the concept of *ambivalence* (considered by Baumbach as synonymous with what Todorov calls *hésitation*) from simple narrative forms (Hesiod and Archilochus) to more complex ones (the travelogue and the novel).

102. On the antithesis between myth and fantasy, see Kloss (2006).

103. *EF* s.v. "Fantasy".

104. On this reading of the *Odyssey*, which has its roots in folktale on the one hand and the *Novellen* (a pre-stage of the novel) on the other, see Hölscher (1988). The 'realistic/mimetic' aspects of the *Odyssey*, seen through the prism of rhetoric, are stressed in the famous essay "Odysseus' Scar" by Erich Auerbach (1953). Halliwell (2002) 303-305 collects passages which reflect the views of ancient scholiasts on the 'life-like' quality of Homeric mimesis.

inscribed into the realm of the fairytale since the age of Eratosthenes[105]. In the celebrated comparison between the dramatic *Iliad* and the mythical *Odyssey* (9.13-14), 'Longinus' criticizes Homer for roving in the fabulous and the incredible (κἂν τοῖς μυθώδεσι καὶ ἀπίστοις πλάνος). Episodes such as the stories about the bags containing the winds of Aeolus or the feeding of Odysseus' comrades like swines in the palace of Kirke are rejected as garrulous (εἰς λῆρον) and utterly absurd (τοῦ Διὸς ἐνύπνια). 'Longinus' concludes that the fabulous prevails over the realistic in the entire epic (πλὴν ἐν ἅπασι τούτοις ἑξῆς τοῦ πρακτικοῦ κρατεῖ τὸ μυθικόν)[106].

The *Odyssey* is a vantage point from which we can observe the substantial difference between myth proper and fantasy in antiquity: myth does not contradict truth or realism[107], still its mutation into something incredible or improbable in terms of reality was immediately noticeable then as it is now. It is in the Hellenistic age that critics became fully aware of the boundaries which separate myth from fantasy, and realistic fiction from fantastic fiction, in consequence of Aristotle's theories on mimesis and the life-like plots of Menander's New Comedy[108]. This assumption stems not only from the views expressed by Eratosthenes about the fabulous character of the *Odyssey*, but also from the Homeric scholia, attributed mainly to Aristarchus[109], who maintains that a poet can depart from what might be called 'historical' into the 'mythical' due to his imagination and poetic licence (ποιητικὴ ἐξουσία). Hellenistic poetry also attests to the fact that fantasy may be a self-contained genre. Callimachus with *Iamb* 1, an inversion of *katabasis* scenes, makes a metapoetic comment on the uses of the fantastic: not only does Callimachus stage the fabulous return of Hipponax from the realm of the

---

105. The *Odyssey, qua* fantasy, is superbly studied within the context of legend and fairytale by Hölscher (1988) 103-169. Renger (2006) reads the *Odyssey*, and especially the *Apologoi*, within the conventions of fantasy, primarily the notions of 'ambivalence' and 'threshold'.

106. Meijering (1987) 67-72; cf. Halliwell (2002) 310-312.

107. Buxton (1994) views Greek myth as an imaginary construct based on, and at the same time juxtaposed with, reality which comprises everyday social contexts, such as landscape, family and religion; he acknowledges that there is a distance between the mythical and the ordinary, but, on the other hand, he maintains that reality and the everyday are the bonds which connect myth with its audience (pp. 77-79).

108. The truth of myth, though, is open to doubt: the *locus classicus* is the proem of Hesiod's *Theogony* where it is said that the Muses have the ability to tell the truth and also falsewoods that seem real (*Th.* 27-28). The issue of truth and lies in poetry is further complicated by the adjacent problem of literary fiction in antiquity, on which see Gill/Wiseman (1993) and especially Finkelberg (1998).

109. For a brilliant analysis of ancient views on fact and fiction in literature, see Meijering (1987) 54-98.

dead within a semi-satirical genre, the iamb, but he also hints at the 'Sacred Scripture' of Euhemerus, a travelogue recounting an imaginary voyage to Panchaia, a novel which became a milestone in utopian writing. The notion of the fantastic was further elaborated in the late Hellenistic and Imperial period, when, for example, Asclepiades of Myrleia, a 1st c. BC grammarian, distinguished between the (ἀληθὴς) ἱστορία and the ψευδὴς ἱστορία or τὸ μυθικόν, corresponding to the potentially historical on the one hand, and the miraculous, the incredible element of mythology on the other[110].

The Gothic mood

Fantasy is the matrix from which the other three concepts, the Gothic, the grotesque and the uncanny, have developed. The *Gothic*, a term coined after the barbaric tribe of the Goths, was introduced by Horace Walpole in 1765 with his novel *The Castle of Otranto* which had the subtitle *A Gothic Story*. Although Walpole through this subtitle intended to suggest that the plot of his book was set in the Middle Ages, this first 'official' use of the term within a literary context demarcates the beginning of an artistic trend that was to become dominant from the Preromantic era to the present day, quite often in low culture manifestations[111]. As a Romantic trend *par excellence*, the Gothic aesthetics, or the Gothic sensibility, is associated with the primitive, the barbarous and the savage, the counter-Classical and the Medieval, the irregular and the obscure; it is thought of as a reaction to the Enlightenment and its rationalism and empiricism, a turn towards the mysterious, the irrational and the paranormal, a preference for the sublime stemming from the supernatural, a fascination with a world beyond reality.

Although the Gothic is a literary tradition both in poetry and novel, it is the latter that has mostly attracted the attention of critics and readers. The Gothic novel includes such landmarks as Ann Radcliffe's *The*

110. Meijering (1987) 76-87.
111. A chronological listing of Gothic works in all artistic media from 1750 until today in Hogle (2002) xvii-xxv. For the definition and description of Gothic aesthetics I rely on the short but illuminating introductory chapter by Trott (2005); helpful, though designed for students of Gothic literature, is Stevens (2000). For a plethora of articles on the main features and primary texts of the Gothic, as well as discussions of its cultural and ideological background, see the four large-scale companions to the Gothic by Punter (2000), Hogle (2002), Bomarito (2006) and Spooner/McEvoy (2007). Both Thompson (1974) and more recently Gamer (2004) stress the affinity of the Gothic with the dark aspects of Romantic fantasy; on the beginnings of the Gothic, see Miles (1993).

Mysteries of Udolpho, Matthew Lewis' *The Monk*, Emily Brontë's *Wuthering Heights*, Mary Shelley's *Frankenstein*, Robert Louis Stevenson's *The Strange Case of Dr. Jekyll and Mr. Hyde* and Edgar Allan Poe's *The Fall of the House of Usher*. At the mention of these titles one may easily recognize the distinguishing features of the genre. The typical setting of a Gothic novel has been succinctly termed *the edifice*, a microcosm and a self-contained world within a real or metaphorical structure representing the past–be it a castle, a labyrinth, a cathedral, a graveyard, a city, a library or just a map–which controls, physically or psychologically, the characters of the story[112]. The Gothic novel is by definition a tragedy, building on scenarios that entail the confrontation of a human with any form of the Other–the past, the devil, the unknown[113]. The lascivious male, the female with its refined sensibility, the villain and the naive girl, are stock characters of the Gothic which either represent, or are subject to the powers of, the Other; therefore, the Gothic features both a male and a female tradition[114]. The encounter with Otherness heightens the tension between the real and the supernatural, the latter of which becomes visible in the appearance of ghosts, goblins, vampires and monsters[115]. Beyond this, Gothic plots explore the breaking of social taboos in describing extreme situations such as persecution, abduction, incest and infanticide; Gothic suspense is as a rule combined with extreme manifestations of sex and violence, of bodily pain and torment: these violations of social and moral laws inform the ideological basis of Gothicism[116].

The Gothic seems primarily to rely on the exploration of two key notions and their effects on the human psyche, terror and horror. For some the former presupposes that evil is due to external circumstances, whereas according to the latter evil is considered to reside in the human psyche and to be largely dependent on the moral ambiguity

112. See especially Aguirre (1990) 91-114, who closes his chapter on the haunted house as the symbolic space of Gothic horror with the following remark (p. 114): "The Haunted Mansion, the Puzzle, the Riddle, the Labyrinth shape the literature of terror. As the genre develops, the labyrinth grows–a labyrinth which no longer signifies merely the *absence* of a numinous power but, quite the contrary, the *presence* of a new Numen in the human world. And at the heart of the labyrinth, the Minotaur waits".

113. The evil appears to possess an 'ontological existence', the 'Numinous Other', as Aguirre (1990) calls it; on the heterotopic character of Gothic fiction, see Botting (2000).

114. For an introduction to the Gothic as a gendered tradition, see Williams (1995) and Heiland (2004).

115. On themes, settings and figures of the Gothic, see Bomarito (2006) 1.230-387.

116. Trott (2005) 487-488. Praz (1970) 53-195 graphically depicts the Gothic as a sensation stemming from the 'beauty of the horrid' in his chapters on "The Metamorphoses of Satan" and "The Shadow of the Divine Marquis".

of the subject[117]. However, the distinction between terror and horror is not clear-cut, and in most cases both terms suggest different hues of the emotion of fear. In any case, the Gothic, as a particular trend of Romanticism, draws on Burke's theory on the sublime effect that derives from the exploitation of fear and explores the pleasures of representing horrifying events in art[118]. The nature of 'artificial terror formed by a sublime and vigorous imagination' is described in the 1773 essay "On the Pleasure Derived from Objects of Terror" written by John Aikin and Anna Laetitia Barbauld:

> The greediness with which the tales of ghosts and goblins, of murders, earthquakes, fires, shipwrecks, and all the most terrible disasters attending human life, are devoured by every ear, must have been generally remarked. Tragedy, the most favourite work of fiction, has taken a full share of those scenes; "it has supt full with horrors"—and has, perhaps, been more indebted to them for public admiration than to its tender and pathetic parts. The ghost of Hamlet, Macbeth descending into the witches' cave, and the tent scene in Richard, command as forcibly the attention of our souls as the parting of Jaffeir and Belvidera, the fall of Wolsey, or the death of Shore. The inspiration of *terror* was by the ancient critics assigned as the peculiar province of tragedy; and the Greek and Roman tragedians have introduced some extraordinary personages for this purpose: not only the shades of the dead, but the furies, and other fabulous inhabitants of the infernal regions.

One cannot deny the 'Englishness' of Gothic aesthetics nor the fact that European Romanticism forms the core of this aesthetics. However, the abovementioned remarks on terror and its effects on the reader help us acknowledge that the critical features of Gothicism transcend the historical and ethnic limits of 18th-19th century literature, and that they can retrospectively apply to other cultural traditions. In exploring borderline cases of human passion, tragedy often verges on the Gothic, if the latter is viewed as a transhistorical discourse and narrative mode. Based on this premise, I intend to show that the concept of the Gothic was not at all alien to poets and critics since antiquity.

---

117. Already distinguished by Ann Radcliffe in her essay "On the Supernatural in Poetry" (1826): "Terror and Horror are so far opposite, that the first expands the soul and awakens the faculties to a high degree of life; the other contracts, freezes and nearly annihilates them...Where lies the great difference between horror and terror, but in uncertainty and obscurity, that accompany the first, respecting the dreaded evil?". In effect, terror-Gothic (e.g. the work of Walpole) has developed into horror-Gothic (e.g. *Frankenstein*): see Hume (1969) and Stevens (2000) 53-54.

118. According to Gamer (2004) 1-26 the common basis between Romanticism and the Gothic is, after William Wordsworth's phrase, 'the pageantry of fear'; cf. Williams (1995) for an identification of the Gothic with (Dark) Romanticism on a similar basis.

It is well known that Aristotle was the first to introduce fear as a concomitant pleasure of the tragic in his famous definition of tragedy (*Poet.*
1449b)[119]. At the same time, though, Aristotle rejects the emphasis on
the monstrous, especially when it derives from the visual, at the expense
of the 'fearful *and* pitiable' stemming from the tragic plot itself (*Poet.*
1453b). It has rightly been observed that "in real life, fear is typically
aroused by the appearance of a particular, perceptible danger to our-
selves; a bad tragedy, like a horror film, might arouse fear of this kind
by its use of such visual effects as terrifying masks"[120]. To travel the
distance between the Gothic of the modern era and its analogy in ancient
times, one needs to distinguish between the Aristotelian type of 'good'
tragedy and the one that arouses pleasure by means of visual, rhetorical
or aesthetic hyperbole. An obvious example of the latter, which we may
call the non-Classical, the Romantic, the 'Gothic' type of tragedy, is
Shakespeare: it is a commonplace of criticism that 'The Bard' was the
inventor of Gothic aesthetics–the famous apparitions scenes of *Macbeth*, *Hamlet* or *Richard III* serve to illustrate the point[121]. The same
'Gothic' feeling is essential to the understanding of Greco-Roman tragedy. To begin from the final phase of ancient tragedy: Senecan dramas
explore, both ideologically and rhetorically, the dark, violent nature of
man and were definitely written under the influence of the bloody spectacles of the Roman arena; it is no wonder that Seneca is considered a
forerunner of Renaissance theatre, and of Shakespeare in particular[122]. At
the opposite end of the spectrum, Seneca draws on Classical Greek

119. On Aristotle's concept of φόβος as arising from the expectation of an imminent
evil and as an aesthetic experience, see Belfiore (1992) 181-189 and 226-238.
120. Belfiore (1992) 232. Konstan (forthcoming, Seneca) draws a prarallel between
instinctive emotions such as horror or disgust and Aristotle's notion of the μιαρόν.
121. Essential for the understanding of Shakespeare's significance for the Gothic, and
for a reading of his plays in the light of Gothic literature, is the collective volume by
Drakakis/Townshend (2008).
122. See the monograph by Boyle (1997), esp. 32-56 on the ideas 'made flesh' in
Senecan tragedy. The main ideas of Seneca that evoke Gothic thematics are among others,
as listed by Boyle (p. 33), "the genealogy and cyclicity of evil; the fragility of social and
religious forms; the fragility of epistemological forms; the failure of reason; civilisation
as moral contradiction; the man as appetite, as beast, as existential victim; power, impo-
tence, delusion, self-deception, the futility of compassion; the freedom, desirability and
value-paradox of death; man, god, nature, guilt, unmerited suffering; the certainty of
human pain; the terror of experienced evil; the inexorable, paradoxical, amoral–even mor-
ally perverse–order of things; the triumph of evil". The macabre in Seneca serves as a
warning against the consequences of uncontrollable emotion: on this Stoic reading of
Senecan macabre, see Mans (1984). Not coincidentally, Seneca focuses on the visual
representation of tragedy, the Aristotelian ὄψις (Staley [2010]), and exploits its potential
to trigger pre-emotions like horror or revulsion in the audience, as Konstan (forthcoming,
Seneca) convincingly argues.

drama and his plays are, in a way, Gothic adaptations of Greek originals, primarily by Sophocles and Euripides.

But already Greek tragedy abounds with Gothic elements, manifest in the gory details of murder descriptions, in the ghostly apparitions of the dead, in the terrifying appearance of gods and demons. Messengers vividly recounting scenes of horror which take place offstage are common in Sophoclean and Euripidean dramas–the hanging of Jocasta and the self-blinding of Oedipus by piercing his eyes with the pins from Jocasta's clothes in *Oedipus the King* (1237-1279), the killing of Glauke and Kreon with a poisonous crown and robe in *Medea* (1136-1221), the dismemberment (*sparagmos*) of Pentheus by his mother Agave and the Bacchants within the supernatural setting of the Cithaeron in the *Bacchae* (677-768), Herakles killing his three children and wife in his madness in *Herakles* (922-1015). Euripides has *Hekabe*–which has been likened to a 'horror story'–introduced by the ghost of her murdered son Polydoros (1-58)[123]; human sacrifice is a recurrent theme in Euripidean drama–*The Trojan Women* and *Iphigenia in Aulis* best exemplify the point. Sophocles was also known for his sublime visualizations. 'Longinus' (15.7) praises the scene where Oedipus dies to the accompaniment of a heavenly sign (*OC* 1620-1665) or when Achilles' ghost is shown to appear *over* his tomb in the lost *Polyxena*[124]. But it was Aeschylus who seems to have been primarily fascinated by similar dark situations, both for their theatricality and their dramatic potential. His famous ghost scenes include the summoning of the dead Dareios at his tomb in the *Persians* (681-842) and the haunting of Orestes by the ghost of Klytaimestra urging the Erinyes to seek revenge for her murder in the *Eumenides* (94-177)[125]. Aeschylus' treatment of the supernatural and the demonic borders on obsession in the pursuit of Orestes by the Erinyes/Eumenides or the juxtaposition of the tortured Prometheus with Zeus in *Prometheus Bound*. The stagecraft of Aeschylus was legendary, and ancient testimonies, from Aristophanes' *Frogs* (833-834) to 'Longinus' (15.5), attest to the fact that he was an

---

123. By Rosenmeyer (1987).

124. On the effect achieved by such φαντασία or εἰδωλοποιία, see Bardel (2005) 83-100.

125. Essential for the study of ghosts in Greek tragedy, and for the treatment of εἴδωλα by ancient literary critics, is Bardel (2005). From the analysis of textual and visual evidence, Bardel (p. 112) reaches two conclusions: that ghostly appearances were very common in (now lost) Greek poetry and that this motif was widely used before Aeschylus' *Persians*, i.e. before 472 BC. Ghosts in Archaic and Classical literature and culture are studied by Johnston (1999). The literary sources concerning the apparitions of ghosts, beginning with the ghost of Patroclus in *Iliad* 23, are collected by Ogden (2009) 146-178.

expert in transforming λόγος to horrifying and spectacular ὄψις[126]. Apart from creating a horror atmosphere in his works, Aeschylus established the pattern of an almost 'Gothic' plot structure with the *Oresteia*, especially the *Agamemnon*, which invites us to read it as a claustrophobic family drama: its protagonists are trapped in the palace of Argos, haunted by the gruesome past of the House of Atreus and unable to escape their cruel fate–Kassandra being the victim of her own horror prophecy[127].

Grotesque nuances

The origin of the *grotesque* (as a word it derives from the Latin *grotta* meaning 'a hollow, a cave') may be traced back to the Renaissance, when artists retrospectively applied the term to the style of the frescoes decorating the walls of Nero's *Domus Aurea*[128]. This style, which had been in vogue in Rome from 100 BC onwards, is ridiculed by Horace in *The Art of Poetry* (1-9). Horace describes grotesque artistic forms (7-8 *vanae / fingentur species*), which originate from the combination of such distinct elements as a human head, a horse's neck, the wings of a bird, the body of a woman and the tail of a fish, as a 'sick man's dreams' (7 *velut aegri somnia*). This aesthetics of the bizarre was also viewed with strong disapproval by Vitruvius (*De Architectura* 7.5.3-4). Like their Roman predecessors, critics of the modern era, such as Vasari and Winckelmann, addressed the grotesque as a new, non-Classical, degenerate class of aesthetics, closely resembling the baroque and the rococo[129].

126. The ancient *Life* offers a vivid description of the impact of Aeschylean ὄψις; it is said that, when Aeschylus introduced the chorus of Furies in the *Eumenids*, the surprise and fear of the audience was such that children fainted and women miscarried (*Vita Aeschyli* test. A1.30-32 TrGF). Contemporary scholars have extensively studied Aeschylus as a *Regisseur* with a preference for the horrific and the dark spectacle, see Taplin (1977) and Easterling (2008).

127. Aeschylus and Shakespeare have often been compared on the basis of employing supernatural elements to heighten the dramatic impact of their tragedies and drawing on popular superstitions and folk traditions of their age: for example, the dark beings that permeate Shakespeare's dramas are likened to the Aeschylean Furies or Dareios' ghost from *Persai* in the "Essay on the Writing and Genius of Shakespear" (1769) by 18th century critic Elizabeth Montagu. However, such remarks suggest the 'parallel lives' between the Greek tragedians and Shakespeare, and do not imply any direct influence, see in particular Suerbaum (1997) and Silk (2004).

128. On the grotesque and the *grottesche*, and its discovery during the Renaissance, I follow Harpham (2006) 27-71.

129. See the history of caricature and the grotesque, written in 1865 by the scholar and antiquarian Thomas Wright (repr. as Wright [2006]). For a theoretical approach to the grotesque, see especially Kayser (1963), Thomson (1972), Harpham (2006) and, accompanied by vivid illustrations, Eco (2007) 106-157.

Definitions of the grotesque fall roughly in three categories: grotesque denotes (a) all things strange, bizarre and out-of-this-world–in Wolfgang Kayser's words "the grotesque is an expression of the estranged or alienated world"–, (b) any form of the paradox, a mingling of the serious with the comic, of the horrifying with the jest, or, (c) a clash, a conflict, a mixture of opposites or heterogeneous elements. A basic problem is whether the grotesque should be classified as a trend of fantasy or realism. The confusion between the two worlds, the imaginary and the real, renders the grotesque an all-encompassing concept[130]:

> If 'fantastic' means simply a pronounced divergence from the normal and natural then the grotesque is undoubtedly fantastic. But if, as we surely must, we insist that the criterion be whether the material is presented in a fantastic, or realistic way, then we are more likely to conclude that, far from possessing an affinity with the fantastic, it is precisely the conviction that the grotesque world, however strange, is yet our world, real and immediate, which makes the grotesque so powerful. Conversely, if a literary text 'takes place' in a fantasy-world created by the author, with no pretensions to a connection with reality, the grotesque is almost out of the question. For within a closed fantasy-world, anything is possible. The reader, once he is aware that he is confronted with such a closed world, accepts the strangest things without turning a hair, for he is not being asked to understand them as real.

The grotesque in literature comprises different notions and modes[131]. Philip Thomson enumerates a good number of the first such as disharmony, the comic and the terrifying, the extravagance and the exaggeration, the burlesque and the playful, and some key terms–the absurd, the bizarre, the macabre, caricature, parody, satire, irony–pertaining to the second[132]. Whether the comic is an indispensable part of the grotesque is debatable. If we take as a point of departure Mikhail Bakhtin's rendering of the grotesque as a literary mode which relates social and political conflicts to human physiology and is closely intertwined with the carnivalesque (the 'grotesque body' being an ambivalent concept celebrating the triumph of life through emphasis on bodily needs), then humor and satire seem essential for its understanding[133]. However, the other 20th

---

130. Thomson (1972) 23.

131. Authors which are more often discussed as examples of the literary grotesque are Jonathan Swift, Emily Brontë, Charles Dickens, Charles Baudelaire, E.T.A. Hoffmann, Edgar Allan Poe, Franz Kafka and Thomas Mann. Theories of the grotesque are applied to literary works, such as "Wuthering Heights", "The Masque of the Red Death" and "Death in Venice", by Harpham (2006) 107-232.

132. Thomson (1972) 20-57.

133. In his 1941 study of Rabelais' *Gargantua and Pantagruel* [Bakhtin (1984) 303-367].

century theorist of the grotesque, Wolfgang Kayser, is the strongest sup-
porter of the idea that the world invoked by the grotesque is inhabited by
demonic powers, that in such a realm animate and inanimate beings are
inseparable, and its quality is often described as sinister, nocturnal, abys-
mal and ominous[134]. There have been also older approaches (some of
them stemming from the heart of 19th century Romantic criticism) which
tend to highlight the negative and strange nature of the grotesque, and to
locate it at the opposite pole of the beautiful and the sublime[135]. Along
the same lines, Victor Hugo in the 'Preface' to *Cromwell* (1827) acknowledges the grotesque, a peculiar mixture of melancholy and irony, as the
quintessence of 'Modern' art, i.e. of Romantic sensibility, 'the supreme
beauty of drama' (§39):

> In the idea of men of modern times, however, the grotesque plays an enor-
> mous part. It is found everywhere; on the one hand it creates the abnormal
> and the horrible, on the other the comic and the burlesque. It fastens upon
> religion a thousand original superstitions, upon poetry a thousand pictur-
> esque fancies. It is the grotesque which scatters lavishly, in air, water, earth,
> fire, those myriads of intermediary creatures which we find all alive in the
> popular traditions of the Middle Ages; it is the grotesque which impels the
> ghastly antics of the witches' revels, which gives Satan his horns, his clo-
> ven foot and his bat's wings...If it passes from the world of imagination to
> the real world, it unfolds an inexhaustible supply of parodies of mankind.
> Creations of its fantasy are the Scaramouches, Crispins and Harlequins,
> grinning silhouettes of man, types altogether unknown to serious-minded
> antiquity...

If we take Hugo's manifesto on the grotesque literally, it is the experimentation with form and deformity, the ambivalent and anomalous
shapes, that leads to strangeness and lack of meaning. This is why the
grotesque is the term usually used to denote both the ornamental chimeras and gargoyles of Medieval cathedrals and the caricatures or the semi-
demonic, semi-comic figures of literature–ranging from Hugo's Quasi-
modo to the protagonist of Kafka's *The Metamorphosis*[136].

Having stressed the transhistorical character of the grotesque, and its
shifting, ambivalent quality, there remains one critical question: how did
antiquity exploit the grotesque for literary and artistic purposes? As seen

---

134. Kayser (1963). Hurley (2007) brings together Bakhtin's grotesque and Kristeva's
notion of the abject as vital ingredients of Gothic horror.

135. E.g. in the famous essay by Walter Bagehot "Wordsworth, Tennyson and Browning; or Pure, Ornate and Grotesque Art in English Poetry" (1864) and in John Ruskin's
study of the Renaissance grotesque in *The Stones of Venice* (1851-1853); for a historical
overview of the concept, see Thomson (1972) 10-19.

136. A collection of papers on the study of Medieval bestiary in Hassig (2000).

above, Roman decorative art and Hellenistic sculpture were deeply influenced by the aesthetics of the bizarre, the absurd and the strange[137].
Roman culture developed a strong affinity with the aesthetics of the grotesque early on, and not only in art and painting: Ovid's *Metamorphoses*
and the works of Petronius, Juvenal and Apuleius are typical examples
that illustrate the point[138]. Yet the grotesque has been a vital part of
Greek culture from its very beginnings, manifest in the merging of different natures in metamorphosis myths or as a quality informing the bestiary of mythology[139]. Extravagant, monstrous or distorted figures–the
Lernaean Hydra, Kerberos, Medusa, Chimera, the Erinyes, the Harpyies
and the Sirens, and, with a comic undertone, Polyphemos, Hephaistos
and Priapos, the Satyrs, the Centaurs and the Cyclopes–form (partly) the
basis of Middle Age grotesqueries[140].

A fascination with extreme monstrosities is probably a by-product of
religious obsession. The theological world view of certain authors, such
as Hesiod and Aeschylus, accounts for the appearance of horrific and
atrocious monsters, expressing the powers of the uncanny. The *Theogony*
abounds with the depiction of monsters, the Typhon, son of Tartarus and
father of the Chimera, the Kerberos and the Sphinx, being the archetype
of the deadly and bizarre creature in all ancient poetry (*Th.* 820-880)[141].
However, this is not yet grotesque. But when poets steer such monstrosities towards the extravagance to enhance the aesthetic effect of their
works, they seem to develop a taste for it. A unique example is the
'Hesiodic' *Aspis*, a fantastic description of the shield of Herakles that
was used in his bloody combat against Kyknos. A *tour de force* of the
shield discourse or a 'pulp' epic, the *Aspis* features horrendous figures
such as the deadly Ares, and also personifications of Fear (*Phobos*),

---

137. The Hellenistic tendency towards the grotesque with a comic undertone is classified as rococo by Pollitt (1986) 127-141. On the contrary, Fowler (1989) 66-78 labels
as grotesqueries small sculptures which represent "real, low-class, often deformed people" with "an attention to detail of anatomy and expression of face and figure often
touching as well as amusing" (p. 66); these include, among others, figures of hunchbacks
and dwarfs, and their 'realistic' style corresponds to the thematics of Herodas' *Mimiambi*.

138. See Callebat (1998) for a general overview and especially Miller (1998) on the
bodily grotesque in Roman satire.

139. That mythic narrative is indispensable for perceiving the alchemy between different substances, the contradiction of the opposites which forms the basis of the grotesque, is argued by Harpham (2006) 76-81. Essential for the study of the bestiary in
classical literature is Murgatroyd (2007), although his insistence to discuss film versions
of ancient monster myths sometimes leads his study to go astray. Wheatcroft (2000)
investigates the complex relation between Classical ideology and Medieval bestiary.

140. For Eco (2007) 34-41, however, such manifestations express horror rather than
the grotesque.

141. See Murgatroyd (2007) 146-154.

Strife (*Eris*) and Death (the *Keres*), to achieve partly a horrific and partly a grotesque effect[142]. 'Longinus' points out the subtle difference between the awesome (as in the depiction of Strife in the *Iliad*) and the repulsive– the 'grotesque body' according to Bakhtin–to be found in the *Aspis*, as follows (9.5): ᾧ ἀνόμοιόν γε τὸ Ἡσιόδειον ἐπὶ τῆς Ἀχλύος, εἴγε Ἡσιόδου καὶ τὴν Ἀσπίδα θετέον· τῆς ἐκ μὲν ῥινῶν μύξαι ῥέον [*Aspis* 267]· οὐ γὰρ δεινὸν ἐποίησε τὸ εἴδωλον, ἀλλὰ μισητόν 'contrast the line about Darkness in Hesiod–if the *Aspis* is by Hesiod: 'mucus dripped from her nostrils.' This gives a repulsive picture, not one to excite awe' [Transl. D.A. Russell].

Towards the uncanny

It has been argued that the grotesque "involves the managing of the uncanny by the comic". This definition is further clarified by the state- ment that the grotesque and the caricature liberate us from repressed fear and childhood desires, while at the same time they may enhance anxiety by evoking strangeness and aggressiveness[143]. According to the same definition psychoanalysis is the key to a proper understanding of this 'strangeness', which came to be known as the *uncanny*[144]. In fact, it was Sigmund Freud who applied psychoanalysis to literary criticism in his 1919 essay "Das Unheimliche" ("The Uncanny")[145]:

> In general we are reminded that the word *heimlich* is not unambiguous, but belongs to two sets of ideas, which without being contradictory are yet very different: on the one hand, it means that which is familiar and cogenial, and on the other, that which is concealed and kept out of sight. The word *unheimlich* is only used customarily, we are told, as the contrary of the first signification, and not of the second. [...] According to Schelling, every- thing is *unheimlich* that ought to have remained hidden and secret, and yet comes to light.

142. 'Hesiod's' *Aspis* is brilliantly depicted as a 'trash' culture remake of the shield of Achilles by Martin (2005). The *Aspis* is only rarely labelled as pure grotesque (e.g. sporadically by Janko [1986]), but has nevertheless been characterized as 'sensational, burlesque, macabre, terrible, weird, degenerate, parasitic', and has even been likened to the art of Goya: for an interesting overview of previous scholarship on the aesthetics of the *Aspis*, see Martin (2005) 154-156. For Toohey (1988) the macabre imagery of the *Aspis* may be read as an unintellectual response to the problem of death.
143. This definition of the grotesque in Steig (1970) 259-260.
144. A full-length study of the uncanny in psychoanalysis, literature and art is offered by Royle (2003). A concise introduction in Punter (2007) and, accompanied by illustra- tions and selected primary sources, in Eco (2007) 310-331.
145. For the quotations from Freud's essay I follow the translation by Alix Strachey, as reprinted in Sandner (2004) 74-101.

The dialectic between that which is familiar, so familiar that it becomes a secret for the outer world, and the sense of the unfamiliar forms the core of the uncanny. As an experience of strangeness or alienation, the uncanny involves a feeling of uncertainty about the nature of things, a crisis of the self, a revelation of something unhomely within a familiar context. The uncanny manifests itself in various ideas and feelings, among others the fear of being buried alive, the sense of *déjà vu*, any form of repetition and coincidence, any situation where reality and illusion converge[146]. The effect is always fear, and this is the point where the uncanny merges with the Gothic[147]. To elucidate his point, Freud analyzes a dark story by E.T.A. Hoffmann, a German author of fantasy and horror, called "Der Sandmann" ("The Sandman"). The story concerns the horrific adventures of a man (including his love affair with an *automaton* called Olympia, his madness and, eventually, his suicide) who is haunted by his childhood fears concerning the *sandman*, a bogeyman who steals children's eyes during their sleep and whom he identifies with the strange, unpleasant Coppelius[148].

In being a reworking of the Romantic notion of fear (or the Gothic) or, to be more precise, a concept on the cusp of Modernism, the uncanny was further elaborated on by other 20th century thinkers. A key notion to the understanding of the uncanny already by Freud is *the double*, a term coined by his contemporary and colleague, the psychoanalyst Otto Rank. In his essay "Der Doppelgänger" ("The Double as Immortal Self"), written in 1914, Rank introduces the idea of the 'second self', the 'soul', that which was primarily thought to be the immortal part of man, and which came to denote the *alter ego*, a splitting of the personality, a terrifying and threatening disturbance of the ego. Another related concept is what Julia Kristeva terms *abjection* or *the abject*, something existing between the object and the subject, the self and the other, anything that disturbs identity, system or order; facing the abject (Kristeva uses the example of the corpse) is always a traumatic, horrific experience. The interesting point in Kristeva's approach to horror by means of the abject is her study of the *Oedipus the King*, *Oedipus at Kolonos* and *Antigone* under this perspective: in the first two plays, the king embodies both the abject and the scapegoat, whereas in the latter the abject is sensed in the clash between the order of the *polis* and the antiquated ethics of the heroine[149].

146. For a full definition, see Royle (2003) 1-38.
147. A collection of essays concering the psychological dimension of the Gothic in Bomarito (2006) 1.301-342.
148. On the uncanny reading of "The Sandman", see Royle (2003) 39-50.
149. In her book *Powers of Horror: An Essay on Abjection* (1982). On the abject, see also Hurley (2007).

Freud warns against too broad a conception of the uncanny, by stressing that "not everything that is connected with repressed desires and archaic forms of thought belonging to the past of the individual and of the race is uncanny"–and enumerates motifs such as the omnipotence of thought or the re-animation of the dead from fairytale narratives which do not amount to the strange encounter of the familiar with the unfamiliar. Therefore, although Greek myths abound with acts that clearly violate natural laws and connect to animistic beliefs, these cannot be collectively regarded as uncanny. An example: although the evil instincts and primeval fears, like the ones described by Freud, loom over Hesiod's cosmos, the *Theogony*, inhabited as it is by gods and characterized by the marvellous, does not communicate an uncanny feeling to the reader. We should instead search for the uncanny in the literary reworkings of mythology. A very interesting case study of a *double* would be that of Achilles in the *Iliad*. Achilles' armour, worn successively by him, his substitute Patroclus and his opponent, Hektor, allows the hero to confront his phantom embodied by Hektor in combat and thus symbolically 'kill' his second self, an act both tragic and uncanny[150].

But, once more, it is tragedy that offers some outstanding examples. Sophocles' *Oedipus the King* represents the clash between the king's nobility and his uncanny deeds, his deeper fears and his premonitions[151]. Sophocles plumbs the mysterious depths of the human psyche in showing how Oedipus is torn between his childhood anxieties and the ominous silence of his fellow-citizens; when he finally discovers the truth about his double crime (to murder the father and sexually possess the mother, the *Oedipus complex*), he blinds himself–a symbolic act that lies at the core of any uncanny and, as such, is brilliantly revived in Hoffmann's "The Sandman"[152]. Other tragedies too have a penchant for the uncanny. In the *Antigone* the fear of, and at the same time the desire for, being buried alive haunts the heroine, in verses such as the following

150. The slaying of Hektor by Achilles is interpreted as a vicarious suicide by Devereux (1978-1979). The killing of the *alter ego* takes the form of suicide in the uncanny narratives of E.T.A. Hoffmann as analyzed by Otto Rank (see Bomarito [2006] 1.312-313).

151. Royle (2003) 325 n. 42 likens the revelation of Oedipus' crimes to an experience of *déjà vu*, a premonition which appears in the form of a dream. This suggestion was already made by Freud in regard to passage *OT* 980-982 where Jocasta consoles Oedipus by saying that many men in the past had dreamt to couple with their mothers.

152. In discussing the horror of losing one's eyes by the sandman, Freud evokes Oedipus: "A study of dreams, phantasies and myths has taught us that a morbid anxiety connected with the eyes and with going blind is often enough a substitute for the dread of castration". For a reading of *Oedipus the King* as an uncanny variant of myth, see Kloss (2006) 151-155.

(848-852): πρὸς ἔργμα τυμβόχωστον/ ἔρχομαι τάφου ποταινίου·/ ἰὼ δύστανος,/ οὔτ᾽ ἐν βροτοῖς οὔτε νεκροῖσιν/ μέτοικος, οὐ ζῶσιν, οὐ θανοῦσιν 'I go to my rockbound prison, strange new tomb–alas, a stranger, I have no home on earth and none below, not with the living, not with the dead'[153]. Two other, utterly different, Euripidean plays, the *Alkestis* and *Hekabe*, may be interpreted against the background of the uncanny: in the former, the *unheimlich* is detected in a series of replacements which occur during the play (Alkestis, the statue and the veiled woman) and in the interchangeability of Alkestis and Admetos in the face of death; in the latter, not only figures and ideas associated with the *unheimlich* permeate the tragedy–doublings, ghosts, death, castration anxiety–, but, more importantly, the fact that Hekabe's character undergoes a transformation during the play, and also the awareness that in the future she will mutate into a dog, illustrate the uncanny[154].

Hellenistic darkness

This lengthy digression on the notions that constitute darkness may serve as an introduction to the study of what I have termed *Hellenistic darkness*. So, the foundation has been laid for the theoretical approach of those Hellenistic poets who in highlighting the darker side of human condition closely resemble Romantic, even Decadent authors of the modern era[155]. But who exactly are they? Limitations of space and methodological principles do not allow for exhaustiveness; thus, I will not address many Hellenistic poets and poems which are pertinent to the idea of darkness, such as Simias of Rhodes, Euphorion of Chalkis, Parthenius of Nicaea, the bucolic poets Bion and Moschus, probably Eratosthenes in the *Erigone*, or some anonymous fragments (e.g. *Actaeonis Epyllium* Epica Adespota fr. 1 CA), and an entire genre, metamorphosis poetry. Nor Theocritus who, despite his Romantic traits, is an isolated case. Instead, I have chosen to focus on four Hellenistic poems which best illustrate the various qualities and different degrees of darkness, namely Apollonius' *Argonautica*, Lycophron's *Alexandra* and Nicander's *Theriaca* and

153. The verses are quoted by Royle (2003) 168 n. 48 to illustrate *Antigone* as a primary example of the 'buried alive' motif.
154. Both readings in Rabinowitz (1993) 78-93 and 114-124 respectively.
155. Papanghelis (1994) 58-82 draws a parallel between this Hellenistic tendency and European Decadence, by tracing trends of Aestheticism back to a taste for the erotic, the morbid and the grotesque which is most evident in post-Callimachean aesthetics. On a parallel study of ancient and modern-day Decadence, see Bonelli (1979).

Alexipharmaca. Neither the fact that these poems are preserved in their entirety nor their generic variety (epic, drama and didactic) are the major reasons behind this choice. It is primarily the belief that in these particular poems the fantastic, the Gothic, the grotesque and the uncanny converge to create a powerful dark effect, thus playing a prominent part in the formation of Hellenistic Romanticism.

The *Argonautica*, in prefiguring features that were to become essential to European Romanticism, marks a major turning point towards Hellenistic darkness[156]. The *Argonautica* parallels a romance in that its plot builds around a heroic quest, during which the central hero confronts tests of honour and identity and love conflicts assume a critical role. Hence the *Argonautica* may be read as a dark romance where the fantastic takes over the heroic[157]. While the quest plot unfolds, the supernatural and the magic elements come to the fore, thus bringing the *Argonautica* closer to Odysseus' *Apologoi*–the Hellenistic epic nevertheless surpasses the Homeric prototype in the depiction of the horrific and the uncanny. The gendered orientation of Apollonius' narrative towards the female, especially Medea, highlights motifs which are recurrent in novels of Romanticism and the Gothic: the solitude of the heroine; her revolt against the authority of the father; the inner conflict of a maiden in love expressed in soliloquies and daydreaming; the adoption of a melodramatic stance in her love affair. The Romantic setting forms another key feature of Apollonius' storytelling. Symbolic places, fantastic geography, a preoccupation with night settings become vital parameters of Apollonius' narrative. Thus, in the *Argonautica* the interplay between the real and the imagined and the exploration of a world 'beyond' are set against the background of a mythological fairytale.

The iambic *Alexandra*, attributed to Lycophron of Chalkis, is a dark poem *par excellence*, dramatizing the prophecy of Kassandra as reported

---

156. On a similar basis Green (1997b) xi-xii has argued that Apollonius looked "old-fashioned" for the mid third century, "a throwback to the Archaic worldview" and certainly less Alexandrian and un-Callimachean in his aesthetics.

157. I refer here to 'romance' as a transhistorical mode that employs the structures and thematic concerns of the original genre (i.e. the historical romance that flourished in Medieval Europe); despite the fact that the theoretical opposition between epic and romance was not known in antiquity, ancient epics may fit into this categorization too, as Beye (1982) and especially Quint (1993) have shown. On a preliminary analysis of the *Argonautica* as a combination of epic and romance, though based on a different theoretical model than my own reading of Apollonius' epic as a dark narrative, see Beye (1982); cf. Cusset (2001c) 74-75 who argues that the *Argonautica* is structured according to the principles of tragedy.

by an anonymous narrator to Priam[158]. The *Alexandra* carries Aeschylus' grand style to extremes, and its linguistic exaggeration contradicts the Callimachean ideals as expressed in the *Aitia*-Prologue[159]. The theatrical qualities of the *Alexandra* reinforce a feeling of *pathos*, thus rendering highly intense its affect upon the reader. Yet the *Alexandra*, in being at the same time a dramatic monologue and a metadramatic comment, reads the Trojan myth from a dual perspective: that of 'Kassandra/ Alexandra' and that of the poet himself. From the viewpoint of the heroine, and her emotional commitment to the tragedies of the House of Priam, her speech may be read as a delirium, where fantasy, dream and illusion converge. Lycophron adapts the Trojan myth for his theatrical medium by offering a dark remake of it: passionate love affairs and violent deaths, unheroic characters involved in bloody acts, Gothic settings, macabre scenaria, hopeless wanderings, suicides and sacrifices constitute the dark world of the *Alexandra*. Moreover, Lycophron condenses previous epic and tragic storytellings of the Trojan myth into expressionist discourse, mainly metaphoric language and enigmatic diction, to multiply their dark effect.

With the third paradigm of Hellenistic darkness, the focus shifts to a plotless genre, namely didactic poetry. Nicander of Kolophon wrote, among others, two didactic hexameter poems on a quasi-scientific subject matter, the *Theriaca* on venomous animals and the wounds they inflict, and the *Alexipharmaca* on poisons and their antidotes. The question I will address is to what degree the influence of science upon literature, most notably of medicine and pharmacology, may be perceived as a turn towards Romantic aesthetics. Taking as a point of departure the fact that Hellenistic scholars were intrigued with the collection of *paradoxa*, it is important to see how and why some of these curiosities found their way into poetry[160]. Nicander is aware that this scientific subject matter verges on the grotesque. To transform it for his artistic medium, he adopts a highly affective, recherché diction, develops a taste for sensuous language and, sporadically, has recourse to mythological narrative, personification and similar literary devices. By poeticizing a discourse

---

158. On the narrative mode of the *Alexandra*, see Lowe (2004); Lowe describes the narrative structure of the poem as follows (p. 308): "The *Alexandra*'s central idea is that Kassandra's prophecy should be presented not diegetically but dramatically, with no overt primary narrator ('Lycophron' does not speak) but within a nested frame of multiple speakers and audiences". More on the issue, see below pp. 138-145.

159. For the opposition between Callimachean and Lycophronean style, see Sens (2010) 308.

160. On the conflict between poetry and didactic in Nicander and on a general overview of his poetic technique, see Jacques (2002) lxv-xcvi.

on reptiles, he creates a unique bestiary. His morbid fascination with poisoning is set against the backdrop of another Alexandrian trend, namely the depiction of human pain: to visualize the body in agony has a special aesthetic appeal for Hellenistic poetry and art, and Nicander works this dark mood into the didactic genre. Nicander, by exploring the curiosities of visuality in his didactic on snakes, poisonous plants and decaying bodies, exploits the potential of scientific observation to stir the dark imagination of his audience.

I. APOLLONIUS *ARGONAUTICA*

THE DARK EPIC

I.1. In quest for the fantastic

Come with us, ye whose hearts are set
On this, the Present to forget;
Come read the things whereof ye know
They were not, and could not be so!
The murmur of the fallen creeds,
Like winds among wind-shaken reeds
Along the banks of holy Nile,
Shall echo in your ears the while;
The fables of the North and South
Shall mingle in a modern mouth.

....

There lives no man but he hath seen
The World's Desire, the fairy queen.
None but hath seen her to his cost,
Not one but loves what he has lost.
None is there but hath heard her sing
Divinely through his wandering;
Not one but he has followed far
The portent of the Bleeding Star;
Not one but he hath chanced to wake,
Dreamed of the Star and found the Snake.
Yet, through his dreams, a wandering fire,
Still, still she flits, THE WORLD'S DESIRE!

H. Rider Haggard-Andrew Lang *The World's Desire* (1890)

Two almost contemporary works, a fantasy novel designed as a sequel to the *Odyssey* written by H. Rider Haggard and Andrew Lang, *The World's Desire* (1890), and the epic remake of the *Argonautica* by William Morris entitled *The Life and Death of Jason* (1867), exploit the potential of heroic fantasies *par excellence*, the adventures of Odysseus and the Argonaut expedition, for an experimentation with the Romantic fantastic[1]. Inspired by the discoveries of Schliemann and the Egyptologist Flinders Petrie, *The World's Desire* (the quest of Odysseus for Helen, the incorporation of ideal beauty) is an amalgam of Greek,

---

1. Nathaniel Hawthorne, a representative writer of Dark Romanticism, also wrote a short story on Jason's adventures with the title "The Golden Fleece". This story is part of the collection *Tanglewood Tales for Boys and Girls*, published in 1853, where Hawthorne rewrites famous Greek myths for children, a sequel to *The Wonder-Book for Girls and Boys* (1852), also a collection of Greek myths with emphasis on the fantastic.

Egyptian and Hebrew mythology with a touch of Medieval travellers' tales. In this novel, as its authors stress in the 'Preface', modern fantasy 'accidentally' coincides with that of ancient Greece. In *The Life and Death of Jason* William Morris rewrites the ancient myth from the perspective of both Medieval romance and Victorian feminist ideology with a taste for visual detail and psychological insight. In contrast to the use of Classical mythology in the Age of Reason, these revivals were a product of Romantic experimentation with the primitive, the fairytale-like and the marvellous. Did Apollonius find himself in a similar position when he undertook to write a mythological epic within an Alexandrian environment? Conscious of his epigonality, Apollonius was faced with many challenges: to adapt the traditional form of the epic to a new aesthetics, to deal with a myth that had its roots in pre-Homeric oral poetry and to differentiate his work from the unsurpassed adventure epic, the *Odyssey*. My claim is that Apollonius chose to treat a quest narrative, which by definition provides ample space for the fantastic, and placed particular emphasis on its dark aspects in order to introduce his 'Romantic' aesthetics into epic[2]. The premise underlying my interpretation is that Apollonius enhances the fantastic element in the *Argonautica* to mark a return to primitive forms of culture—in a manner that parallels the emergence of the fantastic as a reaction to reason in European Romanticism[3].

It is generally accepted that the *Argonautica* is a response to the Homeric epics, the *Odyssey* in particular[4]. Narrative and thematic correspondences apart, the core myth of the poem, the Argonaut expedition, is not only explicitly evoked in *Od.* 12.69-72, probably as the subject of a celebrated pre-Homeric epic, but, more importantly, seems to have served as a model for several Odyssean adventures that are recounted in

2. For the Greek text I have used Vian (1974), (1993) and (1996); translations are taken from Hunter (1998).

3. Romantic criticism associates the fantastic with primitivism. As David Sandner (in Sandner [2004] 319) points out, "whether the fantastic is positioned either in childhood or in the superstitious past may seem to make little practical difference to the genre. In both, the fantastic is related to the immature and the irrational; in both, the fantastic is realized as nostalgia. The development of the child into the reasoned adult and of 'primitive' culture into modern civilized society have an obvious parallel structure." Similarly, Radke (2007) 117-124 terms the emphasis on primitiveness "the childhood of myth" (die Kindheit des Mythos).

4. For a thorough survey of the Homeric reception by Apollonius, as regards both matters of narrative technique and thematic correspondences, see Knight (1995); on the relation between the *Argonautica* and the *Odyssey* in particular, see the dissertation by Dufner (1988). That the *Argonautica* is a variation of the Homeric epics was first argued by Händel (1954). However, recent studies take an ambivalent view of Apollonius as neither an anti-Homer nor as a mere traditionalist, see Fantuzzi/Hunter (2004) 89-132.

the *Apologoi*. This hypothesis, firstly suggested by Karl Meuli in 1921, still holds true, although objections have been raised to the pre-existence of an Argonaut oral epic or even to an early formation of the relevant myth[5]. Whichever the sources of the *Odyssey*, by the Hellenistic period such an Argonaut epic belonged to the dim and distant past and could not have been known to Apollonius. Thus, Apollonius had to reconstruct the 'original' myth, first by using every literary, artistic and scholarly source about the Argonaut expedition available, and second by building episodes of the *Odyssey* into his own *Argonautica*–in effect, by reversing the process initially undertaken by the poet of the *Odyssey*[6].

The plot of each poem may help us understand why these two epics could interact with one another with ease. As is well known, the dominant story-pattern of the *Odyssey* is the homecoming, since the *nostos* is the aim of Odysseus' wanderings; Odysseus the seafarer emerges as the hero of the secondary plot, which is embedded into the primary plot through the *Apologoi* section. The plot of the *Argonautica*, on the other hand, unfolds linearly, from the beginning of the quest for the Golden Fleece until the successful completion of the mission, whereas the whole epic is set against the backdrop of a dangerous sea voyage[7]. It has long been observed that both epics share common ground as regards the series of the challenges with which the protagonist is confronted during the sea voyage. The episodes of the oral, pre-Homeric Argonaut epic that may have influenced the *Odyssey* are the Laistrygonians, Kirke, the *katabasis* to Hades, the Sirens, the Clashing Rocks (called the *Planktai*) and the Cattle of the Sun[8]. However, the register of common episodes is based on speculation. It should be noted that Apollonius has adapted the episodes of Kirke, the Sirens, Skylla and Charybdis, and the Phaeacians

---

5. Meuli (1921); West (2005) also argues for a pre-Homeric *Argonautica* and attempts a systematic comparison between the two wanderings. The theory has been seriously questioned by Hölscher (1988) 170-185, who emphasizes the fairytale motifs that underlie both myths, but does not support the idea that an Argonaut epic was composed prior to the *Odyssey*.

6. For a recent study of the sources used by Apollonius and the reshaping of the Argonaut myth, see Scherer (2006) 9-56, cf. Vian (1974) xxvi-xxxix.

7. It should be noted that the *Argonautica* and the *Odyssey* follow two different patterns of the 'fantastic voyage' narrative, the quest for a desired object or a journey of discovery and the peregrinations of the accursed wanderer unable to reach his destination respectively (see *EF* s.v. "Fantastic Voyages").

8. As registered by West (2005) 59. It is not my intention here to discuss matters of this long-standing debate among Homerists. Two recent overviews of the issue are Kullmann (1992) 125-129 who analyzes several *Odyssey* episodes as motifs borrowed from the oral *Argonautica* and West (2005) esp. 59-61 who suggests that a series of adventures (Laistrygonians to the Cattle of the Sun) were imported *en bloc* into the *Odyssey* from the lost *Argonautica*.

within the context of the Argonaut myth[9]. Yet Apollonius' epic diverges markedly from the Homeric prototype in turning points of the plot: in contrast to Odysseus (and later on, Aeneas), Jason and the Argonauts do not undertake a journey to the land of the dead; the Argonauts pass through the Clashing Rocks on their way to Colchis, whereas Odysseus avoids this site and opts for the passage through Skylla and Charybdis[10]; and there are significant inconsistencies as regards the marine routes followed by the heroes, hence the two geographical views of the world, the Odyssean and the Argonautic, are, in some ways, incompatible[11].

Obviously Apollonius did not intend to write a 'new *Odyssey*', but to offer his own version of heroic epic. Apollonius chose, on the one hand, to differentiate his poem from the archetypal fantasy, the *Odyssey*, and, on the other, to invest the epic genre with a new air of fantasy, a kind of Romantic reconstruction of an imaginary past[12], which is reflected in the choice of subject matter, the combination of various generic conventions and the design of plot, characters and setting of the *Argonautica*. The first of these parameters, subject matter, deserves special attention. The Argonaut expedition clearly predates the Trojan War, the last enterprise of the age of heroes in the chart of mythical chronology; accordingly Apollonius recounts the archaeology of the great Panhellenic myth which forms the basis of the Homeric epics[13]. The very first lines of the *Argonautica* reflect the preoccupation of the narrator with events anchored in the distant past (*Arg.* 1.1-2 παλαιγενέων κλέα φωτῶν/ μνήσομαι 'I shall recall the glorious deeds of men of long ago')[14]. But, furthermore, beneath the surface of the Argonaut plot, a plethora of mythical events is evoked, which are

---

9. It has been argued though that several Argonaut episodes have been modelled on the *Odyssey*: on a systematic comparison between the Kikones and the Colchians, the Lotus-Eaters and the Libyan adventures, the Cyclops and the monsters encountered by the Argonauts etc. as well as on the allusions to Homeric adventures in Apollonius' epic, see Knight (1995) 122-266. Cf. Cusset (2001b) who argues that Apollonius views Italy through a Homeric lens and reproduces Odyssean geography in his epic.

10. See West (2005) 39-43.

11. Scholars mostly emphasize the contrast between the fantastic geography of the *Odyssey* and the more 'realistic', historically accurate view of the world adopted by Apollonius, see e.g. Meyer (2008), cf. Clare (2002) passim.

12. Green (1997a) convincingly argues that Apollonius resists the attempts at rationalizing of myth: though aware of the logical answers provided by geographers and mythographers, Apollonius opts for the Unknown, for a preservation of the mysteries of the mythical past.

13. Sistakou (2008a) 88-100.

14. The exemplarity of the past as a vital parameter of the *Argonautica* is analyzed by Goldhill (1991) 284-333. On time awareness in the *Argonautica*, see Klooster (2007) 63-65.

immersed in an even more distant past[15]. Stories drawn from previous mythological cycles frame the main storyline, thus extending the range of epic memory into a second degree of pastness. Between these two distinct levels of narrative the *aition* functions as a time machine, as a device that highlights the various degrees of mythical temporality. The voyage of the Argonauts is a journey into time, into a less civilized and primitive cosmos, and also into the magic, wonder and mystery surrounding both old and untold stories about this cosmos[16]. In marvelling over the strange encounters during this voyage, the Argonauts operate like any audience of the fantastic; thus, they employ a discourse of marvel and consequently the narrative resonates with the exclamations of their amazement[17].

The aesthetic quality of this thematic choice contextualizes the *Argonautica* into the tradition of the fantastic. To recreate the world *beyond*–beyond order and civilization, and, on a textual level, beyond Homer–Apollonius builds on a variety of literary and cultural traditions. Stories from the whole range of mythology are crossed with the Argonaut plot; the result is an *imaginary* universe where all myths converge[18]. As a rule these 'other' myths exploited by Apollonius in the *Argonautica* have two distinctive features. First, they evoke episodes which according to mythical chronology are prior to the Argonaut expedition, while several of these exploit origins and beginnings. Second, the literary sources for these episodes are non-Homeric; they relate to cyclic variations of heroic epic, which, in turn, show a special affinity with the fantastic[19]. I refer especially to the theogonic and

15. This is what Bakhtin (1981) 15-17 terms 'the absolute past', which reflects the concern for 'beginnings', 'first times', 'founders' and 'ancestors', and is a 'valorized temporal category' of the epic genre.

16. Clauss (2000) offers a thorough description of this world, which dates back to the era of creation: in this sense, he terms the entire epic 'theogonic'. The *Argonautica* is seen as a passage from a primordial world of chaos to order, marked by the establishment of Zeus' power: on this interpretation, see especially Hunter (1993) 162-169.

17. Such as ἐθάμβησαν δ' ἐσιδόντες (1.322), τοὺς δ' ἕλε θάμβος (2.681, 4.682), θάμβησαν (2.922, 4.184), ἐθάμβεον (3.924, 4.74, 4.1363), μέγα θάμβος ἰδέσθαι (1.220), περιθαμβέες (2.1158, 4.1528), τάφον (2.207), οἱ δὲ τάφον...εἰσορόωντες (2.1038) and τεθηπότες (3.215).

18. A thorough analysis of how Greeks perceived the surrounding world as mythical is offered by Ballabriga (1986).

19. It is a commonplace of scholarship that the cyclic epics rely heavily on the exploration of the Romantic, the fabulous and the imaginary, see Griffin (1977) and Burgess (2001) 132-171. In his fundamental article on the distinction between cyclic and Homeric epic, Griffin (1977) 53 concludes that "the strict, radical and consistently heroic interpretation of the world presented by the *Iliad* made it quite different from the Cycle, still content with monsters, miracles, metamorphoses, and an un-tragic attitude towards mortality, all seasoned with exoticism and romance, and composed in a flatter, looser, less dramatic style". For the prominence of magic and the metamorphosis theme in the Epic Cycle, see Forbes Irving (1990).

cosmogonic myths (such as the ones informing Orpheus' song, 1.492-515) and to the intersection between the *Argonautica* and a plethora of heroic legends–two outstanding examples are the myths behind the genealogy of the Argonauts in the catalogue of heroes (1.23-233) and the panorama of epic adventures offered by the decorations on Jason's cloak (1.721-773)[20]. Moreover, the depiction of an era before the dominance of Zeus (Prometheus bound on Caucasus is a characteristic snapshot, 2.1247-1259), the introduction of past heroes–Hypsipyle, Phineus, Phrixos–into the *cosmos* of the Argonauts and the numerous aitiological *analepses* into the narrative past add up to the creation of a primitive atmosphere in Apollonius' epic. The intellectual background of the *Argonautica* and the scholarly preoccupations of Apollonius with the local and the regional also enhance the poem's primitivism. Religious attitudes in the epic date back to the pre-Panhellenic era, since pre-Olympian deities, Rhea/Kybele and Hekate, are worshipped by the Argonauts; strong emphasis is placed upon local rites and hero cults[21]. The primitive stance towards religion in connection with local legends and fairytale motifs (among which magic plays a prominent role) promote the idea of the fantastic within the *Argonautica*[22].

But the cultural background aside, it is the plot that renders the *Argonautica* a fantasy epic. A fantasy may be described as "the story of an earned passage from *bondage*–via a central *recognition* of what has been revealed and of what is about to happen, and which may involve a profound *metamorphosis* of protagonist or world (or both)–into the *eucatastrophe*, where marriages may occur, just governance fertilize the barren land, and there is a healing"[23]. Although the abovementioned

20. See Sistakou (2009a) 388-392.

21. The only systematic account of hero cult in the *Argonautica* in Hitch (2012). Hero cults in the *Argonautica* may have their roots in a widespread trend during Hellenistic times, namely the resurgence of cultural, religious and literary interest for epic heroes and the revival of anything pertaining to hero and tomb cult, see Alcock (1997). The literary antecedent of Apollonius (and Callimachus) in the thematic emphasis on hero cult was Pindar, on which see Currie (2005); Homer does not allude to hero cult as a rule, and the reason behind this thematic choice lies within the Panhellenic (the non-local) character of the epics as argued by Nagy (1979) e.g. 116.

22. The fantastic element in the cyclic epics is explained on a similar basis by Nagy (1990) 72 n. 99: "I would stress that the fantastic and the miraculous elements in the Cycle characterize the religious ideology of local cults, reflecting the more localized interests of individual city-states or groups of city-states. The same goes for the Romantic element of love stories, again for the most part screened out by the Homeric epics: it goes without saying that love affairs lead to conceptions of heroes, a basic theme of genealogical poetic traditions that promote the localized interests of the status quo".

23. *EF* s.v. "Fantasy". In the following study of the fantasy scenario as exploited in the *Argonautica*, I have used technical terms introduced by fantasy theorists (the *quest*, the *dark lord*, the *things bought at too high a cost*, the *land of fable*, the *companions*, the *talents*, the *monsters*, the *imaginary animals* etc.), on which see the authoritative *EF* s.vv.

scenario is roughly outlined, there are some interesting points of contact between this scenario and the *Argonautica*. The *raison d'être* of the expedition is the liberation from a bondage situation caused by the unjust behaviour of the land's king, Pelias. Pelias bears some resemblance to a stock character of fantasy, the *dark lord*, in that he aspires to become the 'prince of this world' first by exercising blasphemy against the gods and second by weaving a web of intrigue against his main antagonist in the struggle for power, Jason (1.6-7): τοῦδ᾽ ἀνέρος ὅν τιν᾽ ἴδοιτο/ δημόθεν οἰοπέδιλον ὑπ᾽ ἐννεσίῃσι δαμῆναι 'destruction caused by a country man whom he should see wearing only one sandal'(cf. 3.333-334 τόνδε τις ἱέμενος πάτρης ἀπάνευθεν ἐλάσσαι/ καὶ κτεάνων βασιλεύς... 'this man has been sent here by someone, a king, who wishes to thrust him out of his homeland and his possessions...')[24]. The situation is explained in the first analeptic narrative of the *Argonautica*, where both Pelias' blasphemy against Hera and his machinations against Jason are made explicit (1.5-17). Although Pelias hovers in the background of the story and never becomes an organic part of it, he is omnipresent in the role of the commanding lord, a role articulated through a series of formulaic expressions: 1.3 βασιλῆος ἐφημοσύνῃ Πελίαο, 1.279 Πελίαο κακὴν βασιλῆος ἐφετμήν, 1.981 Πελίαό τ᾽ ἐφετμάς, 2.624 ἐφιεμένοιο...Πελίαο. The darkness of Pelias' role is further accentuated when first Phineus and then Jason employ the word κρυερός, denoting metaphorically any sentiment, especially fear, that is ice-cold and chilling, to describe the king's terrifying decree (2.210 and 3.390 κρυερὴ ἐφετμή)[25].

Motivated in such a way, the Argonaut plot evolves through two critical phases: the encounter with Phineus who prophesies the success of the voyage (the analogue to the recognition phase in the scheme of fantasy narratives) and the changes Jason and his crew undergo during the Argonaut expedition, which, in turn, becomes a symbol of the transition from chaos to order (the metamorphosis phase)[26]. A fantasy story is characterized by a happy ending, the so-called *eucatastrophe*, denoting the final and unexpected turn of events which result into success, restoration

24. However, the real dark lord of the epic is Aietes, on whom see below pp. 83-85.
25. The only, but rather superficial, discussion of the role of Pelias is offered by Levin (1971) 13-23.
26. That the *Argonautica* culminates with the creation of a new world order is argued by Hunter (1993) 162-169; on a somewhat different approach to the evolutionary model, as a movement towards an eternal Iron Age, in the *Argonautica*, see Clauss (2000). Furthermore, the expedition itself is a symbolic *rite of passage* for Jason, who is akin to figures like Bellerophon, Theseus and Orestes, whose stories reflect generational passage through the accomplishment of difficult tasks (Hunter [1989] 30).

and well-being[27]. Thus, fantasy is by definition not only un-tragic but fundamentally uplifting for the reader[28]. It is no coincidence that the *Argonautica* climaxes with two scenes suggesting a transition from agony to joy and the shaping of a promising future. The *nostos* of the Argonauts nearly goes astray, as the heroes sail across the Cretan sea into the Aegean. A dark night like Hades falls and obscures the view of the heroes, and catastrophe seems to be at hand when Jason starts to pray to Apollo in tears (4.1694-1705). The intervention of Phoibos 'the Gleamer' is the decisive turning point towards the final success, a fact further accentuated by the sudden second person apostrophe to the god (4.1706 Λητοΐδη, τύνη δὲ κατ' οὐρανοῦ ἵκεο πέτρας 'Son of Leto, you heard his prayer and swiftly descended from heaven to the rocks')[29]. In the second scene, a godsent dream prophesies that the divine clod of earth which Euphemos received from Triton will become the island of Thera; thence, Cyrene will be settled, and thus a connection between the Argonaut myth and the Ptolemaic context is firmly established (4.1731-1764). Apart from this optimistic projection into a future well-being, the *Argonautica* closes with two typical happy endings, namely the marriage of Jason and Medea with the concomitant celebrations of the folk (4.1128-1200) and the safe return of the Argonauts to Pagasai (4.1780 ἀσπασίως ἀκτὰς Παγασηίδας εἰσαπέβητε 'and gladly you stepped out on to the shores of Pagasai').

Apollonius has moulded this general pattern into a specific plot type: the *quest*. It is a common assumption that a fantasy inevitably involves a quest; the quest may be oriented towards an external or internal goal, and its typical paradigms extend from Homer's *Odyssey* to J.R.R. Tolkien's *The Lord of the Rings*, from Dante's *The Divine Comedy* to Lewis

27. The term is coined by 20th century fantasy writer J.R.R. Tolkien in his 1947 essay "On Fairy Stories".

28. This is how Tolkien describes the un-tragic quality of fantasy in the essay "On Fairy Stories": "But the 'consolation' of fairytales has another aspect than the imaginative satisfaction of ancient desires. Far more important is the Consolation of the Happy Ending. Almost I would venture to assert that all complete fairy-stories must have it. At least I would say that Tragedy is the true form of Drama, its highest function; but the opposite is true of Fairy-story. Since we do not appear to possess a word that expresses this opposite–I will call it Eucatastrophe. The eucatastrophic tale is the true form of fairytale, and its highest function".

29. It should be noted that for Tolkien the joy aroused to the reader by the eucatastrophic ending has also a religious undertone ("On Fairy Stories"): "This joy, which is one of the things which fairy-stories can produce supremely well, is not essentially 'escapist', nor 'fugitive'. In its fairytale–or otherworld–setting, it is a sudden and miraculous grace: never to be counted on to recur... It denies...universal final defeat and in so far is evangelium, giving a fleeting glimpse of Joy, Joy beyond the walls of the world, poignant as grief".

Carroll's *Alice's Adventures in Wonderland*. The ultimate goal of the Argonaut expedition, the Golden Fleece, never acquires a 'function' in the plot, and its real essence remains a mystery[30]. Its most conspicuous feature, its otherworldly gleaming, is not explained only marvelled at (4.184-185): θάμβησαν δὲ νέοι μέγα κῶας ἰδόντες/ λαμπόμενον στεροπῇ ἴκελον Διός 'the young men stared in wonder at the great Fleece which shone like Zeus' lightning'. The mystery surrounding the object of desire is typical of any quest plot. The Golden Fleece is comparable to the Holy Grail of the Arthurian legend, the Golden Firebird of Russian folktale or the Ark of the Covenant of the Jewish tradition[31]. The Fleece is not only magical but also dark and ill-fated for those who desire it (1.256-259): *When the virgin Helle perished, would that Phrixos too, and his ram, had been covered over by the dark waves* (κῦμα μέλαν)*! But that grim marvel* (κακὸν τέρας) *spoke with a human voice–to store up countless pains* (ἄλγεα μυρία θείη) *and grief* (ἀνίας) *for Alkimede in the future*[32]*!* At the end tragedy awaits Jason and Medea in the sequel to the *Argonautica*. Since the Golden Fleece on the one hand symbolizes material gain, and on the other, though initially rewarding, ends in tragedy, it may be classified among *things bought at too high a cost* typically found in fantasy literature (such as the fruit of knowledge in the Old Testament resulting in the expulsion from the Garden of Eden or the prize that has to be paid by Faust in his pact with the devil). The Golden Fleece lies at the core of the *land of fable* in the *Argonautica*, situated somewhere between the real and the impossible world[33]. In this land of fable heroic, supernatural and divine forces are at work. Within this fantasy context, Apollonius weaves legend, folktale, romance and travelers' tales[34] into a plot which follows a set pattern consisting of: the call, the hero's companions, the voyage (including the encounter with the monsters, the temptations, the deadly opposites and the journey to the underworld), the helpers, the final ordeals and the goal[35]. In what follows, I

30. The Fleece as a magical symbol of power and kingship is appositely described by Green (1997a) 70.

31. Booker (2004) 69.

32. Since ἄλγεα μυρία θείη clearly echoes the opening of the *Iliad* (1-2 μῆνιν...ἣ μυρί' Ἀχαιοῖς ἄλγε' ἔθηκε), Apollonius replaces Achilles' tragic passion, his catastrophic wrath, with a dark symbol, the Golden Fleece, thus contextualizing his epic into the fantasy genre.

33. The best account of this world between reality and fairytale in Harder (1994).

34. These generic traditions as a background to the *Argonautica* are explored by Beye (1982).

35. The pattern of the quest plot, on which I base my reading, is analyzed by Booker (2004) 69-86.

will explore these parameters as incorporated in the *Argonautica* with emphasis on their fantastic and dark elements.

The starting point for the quest is a state of wrongness; as noted above, the *Argonautica* opens with an analeptic narrative describing the injustice exercised by lord Pelias against the gods, the land and Jason. At once the hero feels a compulsion, indeed a haste, to embark on the mission (1.841 *because I am driven on by grievous challenges...*), even though he faces an internal struggle between his desire to accomplish the feat (as expressed by Hypsipyle in 1.888-890 *may the gods keep you...as you bring the Golden Fleece to the king. This is what you want and what your heart desires*) and his proverbial ἀμηχανίη during the joint venture[36].

It is typical for a heroic fantasy that the protagonist gathers around him a group of heroes–either before setting off or along the way–who join voluntarily and represent stock characters of the fantasy genre, such as the bard, the magician, the seer, the gifted child, the woman, the trickster and so on[37]. In accordance with this motif, the Argonauts are volunteers and focus on the acquisition of the common good rather than the glorification of a single *aristos*; in this respect the *Argonautica* closely resembles fantasy and fairytale, whereas, at the same time, it is clearly distanced from heroic epic[38]. In terms of the quest plot the companions are not supporting actors but play, along with the hero, a leading role; therefore, a reading of the *Argonautica* from this viewpoint may answer the thorny question of the whys and the wherefores of heroism within the epic[39]. Their function in the quest narrative has been sketched out as follows: "The band of companions fill the scene, bolster the hero, perform feats he or she cannot, depart upon ancillary quests whose accomplishment will help trigger the climax, and die if necessary"[40]. In contrast both to Odysseus' companions, who are immersed in their anonymity

36. For an analysis of this notion, see Vian (1978). From a different point of view, Toohey (2004) 42-45 argues that this is a symptom of Jason's depression and melancholy.

37. The term used to describe such a group is the 'Seven Samurai' (see *EF* s.v.); it is worth noting that the symbolic number 'seven' has some validity for the *Argonautica*, since Apollonius assignes a special task to only a handful of companions out of a sum of 30 to 50 Argonauts which are found in the traditional lists (for a full account of these lists, see Scherer [2006] 43-56).

38. I am thinking here of the Trojan myth both in its cyclic as well as in its Homeric version. In the former, the joining of the heroes is compulsory (cf. how Odysseus and Achilles attempt to avoid recruitment, Proclus *Chrest.* §22 K. and §27 K.); in the latter, the purpose of their gathering is to obtain τιμή for Agamemnon and Menelaus (*Il.* 1.158-159 ἀλλὰ σοὶ ὦ μέγ' ἀναιδὲς ἅμ' ἑσπόμεθ' ὄφρα σὺ χαίρῃς,/ τιμὴν ἀρνύμενοι Μενελάῳ σοί τε κυνῶπα).

39. The bibliography on this major issue of the *Argonautica* scholarship is summarized by Glei (2008) 6-12.

40. *EF* s.v. "Companions".

and foolishness, and to the leaders of the Achaians, who are ruled by Agamemnon in the *Iliad*, Jason shares a sort of equality with his comrades, and the notion of collective heroism is stressed from the first through the last verse of the epic (1.1 παλαιγενέων κλέα φωτῶν and 4.1773 ἀριστῆες, μακάρων γένος)[41]. Through the genealogies and biographies, which are wedged into the entries of the catalogue and evoke past heroic enterprises, the Argonauts not only assume individual identities but moreover they become heroes, *aristoi*, 'knights' in their own right[42].

Within the body of the Argonauts, as in any group of quest companions, we may observe subtle variations, the most interesting of which are: the hero's *alter ego*, who displays qualities opposed to those shown by the protagonist, and the companions who compliment each other with their highly differentiated talents and add up to 'a whole'[43]. Undoubtedly the hero playing the role of Jason's *alter ego* is Herakles. Herakles and Jason embody antithetical values corresponding to archaic and modern patterns of heroism respectively: strength vs. skill, military prowess vs. seductive allure, primitivism vs. refinement. This is a commonplace of Apollonian scholarship that hardly needs documentation[44]. The fairytale dimension of the epic, however, is significantly enhanced by the exploitation of another motif, the extraordinary and supernatural *talents* with which Jason's companions are endowed. Talents in the literature of the fantastic may be mental and/or physical, and include clairaudience (the ability to hear distant or inaudible sounds), clairvoyance (ability to view far-off or hidden scenes), precognition (knowledge of the future), reading or projecting thoughts, bilocation (being in two places simultaneously), healing by hand, levitation, psychokinesis and the like. The catalogue of the Argonauts opens programmatically with Orpheus, the semi-mythical figure of the bard. In addition to his ability to enchant the rocks on the mountains and the streams of the rivers (1.26-27), Orpheus exercises psychokinetic powers by means of his magical song (1.28-31):

Φηγοὶ δ᾽ ἀγριάδες, κείνης ἔτι σήματα μολπῆς,
ἀκτῇ Θρηικίῃ Ζώνης ἔπι τηλεθόωσαι
ἑξείης στιχόωσιν ἐπήτριμοι, ἃς ὅ γ᾽ ἐπιπρό
θελγομένας φόρμιγγι κατήγαγε Πιερίηθεν.

41. See e.g. Beye (1982) 77-87. However, this observation does not contradict the centrality of Jason as a dramatic hero, see e.g. Clauss (1993).
42. On the biographies of the Argonauts in the catalogue, see Sistakou (2001).
43. Booker (2004) 71-73.
44. See e.g. Clauss (1993) 26-36 and 176-211, Hunter (1993) 25-36 and Clare (2002) 88-104. On the primitiveness of Herakles, see Radke (2007) 124-135.

As signs of his music, the wild oak trees which flourish on the Thracian coast at Zone stand to this day in close-set ranks; he brought them all the way down from Pieria by the bewitching music of his lyre.

Although military prowess and the acquisition of *kleos*, rank high in this, as in any, catalogue of heroes (1.44, 52, 58, 71, 73, 75, 100, 106-108 etc.), with this introductory scene Apollonius places the aesthetics of the fantastic at the heart of his epic. There are more examples that reflect folktale and fantastic motifs. Many heroes boast divine provenance (1.51-54 Erytos, Echion and Aithalides are the sons of Hermes, 1.172-173 Augeias the son of Helios, 1.179-180 Euphemos the son of Poseidon); others inherit the features of their divine parents (1.202-204 Palaimonios is crippled because he is the son of Hephaistos); Argos assists Athena in the construction of the Argo (1.226); Theseus is evoked as the legendary hero who has descended into the underworld (1.101-103); two seers, Mopsos (1.65-66, 80) and Idmon (1.139-145), have been taught the art of augury by Apollo himself, and are aware of their imminent death; the Boreads, the 'birdmen' of the group, are equipped with miraculous golden wings (1.219-223); Aithalides is granted by Hermes 'an unperishing memory of all things' that does not grow dim even in Acheron (1.643-648). However, three stand out for being supernatural, for possessing talents that contradict natural order:

1.153-155 Lynkeus
Lynkeus had the sharpest eyes of any mortal, if the report is true that without trouble he could see even down beneath the earth...

1.158-160 Periklymenos
Poseidon had given him [i.e. Periklymenos] boundless strength, and the ability in battle to become whatever he prayed to be when in the tight corners of war...

1.182-184 Euphemos
Euphemos could run even over the swell of the grey sea: his swift feet did not get wet, for he passed on his watery journey dipping only the very tips of his toes...

Similar paradigms of the mythical taking on a supernatural hue may be found in previous epic[45]. An outstanding case is attributed to the tradition of the *Cypria* (fr. 15 B.), according to which Lynkeus with his extraordinary sight is said to have seen Kastor and Pollux in their hiding place in a hollow oak somewhere in the Peloponnese. The motif of perpetual

---

45. Griffin (1977) 40 lists the following cyclic examples under the heading of the fantastic: the fabulous eye-sight of Lynkeus from the *Cypria*, the snow-white Kyknos and the black Memnon from the *Aethiopis*, and the miraculous daughters of Anius and the transformations of Nemesis and Zeus from the *Cypria* again.

metamorphosis is well known from epic–we may recall the figure of Proteus in Menelaus' narrative from *Odyssey* Book 4. The Hesiodic *Catalogue* (fr. 33a) contains a detailed description of the various shapes– eagle, ant, bee, snake–acquired by Periklymenos, to which Apollonius only elliptically alludes. The third paradigm is a fairytale reworking of the heroic talent of Achilles, his swiftness in running, condensed into the Homeric formula πόδας ὠκὺς Ἀχιλλεύς. It is critical to observe that Apollonius eschews the 'realistic' approach to heroism as found in Homer, while, in refining and extending the cyclic and Hesiodic epic style, he renders the fairytale element a vital part of his epic[46].

The core of the quest narrative, the voyage, is complex and multi-themed. A first pattern concerns the confrontation of the heroes with the *monsters*[47]. The monsters have three different functions within the quest plot: in the active role, the monster is a 'Predator', a creature looking for victims; in the passive role, it becomes a 'Holdfast', a threatening guardian of the 'treasure' or the 'princess'; in the avenging role, the monster as 'Avenger' pursues anyone who challenges his status as a keeper[48]. Paradigms of each category may be found in the *Argonautica*, where the Harpyies correspond to the Predator, the guardian serpent of the Golden Fleece to the Holdfast and Talos to the Avenger. In addition to bad monsters, good monsters too offer their aid to the Argonauts. A prominent example is the wondrous apparition of the sea god Triton in the form of a merman (4.1610-1619); although benevolent in spirit, Triton is depicted as a chimeric, chilling figure, half blessed god (1612 μακάρεσσι φυὴν ἔκπαγλον ἔικτο) and half sea-dragon with a forked tail (1613-1614 δίκραιρα...ἀλκαίη μηκύνετο) and a razor-sharp spine (1614-1615 κόπτε δ' ἀκάνθαις/ ἄκρον ὕδωρ). The plethora of monsters in the *Argonautica* mark a shift from the fantastic element towards the dark and the fearful; the Argonauts fight against the Otherness represented by the fantasyworlds into which, and through which, they move during their journey. We may argue that this emphatically monster plot has obvious parallels with modern-day horror literature[49].

46. On the contrary, such fantasy motifs and the notion of the miracle, popular in the Epic Cycle, are inappropriate to tragic epic, i.e. the *Iliad*, and therefore are carefully suppressed by Homer, see Griffin (1977) 39-43.

47. Some of the monsters encountered by the Argonauts are discussed by Murgatroyd (2007) 119-130.

48. Booker (2004) 31-33 identifies the essential physical, moral and psychological attributes of the monsters and acknowledges their three functions.

49. An essay on how the monsters embody Otherness in each culture may be found in Cohen (1996) 3-25. On mythical monsters as manifestations of horror, see Eco (2007) 34-41.

The commonest monsters in the literature of the fantastic are giants and dragons, both of which play a prominent role in the *Argonautica*. The first encounter of the Argonauts with the giants occurs on an island inside the Propontis. The dwellers of the island, the earthborn men, evoke the Odyssean Cyclopes in their insolence and fierceness (1.942-1011)[50]. Their physical appearance recalls the Hesiodic Hekatoncheires (*Th.* 147-153), and they are horrifying to look at (943 μέγα θαῦμα περικτιόνεσσιν ἰδέσθαι, 950 ἔκπαγλοί περ ἐόντες). They are even likened to the terrible monsters sent by Hera as yet another labour for Herakles who manages to confront them in battle aided by the rest of the Argonauts. However, in reducing their gigantic hands from one hundred to a mere six (944-946), Apollonius places them on the threshold of fairytale. The beginning of Book 2 is also marked by the appearance of a monster-like boxer, Amykos (2.1-97). Although not a mythical creature nor a fairytale giant, Amykos is likened to Typhon or a personification of the Earth in form and stature (38-40)[51]. Amykos, who challenges passers-by to a boxing match, evokes another mythical boxer (who, like Amykos, is a son of Poseidon and a nymph), Kerkyon–the biblical analogue to the Philistine warrior Goliath. Amykos is eventually defeated by the much 'smaller' in size Pollux in a strife realistically depicted in all its gory details[52].

It is not before Book 4 that the Argonauts fight against *the* fairytale giant, Talos (4.1641-1648):

τὸν μὲν χαλκείης μελιηγενέων ἀνθρώπων
ῥίζης λοιπὸν ἐόντα μετ᾽ ἀνδράσιν ἡμιθέοισιν
Εὐρώπῃ Κρονίδης νήσου πόρεν ἔμμεναι οὖρον,
τρὶς περὶ χαλκείοις Κρήτην ποσὶ δινεύοντα.
ἀλλ᾽ ἤτοι τὸ μὲν ἄλλο δέμας καὶ γυῖα τέτυκτο
χάλκεος ἠδ᾽ ἄρρηκτος, ὑπαὶ δέ οἱ ἔσκε τένοντος
σῦριγξ αἱματόεσσα κατὰ σφυρόν· αὐτὰρ ὁ τήν γε
λεπτὸς ὑμὴν ζωῆς ἔχε πείρατα καὶ θανάτοιο.

Among the generation of demigods he was the last survivor of the bronze race of men born from ash-trees, and the son of Kronos gave him to Europa

---

50. Καὶ τὸ μὲν ὑβρισταί τε καὶ ἄγριοι ἐνναίεσκον/ Γηγενέες (1.942) alludes to a stock phrase used by Odysseus each time he arrives in an unknown place (6.120 in regard to Scheria, 9.175 to the island of the Cyclopes, 13.201 to Ithaca).

51. Theocritus in *Id.* 22.44-52 emphasizes the prodigious size of Amykos with grotesque exaggeration; on a comparison of these two Hellenistic reworkings of the same episode, though primarily from a chronological perspective, see Köhnken (1965).

52. For the Amykos episode in Apollonius, and the emphasis on the graphic account of the boxing match, see Levin (1971) 131-149; Knight (1995) 63-66 parallels the scene with *Iliad* 23 and Amykos with the Homeric Epeios, and elsewhere (pp. 131-133) Amykos with Polyphemos.

to watch over the island by travelling three times a day around it on his bronze feet. His whole body and all his limbs were of unbreakable bronze, but below the ankle-tendon there was a vein which carried blood, and the thin membrane covering it held the key to his life and death.

Talos, the bronze man, has a dual function as a fantasy figure. He is an *automaton*, a self-operating machine endowed with human features, a reminiscence of the mechanic assistants in the workshop of Hephaistos as described in the *Iliad* (18.417-421); according to a later source, Apollodorus, Talos was forged by Hephaistos in the form of a bull (*Bibl.* 1.140.3), a version of technofantasy downplayed in the *Argonautica*[53]. By making Talos the last survivor of the Bronze Age of Man, given by Zeus to Europa to guard the island of Crete, and not a robot, Apollonius emphasizes the legendary past and sets the Golden Age as a background to his epic. Moreover, by stressing the anomalous nature of the monster, Apollonius places Talos on the borderline between divine and heroic, natural and artificial, human and animal[54]. Talos also points towards another direction: the standard plot device of fantasy related to the notion of *invulnerability*. Like all undead creatures of supernatural literature, Talos has his own Achilles' heel–the flowing out of his ἰχώρ from his vulnerable ankle[55]. The fantasy dimension of the episode of Talos is reinforced by the fact that he cannot be slain by a heroic (male) force but only by the witchcraft of a female, namely Medea, when she casts the evil eye on him[56].

On the other hand, serpents and dragons form a vital part of the world of the *Argonautica*[57]. Despite the fact that Romantic and Hellenistic poets draw upon different cultural and religious traditions, the serpent, and, in its fairytale version, the dragon inhabit the territory of their fantasylands[58]. It is worth noting that whereas Greek mythology abounds with evil serpentine creatures (for example Typhon, Python or Medusa),

53. On human *automata* in the Classical tradition, see Bruce (1913).

54. Talos as an anomalous creature is analyzed by Buxton (1998) 84-98.

55. On vulnerability as a dominant theme in the myth of Talos, see Buxton (1998) 98-107.

56. Cf. the slaying of the Nazgûl king, for whom it was written 'not to fall by the hand of a man', by a woman and a hobbit in J.R.R. Tolkien's *The Lord of the Rings*. Dickie (1990) argues that Apollonius explains the magic exercised by Medea in terms of Democritean philosophy and paradoxography in the Talos episode; his aim, however, is not to rationalize the heroic myth but, on the contrary, to heighten the sense of horrified wonder to the reader.

57. As well as of other poems by Apollonius, such as the *Alexandreias ktisis* (fr. 4 CA) and the *Canobos* (fr. 3 CA), on which see Sistakou (2008b) 320-322.

58. On the mythological formula of the 'hero killing the dragon' in Hellenistic poetry, see Durbec (2006a). The formula is fully explored within the comparative study of Indo-European poetics by Watkins (1995).

their symbolism is closely associated with primitive cultures (such as the era described in Hesiod's *Theogony* before the dominance of Zeus and Apollo) and, conversely, has no connection whatsoever with the Olympian world order (therefore it is totally absent from the Homeric epics, even the *Odyssey*)[59]. Apollonius captures this primitiveness by furnishing the fantasyworld of his epic with numerous horrific serpents, which, like the rest of the monsters, symbolize the encounter of the Argonauts with the Otherness[60]. All the dragons mentioned in the *Argonautica* have a distinctive identity and represent popular dragons of Greek mythology. The most horrific of these are steeped in past myth, like Typhon who was defeated by Zeus (2.38-40 and 1210-1213) or the serpent killed by Apollo at Delphi, called *Delphune* (2.705-707). Other mythical dragons have left their imprint on the Argonauts' present, and, in particular, on the tasks set to Jason by Aietes. The teeth that Jason has to sow in the field originate from the dragon of Ares which was slain by Kadmos and from whose teeth the citizens of Thebes were initially created (3.1176-1187). But it is the guardian serpent of the Golden Fleece, the sleepless dragon, that Jason has to confront in order to accomplish his mission (2.405-407, 1208-1210, 1269). Described as a 'monster terrible to behold' (2.405 αἰνὸν τέρας) and a son of the Earth (2.1209-1210), the dragon is deliberately left anonymous, a device stemming from folktale rather than myth; this dragon haunts the Argonaut plot and becomes the main obstacle that can only be overcome by means of another folktale device, namely the employment of witchcraft (4.143-161)[61].

As the narrative unfolds and the fantastic element prevails, the atmosphere takes on a darker shading. The Argonauts in Libya are involved in bizarre situations, such as the encounter with the nymphs Hesperides who lament the death of the dragon Ladon (4.1396-1409)[62]. Ladon, the guardian serpent of the golden apples in the garden of the Hesperides, is the dragon of 'the day before', still alive 'just yesterday' (1397 εἰσέτι

59. A notable exception is extra-Homeric but belongs to the thematic cycle of the Trojan saga: it is the strangling of Laokoon and his sons by the huge sea serpents, recorded in the cyclic *Sack of Troy* and Virgil's *Aeneid*; on the episode, see Murgatroyd (2007) 34-43.

60. On how Apollonius depicts the primordial landscape of Colchis and Kirke's island in the *Argonautica* as a reflection of Egypt, see Stephens (2003) 196-208.

61. Behind the killing of the guardian serpent through the use of magic spell, Stephens (2003) 216-218 reads a specific story pattern found in Egyptian underworld books, an episode where Horus confronts the monstrous serpent Apophis. Her argument, although focused on the Egyptian influence, also points to the direction of the common folktale motifs underlying the *Argonautica*.

62. This fairytale adventure has probably been formed under the influence of Panyassis (fr. 11 B.), see Livrea (1987) 186-187.

που χθιζόν παγχρύσεα ῥύετο μῆλα... 'on the previous day Ladon guarded golden apples...'), when he was found and slain by Herakles[63]. The scene verges on the uncanny, since the dragon is depicted as an undead creature (1400-1405):

δὴ τότε γ' ἤδη κεῖνος ὑφ' Ἡρακλῆι δαϊχθείς
μήλειον βέβλητο ποτὶ στύπος· οἰόθι δ' ἄκρη
οὐρὴ ἔτι σκαίρεσκεν, ἀπὸ κρατὸς δὲ κελαινήν
ἄχρις ἐπ' ἄκνηστιν κεῖτ' ἄπνοος· ἐν δὲ λιπόντων
ὕδρης Λερναίης χόλον αἵματι πικρὸν διστῶν,
μυῖαι πυθομένοισιν ἐφ' ἕλκεσι τερσαίνοντο.

Now, however, the snake had been destroyed by Herakles, and it lay against the trunk of the apple tree; only the tip of its tail still moved freely, as it sprawled lifeless from its head to the end of its dark spine. The arrows had left the angry poison of the Lernaean Hydra in its blood, and flies withered on the rotting wounds.

The corpse of Ladon is visualized through reference to horrifying details. The aesthetic pleasure of the reader *qua* spectator stems from the chilling image of the half-dead dragon with the still rattling tail, the dark spine and the flies drying out on the rotten wounds of the serpent. The uncanny effect is further emphasized when the Hesperides, the dramatic spectators of the scene, are transformed, at the sudden approach of the Argonauts, from blond women into dust and earth (1408-1409). But the passage reaches its climax at the point when the poisonous blood of another legendary serpent-like beast, the Lernaean Hydra, is mixed into the blood of Ladon through the arrows of Herakles[64].

A little later in the Libyan episode, the Argonauts encounter the real thing: no more a dragon or a mythical monster but a genuine snake of the Libyan desert, perhaps an asp, which causes death to the seer Mopsos (4.1502-1531). The 'terrible serpent' (δεινὸς ὄφις) and the effects of its black venom (μελάγχιμος ἰός) are described with 'impressionistic physiological realism' most likely echoing the style of iological treatises[65]. However, the scientific style is quickly abandoned for the sake of mythical narration. Apollonius contextualizes the scene into the Argonaut fairytale by ascribing the origin of all serpentine creatures to the archetypal snake monster, the Medusa (4.1513-1517):

63. On Herakles as a figure of 'the day before' in Book 4 of the *Argonautica*, see Sistakou (2009a) 390-392.
64. The scene is a variation on the well-known incident during which Herakles kills Nessos using the arrows that were dipped into the poisonous blood of the Hydra and Deianeira applies Nessos' own tainted blood on a tunic and offers it as a lethal gift to Herakles (Soph. *Tr.* 572-577).
65. Livrea (1987) 188-189; cf. Vian (1996) 199-200.

εὖτε γὰρ ἰσόθεος Λιβύην ὑπερέπτατο Περσεύς
Εὐρυμέδων –καὶ γὰρ τὸ κάλεσκέ μιν οὔνομα μήτηρ–
Γοργόνος ἀρτίτομον κεφαλὴν βασιλῆι κομίζων,
ὅσσαι κυανέου στάγες αἵματος οὖδας ἵκοντο,
αἱ πᾶσαι κείνων ὀφίων γένος ἐβλάστησαν.

When godlike Perseus Eurymedon–for his mother gave him this name as
well–flew over Libya, bringing to the king the head of Gorgon which he
had just cut off, all the drops of dark blood which fell to the ground gave
rise to the race of those serpents.

The aitiological explanation linking the birth of the snakes to the black
blood (κυανέου στάγες αἵματος) of a horrific primordial monster is not
a new idea, as the same origin is elsewhere ascribed to Typhon and the
Titans, whereas the Medusa version is reworked by Nicander in the opening verses of the *Theriaca* (8-12)[66]. The critical point of this passage is the
way in which the narrator visualizes a snapshot capturing one of the darkest pages of Greek myth: Perseus is holding the bleeding head of the
Gorgon while *at the same time* the serpents sprout up from the desert from
each drop of its blood[67]. With the phantom of the Medusa the dragon
discourse of the *Argonautica* reaches its climax; suffice it to say that not
coincidentally the same phantom haunts a great deal of Romantic poetry[68].

Although the legendary dragons are only fleeting images in the *Argonautica*, their dark effect on the reader, the sense that they form part of
this mysterious, horrific, fairytale universe, is deep and sustained. There
are also other monsters in the fantasyworld of the Argonauts, the Harpyies in Book 2 and the Sirens in Book 4. The former, personifications in
Homer and Hesiod of the swift whirlwind, are recontextualized by Apollonius into a monster narrative[69]. Within the framework of Apollonius'
bestiary, the Harpyies, literally the 'Snatchers' of the food of Phineus,
are depicted as winged beasts (2.187-300). Their bird-like form however

66. The various traditions about the origin of the snakes, and the imitations of Apollonius' passage by Late Greek, Latin and European literature, are thoroughly discussed by
Jacques (2002) 77-78.

67. Apollonius offers a darker reworking of the episode from Hesiod's *Theogony*,
where the decapitated Medusa gives birth to Pegasos, the winged horse, and his brother
Chrysaor, two shiny, marvellous creatures (280-286).

68. As mentioned above pp. 3-4, the Medusa became the absolute symbol of dark
beauty during Romanticism, see Praz (1970) 23-52. On the symbolism behind the Medusa
myth, approached from a transcultural and diachronical perspective, see the monograph
by Wilk (2000).

69. The fact that Apollonius is the first to have developed the Harpyies episode into
an independent monster narrative explains the somewhat low-key treatment of the scene
in the *Argonautica*: the emotional pitch is heightented and the scene becomes darker in
its reworkings by Virgil in the *Aeneid* 3.251ff. and by Valerius Flaccus in the *Argonautica*
4.423ff., as has been pointed out by Murgatroyd (2007) 63-69.

is only hinted at through a single reference to their beaks (188 γαμφηλῇσιν)[70] and their ability to speed across the sky (187 διὰ νεφέων ἄφνω πέλας ἀίσσουσαι etc.). The shapelessness of these imaginary animals is an attribute frequent in fantasy literature which heightens the horror effect. Apollonius plays with this device by blurring the boundaries between the avian and the wind-like nature of the creatures; the fact that only the Boreads, two liminal beings between the bird and the wind too (cf. 1.219-223), are able to fight against them retains the same ambiguity. This imprecise depiction of the Harpyies has puzzled critics[71]. However, the Harpyies do not merely suggest a meteorological phenomenon nor does the passage lend itself primarily to a rationalistic reading[72]. A critical detail pointing towards their monstrosity, and thus reinforcing the fairytale dimension of the scene, is the mysterious 'smell' the Harpyies pour over Phineus' meal–a stench so appalling that no man can even approach the remnants of this meal (2.189-193, 228-231)[73].

The Harpyies and the Sirens are two sides of the same coin as regards their function within the quest plot: "the Sirens are only Predators in another guise"[74]. Moreover, the Sirens inhabit the interspace between two major patterns of the voyage phase of the quest plot, namely the monsters and the temptations. The *temptations*, or more accurately, the *temptresses*, have a gendered orientation, as they usually involve "some beautiful and captivating woman" who attempts "to lure the hero to his doom by guile and seduction" by promising some kind of physical gratification, be it sex, wine or food[75]. The Sirens, however, hold the key to another type of sensual pleasure, the enchantment through song. Apollonius' treatment of the Sirens episode, despite some allusions to the related Homeric passages from Book 12 of the *Odyssey*, is quite original and 'Hellenistic' in tone (4.891-921)[76]. An obvious difference

70. The use of γαμφηλαί is ambiguous here, since it may denote both the jaws of animals (*Il.* 16.489) or the beak of birds (Eur. *Ion* 159); the confusion is heightened when Iris calls the Harpyies 'the hounds of mighty Zeus' (2.289 μεγάλοιο Διὸς κύνας). In order to disambiguate the passage, the scholiast notes that κλαγγή may only be used for predatory birds (Sch. A.R. 2.268-269b τοῦτο δὲ ὡς ἐπὶ ὀρνέων ἁρπακτικῶν· καὶ γὰρ ἐκεῖνα πρὸ τῆς ἁρπαγῆς κλάζειν φιλεῖ).

71. See e.g. Vian (1974) 268-269 on v. 189.

72. Levin (1971) 163-166 and Hunter (1993) 81.

73. A second encounter of the Argonauts with fabulous birds takes place near the end of Book 2 on the island of Ares (2.1030-1089). The episode is staged against the backdrof of another legendary battle, the struggle of Herakles against the Stymphalian birds (2.1051-1056).

74. Booker (2004) 75.

75. Booker (2004) 74-75.

76. See the comparative analysis of both episodes in Knight (1995) 200-206.

from the Homeric prototype is the fact that Apollonius provides background information regarding the mythological biography of the Sirens and more accurate details about their physical appearance and their fatal effect upon men. Part women and part birds in form according to Apollonius (898-899 τότε δ' ἄλλο μὲν οἰωνοῖσιν/ ἄλλο δὲ παρθενικῆς ἐναλίγκιαι ἔσκον ἰδέσθαι), the Sirens are introduced as archetypal *femmes fatales*, women whose powers are destructive to men–a narrative pattern which holds a great fascination for Romantic writers too[77]– (892-894 and 900-902):

> ἔνθα λίγειαι
> Σειρῆνες σίνοντ' Ἀχελωίδες ἡδείῃσι
> θέλγουσαι μολπῇσιν ὅ τις παρὰ πεῖσμα βάλοιτο.

Where the clear-voiced Sirens destroyed all who moored beside them with the enchantment of their sweet songs.

> αἰεὶ δ' εὐόρμου δεδοκημέναι ἐκ περιωπῆς
> ἦ θαμὰ δὴ πολέων μελιηδέα νόστον ἕλοντο,
> τηκεδόνι φθινύθουσαι.

They kept a constant look-out from their perch in the lovely harbour: many indeed were the men whom they had deprived of their sweet return, destroying them with wasting desire.

Whereas the Homeric passage is centred upon a macabre snapshot, the heap of the decaying men on site (*Od.* 12.45-46 πολὺς δ' ἀμφ' ὀστεόφιν θὶς/ ἀνδρῶν πυθομένων, περὶ δὲ ῥινοὶ μινύθουσιν 'men's corpses lie heaped up all round them, mouldering upon the bones as the skin decays'), Apollonius highlights the fatal allure of the Sirens. The episode takes an added twist, when Boutes falls a victim to his own hedonism (914 Σειρήνων λιγυρῇ ὀπὶ θυμὸν ἰανθείς) and commits suicide by jumping into the dark sea (915 νῆχε δὲ πορφυρέοιο δι' οἴδματος, 918 ἐν δίναις). Despite the intervention of both Orpheus and Aphrodite, the dramatic act of Boutes downplays the heroic undertone of the episode, while at the same time lends a Romantic shading to an epic story pattern[78]. The main temptress of the *Argonautica*, however, is Hypsipyle, the protagonist of the Lemnian episode (1.609-909). Known in the past as *femmes fatales* responsible for a massive androcide

77. See Praz (1970) 199-300 on the so-called 'belle dame sans merci'. Cf. also the detailed study of women as 'idols of perversity' in 19th century culture by Dijkstra (1986).
78. Hunter (1993) 44 hints at a similarity between the death of Hylas and that of Boutes: the sexual motivation and the mysterious disappearance of both heroes may provide a common basis for a comparison between the two deaths.

(609-619), the Lemnian women offer the Argonauts the typical gifts of seduction–food and wine–, and soon they engage sexually with them[79]. The affair between Hypsipyle and Jason, and the lingering on of the Argonauts on Lemnos, obviously recall the 'temptation' episodes of the *Odyssey* plot, featuring Kirke and Kalypso[80]. Furthermore, the episode (and especially the biographical details about the bloody past of the Lemnian women) foreshadows the 'darker' version of the same story pattern, the Medea plot[81].

The voyage cannot be complete without the passage through *the deadly opposites* and *the journey to the underworld*. Following the tracks of Odysseus, the Argonauts have to travel a narrow sea path between two opposing dangers, which take the form of either destructive rock formations or bloodthirsty sea-monsters[82]. After the encounter with the Sirens, Odysseus is faced with the dilemma of choosing between two opposites, the *Planktai* and Skylla/Charybdis, vividly described in Kirke's prophecy (*Od.* 12.55-110), and opts for the latter (*Od.* 12.235-259). Apollonius has to deal with his own 'poetic' dilemma on how to restage both episodes–literally–against the Homeric subtext[83]. His first choice is to undercut the dramatic impact of the Skylla/ Charybdis episode by turning it into a narrative 'phantom'; the Argonauts bypass Skylla and Charybdis in the actual plot (4.922-923), whereas the sole depiction of the monsters is embedded in Hera's prophetic speech. Hera spares the readers the horrific details of the Homeric prototype, but she nevertheless insists on the dark profile of the Skylla (4.827-831):

79. Hypsipyle offers two gifts to Jason too, which however are first mentioned in Books 3 and 4: a dark robe (φᾶρος κυάνεον) to remind Jason of their lovemaking (3.1204-1206) and a sacred purple robe (πέπλον ἱερὸν πορφύρεον) upon which Dionysus and Ariadne made love (4.423-434). Though these gifts are described in terms of extreme hedonism, they are recalled within a context of black magic and death, the first in the scene where Jason performs rites to Hekate before the bloody contest and the second where Medea lures Apsyrtos to death through the lethal gift.

80. Knight (1995) 162-169 emphasizes the parallels between the Lemnian and the Kirke episodes, whereas she only hints at the similarities with the Kalypso episode (p. 222). Clauss (1993) 132-147 even suggests a comparison between Hypsipyle and Nausikaa.

81. For a systematic comparison between Lemnos and Colchis, see Hunter (1993) 47-52. The Hypsipyle episode is a more 'polite' version of both the romance between Medea and Jason, and the one between Dido and Aeneas (Levin [1971] 59-86). Apollonius models the Lemnian episode on tragedy, especially Aeschylus' *Hypsipyle* and Sophocles' *The Lemnian Women*, see Cusset (2001c) 71-74.

82. These adventures have also been interpreted as a metaphorical *rite of passage* that help Jason mature, see Williams (1991) 133 with n. 9.

83. For a thorough discussion of these episodes against a Homeric backdrop, see Knight (1995) 207-216.

ἠὲ παρὰ Σκύλλης στυγερὸν κευθμῶνα νέεσθαι–
Σκύλλης Αὐσονίης ὀλοόφρονος, ἣν τέκε Φόρκῳ
νυκτιπόλος Ἑκάτη, τήν τε κλείουσι Κράταιιν–,
μή πως σμερδαλέῃσιν ἐπαΐξασα γένυσσι
λεκτοὺς ἡρώων δηλήσεται

Or to pass by the hated cave of Skylla–savage Ausonian Skylla whom night-wandering Hekate bore to Phorkos, she whom men call Krataiis–lest she leap upon them with her terrible jaws and destroy the flower of the heroes...

The second narrative choice of Apollonius is to double the other challenge, by making the Argonauts initially pass through the Clashing Rocks (called the *(Sym)Plegades*) during the outward journey in Book 2 and then through the Wandering Rocks (the *Planktai*) on their way from Colchis to Greece in Book 4; to complicate matters further, Apollonius also applies the alternative name *Kyaneai* to denote the sea passage for which the Argo became famous (e.g. in the proem: 1.2-3 διὰ πέτρας Κυανέας, cf. the prophecy of Phineus: 2.318)[84]. The realistic setting of the rocks and the stormy sea, especially in the lengthy description of the Clashing Rocks (2.549-609), outweighs the fantastic and the fairytale element in both scenes, whereas, at the same time, it heightens the effect of the sublime[85]. But the marvellous eventually comes to the fore, once the Argo, a toy in the hands of the gods, becomes a flying ship[86]: the Nereids lift the Argo and throw it, like a ball, upwards in the air without letting the ship fall to the sea again (4.939-955). What Apollonius visualizes is a long-standing tradition of the Argo flying through the Symplegades, a sublime image captured by the opening verse of Euripides *Medea*–εἴθ᾽ ὤφελ᾽ Ἀργοῦς μὴ διαπτάσθαι σκάφος[87].

The critical phase of the quest plot, the journey to the underworld, does not seem to have formed part of the Argonaut myth in any of its versions[88]. This major omission has been variously interpreted by scholars,

84. Obviously Apollonius identifies the Symplegades with the Kyaneai, as Euripides has done before him (*Med*. 2 κυανέας Συμπληγάδας). There is confusion as to whether the (Sym)Plegades/the Clashing Rocks/the Kyaneai of the *Argonautica* correspond to the Homeric *Planktai*, see Vian (1974) 150-154.

85. According to Williams (1991) 129-145, Apollonius enhances the effectiveness of the scene by focusing not so much on the description of the landscape but rather on the emotional response of the Argonauts.

86. On the intervention of Athena during the passage through the Clashing Rocks, see Byre (1997) and Knight (1995) 41-48; on Hera, Iris and Thetis in the scene of the Wandering Rocks, see Knight (1995) 297-305.

87. Cf. the ancient hypothesis which praises the emotional style of the opening of the *Medea*: ἐπαινεῖται δὲ ἡ εἰσβολὴ διὰ τὸ παθητικῶς ἄγαν ἔχειν.

88. However, the topography of the Homeric *Nekyia* must have been formed under the influence of the epic tradition about the voyage of the Argo, see West (2005) 54-56.

some of which read the entire Argonaut myth as a voyage to the land beyond, a 'Jenseitsreise'[89]. Within this framework, the Clashing Rocks and the Wandering Rocks on the way to Colchis and Greece respectively, represent the gates to the underworld, and, by extension, render the voyage of the Argo a kind of *katabasis*[90]. The journey to the dead has a double function within the quest plot, firstly to put the hero to the test through the horrific experience of the contact with the dead, and secondly to inform him about the outcome of his enterprise by means of a prophecy[91]. Apollonius naturally eschews the adventure to Hades (constricted as he is by the mythological tradition), but incorporates these two functions into other episodes of his epic. Prophecy is assigned to Phineus in Book 2. As for the former function, the tone in the epic is often 'infernal'[92] and a web of death is systematically weaved around the protagonists of the *Argonautica*[93]. Dead companions, tombs, ghostly apparitions, infernal gods, such as Hekate, and the murderous couple, Jason and Medea, are omnipresent in the epic. Even the geography is oriented towards Hades, and explicitly so when the Argonauts reach the Acherousian headland in Book 2–immediately after the passage through the Clashing Rocks–or when they traverse the Libyan desert in Book 4 and come across deadly experiences[94].

No quest plot is complete unless the heroes encounter, on their way to the ultimate goal, a number of mysterious, beneficial figures, the *helpers*. Gods are by definition helpers in any epic, and Apollonius exploits the full potential of divine machinery, though in a different manner in comparison with the Homeric epics[95]. Zeus' central plan is marginal for

89. Bibliography in West (2005) 54 n. 52. The never accomplished journey to the underworld becomes a rhetorical topos in the *Argonautica*, according to Clare (2002) 84-88.

90. This is the view held by Nelis (2001) 228-235. Cf. Kyriakou (1995) who associates the theme of the *katabasis* in the *Argonautica* especially with Herakles.

91. Booker (2004) 76-77.

92. See the analysis by Hunter (1993) 182-188, also in comparison with *Aeneid* Book 6.

93. This is how Stephens (2003) 218 summarizes the deathly atmosphere of the *Argonautica*: "The fact that the voyage of the Argo often takes place in a landscape populated with chthonic creatures and figures imagined or hallucinated, in which both narrative and protagonists seem to have lost direction, until at last they emerge from the Stygian darkness into the light of dawn, has prompted a number of interpreters, both ancient and modern, to understand the story as in part a *katabasis*."

94. Williams (1991) 145-150 and Stephens (2003) 218-237 read Book 4 of the *Argonautica* as a Hellenic version of the journey of the Sun as found in the Egyptian underworld books.

95. Gods in the *Argonautica* have a 'literary' nature and are depicted as characters within the epic, see Hunter (1993) 75-90. Feeney (1991) 57-98 stresses the distance between gods and humans in Apollonius' epic. For a comparison between the gods in Homer and Apollonius, see Knight (1995) 267-305.

the development of the plot, Apollo assumes a key role only in turning points of the *Argonautica*, Aphrodite and Eros motivate the secondary plot of the poem, the encounter between Jason and Medea, whereas it is the female goddesses, primarily Hera and Athena, and indirectly Thetis, that intervene as helpers and saviours in critical phases of the voyage[96]. There are two innovations introduced by Apollonius as regards the treatment of the Homeric gods in his epic. Firstly, "the element of the miraculous and the magical is far more important than in Homer generally", and secondly Apollonius reduces the communication of his heroes with the prominent Olympians, whereas, at the same time, "the Argonauts only have contacts with minor divinities–Glaukos, Thetis and the Nereids, the Libyan 'heroines', the Hesperides, Triton"[97]. By extension, and so as to accentuate the dark and mysterious forces that underlie the Argonaut expedition, Apollonius highlights infernal and Oriental gods (such as Hekate and Rhea/Kybele), the Titan Prometheus, minor divinities of water, nymphs, and semi-divine heroes like Herakles, the Dioskouroi and Orpheus[98].

The gods apart, the thematic category of the helpers in folktale and legend typically comprises "a benevolent, usually wise old man, and a beautiful young (though mysteriously ageless) woman" who, in being invested with supernatural powers, act as guides and advisers for the heroes[99]. We may easily identify the former figure with Phineus[100]. Phineus, who is endowed with the gift of prophecy by Apollo himself (2.178-182), a combination of Kirke and Teiresias from the *Odyssey*, is depicted as a male Sibyl–so heavy is the burden of old age upon him! In visualizing the aged Phineus, likened to 'a ghostly dream', feebled and dessicated, who can hardly get up from his bed supporting himself on a staff (2.197-205), the narrator renders the subsequent prophetic scene more effective, as the Argonauts watch and listen in amazement (2.206-207 οἱ δέ μιν ὡς εἴδοντο, περισταδὸν ἠγερέθοντο/ καὶ τάφον)[101]. Needless to say that the female figure, the young, beautiful woman is Medea, whose supernatural power, her fairytale talent, is not prescience

96. Apart from the abovementioned bibliography, on the role of Hera and Thetis in particular, see also Hunter (1993) 96-100 and Clare (2002) 139-144. On Hera and Athena, also from a narratological viewpoint, see Berkowitz (2004) 102-127.

97. Two fine remarks made by Hunter (1993) 77-78. On the plurality of divinities assisting the Argonauts, see Berkowitz (2004) 98-102.

98. A point made by Knight (1995) 274-277.

99. Booker (2004) 77.

100. On the Phineus episode, see Hunter (1993) 90-95 and Clare (2002) 74-83. Phineus as a version of the Homeric Kirke is discussed by Knight (1995) 169-176.

101. On the description of Phineus as a living dead, see Hunter (1993) 91 and n. 81.

but magic[102]. But help comes unexpectedly also from another direction that requires to be mentioned separately: the sons of Phrixos. Their course from Colchis towards Orchomenos, in a direction opposite to the one followed by the Argonauts, is violently interrupted by a shipwreck near the island of Ares; soon after their rescue by the Argonauts, the sons of Phrixos join the mission and retrace their route back to Colchis (2.1090-1230)[103]. This secondary voyage may also be classified as a quest plot[104]. Within its context the sons of Phrixos gain additional fairy-tale features, since, on the one hand, their failure to reach their final destination, Orchomenos, makes them a kind of *eternal wanderers* (are we ever informed by the narrator of their safe homecoming?), and, on the other, Aietes twice puts a *curse* upon them (3.584-608) for being the avatars of Phrixos and the allies of the 'pirates' Argonauts. Their helping role towards the Argonauts, as clearly foretold by Phineus (2.1090-1092), is to show them an alternative way back to Greece (4.257-293); the instructions given by Argos are marked by a divine portent, a heavenly light (4.294-297), which highlights the fairytale dimension of this episode.

The final goal, the acquisition of the Golden Fleece, remains to be achieved. The terrifying last ordeals will have to be faced with the aid of the dark helper of the *Argonautica*, Medea, to whom the next chapter is dedicated.

---

102. Medea is classified as a helper-maiden by Clauss (1997).

103. On the episode of the Phrixids, see Levin (1971) 197-211 and Clare (2002) 104-118.

104. See Clare (2002) 106: "All four essential ingredients of an epic quest as exemplified by the opening verses of the *Argonautica* are in place here [in verses 1.1093-1096], namely a group of *heroes* (1) embarked upon a difficult *voyage* (2) in obedience to the *command* (3) of another and with a specific *purpose* (4) in view."

I.2. The phantoms of Medea

> So said she, and with pale and languid face
> And half-shut eyes, unto the guarded place,
> Where was her golden bed, the maiden came.
> And in her dreams at first saw blood and flame
> O'er all the world, and nothing green or fair;
> Then in a snowy land, with body bare,
> Went wandering long, be-mocked of uncouth things:
> Then stood before the judgment-seat of kings,
> Knowing no crime that she was charged withal,
> Until at last deep sleep on her did fall
> Like death itself, wherein the troublous past
> And fearsome future in one tomb are cast.

William Morris *The Life and Death of Jason* 12.275-286 (1867)

In the Victorian remake of the Argonaut myth by William Morris, a poem entitled *The Life and Death of Jason* in 17 books, Medea is portrayed as a Romantic heroine. Having fallen a victim to her love affair with Jason, she is given over to visions of 'blood and flame' and to a deep sleep 'like death itself'. Morris' Medea, in her subtle psychological portrayal, is the dark reincarnation of Apollonius' own Medea. Both heroines experience the entire range of emotions from sentimentality to horror, from love to guilt; in fact, the latter seems to have served as a model for the revival of Medea by William Morris. And justly so, since Books 3, and, to a certain degree, 4 of the *Argonautica* show a close affinity with Romantic aesthetics and, conversely, are markedly differentiated from the contexts of heroic epic[105].

The opening of Book 3 of the *Argonautica*, the second proem of the epic addressed to the Muse Erato, marks the transition from the quest plot to the love story[106]. If, until this point, the narrator had to deal with *the glorious deeds of men* (κλέα φωτῶν), it is now *the power of love* (Κύπριδος αἶσαν) that attracts his attention. In terms of genre, the shift from the heroic/fantastic to the love element thematizes the divide between the epic and the novelistic, and it is not surprising that Apollonian scholarship has

---

105. The first to have interpreted Book 3 of the *Argonautica* in the light of 19th century Romantic literature was Sainte Beuve in his 1845 essay "De la Médée d'Apollonius".

106. In contrast to Books 1, 2 and partly 4 where Apollonius gives his own version of heroic epic, in Book 3 he reworks tragic sources—Euripides *Medea* and a series of lost tragedies by Aeschylus and Sophocles on the Argonaut myth: for a list of the underlying tragedies, see Nelis (2005) 360.

viewed Book 3 as the precursor of ancient novel, and consequently Medea and Jason as protagonists of a love and adventure romance[107]. The proem to Book 4, however, alters dramatically the thematic core of the *Argonautica* by highlighting the dark side of Medea's passion, her sufferings (κάματον) and secret thoughts (δήνεα) as a consequence of her love for Jason. The narrator's opinion is split over the motivation of Medea's flight from Colchis (4.4-5): *I ponder whether I should call it the mad, sickening burden of desire* (ἄτης πῆμα δυσίμερον) *or a shameful panic* (φύζαν ἀεικελίην) *which caused her to abandon the tribes of the Colchians.* Δυσίμερος 'sickening desire' is a very strong adjective, used once more in the *Argonautica* in 3.961 to denote the unhealthy effects (κάματον δυσίμερον) roused by the attractiveness of Jason, which are likened to the misery (ἄσπετον ὀιζύν) brought to the flocks when Sirius, brilliant to behold, rises to the sky (3.956-961). As for ἀεικέλιος 'disgraceful, ignominious', it suggests that the passion felt by Medea for Jason has a heavy burden of guilt[108].

So, this is the story of a female, racked with fear and guilt for an intimate love affair with a stranger; dominated by her anxieties and the death drive, she experiences an inner conflict between family duty and sexual desire; her dark passion develops under the shadow of a tyrannical father; to achieve her goal, the marriage with the alluring stranger, she resorts to black magic; eventually, a victim of her own nightmares, she violates social and moral laws and becomes an outcast. Medea's two-sidedness is not a result of incoherence or design fault on the part of Apollonius[109]; my claim is that Apollonius casts Medea into a dark romance scenario which, *mutatis mutandis*, shows some interesting parallels with 18th and 19th century Romantic, in particular Gothic, novel. Although it is daring to offer a comparative reading between two historically and culturally

107. Rohde (1960) provides the basis for detecting the roots of the ancient novel in Hellenistic love poetry; on the *Odyssey* and the *Argonautica* in particular as the predecessors of the ancient novel, see Konstan (1994) 170-178. Beye (1982) 120-166 proposes the 'comedy of manners' as a model for the 'sweet talk' of Book 3, but he often compares Books 3 and 4 with the novel too. The features of romance in the *Argonautica* deviate from the Homeric epics and stem from the Cycle according to Fantuzzi/Hunter (2004) 96-97. Already Phinney (1967) has analyzed the so-called 'Medea-Jason romance'; on Jason as a novelistic hero (*personnage romanesque*) who refuses traditional epic values, see especially Cusset (2001a).

108. On ἀεικέλιος as a synonym of ἀεικής, see Rengakos (1994) 36; Vian (1996) 147 on v. 5 and 212 on v. 5 rejects the moral judgement inherent in ἀεικέλιος=ἀεικής, and thinks that the adjective has rather a nuance of condolence towards Medea.

109. The dichotomy in Medea's character who is depicted as an innocent maiden in Book 3 and a sorceress in Book 4 has provoked intense debate between scholars: for an overview of the main arguments, see Glei (2008) 14-15.

distinct genres, and despite the fact that the *Argonautica* does not always
follow the typical story pattern of the Gothic novel, as has been described
in the introductory chapter, some key notions of the latter may throw new
light on the interpretation of Apollonius' epic, and the figure of Medea in
particular.

A stock female character of the Gothic scenario is 'the damsel in
distress', a young, beautiful maiden kept imprisoned by a villain in a
tower or a castle, waiting to be rescued by an errant knight, who eventually falls in love with her and marries her; its Greek archetype is
Andromeda, and it is featured primarily in fairytale and Medieval
romance. Medea does not fit into this pattern–at least the Medea which
is depicted as a demonic witch that abandons her home for the love of
Jason in Pindar's *Pythian* 4 and Euripides' *Medea*. Although Apollonius
has inherited the tradition which makes Medea an evil witch and thence
a dynamic woman, he recasts this black and white figure into a new
mould. In a way, this new Medea is more passive, a victim of the gods'
plans and Aietes, kept in a palace in the far away land of Colchis, and
waiting for the 'knight' Jason to set her free by marrying her; after this
first, 'romance' section, the union of the two lovers occurs, symbolically marked by their common flight from Colchis, thus setting the
darker section of the narrative about the aftermath of this union in
motion[110]. The key to understanding this new Medea is the female perspective adopted throughout Book 3 and, to an extent, Book 4. Despite
the fact that the *Argonautica* represents the male authorial tradition, and
its plot is set within the broader context of a heroic epic tending towards
the fantastic, the dark love story of Medea primarily concerns a female
in search of her identity within a society dominated by the male hero.
If construed thus, the *Argonautica* seems to explore ideological issues
pertaining to the role of the female within a patriarchal system, who, in
her inability to revolt against this system, becomes emotionally disturbed, and is often led to paranoid behaviour and violent action. This
is exactly the point of departure for the formation of the Gothic aesthetics, centred around the cultural connotations of the 'female', as a reaction to the 'male' oriented qualities privileged by Classicism and the

---

110. Interestingly enough, Newman (2008) 415-416 suggests that the threads of two
tales have crossed in the *Argonautica*: the first is the quest, the second tells of the hero's
confrontation with the monster dragon, his marriage to the princess after her rescue and
his ascension to her father's throne (as exemplified by the tale of Perseus and Andromeda
or Theseus and Ariadne). But, as Newman rightly points out, the story of Medea does not
develop in the expected way, since the sequel to the story in Corinth has Medea transformed into the dragon and Jason into her victim.

Age of Reason[111]. I will explore the heuristic value of this analogy for a deeper understanding of Apollonius' generic experimentation with epic and romance–or, to be more accurate, with epic *vs.* romance. In what follows the Medea story will be read as a predated version of a Gothic narrative.

A fundamental parameter of the Gothic is the setting, labelled *the edifice*, which has a physical entity (be it a castle, a tower or a city) but is foremost a symbolic structure, suggesting the way in which the past or any supernatural power controls the characters of the narrative, and the terror stemming from it. My claim is that the *Argonautica* features an edifice: it is the secluded land, Colchis, and the palace of Aietes, and, on a symbolic level, the hidden object, the Fleece, the emblem of the ancestral curse associated with Phrixos[112]. Phrixos haunts the narrative as a figure having the power to cause doom and destruction from the distant past. Two passages reinforce this portrayal. In the first, the women of Iolkos (1.256-259) and then Alkimede herself (1.290-291) claim that the legendary escape of Phrixos over the Hellespont is the fate that blights the present and the future of Jason and the Argonauts. The second passage originates from the speech of Argos, who claims that the curse of Phrixos is hereditary (3.336-339): *the family of Aiolidai will not escape* (οὐδ' ὑπαλύξειν) *from the bitter wrath* (θυμαλγέα μῆνιν) *of implacable Zeus, from his anger* (χόλον) *and from the appalling pollution* (ἄτλητον ἄγος) *and punishment* (ποινάς) *arising from Phrixos until the Fleece comes to Hellas*. The symbolism apart, the edifice in itself as part of the *Argonautica* setting will be treated in detail in the following chapter[113]; my present focus is the family.

If there is a myth essential to the formation of a genre, a myth informing its 'deep structure', then 'the Gothic myth' is *the patriarchal family*. A family based on the power and supremacy of the father and the tensions generated between male and female on the basis of inequality and oppression is a key theme in any Gothic plot. " 'Gothic', in contrast to other form of romance (or any mode of literary expression), is determined–indeed 'overdetermined'–by the rules of the family...Literally and metaphorically, Gothic plots are family plots, Gothic romance is

111. This is the fundamental definition of the Gothic aesthetics given by Williams (1995) e.g. 19: " 'Gothic' is an expression (in the Freudian 'dream-work' mode) of the ambivalently attractive, 'female', unconscious 'Other' of eighteenth-century male-centred conscious 'Reason' ".

112. The curse, associated with the haunted house and the family, is a fundamental motif of the Gothic, on which see the essay by Robert Mighall in Bomarito (2006) 1.290-301.

113. See pp. 114-117.

family romance"[114]. The analogy between this Gothic myth and the structuring of the Medea plot in the *Argonautica* is remarkable. The background of Medea is one of the less studied parameters of the epic, yet we may gain a deeper understanding of the *Argonautica*, if we interpret it as a family drama. As the Argonauts pass through the gardens and the halls of Aietes' palace, the narrator gives a full account of Medea's family; the successive description of the edifice and the family dwelling in it, in effect the interconnectedness between the two implied by the narrator, foreshadows the domestic drama that is about to unfold[115]. The patriarchal structure of the family is reflected in the hierarchical ordering of the royal apartments within the palace, which is divided into two wings, the one comprising the high buildings, and the other a series of bed-chambers on both sides of an inner court. King Aietes and his queen symbolically dwell on the loftiest of the high buildings (3.239-240 τῶν [i.e. δόμων] ἤτοι ἄλλον μέν, ὅ τις καὶ ὑπείροχος ἦεν,/ κρείων Αἰήτης σὺν ἑῇ ναίεσκε δάμαρτι). A prominent place, also in one of the high buildings, is granted to the other male member of the family, Apsyrtos (3.238-241), whereas the king's daughters dwell, along with the servants, in the bedchambers of the lower wing of the palace (3.247-248 τοὺς δ᾽ [i.e. θαλάμους] ἔχον ἀμφίπολοί τε καὶ Αἰήταο θύγατρες/ ἄμφω, Χαλκιόπη Μήδειά τε)[116].

Head of Medea's family is the commanding lord, king Aietes, while Apsyrtos represents the heir to the throne passed through the male line of the family. The mother, the Okeanid Eidyia, is a shadowy figure. Although mentioned twice by name (3.243, 269), in effect she remains *nameless*, a symbol of the beloved mother, from whom Medea will be violently separated (4.27-31). However, there are two mother substitutes in the family, emblematic of the 'good' and the 'bad' mother respectively. The first is Chalkiope, Medea's sister who assumes the stock role of the confidante. Medea has a peculiar mother-daughter relationship with Chalkiope, when she declares that *I am both your sister and your daughter* (φημὶ κασιγνήτην τε σέθεν κούρην τε πέλεσθαι), *since mother often used to tell me that when I was a baby you took me to your*

114. Williams (1995) 22-23; on her analysis of the family plots of the Gothic, see especially pp. 87-96.

115. The enumeration of the apartments of Aietes, Chalkiope, Medea and Apsyrtos, correspond to different storylines throughout Books 3 and 4, see Danek (2009) 283-284.

116. There is an asymmetry in the stucturing of the royal buildings, corresponding to the discrimination between the males and the females of the royal family; on the 'geography' of the palace, see Vian (1995) 119-120. Cf. Elliger (1975) 306-307 who stresses the similarities between the description of Aietes' palace with that of Alkinoos, and of his garden with Kalypso's grotto, in the *Odyssey*.

breast (τεῷ ἐπαείραο μαζῷ) *just like your sons* (3.732-735). Her counterpart is Kirke. Kirke's motherhood relationship with Medea is not only based on their ties of kinship (her flashing gaze in 4.727-729 reveals that she is the daughter of Helios)[117] but also suggested by their similarities, most obvious of which is the use of witchcraft[118]. Being a witch disturbed by nightmares (4.662-664, 685-686), one who purifies murderers by means of blood (4.704-709)[119], Kirke also assumes the role of the dark mother towards Medea. Their encounter in Book 4 brings a problematic relationship to the fore: the 'daughter's' guilt for the fratricide forbids her from confessing her crime, for which no atonement by the 'mother' is granted; consequently, the expulsion from Aiaia, a double of her homeland Aia, symbolizes the rejection by the mother, which results in the eternal lamentation experienced by the daughter (4.718-752)[120].

To understand how the patriarchal authority controls the Medea plot, we have to study the function of Aietes within the narrative. Aietes assumes a dual role in the 'dual' plot of the *Argonautica*. Like Pelias who sets the quest in motion, he is *the dark lord* to be faced by the Argonauts during their quest for the Fleece; from the viewpoint of the family, he is also the tyrannical father figure who confronts the feminine Otherness represented by Medea. Aietes' profile as a savage and cruel king, with a terrifying voice and great stength that evoke Ares, who is equalled only by the dragon monster guarding the Fleece, is first given by Argos (2.1202-1206); later on, during his arming scene, Aietes is depicted as a god, an Ares, Helios or Poseidon to behold (3.1225-1245)[121]. This awesome king is hostile both to the sons of Phrixos–whom he addresses as an authoritative *pater familias* in v. 304 παιδὸς ἐμῆς κοῦροι Φρίξοιό τε...–and to the Argonauts from their very first meeting at the palace (3.302-438). In Aietes' mind Jason represents a threat to his royal power, thus indirectly suggesting that the stranger will marry the princess to ascend to the throne (375-376), and therefore he and his companions

117. On the formidable and fatal gaze of the descendants of Helios in the *Argonautica*, see Vian (1995) 66 n. 2 and 138 on v. 886.

118. On a literary level, the Homeric Kirke is used as a model for Apollonius' Medea, especially since both match the scenario 'use of witchcraft and sexual interest in their visitors before helping them in their efforts to return home', see Knight (1995) 176-184.

119. Purification from family murder is found in tragedy, e.g. in Aeschylus *Eumenids*. Knight (1995) 191 n. 216 remarks that "the sacrifice gives mystery and leads to the 'tragic scene' of recognition".

120. Knight (1995) 194 rightly points out that "[Kirke's] angry rejection of her niece further weakens the links between Medea and Colchis, which are to be broken completely on Drepane". On the portrayal of Kirke in Apollonius, see Dyck (1989) 462-464.

121. The divine illusion of the scene is discussed by Clare (2002) 198-201; on Aietes' depiction as an Ares-hero, see Harrauer (2004).

deserve to suffer excruciating torture to death (377-379): εἰ δέ κε μὴ
προπάροιθεν ἐμῆς ἥψασθε τραπέζης,/ ἦ τ᾽ ἂν ἀπὸ γλώσσας τε
ταμὼν καὶ χεῖρε κεάσσας/ ἀμφοτέρας, οἵοισιν ἐπιπροέηκα πόδεσ-
σιν 'if you had not already eaten at my table, I would have cut out your
tongues and chopped off both your hands and sent you packing with only
your feet left'[122].

Instead the evil king forces Jason to go through three deadly ordeals
before granting him the Golden Fleece. Aietes reveals himself as a dark
lord, and the narrator discloses the hidden thoughts of this character, in
the long indirect speech addressed to the Colchians by the king (3.576-
608). Although Aietes is not yet aware of Medea's plotting against him,
he emphatically summons his people to a location far away from the
palace (577 νόσφιν ἑοῖο δόμου). Towards the end of the speech, he
recalls the enigmatic prophecy given to him by Helios that treachery
awaits him from his own offspring; according to his understanding, the
curse would be fulfilled in the sons of Chalkiope (597-605). But the narrator has Aietes–unconsciously–foreshadow the threat represented by
Medea when he ironically declares that *he had no fear at all that his
daughters might devise some hateful scheme* (602-604). Book 4 opens
with a counter-scene (6-10). Aietes meets the Colchians in an overnight
session in the palace (8 οἷσιν ἐν μεγάροις); while devising treachery
against the heroes, he is deeply aware that the success of Jason in the
contest could not have been achieved without the help of his daughters
(9-10 οὐδ᾽ ὅ γε πάμπαν/ θυγατέρων τάδε νόσφιν ἐῶν τελέεσθαι
ἐώλπει). The contrast between these scenes indicates that the roles of
Aietes are reversed during the course of Book 3: no longer the cruel king
but the dark father comes to the fore[123].

After this turning point, Aietes exacts revenge not on the Argonauts
but especially on Medea, by commanding the Colchians to bring back
the maiden from land or the open sea–this being the only way to sate his
rage (4.231-233 εἰ μή οἱ κούρην αὐτάγρετον ἢ ἀνὰ γαῖαν/ ἢ πλωτῆς
εὑρόντες ἔτ᾽ εἰν ἁλὸς οἴδματι νῆα/ ἄξουσιν). Medea's flight is a
flight from the house of the father[124]. Although initially the desire to flee
enters unconsciously Medea's phantasies in Book 3, it is expressly stated

122. Vian (1995) 23-31 offers a detailed psychological profile of Aietes.
123. On the contrasted scenes of the assembly, see Clare (2002) 216-219.
124. The idea that Medea 'escapes' the palace is probably suggested by the enigmatic
simile of 4.34-39, especially if we follow the interpretation of the ancient scholia of
διειλυσθεῖσα as λάθρα διεξελθοῦσα τοῦ δόμου, ἀποδράσασα, φυγοῦσα. The opposite view of the simile, i.e. that it suggests a girl not escaping from but taken into slavery,
is supported by Hunter (1987) 136-137.

in Book 4, in the scenes with Kirke (735-736) and Arete (1014-1024), to whom the heroine points out the terrors of the tyrannical father. The wrath of Aietes *qua* father is usually overlooked by the interpreters of the *Argonautica*, though it has a strong dramatic effect on the characters and it is undoubtedly a source of the sublime for the reader[125]. Thus, when Arete decides to rescue Medea, she illustrates the dark and savage relationship between father and daughter by three mythological examples. The first is about Nykteus, the mythical king of Thebes, who punished his daughter Antiope when she fled to Sicyon to marry Epopeus (1090); the second tells of how Danae was cast with the newborn Perseus into the sea in a wooden chest by her father Akrisios (1091-1092)[126]. The third is more extensive and treats the story of Echetos, an obscure figure only known from the *Odyssey*, who blinded and imprisoned his daughter for a secret love affair (1092-1095)[127]:

> νέον γε μὲν, οὐδ᾽ ἀποτηλοῦ,
> ὑβριστὴς Ἔχετος γλήναις ἔνι χάλκεα κέντρα
> πῆξε θυγατρὸς ἑῆς, στονόεντι δὲ κάρφεται οἴτῳ,
> ὀρφναίῃ ἐνὶ χαλκὸν ἀλετρεύουσα καλιῇ

Recently, and not far away, the violent Echetos pierced his daughter's eyes with bronze pins and her life wastes away in grief-filled doom as she grinds bronze in a dark hut[128]...

The story of Echetos is based on a scenario that would become central to the Gothic novel: the female heroine is kept imprisoned in the secret chambers and dungeons of the dark edifice as a punishment for transgressing the boundaries imposed by the tyrannical father[129].

If Aietes, in representing the wrath of the father, may be associated with the idea of terror, the reading of the *Argonautica* from a feminine

---

125. Cf. the interpretation given by Williams (1995) 77 on how Burke perceives the 'masculine' sublime: "Burke links the sublime with the attributes of God the Father according to Christian theology, notably power, infinity, wrath, justice, wisdom. Nothing is more sublime, he writes, than the wrath of an angry God. Human fathers also properly evoke awe, according to Burke, but love (evoked by beauty) is the mother's province". It is no coincidence that Apollonius stresses the god-like essence of Aietes, on which see above pp. 83-84.

126. See Vian (1996) 185 on vv. 1090-1092.

127. In *Od.* 18.85-87 Echetos is mentioned by Antinoos as a bogeyman, a savage killer who will cut Iros' nose and ears and genitals with a knife and throw them to the dogs; interestingly enough, Aietes is depicted in similar terms when he threatens to cut the tongues and hands of the Argonauts in 3.377-379.

128. The translation of ὀρφναίῃ καλιῇ as 'in a dungeon's gloom' by R.C. Seaton in the 1912 Loeb edition captures more accurately the 'Gothic' atmosphere of Echetos' story.

129. For an analysis of the Gothic novels based on this scenario, see Williams (1995) 1-12.

perspective brings horror to the fore. This horror is internalized, as it deals with the fantasies and fears of the female psyche; in this respect the interpretation of the Gothic scenario presupposes a study of the feminine unconscious and a recourse to 'hysterical readings' of Romantic literature[130]. An approach to Medea *from within*, from a psychological viewpoint is, as critics have already pointed out, the great innovation of Apollonius, and to this I will now turn my focus[131].

Medea shows a great tendency towards isolation, and in this isolation she evokes the melancholy hero of Romanticism. Although on the fatal day of the wounding by Eros Hera keeps Medea at the house by means of divine force (250 Ἥρη γάρ μιν ἔρυκε δόμῳ), we are told that she avoids the palace (3.250-251 πρὶν δ᾽ οὔ τι θάμιζεν/ ἐν μεγάροις) and regularly finds shelter at the shrine of Hekate (251-252 Ἑκάτης δὲ πανήμερος ἀμφεπονεῖτο/ νηόν). There is a tension created between these distinct spaces: the house of the father, a closed and threatening place, and the shrine of Hekate, where Medea establishes contact with the dark powers of nature. Medea the witch frequents a secluded landscape with features that recall Romantic aesthetics. Not only a landscape inspiring melancholy (the stars and the moon being its main traits) but primarily a natural space where human and divine forces converge to produce a sublime effect. All these characteristics are explicitly mentioned by Argos in the depiction of Medea's ability to control nature by her spells (3.528-533): *There is a young girl who lives in Aietes' palace; the goddess Hekate has taught her extraordinary skills in handling all the drugs which the dry land and the boundless waters produce; with these she charms the blast of unwearying fire, stops still the flow of crashing rivers, and puts bonds on the stars and the holy paths of the moon*[132].

The nocturnal visits of Medea to the shrine of Hekate or its natural surroundings to collect magical herbs mark a symbolic distancing from the house of the father and, by extension, a revolt against patriarchal

130. See especially the essay by Ronald Thomas (2006) on the relationship between dreams and Gothic literature, and the discussion of 19th century female Gothic under the perspective of psychoanalysis by Elaine Showalter (in Bomarito [2006] 1.210-220).

131. Cf. the detailed account of the role of Medea by Vian (1995) 39-48.

132. In Burke's and Kant's notion, the encounter of man with the infinite power of God or the universe that occurs within the natural landscape is a source of sublimity. In Romantic literature written from a female perspective, Mother Nature becomes a friend and a co-worker, an ally of the female, whereas, in other cases, the sublime landscape may function as a solace and a shelter, an alternative to the claustrophobic castle, see Mellor (2005) 187-188. Both functions of nature may serve as key to the understanding of the Medea plot.

authority. Two scenes that highlight Medea's search for the self far away from the palace of Aietes, within the isolation offered by nature, stand out for their Romantic and dark tone. In the first the narrator tells of how Medea once compounded 'the drug of Prometheus' after performing a ritual for Hekate (3.844-866). The setting is a sublime landscape, full of awe, horror and grandeur: situated between Caucasus and the Caspian sea, the place is haunted by the infernal Hekate, the dark Brimo 'the Roarer'; within this landscape flourishes the *Prometheion*, a herb grow-ing from the dripping ἰχώρ of the Titan; to cut its root, as Medea does, causes the dark earth to groan and shake and Prometheus to writhe in pain! One should not overlook the fact that Medea has a dual identity, as she is torn between the sorceress and the lover. Medea's split between her two selves is recorded during her flight from the palace in Book 4. The landscape acquires again a sublime dimension, which stems from the personification and the soliloquy of the Moon. As the goddess *Mene* bitterly confesses, magic and eros are conflicting notions in her relation-ship with Medea–a relationship that has brought the heroine and the powers of nature together many times in the past (4.59-61): *Ah! How many times have your treacherous incantations caused me to hide when my mind was full of love, so that in the gloom of the night and without disturbance you could work with your drugs...*[133]

It is the complex relationship of Medea with the house of the father that invites a psychological reading of the female in the *Argonautica*. The beginning of Book 3 records the thoughts, words and actions of a (pas-sive) woman in love staying indoors: this I will call the 'romance' phase of the narrative. As the narrative progresses Medea gradually becomes more susceptible to hysterical and paranoid reactions: this is the 'Gothic' phase[134]. In my analysis I will focus on what I call the *phantoms* of Medea, her visions, fantasies and nightmares, and also on the aftermath of these *phantoms*, the triad magic-murder-marriage[135].

133. For a full discussion of this critical scene, see Fantuzzi (2008) 301-307.
134. The difference in tone and thematics between Books 3 and 4 may again be inter-preted by means of an analogy with modern poetics. E.g. to distinguish between the sub-categories of mass-produced romances, the so-called Harlequins and the Gothics, Modleski (2008) 51-57 offers a plausible explanation: the 'romance' corresponds to courtship, the 'Gothic' to the marital stage of a woman's life; in the former the heroine is preoccupied with getting a man, in the latter with dealing with the problems once the union has been formed; the psychic transformations the heroine has to undergo are from fear into love in the first case, and from love into fear in the second. This pattern may also explain the differences between the Medea *before* and the Medea *after* the flight from Colchis.
135. Toohey (2004) 61-65 explores the relation between lovesickness and melancholy, as well as that between love and violence, in Apollonius' depiction of Medea.

The first category comprises daydreaming, one of the symptoms of erotic pathology. The big scene of daydream takes place after the walk-out of the Argonauts from the meeting with Aietes. By analogy with the Lemnian episode, Jason walks through the hall shining with grace and beauty. As he exits Medea's soul follows his steps *like a dream* (3.446-447 νόος δέ οἱ ἠΰτ' ὄνειρος/ ἑρπύζων πεπότητο μετ' ἴχνια νισομένοιο)[136]. The contrast between ἑρπύζων and πεπότητο suggests the image of a sleeper who in his dream is incapable of reaching his goal despite his efforts; the model for this nightmare situation is *Iliad* 22.199-201, where the same simile is used to describe Achilles' futile attempt to catch Hektor[137]. It is made explicit that, from this point on, Medea will become a victim of her own fantasies, as her perception will be controlled by her emotions and anxieties; in terms of narrative, this renders Medea the 'focal character', and her 'internal focalization' dominant in Books 3 and 4 of the *Argonautica*. Hence, there are two levels of *reality* running parallel in these books: the events as seen from the perspective of the omniscient narrator and the events as filtered through Medea's point of view[138]. A telling example is the scene under discussion, the meeting between Aietes and Jason in the palace. After the end of the scene (3.268-448), the narrator has Medea take a leap back in time and recreate it once more in a *vision* (453-458)[139]:

προπρὸ δ' ἄρ' ὀφθαλμῶν ἔτι οἱ ἰνδάλλετο πάντα,
αὐτός θ' οἷος ἔην, οἵοισί τε φάρεσιν ἧστο,
οἷά τ' ἔειφ', ὥς θ' ἕζετ' ἐπὶ θρόνου, ὥς τε θύραζε
ἤιεν· οὐδέ τιν' ἄλλον ὀίσσατο πορφύρουσα
ἔμμεναι ἀνέρα τοῖον· ἐν οὔασι δ' αἰὲν ὀρώρει
αὐδή τε μῦθοί τε μελίφρονες οὓς ἀγόρευσε.

Everything still danced right before her eyes–how he looked, the clothes he wore, how he spoke, the way he sat on the chair, how he walked towards the door. As she pondered she thought that there could never have been another such man. In her ears rang his voice and the honeyed words he spoke.

136. On the mind's dream-like detachment from the body, see Campbell (1994) 367-368.
137. Vian (1995) 69. The same feeling is thus described in Mary Shelley's *Franken-stein* (Ch. 20): "But I was overcome by the sensation of helplessness, so often felt in frightful dreams, when you in vain endeavour to fly from an impending danger, and was rooted to the spot".
138. The contrast between the omniscient narrator and the internal focalization of the action by Medea in Book 3 is thoroughly discussed by Fusillo (1985) 347-355.
139. On the models of this dream-scene, and its Sapphic undertone, see Campbell (1994) 370-371.

The immediate replay of the previous scene interrupts the linearity of the plot. Medea *qua* narrator focuses on the visual and aural highlights of Jason's presence in the palace, thus adding to the passage a cinematic quality[140]. Suddenly Medea's reverie takes a dramatic turn–it becomes a nightmare. Her initial fear for the ordeals Jason will have to face (459 τάρβει δ' ἀμφ' αὐτῷ), an anxiety oriented towards the future, gives its place to the actual mourning for the death of the hero as if it has already taken place (460-461): ὀδύρετο δ' ἠύτε πάμπαν/ ἤδη τεθνειῶτα 'she grieved as though he were already dead and gone'. From daydreaming to mourning, this is the first in a series of scenes which begin as Romantic dreams only to end as Gothic nightmares.

The fantasies of Medea are once more brought to the fore in the scene of the dream (3.616-644)[141]. Unlike the dreams of epic and tragedy, Medea's dream overrides traditional classifications: it is not allegorical, godsent, admonitory or prophetic but rather a reflection of the heroine's complex bodily and emotional state[142]. Apollonius' notion of the dream diverges significantly from the religious concepts of dreaming; in viewing the dream of Medea as a product of psychic disturbance, Apollonius anticipates both the Romantic and Gothic notions of dreaming as well as the claims of Freudian psychoanalysis[143]. More importantly, the dream is a gendered literary device, closely connected with the female: this feature too is characteristic of the Gothic novel, where only females are expected to have dreams, illusions and fantasies because they are associated with subjectivity, superstition and insanity, whereas men represent reason, knowledge and positivism and therefore may only rarely dream[144]. The Gothic heroine is a female of morbid perceptiveness, her irrational-

140. The device introduced by Apollonius closely resembles the 'point of view shot' in cinema, which refers to how a character views an object. Cf. Campbell (1994) 368 who notes that "a rapid succession of visual impressions recapturing the departed Jason present themselves in cinematographic fashion 'in front, in front...of her eyes'–she is reenacting a 'dream-experience' ".

141. On Medea's dream, see Kessels (1982) 156-161 and especially Fusillo (1994). The literary model for this scene is Nausikaa's dream from the *Odyssey* (Knight [1995] 232-244). On dreams and their interpretation in the Graeco-Roman tradition, see Walde (2001) esp. 13-33.

142. As a rule Hellenistic writers accept the notion (fully explored by Aristotle) that dreams are not sent by the gods but are products of the human *psyche*, see Kessels (1982) 155-156 and Plastira-Valkanou (1999) esp. 127-129 with bibliography. On dreams reflecting the waking preoccupations of a person in ancient novels, see MacAlister (1996) 70-73.

143. Fusillo (1994) claims that Medea's dream represents, according to the explanation of Freud "the fulfillment of a desire"; cf. Thomas (2006) on nightmares in 19th century literature.

144. On a reading of female dreams in the Gothic novel from this perspective, see the excellent analysis by Doody (1977).

ity is an expression of inner pain and anxiety, and her 'dreams' are the product of the blurring of the boundaries between reality and illusion, thus allowing the 'nightmare' terror to take control over her thoughts and actions[145].

Within this context, Medea's dream is at the same time a symptom of illness and an attempt at recovery from it[146]. Apollonius captures this subtle shading in the introductory verses of the dream scene (616-617)– especially if we interpret ἄχος as 'pain': κούρην δ' ἐξ ἀχέων ἀδινὸς κατελώφεεν ὕπνος/ λέκτρῳ ἀνακλινθεῖσαν 'the young girl found respite from her *pains* in exhausted sleep which came over her as she lay stretched on the bed'[147]. The dream of Medea is twofold as the plural ὄνειροι and its two antithetical attributes imply: as the narrator explicitly states, it is both ἠπεροπεύς 'seductive' and ὀλοός 'fatal'[148]. Probably these attributes correspond to the two episodes of the dream, which in its first part reflects the wishes of the dreamer (619-623 the desire of Jason for Medea) and in its second the aftermath of this desire (623-632 the conflict between Medea and the family)[149]. The dream brings the female unconscious to the surface, which is haunted by the repressed sexual desire on the one hand and the confrontation with parental authority on the other[150]. Medea fantasizes that the only motive behind Jason's voyage is a love conquest; in her dreamworld the masculine view of the Argonaut expedition *qua* heroic quest gives its place to the female obsession with love and marriage. *She imagined that the stranger undertook the challenge, not at all because he wanted to recover the Fleece–it was not for that that he had come to Aietes' city–but to take her back to his own home as his properly wedded wife.* This marks a turning point in Medea's behaviour, since it is this 'fantasy' situation that will define the heroine's notion of self and her subjective understanding of 'reality'. For this reason, the finale of the dream should not be regarded as prophetic but as a

145. Doody (1977). Cf. a similar scene where the heroine has a vision of her dead father from Ann Radcliffe's *The Mysteries of Udolpho* (Ch. 8): "Retired to her lonely cabin, her melancholy thoughts still hovered round the body of her deceased parent; and, when she sunk into a kind of slumber, the images of her waking mind still haunted her fancy. She thought she saw her father approaching her with a benign countenance…".

146. Chalkiope also suggests that Medea suffers serious illness in verse 3.676: ἦ νύ σε θευμορίη περιδέδρομεν ἅψεα νοῦσος 'has a god-sent sickness seized hold of your body?'.

147. Cf. the translation of the passage by Seaton in the Loeb edition and especially the medical terminology 'now a deep slumber had *relieved* the maiden from her *love-pains*…'.

148. This interpretation of attributes in Kessels (1984) 159-161.

149. See Papadopoulou (1997) 663.

150. Therefore I do not agree with Kessels (1984) 158 who stresses the prophetic value of the second part of Medea's dream.

sequel to the 'romance' with Jason: the resistance to paternal control is Medea's hysterical response to the conflict between love and family, and, by extension, to her divided self[151]. *From this arose a bitter dispute between her father and the strangers, and both allowed her to choose whatever outcome her mind desired. Without thought of her parents she immediately chose the stranger*[152].

In the subsequent scene, Medea becomes a true Gothic heroine: she is awaken by the screams of her parents–in her dream!–(631-632 ἐκ δ' ἐβόησαν/ χωόμενοι. τὴν δ' ὕπνος ἅμα κλαγγῇ μεθέηκε), she is filled with anguish and terror (633 παλλομένη δ' ἀνόρουσε φόβῳ), she desires to rush–barefoot and in her robe (646 νήλιπος οἰέανος)–into her sister's chamber but to no avail (645-653), she is haunted by the image of the unlucky bride (suggested by the extended simile of vv. 656-663), she falls on her bed and bursts into tears (654, 664), and eventually narrates her dreadful dream to her sister (690-691 τοῖα κατακνώσσουσα μινυνθαδίῳ νέον ὕπνῳ/ λεύσσω ὀνείρατα λυγρά). From then on, the plot takes a dramatic turn, as the dilemmas visualized in the dream gain control over Medea's psyche. The much discussed 'inner struggle' of the heroine[153], which takes the form of successive monologues in the rest of Book 3[154], is a conflict between her deepest anxieties, fear vs. guilt, desire vs. shame, duty vs. disgrace. As said "Gothics are never about women who experience delusions of grandeur and omnipotence (a form paranoia occasionally takes); the Gothic heroine always feels helpless, confused, frightened, and despised"[155]. Nothing could describe more accurately Apollonius' Medea. This Medea, as any Gothic heroine, is torn between two archetypal males, the father and the lover, and it is her

151. For this psychoanalytical reading of Romanticism, see Roberts (2005).

152. Apollonius has elsewhere used the female obsession with marriage as a means of characterization of the hysterical heroine: like Medea, Peisidike fantasizes that she will become the bride of Achilles upon the death of her family in the *Lesbou ktisis* (fr. 12 CA), see Sistakou (2008b) 331-336.

153. On the psychological characterization of Medea and the depiction of her inner self, especially in verses 3.744-824, see the systematic overview by Barkhuizen (1979); cf. the rather psychoanalytical approach by Beye (1982) 132-140, and for an earlier reading of the psychology of Medea in love, see Carrière (1959).

154. Narratologically Medea's divided self is expressed by means of an 'interior monologue'. The idea that Apollonius with this scene introduces the interior monologue belongs to the theorists Robert Scholes and Robert Kellogg: Papadopoulou (1997) 654-664 offers some preliminary remarks on this literary device as used by Euripides and Apollonius in order to give a positive characterization of Medea, whereas Fusillo (2008) fully explores Apollonius as the 'inventor' of the interior monologue and the 'stream of conciousness' device, and illustrates his argument by reference to examples from Homer, Apollonius and the modern novel.

155. Modleski (2008) 57.

inability to overcome the one in favour of the other that soon drives her to paranoia[156].

This set of conflicting feelings comes again to the fore after Medea's promise to Chalkiope that she will rescue the Argonauts and the Phrixids (741-743):

τὴν δὲ μὲν αὖτις
αἰδώς τε στυγερόν τε δέος λάβε μουνωθεῖσαν,
τοῖα παρὲξ οὗ πατρὸς ἐπ' ἀνέρι μητιάασθαι.

Medea, now left alone, was prey again to shame and hateful fear, because she was devising such help for a man behind her father's back.

Though the night falls and people are fast asleep (744-750), Medea suffers from insomnia (751)[157]. Her dreams are replaced by nightmare scenaria about the future[158]. Medea fantasizes how Jason would perish from the fury of the bulls in the field of Ares (752-754); that she would give the charms to the hero (766-767); that she would not give him the charms and she would herself perish (767); that she would neither give him the spells nor die but only endure her miserable love (768-769); how she would be disgraced and mocked after death for betraying her family (791-798)[159]. Dominated by these phantoms, Medea decides to kill herself with a murderous drug (802-809); the motif of suicide heightens the dramatic tension and highlights the Romantic sensibility of Medea[160]. Now in front of her eyes new visions arise, the visions of the pleasures of life (811-812): ἀμφὶ δὲ πᾶσαι/ θυμηδεῖς βιότοιο μεληδόνες ἰνδάλλοντο

156. Along the same lines, Beye (1982) 136 offers a Freudian interpretation of the plot, in pointing out that "the Fleece is somehow symbolic of Medea's virginity, and Aietes' anger at losing the Fleece is a father's anger at losing his daughter to another man".

157. The juxtaposition of nocturnal calm and inner agitation of a hero is as old as Homer and a recurrent device in Greek literature, see Vian (1995) 132-133 on v. 744.

158. A passage from Oscar Wilde's *The Picture of Dorian Gray* captures the dark mood of this nightmarish reverie (Ch. 11): "There are few of us who have not sometimes wakened before dawn, either after one of those dreamless nights that make us almost enamoured of death, or one of those nights of horror and mishappen joy, when through the chambers of the brain sweep phantoms more terrible than reality itself and instinct with that vivid life that lurks in all grotesques, and that lends to Gothic art its enduring vitality, this art being, one might fancy, especially the art of those whose minds have been troubled with the malady of reverie".

159. Barkhuizen (1979) 43 points out that the visions of the women mocking 'the maid who disgraced her home and parents' and 'the maid who cared so much for a stranger' emerge from her subconscience and have a dream-like quality.

160. Similarly 'Romantic' in its effect is the motif of suicide in Greek novel; as MacAlister (1996) 54-70 notes, dramatic suicides in the novel are an expression of inner conflict and despair, whereas the Classical notion of suicide is associated with moral values, such as dignity and honour.

'all the delightful pleasures of life danced before her'[161]. Here the use of ἰνδάλλοντο, and the fleeting images of the maiden's girlfriends and of the shining sun, once more evoke Medea's oneiric viewing of reality. As day breaks and Medea moves symbolically from the palace to the shrine of Hekate, the final act of the romance is about to unfold (828-1155). After her romantic meeting with Jason, Medea for one last time drifts off into a reverie of love (1151-1152): ψυχὴ γὰρ νεφέεσσι μεταχρονίη πεπότητο./ αὐτομάτοις δὲ πόδεσσι θοῆς ἐπεβήσατ' ἀπήνης 'her soul was flying aloft amidst the clouds...by themselves her feet mounted the swift wagon...'. Once more Medea is "in a dreaming–indeed a sleep-walking–state"[162].

At this point the romance of Medea and Jason reaches its climax, and Medea eventually resolves her dilemma. Once she leaves the palace and joins the Argonauts, the heroine comes into a new conflict with the world around her; under the delusion that Jason and the Argonauts are conspiring against her, Medea develops an almost paranoid behaviour. And although scholars provide an in-depth study of Medea's psyche in Book 3, the psychological disturbance of the heroine in Book 4 with its tragic undertones has gone unnoticed[163]. After the repressed anxieties of separation from home are materialized and Medea leaves Colchis for Greece, she is beset by the thought that Jason will abandon her. Apollonius has Jason foreshadow the idea of abandonment by reference to the mythological example of Ariadne (3.997-1004, 1096-1099). Of course, Jason emphasizes the first part of the story, how Ariadne rescued Theseus against the will of Minos, to urge Medea to help him; it is Medea, who, although ignorant of the end of the story (3.1074-1076), fantasizes that she will too be abandoned[164]. Medea's anxiety of abandonment, another typical trait of the Gothic female who feels victimized and persecuted by

161. Cf. the translation of the passage by Seaton in the Loeb edition 'and all around her thronged visions of the pleasing cares of life'.

162. Campbell (1994) 368.

163. Cf. however the tragic reading of Medea by Fusillo (2008) 159: "Although Medea finally decides to help Jason and elope with him, and not to commit suicide, the negative *Stimmung* of the last monologue [i.e. 3.770-801] will always follow her in the narration of the adventurous voyage to Greece, rich in its foreshadowing of the Euripidean tragedy. In fact there is no major difference with respect to the heroines that will come after her, whose stories will all end with a tragic and sublime suicide–from her immediate descendant, Virgils' Dido, to a very distant one, Tolstoy's Anna Karenina, who is torn between social codes and love, and between her maternal role her relationship with Vronsky. Their conflictuality is equally insoluble, and produces a deep sense of frustration".

164. However, in vv. 3.1106-1108 Medea declares that Aietes is no Minos and she no Ariadne, cf. Dyck (1989) 460. The abandonment of Ariadne is mentioned by the narrator in vv. 4.431-434, just before the killing of Apsyrtos, thus reinforcing the antithesis between Ariadne and Medea.

the male counterpart[165], is a recurrent theme in her speeches and a vital parameter of her actions throughout Book 4. As I intend to show below, Book 4 is designed so as to highlight the interconnectedness between the 'abandonment' speeches of Medea, which are formulated as supplications[166], and her dark actions, i.e. the exercise of magic, the murder of Apsyrtos and the marriage with Jason[167]; the former correspond to Medea's fear[168], whereas the latter to her madness, two conflicting psychological states which are programmaticaly advertised in the proem to Book 4 (cf. 4-5 ἄτης πῆμα and φύζα ἀεικελίη)[169].

Immediately after her flight, Medea becomes an ἱκέτης of the Argonauts (4.83-91). Jason responds to her anguished cry for help (92 ἴσκεν ἀκηχεμένη) by taking an oath of marriage–once the Argonauts return safely to Iolkos (94-98). In exchange for this vague promise, Medea leads the Argonauts into the sacred grove where the dragon guards the Golden Fleece (100-108). Medea's active participation in the acquisition of the Fleece calls attention to her dark role as a sorceress[170]. Although Medea is introduced as a servant of Hekate from her first appearance in Book 3, and despite the fact that she has already given her spells to Jason to help him survive the ordeals of Aietes, it is in Book 4 that her witchcraft becomes dramatically significant[171]. In portraying Medea as a witch, the narrator reveals the Otherness, the uncanny nature of his heroine[172], and creates an effect of horror to the reader. The flight of Medea during the night is set within a fairytale atmosphere: the bolts of the palace doors yield automatically to her magic song (41-42) and her feet

165. For this reading of female paranoia in Gothic literature, see Modleski (2008) 51-76.

166. The supplication typology of Medea's speeches in Book 4 are discussed by Plantinga (2000) 116-126.

167. Plantinga (2000) 116 notes that "the suplication in 4.81-100 marks the beginning of a series of supplications which each time mark moments of great anxiety and crisis".

168. Vian (1996) 3-5 points out that the dominant feeling in Book 4 is fear; cf. the powerful simile of vv. 11-13 where Medea is likened to a young fawn terrified by the baying of the dogs in the forest.

169. According to Dyck (1989), Medea in Book 4 is portrayed as a tragic heroine, capable both of good and evil, a victim and a victimizer at the same time. Cf. Hunter (1987) who likens Medea in Book 4 both with Euripides' Medea and the Homeric Helen.

170. Dyck (1989) 458-459 argues that the Fleece functions as a token of passage or a dowry which facilitates Medea to move from the barbaric society of Aietes to the Greek society of Jason and the Argonauts.

171. On how Medea uses her witchcraft and rhetorical skill for her self-preservation throughout Book 4, see Dyck (1989).

172. Apollonius has modelled Medea on Nausikaa by assigning her the role of the 'helper-maiden'; however, Medea diverges significantly from the Homeric model in that she is depicted as a terrifying and passionate heroine, representing Otherness rather than normality: see Clauss (1997).

hastily carry the maiden to the Argonauts (66)[173]. Horror, however, lurks in this magical setting (50-53):

οὐ γὰρ ἄιδρις
ἦεν ὁδῶν, θαμὰ καὶ πρὶν ἀλωμένη ἀμφί τε νεκρούς
ἀμφί τε δυσπαλέας ῥίζας χθονός, οἷα γυναῖκες
φαρμακίδες

She knew the roads well, as often in past days she had roamed in search of corpses and poisonous roots in the earth, as women who work in drugs do...

The path taken by Medea is covered with dead bodies. To search between corpses for magic spells is an extremely horrific action[174], one that produces what might be called a Gothic effect[175]. The fantastic and the horrifying are combined in the further portrayal of Medea as a witch in two highly effective scenes that frame Book 4. In the first Medea takes the Fleece by hypnotizing the guardian serpent (145-161); in the second she uses the same mesmerizing device against Talos (1659-1672)[176]. In both scenes Medea, in invoking the spirits of the underworld (147-148 αὖε δ᾽ ἄνασσαν νυκτιπόλον, χθονίην, 1665-1666 θέλγε τε Κῆρας/ θυμοβόρους, ᾿Αΐδαο θοὰς κύνας), represents the powers of darkness and death, the uncanny powers of a female psyche in despair.

Every supplicant has a potential 'threatening power', which in the case of Medea is her ability to exercise black magic. But horror escalates further, after the second, more intense 'supplication' of Jason by Medea

173. As Vian (1996) 73 n. 2 notes, πόδες φέρον suggests 'mechanical walking'.

174. Typically Medea and her helpers collect herbs to produce their drugs: this dark act, which however does not involve corpses, is described in the remains of Sophocles' lost play *Rhizotomoi* (fr. 534-536 TrGF).

175. One cannot resist recalling the famous scene from Mary Shelley's *Frankenstein* where Victor Frankenstein searches among the corpses to study the mysteries of life and death (Ch. 4): "To examine the causes of life, we must first have recourse to death. I became acquainted with the science of anatomy, but this was not sufficient; I must also observe the natural decay and corruption of the human body...Darkness had no effect upon my fancy, and a churchyard was to me merely the receptacle of bodies deprived of life, which, from being the seat of beauty and strength, had become food for the worm. Now I was led to examine the cause and progress of this decay and forced to spend days and nights in vaults and charnel-houses. My attention was fixed upon every object the most insupportable to the delicacy of the human feelings. I saw how the fine form of man was degraded and wasted; I beheld the corruption of death succeed to the blooming cheek of life; I saw how the worm inherited the wonders of the eye and brain".

176. Hypnotism is a motif rarely found in Greek literature (for hypnotism as a practice of the magicians, mostly in technical texts, see Ogden [2009] 171-175). However, the idea of hypnotizing the dragon should be probably attributed to Antimachus (fr. 73 Matthews). Black magic and hypnosis are key themes of fantasy literature, on which see also below pp. 129-130.

96 THE AESTHETICS OF DARKNESS

in vv. 350-390. When Medea discovers that the Argonauts have come to
an agreement with the Colchians to surrender her to Apsyrtos (338-349),
her rage is turned against Jason. It is dramatically significant that whereas
the narrator stresses the collective responsibility of the Argonauts for the
negotiations with the Colchians (338-340 Μινύαι...πάροιθεν συνθε-
σίην, μέγα νεῖκος ἀλευάμενοι, ἐτάμοντο 'the Minyans...avoided this
great strife by first reaching an agreement'), Medea, as a focalizer of the
subsequent scene (350 ἔνθα δ' ἐπεὶ τὰ ἕκαστα νόῳ πεμπάσσατο
κούρη 'when the young girl had thought this all over in her mind'),
personalizes her criticism by specifically accusing Jason (352-353 αἶψα
δὲ νόσφιν Ἰήσονα μοῦνον ἑταίρων/ ἐκπροκαλεσσαμένη 'straightaway she called Jason aside, away from his companions')[177]. Medea is
stricken by sudden anguish as in a crisis of madness (351-352 δή ῥά μιν
ὀξεῖαι κραδίην ἐλέλιξαν ἀνῖαι/ νωλεμές 'her heart was wracked by
violent waves of bitter pain'). Female paranoia, roused by the conspira-
cies of the male, is put on display in Medea's highly emotional and
threatening speech[178]. The argumentation, which focuses on the invalid-
ity of Jason's oaths and the desolation of Medea, summarizes the core
arguments of Euripides' *Medea*[179]. The most impressive feature of this
speech, however, is its gendered orientation; Medea explicitly states that
Jason represents now all the males potentially associated with a female–
the father, the husband and the brother (368-369 τῷ φημι τεὴ κούρη τε
δάμαρ τε/ αὐτοκασιγνήτη τε μεθ' Ἑλλάδα γαῖαν ἔπεσθαι 'for this I
tell you that I follow you to the land of Hellas as your daughter, wife,
and sister')[180]. In deciding to kill Apsyrtos (411-420), Medea kills the
phantoms of her family; Jason becomes a father and a brother substitute,
when he symbolically slaughters Apsyrtos, the representative of Aietes,

177. On the narrative devices used in this scene, see Byre (1996) 5-6. I do not agree
however with Byre's point that the reader senses a 'psychic distance' from Medea's inner
thoughts in Book 4; in my opinion, only the narrative devices of characterization in Book
4 have changed, in the sense that the psychological state of Medea is not revealed through
the interior monologues of the heroine as in Book 3 but through her speeches and actions.
178. The motivation behind Jason's actions is deliberately left ambiguous by the narrator, a feature regularly used in Romantic and Gothic literature. Cf. Byre (1996) 8 who
notes that "we know that Jason is contemplating treachery, but we do not know who is
his primary object, Medea or Apsyrtos; nor whether Jason is motivated chiefly by love
for Medea or by concern for the success of his expedition and the safety of himself and
the Argonauts".
179. Byre (1996) 6-8.
180. Apollonius reworks here a famous phrase addressed to Hektor by Andromache
(*Il.* 6.429-430)–but by eliminating the parameter of the mother: Ἕκτορ ἀτὰρ σύ μοί
ἐσσι πατὴρ καὶ πότνια μήτηρ ἠδὲ κασίγνητος, σὺ δέ μοι θαλερὸς παρακοίτης; cf.
Vian (1996) 162 on v. 369 and Byre (1996) 8-9.

with his own hands[181]. The scene is staged as a Greek tragedy–the peplos sent to Apsyrtos strongly recalls the fatal wedding presents offered to Glauke in Euripides' play, whereas the *exempla* of Ariadne and Hypsipyle suggest the tragic implications of love[182]. The tragic elements apart, the emphasis upon the appalling details of the murder and the mutilation of the corpse, the image of the blood welling from the wound, the sidelong glance of the Erinyes, the rite of licking and spitting the blood and the burying of the dead body (464-481)[183], all visualize the uncanny and the horror stemming from Medea's *eros*[184].

As the Argonauts come across sites and characters from the *Odyssey*, Medea twice assumes the role of the supplicant. In the Kirke episode, however, her supplication has practically no results[185]. On the contrary, the supplications addressed first to Arete (1014-1028) and then to the Argonauts (1031-1052) achieve their aim, and the Phaeacian episode ends with the celebration of the couple's wedding[186]. A closer look at Medea's speeches reveals the heroine's obsession with the authority of the father as well as with the notion of marriage. The nightmare of being returned to the vicious Aietes still haunts Medea (1014-1015, 1042-1044); she stresses her virginity, an idea closely associated with her life as a maiden in the house of the father (1024-1025 ἔτι μοι μίτρη μένει ὡς ἐνὶ πατρός/ δώμασιν ἄχραντος καὶ ἀκήρατος 'my virgin's belt remains unstained and untouched, just as it was in my father's house'). Being a fugitive from paternal authority, Medea's last resort is marriage; it is no coincidence that before fleeing the palace, she takes leave of her maidenhood by cutting off a lock of her hair (27-29 χερσί τε μακρόν/ ῥηξαμένη πλόκαμον, θαλάμῳ μνημήια μητρί/ κάλλιπε παρθενίης 'she cut off a long lock of her hair, and left it in her room for her mother as a memorial of her virginity')[187]. Apparently the idealized fulfillment of Romantic love,

181. For an extensive discussion of the episode, see Byre (1996), cf. Dyck (1989) 460-462.

182. On the tragic undertones of these references, see Byre (1996) 10-12.

183. The allusions of this scene to Orestes' killing of Aigisthos in Euripides' *Electra* are pointed out by Porter (1990) 260-267. On the mutilation theme and the expiation rites in tragedy, see Vian (1996) 167 on vv. 477, 478.

184. Visualization of horror as a vital parameter of the scene is emphasized by Byre (1996) 13: "The killing itself, narrated in 464-479, is horrible; but the horror is almost impersonal...No speech, no thoughts or feelings are reported; the characters are shown acting only, in a sort of surrealistic dumb show"; cf. Dyck (1989) 462 who speaks of a vivid dramatization by means of a series of mimic gestures.

185. Plantinga (2000) 119-123.

186. See Dyck (1989) 464-467 and Plantinga (2000) 123-126.

187. For an introduction on the adolescent hair-cutting ritual, an act symbolizing, among other things, sexual maturation, see Leitao (2003).

this marriage has uncanny undertones. Medea fantasizes herself as Jason's bride-to-be in the dream scene of Book 3, when *she imagined that the stranger undertook the challenge to take her back to his own home as his properly wedded wife*. Upon awakening, Medea is faced with the harsh realities of the unhappy marriage, brilliantly depicted in the extended simile of the widowed bride (3.656-664)[188]. Soon the imaginary promise of marriage (625 ὑποσχεσίης)[189] becomes an oath on the part of Jason– but one that binds him with the bridal chamber until death (3.1128-1130, cf. 4.1083-1085). Throughout Book 4 we watch the preparation of a wedding, marked by the prenuptial rite performed by Medea before leaving the palace (26-33), the nuptial associations of the full moon (166-171)[190] and the Fleece offered to Jason as a wedding gift (162-182)[191]. These arrangements culminate in the love making of the couple in the sacred cave of Corcyra and the ensuing wedding ceremony (1128-1222), an event marked both of joy and fear[192]. But the marriage is soon to end in horror–and the narrator foreshadows its dark outcome by having Medea and Jason make love on the ominous object of desire, the Golden Fleece which covers their bridal chamber. Apparently, the romance has a 'happy ending'; however, beneath the surface of this light-hearted closure hovers the threatening figure of Medea who has already made her debut in literature as a *femme fatale* in Euripides' tragedy.

By mid 20th century Gothic literature came into vogue in the form of mass-market paperbacks. The covers of these paperbacks illustrated the basic 'scenario', 'setting', 'characters' and 'tone' of this popular romances, which have been described as follows[193]:

> These books asked to be judged by their covers, which invariably depicted the heroine and an imposing, ancient edifice set in a wild landscape. Usually it was night, dimly illuminated by a moon half-hidden in clouds. The

188. Cf. the story of another unhappy bride, Kleite, the wife of Kyzikos, who hangs herself upon the death of her husband (1.1053-1069).
189. Equally 'imaginary' is the promise given by Achilles to Peisidike and the ensuing vision of the heroine that she will become Achilles' bride and a daughter-in-law of Thetis in the palace of Phthia from the *Lesbou Ktisis* (fr. 12.14-18 CA): see Sistakou (2008b) 334-336.
190. A thorough discussion of the nuptial symbolism of the scene is offered by Bremer (1987).
191. The nuptial connotations of the Golden Fleece become evident, when Jason's excitement on its acquisition is likened to the joy of a maiden trying on her wedding dress (Bremer [1987] 424-425); for the allusions to the deadly garments in Euripides' *Medea*, and the tragic undertones of Medea's marriage, see Knight (1991).
192. For this ambivalent viewing of the wedding, see Dyck (1989) 467.
193. By Williams (1995) 101; for a similar description of the cover illustrations of the Gothic romances, see Modleski (2008) 51.

heroine was always fleeing the house (dark except for one lighted window high in a tower); she wore a look of terror and a diaphanous garment that might be either ball gown or nightgown...

In a way this illustration captures the essence of any Gothic narrative. Although writing within a different historical and cultural context, Apollonius has staged the flight of Medea in Book 4 in similar terms, centuries before Gothic aesthetics were invented. *This was how the lovely girl rushed from her home... On naked feet Medea ran through the narrow streets; with her left hand she held up her robe above her eyes to conceal her forehead and lovely cheeks, and with her right she lifted the hem of her tunic off the ground. Swiftly she passed in terror out of the walls of the broad city by a lonely path... Her heart trembled and quaked with fear. The daughter of Titan, the goddess Moon, was just rising from the horizon and saw her in her mad haste...* There is a striking similarity between the covers of subliterary Gothic and Apollonius' passage: the scenario is a flight during the hours of darkness; the setting is an edifice (a castle or a palace left behind) and a wild landscape (the moonlit scenery outside the city walls); the character is a heroine running in bare feet wearing only her robe; the tone is that of darkness, fear and terror. Apollonius' achievement is the introduction of a modern (:non-Classical) sensibility into heroic epic; therefore, he may be considered the forerunner not only of ancient novel but of Romantic aesthetics as well.

I.3. Sites of fantasy, sites of horror

> "Listen to me," said the Demon as he placed his hand upon my head. "The region of which I speak is a dreary region in Libya, by the borders of the river Zaire. And there is no quiet there, nor silence. The waters of the river have a saffron and sickly hue; and they flow not onwards to the sea, but palpitate forever and forever beneath the red eye of the sun with a tumultuous and convulsive motion. For many miles on either side of the river's oozy bed is a pale desert of gigantic water-lilies. They sigh one unto the other in that solitude, and stretch towards the heaven their long and ghastly necks, and nod to and fro their everlasting heads. And there is an indistinct murmur which cometh out from among them like the rushing of subterrene water. And they sigh one unto the other. But there is a boundary to their realm—the boundary of the dark, horrible, lofty forest. There, like the waves about the Hebrides, the low underwood is agitated continually. But there is no wind throughout the heaven. And the tall primeval trees rock eternally hither and thither with a crashing and mighty sound. And from their high summits, one by one, drop everlasting dews. And at the roots strange poisonous flowers lie writhing in perturbed slumber. And overhead, with a rustling and loud noise, the gray clouds rush westwardly forever, until they roll, a cataract, over the fiery wall of the horizon. But there is no wind throughout the heaven. And by the shores of the river Zaire there is neither quiet nor silence. It was night, and the rain fell; and falling, it was rain, but, having fallen, it was blood. And I stood in the morass among the tall and the rain fell upon my head—and the lilies sighed one unto the other in the solemnity of their desolation."

Edgar Allan Poe Silence-A Fable (1838)

Edgar Allan Poe's short story "Silence" is set in an exotic place, vaguely described as 'a dreary region in Libya, by the borders of the river Zaire'. Despite this superficial connection to the real world, soon the reader becomes aware that the background of the story is a dream-scape or, more accurately, a nightmare-scape. Inhabited by a demon, this landscape becomes a symbol of everything dark Romanticism stands for: morbid spiritualism, metaphysical horror, the disturbed relationship between man and god, the sublime yet terrifying dimension of nature. In Poe's symbolic fable the landscape undergoes a transformation from the real to the fantastic and thence to pure horror. In Apollonius' *Argonautica*, where landscape serves as a dramatic background against which the narrative is set[194],

194. For a thorough study of the landscape and its function in the *Argonautica*, see the dissertation by Williams (1991); on time and space in the *Argonautica* see Danek (2009). The classic work focused upon the geography of the *Argonautica* is Delage (1930). Geography in the *Argonautica* has attracted considerable attention, see e.g. Vian (1987) who discusses the return journey; on geography seen from a scholarly perspective, see

a similar process takes place. Although the Argonauts set out on a journey into the known world from mainland Greece to the Black Sea, they gradually enter a fantastic realm in which they are eventually trapped; to find their way to salvation they have to traverse a horror landscape, which culminates with the passage through the Libyan desert–a site as awesome and horrific as Poe's imaginary Libya.

But how exactly does this pattern apply to the *Argonautica*? As the narrator declares in the proem to the epic, the *Argonautica* thematizes a fantastic voyage (1.1-4): *men of long ago propelled the well-benched Argo through the mouth of Pontos and between the Dark Rocks to gain the Golden Fleece*. The passage of the Argo through the Symplegades constitutes a *portal*, demarcating the world of fantasy where the Fleece is situated[195]. Since the Argonautic enterprise belongs to the generic category of the fantastic, Apollonius' epic records the descent to a *land of fable*. According to a definition "lands of fables can be found somewhere between the identifiable real world–in which all supernatural fiction and many kinds of fantasy are set–and impossible worlds: a land of fable always has its roots in this world, but in at least some aspects is an impossible one"[196]. The distinction between the real and the impossible world is not clear-cut in the *Argonautica* either. As said, the Argonauts travel from Pagasai to Colchis and back again (via the river Istros, the western Mediterranean and the Libyan desert) within the limits of a historical map, and the narrator stresses the 'historicity' of the places visited–thence the plethora of toponyms, the insistence on geographical and navigational detail, and the exploitation of the *periplous* as a generic model[197]. But, as the quest progresses, the setting paves the way for the dark and the horrific to unfold. The universe of the *Argonautica* is inhab-

---

Meyer (2008). Harder (1994) explores the travel descriptions in the epic, and makes useful distinctions between the outward and the homeward journey. Cusset (1998), (2001b) and (2004) emphasizes the intertextual background and the dramatic function of Apollonius' geography. The sociopolitical implications of Apollonius' conception of geography and space are explored in terms of territorial expansion in an unpublished dissertation by Rubio (1992) (for an overview of Rubio's arguments, see Meyer [2008] 284-285); for an interpretation of the *Argonautica* geography within a Ptolemaic context and from the perspective of colonization, see Stephens (2000).

195. Portals signal the transition between this world and an otherworld, and, as is also the case with the Symplegades, they are woven around conditions and prohibitions; see *EF* s.v. "Portal".

196. *EF* s.v. "Land of Fable".

197. The geographical realism of the *Argonautica* is emphasized by Meyer (2008) who also reconstructs the imaginary *periplous* map of the epic. According to a similar view held by Endsjø (1997), Apollonius "places the unplaceable" of the Homeric geography within the limits of the real world. For an overview of the journey of the Argonauts on a geographical basis, see Vian (1996) 11-46.

ited not only by the Argonauts and Medea, but also by gods, dead heroes, monsters and supernatural creatures. This is an impossible world, consisting of mythical, fairytale and literary sites; I will first discuss those aspects of space which help create a fantastic background to the Argonaut plot in Books 1 and 2, and then move to the horror landscapes of Books 3 and 4[198].

My aim is not to offer yet another geographical reading of the *Argonautica* nor to explore isolated elements of landscape within their immediate context. The following analysis is based on two premises. That in this (as in any) narrative spatial environment is inconceivable without the temporal dimension and that the spatio-temporal matrix underlying a narrative is indicative of its genre. There is a theoretical concept that in a way covers both premises. Bakhtin has introduced the term *chronotope* to suggest the implicit interconnectedness of time and space, and has shown, by studying ancient and modern novel, that each literary genre is set within a particular spatio-temporal framework which is representative of this genre[199]. Bakhtin's concept, albeit its originality, is restrictive; therefore, in the present analysis, the term 'chronotope' will be used more broadly to denote both the temporal dimension of space in Apollonius' *Argonautica* and the affinity between the spatio-temporal factors of the narrative and the specific *tone* created by them[200]. As seen, the *Argonautica* plot alternates between the quest for the Golden Fleece and the love story of Jason and Medea; I intend to show how the chronotopes chosen by Apollonius resonate with the fantastic and the Gothic aesthetics of these plots respectively.

In Book 1 the basic antithesis underlying any quest plot is found: that between civilization and savagery. To leave behind the civilized world is the first act of the *Argonautica*, marked by the departure from the city— i.e. Iolkos, the city with the well-built streets (1.317-318 ἐπεί ῥα πόληος ἐυδμήτους λίπ᾽ ἀγυιάς,/ ἀκτήνδ᾽ ἵκανεν Παγασηίδα...), and

198. A standard feature of fantasy is that landscape is supplementary to the plot, i.e. that the landscape is inextricably interwoven with the action, see *EF* s.v. "Landscape": among its most characteristic parameters are the *land of fable*, the *otherworld*, the *forests* and *trees*, the *dragons*, the *animals unknown to science*, the notion of *into the woods*, of *timeslips* and *time travels*, on which see *EF* s.vv. Williams (1991) 15-16 argues that landscape in the *Argonautica* assists the plot, foreshadows events, reinforces characterization and creates emotion.

199. Bakhtin (1981) 84-258; on this vague, almost enigmatic term, cf. *RENT* s.v. "Chronotope".

200. *Tone* is used here in its general sense to denote "an intangible quality which is metaphorically predicated of a literary work or of some part of it such as its style, and often felt to pervade and 'color' the whole, like a mood in a human being, so that the tone becomes its pervading 'spirit', 'atmosphere', or 'aura' " (*NPEPP* s.v. "Tone").

the other Greek cities from which the Argonauts gather. Every quest is a journey through–and eventually into–Otherness[201]. Even the first stop, the island of Lemnos, is a blending of familiarity and strangeness. Although it possesses the characteristics of a big and lawful city–it has new-built houses, city gates and a glorious palace (1.774-790), while its female population complies with the rules of the ἀγορή 'assembly' (1.653-654)–, Lemnos is haunted by the uncanny deeds of Hypsipyle and her comrades. The murder of the males has transformed them into fierce warriors likened to 'bacchants who devour raw flesh' (1.636 Θυιάσιν ὠμοβόροις ἴκελαι)[202].

However, the areas traversed during a quest primarily include wild landscapes; a desert, a forest or a mountain; a countryside inhabited by dangerous men and beasts; and, of course, the stormy sea[203]. The world between Iolkos and Colchis is full of such alien and unexplored sites. Upon entering the Hellespont, the Argonauts arrive at an unknown island with the strange name Mountain of the Bears where they come across the savage earthborn men. Thereupon they are welcomed by the neighbouring people, the Doliones. Only after the deadly clash with the Doliones and the tragic death of their king Kyzikos do the Argonauts enter the realm of fantasy. The winds prevent the heroes from sailing for twelve days and twelve nights (1.1078-1080)–the number has obvious magical associations which mark the transition into a fairytale narrative[204]. Action is again resumed on the following night, more precisely in the third

201. In analyzing the *Argonautica* as an encounter with Otherness, Stephens (2003) 183-196 draws an interesting parallel between Apollonius' epic and travel literature about Africa or Latin America of the 17th and 18th century. Three narrative patterns link these different traditions: (a) the travellers experience fantastic adventures with monsters in an alien region, (b) thereupon follows a scientific exploration of this region, and (c) a Romantic encounter occurs between the European male and a native woman who betrays her own culture.

202. For a comparison between the Lemnian women and the Amazons, see Cusset (2004) 47-50.

203. Booker (2004) 73. On the open space, primarily the sea, defining the quest plot, see Aguirre (1990) 16-20.

204. Vian (1974) 18-19 and (1996) 12-13 has convincingly shown (in tables) that Apollonius marks the passage of days throughout Books 1-3 and partly Book 4. As a rule Apollonius avoids referring to blocks of time without any action (Fusillo [1985] 251-252 remarks that even the 'tempi morti' of the voyage usually take the form of geographical catalogues). References of the type 'the winds blew for twelve days and nights' (cf. the two days of inaction in 1.588-589, the three days of mourning in 1.1057-1058 and the nine days of tempest in 4.1232-1234) mark a deviation from the 'realistic' concept of time and may be construed as stock phrases of epic and/or as markers of fairytale narratives in the *Argonautica*. The passage probably alludes to *Od.* 19.199 where the Achaians are held in Crete by violent winds for twelve days. Cf. the fairytale dimension of similar temporal markers (3, 6 or 9 days of sailing) in the *Odyssey* (9.74-75, 9.82-83, 10.28-29, 10.80).

watch of that night, when dawn draws near and dreams are prophetic
(1080-1083)[205]. The fairytale atmosphere is further accentuated by the
motif of the prophetic bird: a halcyon brings the message that the Great
Mother of the Gods must be honoured so that the Argo can sail again
(1084-1102)[206]. The sacrifice to Rhea/Kybele on Mount Dindymon has a
religious background, as the context clearly suggests. The cult in honour
of Kyzikos, who symbolizes the young dying hero, the association of his
death with the withering of the vegetation, and the hymnic tone of the
entire episode cannot be overlooked[207].

Its mystical connotations apart, the mountain episode reveals Apollonius' emphasis on the sublime dimension of nature[208]. From the top of
Dindymon the Argonauts have a panoramic view of the entire Propontis
(1112-1116). The landscape is focalized through the eyes of the Argonauts, and their subjective perception is further reinforced as the heroes
enter the forest. The vine is sturdy (1116 στιβαρὸν στύπος ἀμπέλου),
the tree exceedingly old (1117 πρόχνυ γεράνδρυον), the hill rugged
(1120 ἐπ' ὀκριόεντι κολωνῷ), the oaks lofty (1121 φηγοῖσιν ἀκρο-
τάτῃσιν) and their roots the deepest of all (1122 αἵ ῥά τε πασάων παν-
υπέρταται ἐρρίζωνται): the reader shares the 'visual direction' of the
Argonauts' eyes and becomes immersed into the extraordinary landscape[209]. Soon the forest is transformed into a *locus amoenus* under the
spell of Rhea/Kybele (1141 ἐοικότα σήματ' ἔγεντο, 1146 ἄλλο θῆκε
τέρας). In playing the role of Mother Nature, the goddess renders the
forest an eutopia with blossoming trees, flowers and fruits in abundance,
tamed animals and unceasing streams of water (1142-1149). The magic

205. The division of the night into three parts is a Homeric device, see Vian (1974)
101 n. 1. Cf. the dream of Europa in Moschus' epyllion which is also set in the τρίτατον
λάχος of the night (1-2), obviously due to the influence of Apollonius' passage.

206. It seems that Apollonius retains an ambivalence as regards the motif of the talking bird: although it is expressly stated that the bird communicates the message via its
voice (1085 ἀλκυονὶς λιγυρῇ ὀπὶ θεσπίζουσα/ λῆξιν ὀρινομένων ἀνέμων), only
Mopsos can convey its meaning to Jason. According to the Sch. A.R. 1.1085-1087a, Apollonius draws upon Pindar for the story of the halcyon; see Vian (1974) 36-37.

207. Vian (1974) 34-38. On the tragic undertones of the Kyzikos episode, see Cusset
(2001c) 68-69.

208. The mountain in the *Argonautica* has a dual function: it is the dwelling of the
gods and therefore has religious connotations, and it is a distant place, inhabited by primitive people and wild beasts (Williams [1991] 79-83). For 19th century Romantics, the
mountain is a site where man contemplates nature and experiences the sublime, see William Wordsworth's *The Prelude* (Book 14 Conclusion) or the eutopic description of the
mountain in Percy Shelley's "Mont Blanc". On how the Romantic poets perceive the
'materiality of nature' and the sublime effect stemming from it, see Oerlemans (2002).

209. The device of 'visual direction' plays a central role in the episode, see Williams
(1991) 83-92.

of the mountain on which god and man are gloriously united comes to an end at the crack of dawn[210].

Night, as opposed to dawn, is the key to the understanding of the chronotopes in the *Argonautica*[211]. As has been remarked, "it is a time of emotion and fear, treachery, murder, theft, mistakes and foreboding, and its arrival signals imminent misfortune"[212]. Moreover, night implies darkness, and it is no coincidence that Apollonius, in contrast to the conventions of the Homeric epics, has each and every critical action, associated either with the fantastic or the horrific, occurring during the night[213]. In Book 1 the departure from Pagasai is ominously set at dusk (450-459), and it is nightfall when the Argonauts perform a sacrifice by the tomb of Dolops (580-591); the first stop, Lemnos, is also reached by evening (607-608), and the Lemnian women watch the Argo arriving at Myrina by night (633-639, 650-652); it is evening when the Argonauts are initiated into the mysteries of Samothrace (913-921) and dark when they eventually pass through the Hellespont into the Propontis (922-935). Up to this point the nocturnal setting of these episodes does not have a genuine dramatic function but rather darkens the mood of the narrative in being Romantic in essence[214].

Night sets also the mood for the episode of the abduction of Hylas. The Argonauts reach the land of Kios by evening, as illustrated by the image of the farmer returning to his hut for the meal (1172-1178), and the preparations for fire, dinner and sacrifice are made at nightfall (1186 ἐπὶ κνέφας). Darkness and light alternate to produce a dramatic contrast during the nocturnal sequence. Thus, the sexual passion of a nymph is aroused when the beauty of the young Hylas glows in the rays of the full moon (1228-1232)–

210. According to Williams (1991) 82, in a similar scene from Book 2, where Prometheus is shown as hanging on Caucasus (2.1246-1259), the mountain symbolizes the separation between gods and men.

211. For a full analysis of the dramatic role of night and dawn in the *Argonautica*, see Williams (1991) 25-51.

212. Williams (1991) 33.

213. Williams (1991) 27 makes a sharp distinction between the usage of the time of day by Homer and Apollonius (who probably draws on the tragedians for this device) in emphasizing that a) the latter links the time of day to the mood of his characters and the impression he wishes to create, b) in the *Argonautica* dawn is consistently positive while night is a time for misfortune and anxiety, and c) night and dawn are used to foreshadow events.

214. Evening and night, which express the quintessence of Romantic sensibility, are explored by Miller (2006). Moreover, darkness is a vital parameter of the sublime according to Burke who declares (2.15) that "darkness is more productive of sublime ideas than light".

ἡ δὲ νέον κρήνης ἀνεδύετο καλλινάοιο
Νύμφη ἐφυδατίη. Τὸν δὲ σχεδὸν εἰσενόησε
κάλλεϊ καὶ γλυκερῇσιν ἐρευθόμενον χαρίτεσσι·
πρὸς γάρ οἱ διχόμηνις ἀπ' αἰθέρος αὐγάζουσα
βάλλε σεληναίη

The nymph of the spring, however, was just rising from the fair-flowing
water when Hylas came, and she saw close at hand how the sweet grace of
his beauty blushed red in the rays of the full moon which shone from the
sky...

The Romantic sensibility associated with the moonlight is further reinforced by the fairytale connotations of the landscape.

Apollonius employs cinematic devices as his focus gradually zooms
in on the landscape to highlight first the mountain (1178 Ἀργανθώνειον
ὄρος), then the forest (1188 εἰς ὕλην) and finally the spring (1208
κρήνης ἱερὸν ῥόον)[215]. These spaces do not operate individually but
interact with each other to accentuate the symbolism of the episode. To
contextualize it into the fantastic, one has to acknowledge that at least
one out of the three spaces, namely the forest, suggests a liminal landscape where a transition from one life to another, a *rite of passage*, takes
place. To go *into the woods* implies a solitary journey into the unknown;
wandering through the woods signals the cutting-off from the former
self and the acquisition of a new identity[216]. A sense of withdrawal from
the group and solitary wandering pervades the scene: Herakles finds a
pine tree wandering about (1190 ἀλαλήμενος); isolated from the Argonauts (1207 νόσφιν ὁμίλου), Hylas goes further afield in search of
water (1208 δίζητο κρήνης ἱερὸν ῥόον)[217]; Polyphemos too follows
the path of Herakles (1241 ἰὼν προτέρωσε κελεύθου), when he hears
the cries of Hylas and rushes to the site of the abduction (1243 βῆ δὲ
μεταΐξας Πηγέων σχεδὸν)[218]. The scene of the crime is a spring

215. However, it should be noted that the mountain functions as a *frame* whereas the
forest and especially the spring constitute the immediate *setting* of the episode: on these
different functions of space, see Ronen (1986).
216. The *locus classicus* for this notion of the woods are the opening verses of Dante's
The Divine Comedy (1-3): *Nel mezzo del cammin di nostra vita/ mi ritrovai per una selva
oscura,/ ché la diritta via era smarrita* "Midway in the journey of our life I came to
myself in a dark wood, for the straight way was lost". The forest as the setting where
multiple changes of identity take place is also the central theme in Shakespeare's *A Mid-
summer Night's Dream*.
217. Cf. Sch. A.R. 1.1208 δίζετο: πρὸς τὸ ἄπειρον τῶν τόπων τὸ δίζεσθαι.
218. Cf. Clare (2002) 95 who observes that "by introducing the third actor Apollonius
makes the whole episode revolve around the question of orientation, and the result in
terms of visualisation is a complex and occasionally bewildering sequence of stage-direc-
tions".

known by the fairytale name *Pegai* 'Springs'. Each night around this spring the nymphs–the equivalent to the *fairies* of folktale–gather and dance. In being ruled by the nymphs, the space equals a *faerie*[219]; according to the most plausible scenario a creature from the fairie must fall in love with a human[220]. In this realm all three elements of space merge to create an *otherworld* (1226-1229)[221]. *Some were nymphs of the mountain peaks and the glades; others were forest-nymphs who had come from far away. The nymph of the spring, however, was just raising from the fair-flowing water...* The emergence of the nymph from within the water foreshadows the subsequent apparition of Glaukos from the sea (1310-1313)[222]. *From the depths of the sea Glaukos, the wise spokesman of divine Nereus, appeared to them. His shaggy head and chest emerged out of the water as far as the waist...* Apollonius leaves no doubt to the reader of his epic that this is an otherworld, wherein the three protagonists are forever trapped with no hope of escaping–Hylas is literary swallowed up by the enchanted wood and its magic spring, Herakles follows his destiny far from Colchis and Polyphemos founds a city in the neighbouring Mysia[223].

After leaving this fantasy site the Argonauts re-enter the real world at dawn. Throughout Book 2 the course of the Argonauts takes the form

219. The *faerie* or *fairyland* (see *EF* s.v. "Faerie") is the realm of the fairies, an otherworld in fantasy literature, accessed by going into the woods or by being transported by water, the wind, or even a dream into it.

220. Modern adaptations of this theme include the fairies and water spirit legends of European fairytale, which had a great appeal for Romantic writers: see especially the influential novel *Undine* (1811) by Friedrich de la Motte Fouqué and *The Little Mermaid* (1837) by Hans Christian Andersen.

221. Accepting the notion of the otherworld, of a fairyland with its own laws means to reject the recurrent interpretation of the Hylas episode as a shattering of the idyllic *locus amoenus*, see Williams (1991) 175-184.

222. On this odd apparition, see Feeney (1991) 71.

223. Apollonius stresses the divide between this world and the otherworld. First, by providing two different explanations for the mystery surrounding Hylas' fate: in the fairyworld, as Glaukos the representative of this world states, he has become the husband of the nymph (1324-1325 Ὕλαν φιλότητι θεὰ ποιήσατο Νύμφη/ ὃν πόσιν), whereas in the 'real' world of the heroes he is reported missing (1349-1350 ὁππότε μή οἵ/ ἢ ζωοῦ εὕροιεν Ὕλα μόρον ἠὲ θανόντος). Herakles crosses the boundary between man and god by the end of the *Argonautica* by becoming himself a god, see Feeney (1991) 94-98. Moreover, the fact that the Argonauts only see his mirage in 4.1477-1484 reinforces the idea that the hero vanishes in the otherworld, cf. Sistakou (2009a) 392. Herakles is "literally lost from view" by characters, narrators and narratees after this episode, which marks a "bifurcation of storylines", as argued by Danek (2009) 280. As for the third, Polyphemos, he is never restored into the world of the Argonauts but dies while searching for the Argo (4.1473-1475 ἔβη διζήμενος Ἀργώ...τόθι μιν καὶ Μοῖρ' ἐδάμασσε).

of a *periplous* along the coast of Bosporos[224]. People with which the Argonauts come into contact include the Bebrykians, the Mariandynoi, the Amazons, the Chalybes, the Tibarenoi and the Mossynoikoi; in his prophetic speech Phineus gives a geographical and ethnographical account of the areas that will be visited by the Argonauts until they reach Colchis (317-407)[225]. Although the route of the Argonauts can be retraced on a historical map and there is remarkable precision as regards the navigation of the Argo, it also provides glimpses into a world beyond the mundane, an otherworld located in a different spatial and temporal dimension. Venues of the fantastic in Book 2 of the *Argonautica* alternate with actual geography, and include places of divine apparitions, the land of the dead and the mythical sites: to these I will now turn my attention.

In contrast to the *Iliad* and the *Odyssey*, where the gods are omnipresent and operate as characters in the world of men, Apollonius is highly sceptical about the appropriate mode of presentation of the divine in his epic[226]. The divide between heaven and earth is highlighted in two scenes: when the gods look down from the sky (οὐρανόθεν) on the departure of the Argo (1.547-549), and in the opening verses of Book 3 when Hera, Athena and Aphrodite hold a meeting in their heavenly palace. Semi-divine creatures sometimes inhabit marginal spaces of the human world, like the nymphs who view the Argo from the topmost heights of Mount Pelion (1.549-552); other demonic figures, like the water nymphs and Glaukos in the episode of Hylas, occupy a secluded space, the fantasyland. The descent of the gods from heaven to earth is an extremely rare phenomenon in the *Argonautica*. Two of these descents occur in Book 2, in spaces where the real and the fantastic worlds converge into one[227]. The passage between the Symplegades—which, as said, mark a portal into the otherworld—is aided by Athena. Apollonius leaves no doubt as to the corporeality of her presence at the site—*without delay she leapt on to a light cloud which could bear her great weight swiftly* (538-539)–, which however passes unnoticed by the Argonauts. *Qua* humans they are not

224. See Vian (1974) 128-168, Cusset (1998) and Meyer (2008). In Book 2 the divine and human map converge, see Hunter (2008a).

225. In effect, the itinerary of the Argonauts is described twice during the course of Book 2, once by a secondary narrator, Phineus, and a second time by the primary narrator; on a comparative reading of this double itinerary, see Cusset (1998) 102-105.

226. For the presentation of the divine in the *Argonautica*, see Feeney (1991) 69-80.

227. To describe these liminal places, the theorists of the fantastic use the term *crosshatch* to denote that two or more worlds may simultaneously inhabit the same territory: see *EF* s.v. "Crosshatch".

allowed to view the divine, only to marvel at the work of the gods (611-618)[228].

A few verses later, the Argonauts reach the deserted island of Thynias. The temporal setting foreshadows the forthcoming miracle: it is a brief period of time between night and day (669-670 ἦμος δ' οὔτ' ἄρ πω φάος ἄμβροτον οὔτ' ἔτι λίην/ ὀρφναίη πέλεται), an hour of darkened light (670 λεπτὸν δ' ἐπιδέδρομε νυκτὶ/ φέγγος) so unearthly that it is recorded only in literature by the Homeric hapax ἀμφιλύκη[229]. This deserted island with its fading light sets the stage for the apparition of Apollo. Apollo's epiphany has been justly described as "an eerily random and puzzling event", since the god does not appear in disguise, as is usual in the Homeric epics, but in full splendour[230]. The epiphany cannot be construed as a mere hallucination (still less an allegory of dawn) because the presence of the god is almost tangible and it produces a dramatic effect on the natural surroundings (675-680). *The son of Leto, travelling afar from Lykia to the countless race of the Hyperboreans, appeared to them. On both sides of his face golden curls like bunches of grapes waved as he proceeded; in his left hand he carried a silver bow, and his quiver was slung around his back from the shoulder. Under his feet the whole island shook and waves washed over the dry land.* Mystified by this experience the Argonauts respond with amazement, and avert their gaze from Apollo at once; yet the god remains indifferent as he passes through the air and heads towards the sea (681-684)[231]. This is a liminal space, somewhere between the human and the divine territory, where such an encounter is possible and 'real' but still a marvellous incident that further stresses the divide between the two worlds.

After this episode, the Argonauts reach the land of the Mariandynoi and the Acherousian headland, a historical venue which at the same time is a portal to the underworld. Apollonius clearly alludes to the archetypal depiction of the underworld in the Homeric *Nekyia*, but in effect downplays its fantastic elements by situating the Acherousia on

228. For this interpretation of the episode, according to which human and divine experiences are not interlocking in the *Argonautica*, see Feeney (1991) 72-75. In a similar incident in Book 4, Apollo appears on the Melantian Rocks and creates light for the Argo but remains invisible to the Argonauts (4.1706-1712).

229. On the philological colouring of ἀμφιλύκη, see Rengakos (1994) 49.

230. Feeney (1991) 75-77.

231. Danek (2009) 281 argues that here the two storylines, that of the Argonauts and that of Apollo, do not intersect with each other, highlighting the fact that "innumerable different storylines potentially intersect with one another in ways that are beyond our control".

a historical map[232]. For several verses action comes to a standstill and description takes over (720-751): the digression on the natural landscape of the Acherousia introduces the theme of death into the *Argonautica*[233]. In this section–as also in its doublet in 4.1485-1536 which unfolds against the backdrop of Libya–the death of two Argonauts is foreshadowed by the description of the "infernal landscapes"[234]. Apparently the site has nothing infernal (the arrival of the Argo is markedly set at dawn!)[235] but rather resembles a *locus amoenus* with its light breeze, its wood and trees, its waters and safe anchorage. It is an ominous place, however, whose steep cliffs and thundering waves, visualized with precision and detail, evoke the threatening sea routes followed by the Argonauts and especially the Symplegades and the Wandering Rocks[236]. The cave of Hades breathes out a chilling wind from its depths (736-737 ἀυτμὴ/ πηγυλίς, ὀκρυόντεος ἀναπνείουσα μυχοῖο) which becomes a blazing white frost in the open air (738 ἀργινόεσσαν ἀεὶ περιτέτροφε πάχνην)–yet easily melts in the midday sun (739 ἥ τε μεσημβριόντως ἰαίνεται ἠελίοιο). Silence is not a feature of the landscape (740 σιγὴ δ᾽ οὔ ποτε τήνδε κατὰ βλοσυρὴν ἔχει ἄκρην), which is agitated by the groaning of the sea (741 ἀλλ᾽ ἄμυδις πόντοιό θ᾽ ὑπὸ στένει ἠχήεντος) and the rustling of the leaves (742 φύλλων τε πνοιῇσι τινασσομένων μυχίῃσιν). The acoustics of the Acherousia–markedly characterized as βλοσυρὴ ἄκρη 'grim headland'–ambiguously refer to the natural sounds of the sea and the forest but also to notions associated with death, such as the idea of sigh or lament echoed by the verb στένω[237].

232. Cf. Kyriakou (1995) 257.

233. In this, as in any, epic, death plays a prominent role, see Hunter (1993) 41-45 and Durbec (2008); Williams (1991) 145-150 points out that the Acherousian landscape foreshadows the coming deaths of Book 2. To suggest the theme of death Apollonius draws on the *katabasis* scene of the Homeric *Nekyia*, see Kyriakou (1995).

234. This is a term used by Beye (1982) 113 to denote not only the Acherousia but also the subsequent settings of the tomb section and even the Caucasian site where Prometheus is chained.

235. In contrast to the extensive description of the night which sets the tone for the *katabasis* of Odysseus in the *Nekyia* (11.14-19).

236. The contrast between the idyllic and the wild dimension of the Acherousia is pointed out by Williams (1991) 148. For the symbolic dimension of this 'landscape of death', see Cusset (1998) 106-109.

237. In stressing the acoustic properties of the landscape, Apollonius elaborates on a single detail from the Hades description in the *Odyssey*, the loud-roaring rivers of the underworld (*Od*. 10.515 πέτρη τε ξύνεσίς τε δύω ποταμῶν ἐριδούπων); cf. Kyriakou (1995) 257. At this point, however, another methodological anachronism is necessary. The same acoustical effects, created by the flowing waters and the tall trees, reign in the nightmarish landscape of Poe's "Silence-A Fable": "The waters of the river flow not onwards to the sea, but palpitate forever and forever beneath the red eye of the sun with

Darkness, coldness and silence are evoked by this description but do not add to the creation of a truly Romantic atmosphere. Soon actual deaths occur, this time set against a gloomy background: the tombs of the dead heroes[238]. From the outset of their voyage, the Argonauts come across the tomb of Dolops to which they sacrifice sheep by night (1.585-591); on their way to Colchis, they kill Kyzikos and then build a tomb in his honour (1.1057-1062). The religious undertones of the hero cult apart, scenes set by tombs are recurrent in the *Argonautica* and help create a dark mood[239]. Thus, the deaths of four Argonauts Idmon and Tiphys in Book 2, and Kanthos and Mopsos in Book 4, are followed by lamentation and conclude with the erection of their tombs, a token of their *kleos* for posterity. In one case, however, the view of the tomb is followed by a ghostly apparition[240]. It is the ghost of Sthenelos, the comrade of Herakles, who was killed on the beach struck by an arrow (2.915-922):

ἧκε γὰρ αὐτή
Φερσεφόνη ψυχὴν πολυδάκρυον Ἀκτορίδαο,
λισσομένην τυτθόν περ ὁμήθεας ἄνδρας ἰδέσθαι.
Τύμβου δὲ στεφάνης ἐπιβὰς σκοπιάζετο νῆα,
τοῖος ἐὼν οἷος πόλεμόν δ᾽ ἵεν, ἀμφὶ δὲ καλή
τετράφαλος φοίνικι λόφῳ ἐπελάμπετο πήληξ.
καί ῥ᾽ ὁ μὲν αὖτις ἔδυ μέλανα ζόφον, οἱ δ᾽ ἐσιδόντες
θάμβησαν.

Persephone herself sent up the tearful shade of the son of Aktor, who had begged her to be allowed to see his compatriots even for a short while. Stepping upon the crest of the tomb he gazed out at the ship; he looked as he did when he went to war, and his beautiful fourhorned helmet with its scarlet plumes gleamed afar. Then he retreated back into the dark gloom leaving the onlookers full of amazement.

According to the scholia Apollonius draws upon the local historian Promathidas for the story of Sthenelos—however, the apparition of the ghost is his own invention (Sch. A.R. 2.911-914 τὴν δὲ περὶ Σθενέλου

a tumultuous and convulsive motion…And there is an indistinct murmur which cometh out from among them like the rushing of subterrene water. And they sigh one unto the other. But there is a boundary to their realm—the boundary of the dark, horrible, lofty forest… And the tall primeval trees rock eternally hither and thither with a crashing and mighty sound."
   238. On the tomb section of Book 2, see Said (1998) 17-19 and Durbec (2008) 63-65.
   239. On the chthonic undertones of the tomb section, see Hitch (2012).
   240. The tomb serves as a setting for the apparition of the ghost of Dareios in Aeschylus' *Persai* 684-688. Plato explains why ghosts are visible around the graves on the basis of Pythagorean theories about reincarnation in *Phaedon* 81c-d: ἡ τοιαύτη ψυχὴ βαρύνεταί τε καὶ ἕλκεται πάλιν εἰς τὸν ὁρατὸν τόπον φόβῳ τοῦ ἀιδοῦς τε καὶ Ἅιδου, ὥσπερ λέγεται, περὶ τὰ μνήματά τε καὶ τοὺς τάφους κυλινδουμένη, περὶ ἃ δὴ καὶ ὤφθη ἄττα ψυχῶν σκιοειδῆ φαντάσματα, οἷα παρέχονται αἱ τοιαῦται ψυχαὶ εἴδωλα.

ἱστορίαν ἔλαβε παρὰ Προμαθίδα, τὰ δὲ περὶ τοῦ εἰδώλου αὐτὸς ἔπλασεν). Epic and tragedy abound with such apparitions which as a rule have a specific dramatic function to fulfill: ghosts address warnings or demands or seek revenge, and always strike terror into the hearts of men[241]. Unlike epic and tragic apparitions, Sthenelos' apparition is only motivated by his burning desire to contemplate his living comrades[242]. His return from the realm of the dead is a melancholy action as the adjective πολυδάκρυον 'much-weeping' suggests[243]. The visual aspect of a ghostly apparition in poetry is praised by 'Longinus' as a source of the sublime[244]. Apollonius in this passage exploits the dynamics of visualization by stressing the corporeality of the ghost (Sthenelos has the appearance of a warrior in full armour) and by highlighting the detail of his gleaming, crimson helmet which stands in marked contrast with the gloomy darkness of Hades[245]. The effect upon the viewers is not that of terror but of pure amazement, a response suggestive of the supernatural undertones of the scene.

Many levels of reality are at work in Book 2 of the *Argonautica*–the historical, the heroic, the divine, the chthonic and the mythical. The term *mythical space*, or rather *mythical chronotope*, applies to sites associated with stories or characters drawn from mythological cycles, which, seen from the viewpoint of the Argonauts, belong to a distant past. Apollonius clearly distinguishes between the chronological strata

241. Well-known examples include the apparition of Achilles on his tomb in the cyclic *Nostoi* (Proclus p. 106 K.), the ghost of Klytaimestra in Aeschylus' *Eumenides* (94-116) and the ghosts of Polydoros and Achilles in Euripides' *Hekabe* (1-58). On the restless dead who die unavenged, see Johnston (1999) 127-160.

242. This is perhaps a remake, with significant alterations, of the apparition of Elpenor to Odysseus in the *Nekyia* (*Od.* 11.51-83). Descriptions of the dead in Greek literature are studied by Johnston (1999) 3-35.

243. A similar use of πολύδακρυς within a nostalgic context in Eur. *Ph.* 366-370, where Polyneikes, upon his arrival at Thebes, confesses: πολύδακρυς δ' ἀφικόμην,/ χρόνιος ἰδὼν μέλαθρα καὶ βωμοὺς θεῶν/ γυμνάσιά θ' οἷσιν ἐνετράφην Δίρκης θ' ὕδωρ·/ ὧν οὐ δικαίως ἀπελαθεὶς ξένην πόλιν/ ναίω, δι' ὄσσων νᾶμ' ἔχων δακρύρροον.

244. Ghosts belong, according to 'Longinus', to the means of poetic exaggeration and to the incredible stemming from the fable-like (15.7-8): καὶ κατὰ τὸν ἀπόπλουν τῶν Ἑλλήνων ἐπὶ τἀχιλλέως προφαινομένου τοῖς ἀναγομένοις ὑπὲρ τοῦ τάφου, ἣν οὐκ οἶδ' εἴ τις ὄψιν ἐναργέστερον εἰδωλοποίησε Σιμωνίδου...οὐ μὴν ἀλλὰ τὰ μὲν παρὰ τοῖς ποιηταῖς μυθικωτέραν ἔχει τὴν ὑπερέκπτωσιν, ὡς ἔφην, καὶ πάντη τὸ πιστὸν ὑπεραίρουσαν 'and in the appearance of Achilles over his tomb at the departure of the Greek fleet. Simonides has perhaps described this scene more vividly than anyone else... the poetical examples, as I said, have a quality of exaggeration which belongs to fable and goes far beyond credibility' [Transl. D.A. Russell].

245. Durbec (2008) rightly observes that the scene is built on glances ("the Argonauts look at Sthenelos who has returned from Hades to see them"), a feature which he attributes to the influence of the ecphrastic epigram.

of myth ranging from the theogonic beginnings to the heroic era and beyond to the narrator's 'present'[246]. An obvious example is the distinction between two categories of *aitia*, the ones encountered by the Argonauts *en route* as souvenirs from the past, and the ones created by the Argonauts themselves during their voyage for future generations to behold[247]. Especially in the former case, the aitiological remains of a story, and their incorporation into the real cosmos, are a means of rationalizing the mythical; yet, in evoking a world beyond and an era during which gods and heroes still lived together in harmony, Apollonius transforms this 'real' cosmos into a land of fable. Thus, a natural phenomenon, the Etesian winds, are attributed to an old story according to which Kyrene bore Aristaios to Apollo (500-528): *Among men of an earlier age, it is said, a girl called Kyrene...* Reflections of stories of old are omnipresent in this land of fable. By the river Kallichoros in front of a cave, did Dionysus, according to legend, establish his orgiastic rites (904-910); the Assyrian territory, reached by night, is the site where once Zeus gave a home to Sinope (946-954); the land of the Amazons is the place where Melanippe, the daughter of Ares, was captured by Herakles (966-977); the island where Kronos, disguised as a horse, made love to Philyra (1231-1241).

The more the Argonauts approach Colchis, the more they are immersed in this land of fable. "By night the Argonauts enter a pre-Olympian world which is no more their own" as has been succinctly observed[248]. Just before reaching their destination, they are no more exposed to mere reflections of past legend but watch 'myth' unfold before their eyes. Apollonius visualizes a scene known for its sublimity since Hesiod and Aeschylus, namely Prometheus bound on Caucasus (1246-1261)[249]. Visual details and chilling sound effects heighten the horror of the scene. The setting is almost apocalyptic, as the gulf of the sea is juxtaposed to the steep crags of Caucasus (1247-1249). Prometheus with his limbs bound by bronze chains on the rocks is present, albeit as an optical illusion created by the legendary setting (1248-1250). The focus of the scene, what is actually witnessed by the Argonauts (1251 ἴδον ~ 1256 ἄιον), are the eagle with its monster-like appearance, *which was not that of a bird of the*

---

246. On the chronological span of the *Argonautica*, see Klooster (2007) 65-67.

247. The best discussion of the different types of the *aitia* in the *Argonautica* in Harder (1994) 22-26. On the *aitia* as ruins from the epic past, see Sistakou (2009a) 392-393.

248. By Vian (1974) 174.

249. Cusset (2001c) 66-67, who stresses the tragic subtext of the scene, suggests that the sufferings of Prometheus foreshadow the sufferings of the Argonauts in Colchis.

air, but it plied its wings like well-planed oars (1251-1255)[250], and the agonizing cries of the Titan–*they heard Prometheus' wretched groans as his liver was torn out*–filling the landscape (1256-1259)[251]. This is an overture to the horrific site of Colchis, as it appears to the heroes' expectant eyes at dawn[252]. The 99th day of the Argonaut voyage has just begun.

Book 3 and the first part of Book 4 are set in Colchis. Although Colchis is situated at the end of the earth, Apollonius refrains from depicting it as a purely alien and barbaric place; to chart its wild geography seems to be of minor importance for the development of the plot[253]. In contrast to the changing landscapes of the first two books, Apollonius renders Colchis a static place, almost a theatrical stage, where the domestic drama unfolds. The characters of this drama move between a handful of settings: the palace of Aietes; the shrine of Hekate; the plain of Ares; the grove where the Golden Fleece is situated; and the Argo[254]. In the narrative economy of Book 3, the deadly landscape of Colchis along with the palace of Aietes constitute the *edifice*; other threatening places, where the authority of Aietes is strongly felt, include the plain and the grove of Ares. At the opposite end of the spectrum, the Argo offers a safe haven for the Argonauts, and the shrine of Hekate is the place where Medea often seeks refuge from the palace[255]. The theatrical dimension of

250. Apollonius vaguely alludes to the genealogy of the eagle from Typhon and Echidna known to Pherekydes and Akousilaos, see Vian (1974) 236 n. 3.

251. Apollonius thus indirectly suggests the presence of the Titan on site, cf. 3.864-866 for the same effect.

252. Ἐελδομένοις in the last verse of Book 2 captures a subtle psychological detail: that dawn brings relief to the heroes after an oppressive night (Vian [1976] 175). With this particular word Apollonius emphasizes that the Prometheus scene, and the last phase of the journey in general, was meant to produce a horrific, agonizing effect both to the characters and the readers of the *Argonautica*.

253. The scanty data about the topography of Colchis (the river Phasis, Mount Caucasus, the plain of Ares and the sacred grove) are discussed by Vian (1995) 16-19. A summary description of the Colchian topography, as seen from the perspective of the heroes, is given in 2.1260-1270, on which see Williams (1991) 242-243. The cultural differences between Greeks and barbarians are projected on the characters not the setting (Vian [1995] 19-23).

254. An additional setting, where the divine plot unfolds, is the abode of the gods, Olympos. Vian (1995) 4-5 likens Book 3 to a tragedy, and distinguishes 5 acts, where 'psychological' and 'epic' scenes alternate with each other; cf. Beye (1982) 124. Danek (2009) 288-289 recognizes triangular patterns in space behind the movement of the characters between different locations, i.e. Olympos, river and palace at the beginning of Book 3, palace, river and temple in the middle of the same book.

255. The Argonaut scenario reflects the scheme according to which the edifice dominates the characters in a fantasy of Gothic plot (*EF* s.v. "Edifice"): the ruler of the edifice (often a *dark lord*) is identified with his abode; protagonists raised within edifices must escape (by undergoing a *rite of passage*); and heroes who come to edifices do so in the furtherance of quests.

space is further reinforced by the compression of time. Books 1 and 2 cover a *fabula*-time of 98 days of journey (and Book 4 more than 50), whereas the sojourn in Colchis comprises only four days of intense action[256]. Here, as in the former books, night and dawn mark turning points of the plot.

Upon their arrival, the Argonauts invoke the Earth, the local deities and the souls of the dead heroes–a sign that "they will be trapped, entombed in this strange Hades-like landscape"[257]. As they enter Colchis, and especially when they head towards the palace of Aietes, the reader has the expectation of an alien, horrendous place. And indeed their first impression is that of horror and death (198-203):

> ἄφαρ δ᾽ ἀνὰ νηὸς ὑπὲρ δόνακάς τε καὶ ὕδωρ
> χέρσον δ᾽ ἐξαπέβησαν ἐπὶ θρωσμοῦ πεδίοιο.
> Κιρκαῖον τό γε δὴ κικλήσκεται· ἔνθα δὲ πολλαί
> ἐξείης πρόμαλοί τε καὶ ἰτέαι ἐμπεφύασιν,
> τῶν καὶ ἐπ᾽ ἀκροτάτων νέκυες σειρῇσι κρέμανται
> δέσμιοι.

They wasted no time in disembarking above the reeds in the river on to the dry land where the plain sloped upwards. This area is called the Plain of Kirke. Here rows of elms and willows grow in profusion, and from their topmost branches corpses are hung by ropes.

In passing through this "aisle of tombs"[258], the Argonauts watch the awesome spectacle of an avenue made of corpses; even its name, *the plain of Kirke*, is a detail carefully chosen to create an uncanny effect[259]. The fact that this site is explained on the basis of a local burial custom further heightens the sinister atmosphere of the scene (203-209). As the Argonauts move forward, Hera spreads a thick mist through the city (210-212). Although her intention, as stated by the narrator, is to render the Argonauts invisible to the Colchians, her action produces the opposite result: the fog blocks the Argonauts' view of the palace (213-214). Within this gloomy context, the eutopic depiction of Aietes' garden, modelled upon the description of Alkinoos' palace and Kalypso's garden in the *Odyssey*, comes as a narrative surprise to the reader[260]. A closer look, though, reveals that the magical elements prevail in Apollonius'

256. From the 99th to the 102nd, see Vian (1996) 12.
257. Beye (1982) 114.
258. The adverb ἐξείης suggests "une allée des tombeaux" (Vian [1995] 117 n. 201).
259. This is another example that shows how Apollonius uses a historical source (in this case Timaios, see Vian [1995] 117 n. 201), to achieve a powerful dramatic effect.
260. For a comparative reading of the Apollonian and the Homeric passages, and the narrative function of the description of Aietes' palace, see Williams (1991) 151-162 and Bettenworth (2005).

passage. Once Hera disperses the fog, the Argonauts assume the role of the enchanted viewers (215 τεθηπότες) as they watch the engineering marvels fashioned by Hephaistos, namely the four ever-flowing fountains gushing milk, wine, fragrant oil and water, the bulls of bronze which breathe out terrible flames of fire and the plough made of unbreakable adamant (221-234). The divine marvels of the garden are framed by the panoramic view of the palace with its gates and columns (215-218) and by the description of the architecture of the inner court and the royal apartments (235-248)[261].

Day 99 of the voyage begins with a tour into the land of fable–but it continues as an intense domestic drama; it thus becomes the longest day in the entire epic, covering almost 830 verses of text time. The palace and the Argo serve as counterparts in the staging of Book 3, where the meeting with the king and the assemblies of the Argonauts are set respectively. The antithesis underlying the quest plot, the one between savagery and civilization, is reversed in these scenes: the Colchian palace is presented as an architectural wonder, and is therefore seen as an emblem of an organized universe, whereas the Argo is anchored in a swamp, a symbol of the savage and secluded space (2.1283 δάσκιον ἕλος, 3.6-7 οἱ μὲν πυκινοῖσιν ἀνωίστως δονάκεσσι/ μίμνον ἀριστῆες λελοχημένοι 'so the heroes waited in hiding, out of sight in the dense reeds'). Through this shift in perspective Apollonius highlights a reversal not only in scenery but also in roles, as the Argonauts become the victims and Aietes the authoritative king, and marks, by extension, a transition from the fantastic to the Gothic plot.

The palace becomes the centre of the narrative world, in which the heroes and especially Chalkiope and Medea are confined. To abandon the royal hall means to flee from Aietes' power. This is what the Argonauts do when they leave the palace for the Argo (442 οἱ δ' ἤεσαν ἐκ μεγάροιο, 448 οἱ μὲν ῥα δόμων ἐξήλυθον ἀσχαλόωντες), and also Chalkiope when she rushes into her bedroom (449-450 Χαλκιόπη δὲ χόλον πεφυλαγμένη Αἰήταο/ καρπαλίμως θάλαμον...βεβήκει 'Chalkiope quickly retreated to her chamber to avoid Aietes' anger'). Space thus becomes a vital parameter of the developing drama of Book 3. Some verses later, the inner conflict of Medea takes the form of a to-and-fro movement in her chamber (645-655). *So saying, she raised herself and opened the doors of her chamber; she was barefoot, and wearing only her dress. She longed to go to her sister, to cross over the threshold into the court. For a long time she remained there in her ante-chamber:*

261. On the dramatic function of the architecture of the place, see above pp. 81-82.

shame would not allow her to go further. Then she turned around and
went back in again, but then came out again, and then hid away inside
again; her feet carried her this way and that, all to no purpose. Whenever
longing gripped her, shame kept her inside; when she was held back by
shame, reckless desire pushed her on. Three times she tried, and three
times she stopped short; on the fourth time she whirled around and col-
lapsed face down on her bed. The emphasis on the closed and limiting
space of the chamber, suggesting the heroine's physical and psychological imprisonment in the palace, has a Gothic undertone[262]. And since the
temporal marker is inseparable from the spatial dimension, and both interact with the plot, the various stages of the night are closely monitored in
connection with Medea's insomnia to suggest an increasing premonition
of death[263]. First darkness falls; then the stars appear in the sky; not only
the wanderer and the warder but even the mother whose children are dead
fall into sleep; silence reigns over the city, animals and men; dead silence
deepens the impression of blackness (744-750). The expectation of dawn,
light as opposed to darkness, signals a dramatic turn of the plot, namely
Medea's decision to help Jason (819-824).

Consequently the setting changes too, and the events of day 100 are
staged at the shrine of Hekate; Jason's preparations on the following
night are also set in a landscape where the presence of Hekate is strongly
felt. There is a dichotomy in the depiction of the two 'sites of Hekate',
depending on the perspective of the viewer. Focalized through Medea's
eyes, the shrine appears to be a beautiful place (842 εἰς Ἑκάτης περι-
καλλέα νηόν). The primary focus is not on the holy site but on its
paradise-like natural surroundings[264]. Within this scenery Medea is transformed from a *rhizotomos*, a cutter of magical herbs–an image suggested
by the digression on the horrific landscape where the *Prometheion* grows
in vv. 844-866–into an innocent maiden–implied by the contrasting scene
of the girls picking flowers from the flourishing plain in vv. 896-899

262. The solitude and obscurity of the chamber becomes emblematic of the Gothic
novel, e.g. in Ann Radcliffe's *The Mysteries of Udolpho* and Emily Brontë's *The Wuther-*
ing Heights. Cf. a passage from Mary Shelley's *Frankenstein* recording the interaction
between the protagonist's anxiety and the closed space of his chamber (Ch. 5): "Unable
to endure the aspect of the being I had created, I rushed out of the room and continued a
long time traversing my bedchamber, unable to compose my mind to sleep. At length
lassitude succeeded to the tumult I had before endured, and I threw myself on the bed in
my clothes, endeavouring to seek a few moments of forgetfulness. But it was in vain; I
slept, indeed, but I was disturbed by the wildest dreams".

263. On the dynamics of emotion and background in a night which suggests anxiety,
fear, depression and death, see Williams (1991) 39-41.

264. The fantasy dimension is present here too; cf. the speaking crows in v. 929 which
evoke the recurrent motif of the prophetic birds. See also above p. 104 with n. 206.

(esp. 898-899 τὰ δὲ καλὰ τερείνης ἄνθεα ποίης/ λεξάμεναι τότ᾽ ἔπειτ᾽ αὐτὴν ἀπονισσόμεθ᾽ ὥρην)[265]. On the same site the wirlwind romance between Medea and Jason takes place (948-1024).

When, on day 101, Jason performs a ritual to Hekate by the river Phasis and the holy site is seen from his perspective, the mood changes dramatically. Not only does the hero perform the ritual by night (1191-1198) but at its most terrifying moment: on the stroke of midnight (1029 δὴ τότε μέσσην νύκτα διαμμοιρηδὰ φυλάξας). This second 'site of Hekate' has the features of a Romantic landscape: it is deserted (1197 ἐς ἐρημαίην), isolated (1201-1202 χῶρον ὅ τις πάτου ἔκτοθεν ἦεν/ ἀνθρώπων) and sacred (1203-1204 ποταμοῖο...θείοιο), a natural scenery evoking the sublime by being plain and majestic at the same time (1202 καθαρῆσιν ὑπεύδιος εἰαμενῆσιν 'open to the skies in the midst of pure water-meadows')[266]. The Romantic sensibility of the scene is also conveyed by the jet black robe worn by Jason (1204-1205 φᾶρος... κυάνεον), a souvenir of his lovemaking with Hypsipyle (1206 ἀδινῆς μνημήιον εὐνῆς). Suddenly there is a shift in tone, as Hekate responds to Jason's invocations (1212-1220):

> ἡ δ᾽ ἀίουσα
> κευθμῶν ἐξ ὑπάτων δεινὴ θεὸς ἀντεβόλησεν
> ἱροῖς Αἰσονίδαο. Πέριξ δέ μιν ἐστεφάνωντο
> σμερδαλέοι δρυΐνοισι μετὰ πτόρθοισι δράκοντες·
> στράπτε δ᾽ ἀπειρέσιον δαΐδων σέλας· ἀμφὶ δὲ τήν γε
> ὀξείῃ ὑλακῇ χθόνιοι κύνες ἐφθέγγοντο.
> Πείσεα δ᾽ ἔτρεμε πάντα κατὰ στίβον· αἱ δ᾽ ὀλόλυξαν
> Νύμφαι ἑλειονόμοι ποταμηίδες, αἳ περὶ κείνην
> Φάσιδος εἰαμενὴν Ἀμαραντίου εἰλίσσονται.

Hearing the call, the dread goddess came from the furthest depths to accept the sacrifices of the son of Aison. Around her head was a garland of terrible snakes entwined with oak-branches, and her torches flashed out a blinding brightness; all around her was the piercing bark of hellish dogs. All the fields trembled at her approach; the marsh-dwelling nymphs of the river who dance around that meadow of the Amarantian Phasis screamed aloud.

The landscape is at once filled with sound (ὀξείῃ ὑλακῇ, ὀλόλυξαν), light (ἀπειρέσιον δαΐδων σέλας) and movement (ἔτρεμε, εἰλίσσονται). The ascent of Hekate from the Underworld (κευθμῶν ἐξ ὑπάτων, cf. χθόνιοι κύνες) conveys a strong feeling of death; the divine epiphany and the influence it exerts on the inanimate and animate universe

265. This portrayal of Medea evokes Nausikaa, and also alludes to the *Homeric Hymn to Demeter*, see Vian (1995) 88 n. 3.

266. On the Romantic sensibility and the sublime effect created by a lonely man contemplating a natural landscape, see pp. 86, 104 and 158-159.

creates a sublime effect[267]. Although the passage, developed around Jason's ritual, draws heavily on the beginning of the *Nekyia*[268], the expectation of the reader that an apparition of the dead is about to take place is not fulfilled. The depiction of Hekate, and especially the detail of her Medusa-like garland[269], and Jason's fearful reaction at her sight (1221-1222 Αἰσονίδην δ' ἤτοι μὲν ἕλεν δέος, ἀλλά μιν οὐδ' ὧς/ ἐντροπαλιζόμενον πόδες ἔκφερον 'the son of Aison was seized by fear, but even so he did not turn around as his feet carried him back') establish this setting as a site of horror.

Day 102 is divided into day action and night action, each of which corresponds to a different setting, namely the plain and the grove of Ares respectively. These settings are nightmarish, spaces inhabited by creatures drawn from the darkest dreams, ones that articulate the horrors of the inner self. The fact that the scene is set at daylight reinforces the notion that reality itself becomes a nightmare, and the emphasis on this daylight nightmare heightens its Gothic effect. The plain of Ares, first described by Aietes as the theatre of the dreadful contest, is a fantasy site with three main features: it can only be ploughed by bulls with bronze feet that breathe fire; it cannot be sown with seeds but only with the teeth of a terrible dragon; its crop is a body of armed men that can only be harvested by a spear (407-418)[270]. This site, something between a ploughland and a battlefield, is 'realistically' situated in the topography of Colchis, on the opposite side of the city, by the river Phasis and beneath the Caucasian heights (1271-1277); the king and the Colchians, *qua* audience, have a panoramic view of the site and, thus, the plain is visualized as "the orchestra of a theatre"[271]. The contest takes place on this huge stage, and it is monitored in minute detail by the omniscient narrator (1278-1407). In this extended scene, space is vital to the development of the action which is eventually accomplished at the setting of the sun (1407 ἦμαρ ἔδυ, καὶ τῷ τετελεσμένος ἦεν ἄεθλος 'nightfall came, and Jason's task was at an end'). This site abounds with

267. The sublime here is produced by a combination of what 'Longinus' calls τὸ μεγαλοφυές 'greatness of thought' regarding the representation of gods (*On the Sublime* 9.8), and his notion of visualization of a divine epiphany (15.6).

268. Vian (1995) 141 on v. 1029.

269. The detail is probably reminiscent of the depiction of Hekate in Sophocles' lost play *Rhizotomoi* (fr. 535.5-6 TrGF στεφανωσαμένη δρυΐ καὶ πλεκταῖς/ ὠμῶν σπείραισι δρακόντων), see Vian (1995) 145 on v. 1215. That the scene is also modelled upon the epiphany of Apollo from the *Homeric Hymn to Apollo* is suggested by Vian (1995) 145 on v. 1216.

270. Apollonius' sources for the description of the contest and the dreadful site are Pherekydes, Sophocles, Eumelos and Pindar's *Pythian* 4, see Vian (1995) 7-8.

271. Vian (1995) on v. 1277.

horror snapshots, the most impressive of which I will highlight here. The first is the entrance of the bulls into the plain (1289-1292): *They have some hidden lair in the earth, where their strong pens are thick with smoke; from there, they both rushed forth together, exhaling glowing fire.* The χθόνιος κευθμών, filled with fire and smoke, from which the bulls suddenly emerge suggests an ascension from the underworld[272], and the fearful reaction of the heroes at their sight (1293 ἔδδεισαν δ' ἥρωες ὅπως ἴδον) confirms the Hades-like effect of the scene. In the second snapshot the springing up of the earthborn men from the 'groaning clods' of the field (1333-1334 δεινὸν δ' ἐσμαράγευν...βώλακες) is both terrifying and sublime; the latter effect is produced by enlarging upon the detail of the otherwordly shine of the warriors' armour whose flashing gleam reaches heaven (1354-1362)[273]. The grotesque nature of this strange crop, which at the same time has the features of a plant and a man[274], is highlighted by the closing snapshot of its slaughtering (1391-1392). *Just so did Jason cut the crop of the earthborn. The furrows were filled with blood as irrigation-channels fill with streams from a well.* In a passage full of metaphors and similes drawn from agriculture (the farmer who cuts the crop with his sickle and the storm which cuts off the plants by its roots), the rise and the fall of the earthborn men render the plain of Ares a waste land and a bloody battlefield at the same time.

Book 4 begins with the night flight of Medea. Later on the same night, in the early hours (109-113), the last act of the Colchian adventure takes place, namely the obtaining of the Fleece from the grove of Ares. As the Argonauts approach the site from the river bank, they first enter a grassy spot bearing the telling name *the Ram's Bed*, then they proceed to the altar set up by Phrixos to Zeus and eventually they arrive at the forest where the Fleece is kept (114-126). The forest setting constitutes a vital parameter of fantastic literature: it is dark, mysterious and impenetrable, an ancient site—one that could "have existed almost forever" and inhabited by "creatures or spirits from the dawn of time"—associated with the

272. Although it has no verbal analogies, the scene evokes the emergence of the dead from the trench dug by Odysseus in the *Nekyia* (11.36-37): ἐς βόθρον, ῥέε δ' αἷμα κελαινεφές· αἱ δ' ἀγέροντο/ ψυχαὶ ὑπὲξ Ἐρέβευς νεκύων κατατεθνηώτων.

273. The detail was also emphasized by Sophocles in his lost play *Colchides* (fr. 341 TrGF); on the simile of the shining stars which stand in sharp contrast to the dark sky, see the Homeric parallels collected by Vian (1995) 108 n. 3.

274. This double nature is brilliantly captured by the image of the gradual emergence of the earthborn men from the ground, e.g. 1382-1385 πολέας μὲν ἔτ' ἐς νηδὺν λαγόνας τε/ ἡμίσεας δ' ἀνέχοντας ἐς ἠέρα, τοὺς δὲ καὶ ἄχρις/ γούνων τελλομένους, τοὺς δὲ νέον ἑστηῶτας, τοὺς δ' ἤδη καὶ ποσσὶν ἐπειγομένους ἐς ἄρηα. See the explanatory notes on this difficult passage in Vian (1995) 109 n. 1 and 160 on v. 1384.

land of *faerie*, a mysterious place with hidden secrets[275]. All these features are present in Apollonius' description. The grove of Ares is dense (161 πολυπρέμνοιο ὕλης), shadowy (166 πολύσκιον ἄλσος) and infinite (130 ἄσπετον ἄλσος). The introductory aitia which trace the origins of the site back to the arrival of Phrixos at Colchis testify to its primitiveness–in effect, the passage of the heroes from the Argo into the forest is a passage from the present into the distant past. To penetrate into the forest, where wonder and horror coexist, represents the ultimate challenge for the Argonauts and the goal of every quest[276]. Wonder pertains to the unearthly shining of the Fleece (124-126, 167-173, 184-185); yet the visual and sound effects produced by the dragon render horror the dominant tone of the scene. Through the accumulation of adjectives, images and similes, this dragon becomes the absolute symbol of the fantasyland[277]. As a rule, fairytale dragons are servants of the dark lord–in this case, of Aietes. Their task is to guard a treasure and to pursuit anyone attempting to steel it–the treasure here being the Golden Fleece. To kill the dragon, or to defeat it, means to become a king –Jason, aided by Medea, aspires to become both a hero and a king through this contest[278]. Fairytale dragons are both wise and intelligent, dangerous and uncanny– the sleepless eyes allude to the former features (128 ἀΰπνοισι ὀφθαλμοῖσι), whereas the endless coils and awful hissing and murderous jaws to the latter (143-144 ἀπειρεσίας ῥυμβόνας, 129-130 ῥοίζει δὲ πελώριον, 155 ὀλοῇσι γενύεσσιν). The charming of the dragon by Medea, introduced by the invocation to Sleep and the Lady of Darkness, Hekate, has death connotations (145-148)[279]. Moreover, by coupling Sleep to Hekate, Apollonius renders the dragon a liminal creature, one that represents a state between life and death[280]. As always, the horror

275. In reference to the Arthurian legend, Aguirre (1990) 18 describes the symbolism of the forest as follows: "Whereas the Court, and the Table within, are microcosmic images of the ordered universe, the labyrinthic Forest symbolises the realm of lawlessness: inimical, yet rewarding, populated by white stags and other fantastic creatures, full of dangers yet full of promise too".

276. The forest lies at the core of the fantasylands in William Morris' romances *The Wood Beyond the World* (1894) and *The Well at the World's End* (1896), which in turn become the models for the mythography of J.R.R. Tolkien. It is worth noting that the fairytale topography of the works of Tolkien features more than 40 (!) different forests.

277. On dragons in the literature of the fantastic, see Williams (1996) 202-207.

278. This scene, especially through the reversal of sexual roles between Jason and Medea, strongly evokes a *rite of passage*, see Hunter (1993) 17.

279. Hunter (1993) 182-188 points out the influence of this Apollonian passage on the formation of the underworld scenes of the *Aeneid*.

280. Cf. the apposite remark by Hunter (1993) 183: "In the *Argonautica*, the linking of Hypnos with infernal Hekate creates a powerful ambivalence in the fate of the dragon: modern critics should not be so certain that he is going to wake up".

sensation of the scene is primarily experienced by the characters themselves, here Jason (149 εἵπετο δ' Αἰσονίδης πεφοβημένος)–but has
also a universalizing effect on faraway lands, on young mothers and their
newborn babies (131-138).

The coming of the day marks the beginning of the homeward journey.
The juxtaposition of fact with fiction, of geography with fairytale topography is once more the key to the understanding of the travel descriptions
of Book 4. On their return journey, the Argonauts programmatically
bypass the Okeanos, the milestone of the mythical conception of the universe. Apollonius exploits up-to-date geographical knowledge (probably
drawn from Timagetos, the author of the Περὶ λιμένων) by outlining an
itinerary from the Black Sea via the river Istros to the Adriatic[281]. Space
becomes dramatically significant again when the Argo takes the western
route, where the Argonauts first come across Odyssean sites and then
enter a new land of fable, conventionally identified with the desert of
Libya. Historical geography is downplayed in favour of a more sophisticated conceptualization of the fantastic travelogue; moreover, Apollonius' penchant for the fantastic and the horrific is reflected on his idiosyncratic adaptation of the wanderings of Odysseus throughout Book 4[282].

From all the Odyssean sites, it is the treatment of the abode of Kirke
that brings dark aesthetics to the fore[283]. A comparison between the
Homeric passage and Apollonius' account is quite revealing[284]:

Od. 10.210-222
*In the glades they found the palace of Kirke, built of smooth stones on open
ground. Outside, there were lions and mountain wolves that she had herself
bewitched by giving them magic drugs. The beasts did not set upon my men; they
reared up, instead, and fawned on them with their long tails. As dogs will fawn
around their master when he comes home from some banquet, because he never
fails to bring back for them a morsel or two to appease their craving, so did these
lions, these wolves with their powerful claws, circle fawningly round my comrades. The sight of the strange huge creatures dismayed my men, but they went*

281. On how geographical knowledge changed the mythical account of the voyage of
the Argo, see Endsjø (1997). Cf. Vian (1996) 16-20 and 23-35 on the *periplous* of the
Adriatic; for a thorough discussion, see Meyer (2008).
282. E.g. Harder (1994) 26-29 points out that Apollonius does not make use of the
first-person narrative, as is the case with the *Apologoi*, thus downplaying the relevance of
truth to his travel narrative. On the treatment of Odyssean geography by Apollonius, see
also above pp. 54-56.
283. The best account of the treatment of Odyssean sites in the *Argonautica* in Cusset
(2001b).
284. For a comparison between the two passages, see Knight (1995) 184-200. The
non-epic, tragic character of the episode is stressed by Vian (1996) 38-39.

on and paused at the outer doors of the goddess of braided hair. And now they could hear Kirke within, singing with her beautiful voice... [Transl. W. Shewring]

Arg. 4.662-682
There they found Kirke purifying her head in the flowing salt waters because she had been much disturbed by dreams during the night. All the chambers and courts of her house seemed to drip with blood, and flame consumed all the drugs with which it had been her habit till then to bewitch any stranger who arrived; she herself doused the raging fire with the blood of a slaughtered victim which she gathered up in her hands, and this put an end to her deathly fear. Because of this dream she had gone to purify her hair and clothes in the flowing waters of the sea as soon as she woke with the arrival of dawn. Her beasts–which were not entirely like flesh-devouring beasts, nor like men, but rather a jumble of different limbs–all came with her, like a large flock of sheep which follow the shepherd out of the stalls. Similar to these were the creatures which in earlier times the earth itself had created out of the mud, pieced together from a jumble of limbs, before it had been properly solidified by the thirsty air or the rays of the parching sun had eliminated sufficient moisture. Time then sorted these out by grouping them into proper categories. Similarly unidentifiable were the forms which followed after Kirke and caused the heroes amazed astonishment.

The *Odyssey* passage is introduced by a laconic description of the exterior of the palace: it is a building made of stone set within a glade. There is no such association with the real-world in the visualization of the palace in the *Argonautica*: focalized through Kirke's eyes–or, to be more accurate, filtered by Kirke's subconscious–, the palace becomes an imaginary space filled with horror[285]. The night before the arrival of the Argonauts, Kirke dreams that the entire palace with its chambers and walls runs with blood; that her drugs are consumed by fire; and that she douses the flames by pouring copious amounts of blood with her hands. Apollonius probably draws his inspiration from the *Odyssey*, from a scene where the seer Theoklymenos has a vision that when the suitors will fall dead during the night the walls will be covered with blood and the chambers be filled with ghosts (*Od.* 20.351-357). As said, this is "the most eerie passage in Homer" whose fantasy and horror qualities have not gone unobserved by Apollonius[286]. On the other

285. In modifying Genette's notion of focalization, Mieke Bal "distinguishes between perceptible and imperceptible 'focalizeds' (objects of focalization)–things visible in the real-world as opposed to things visible only in a character's consciousness or imagination" (in *RENT* s.v. "Focalization"). The latter is the case in Kirke's dream-like rendering of her palace.

286. Russo etc. (1992) on *Od.* 20. 351-357, who emphasize the non-Homeric character of the passage and note further parallels from Greek tragedy and Celtic saga. See Dodds (1951) 64-101 who explains the Homeric passage within the context of madness; he observes, among others, that this is a sensational scene, recalling primitive forms of prophetic madness and evoking the tragic visions of Kassandra in the *Agamemnon*.

hand, the symbol of fire evokes tragic contexts–it is perhaps a reminiscence of Euripides' lost play *Alexandros*, where Hekabe has a dream
that she will give birth to a firebrand that will burn down the entire city
(Apollod. 3.148 ἔδοξεν Ἑκάβῃ καθ᾽ ὕπνους δαλὸν τεκεῖν διάπυ-
ρον, τοῦτον δὲ πᾶσαν ἐπινέμεσθαι τὴν πόλιν καὶ καίειν). Various
interpretations have been given as to the dramatic function of this
dream[287], but it is the nightmare sensation it conveys that renders Apollonius' passage unique.

Both passages focus on the animals surrounding the palace. In the
Odyssey the magical element is downplayed, and the only transformation
the animals have undergone concerns their behaviour: despite their wild
origin, Kirke's lions and wolves become substitutes for domesticated
dogs. By analogy, Kirke's beasts in Apollonius are likened to sheep,
however they cannot be identified with any species of animals or men.
The key phrase of the passage is repeated twice: they are a strange
assortment, a pastiche of various, non-compatible limbs. Obviously the
passage has philosophical undertones, and the digression on the creatures
made of mud clearly evokes Empedocles' cosmology[288]. Time (αἰών),
marking the borderline between the shapelessness of the creatures and
their ordering into distinct categories, is an innovation introduced by
Apollonius, implying the setting of his epic within a pre-cosmogonical
context[289]. Yet the primary function of the narration about these beasts is
to produce an uncanny effect. As monsters belonging to an era before the
theories of evolution were even conceived, they may be classified as
animals unknown to science, a category which became popular in the
literature of the fantastic. Despite the fact that these chimeric creatures
are unseen before (ἀίδηλοι), Apollonius stresses the divide between
these proto-animals and common mythological monsters[290]. The reaction
of the respective 'audiences' is also different: the men of Odysseus
experience fear, whereas the Argonauts respond, as ever, with immense
astonishment.

287. The fullest explanation in Vian (1996) 99 n. 3 who notes that the blood symbolizes the murder of Apsyrtos, the flame foreshadows the failure of Kirke's magic charm in
v. 687 and the blood by which the fire is extinguished announces the expiatory sacrifice
of a sow in vv. 704-707. Kessels (1982) 163 summarizes its function as follows: "Kirke's
dream serves as an allegorical prediction of coming events, as a means of building up an
atmosphere of fear and tension, but it also conditions Kirke's behaviour towards Medea".
   288. See Kyriakou (1994) 317-318 and Vian (1996) 172 on v. 681.
   289. Instead of the Empedoclean notions of Love and Strife, see Vian (1996) 173 on
v. 681.
   290. Apollonius creates a protoscientific context for this scene by drawing a line
between the genre of fantasy biology and mythological fantasy (see *EF* s.v. "Biology");
therefore, he uses scientific terminology (Knight [1995] 188 n. 201).

The passage from the island of the Sirens, Skylla and Charybdis, the *Planktai*, and the arrival among the Phaeacians complete the Odyssean phase of the return journey; thereupon follows the Libyan adventure which, along with Crete and Anaphe, marks the end of the Argonaut voyage. In his account of the Libyan itinerary of the Argonauts, Apollonius has combined historical/geographical sources, especially Herodotus and Timaios, with mythological/poetic traditions stemming from Hesiod and Pindar's *Pythian* 4; the blending of realism and poetry in the depiction of the Libyan landscape cannot be denied[291]. Chronotope becomes once more important for the interpretation of this episode, whose spatio-temporal setting anticipates in part the so-called 'adventure-time' and 'alien world' settings of later Greek novel[292]. Now, the Argonauts during their quest come across many forms of Otherness—mythical, divine and literary landscapes, routes into unknown and wild territories, countries at the end of the earth. The Libyan adventure best exemplifies Apollonius' taste for exoticism, as it records the transition into an unknown land set within fantasy-time[293]. Nine days and nine nights, a symbolic number of fantasy and fairytale, suffice to transfer the Argonauts into "an unmapped and unmappable space"[294], from where no return is ever possible (1235-1236 ἵν' οὐκέτι νόστος ὀπίσσω/ νηυσὶ πέλει). The sea of Syrtis is strange and unfriendly (1237-1244), but the land extending beyond it, depicted as misty (1246 ἠέρα), vast (1246-1247 μεγάλης νῶτα χθονὸς ἠέρι ἶσα/ τηλοῦ ὑπερτείνοντα διηνεκές), deserted (1247-1248 οὐδέ τιν' ἀρδμόν,/ οὐ πάτον) and dead calm (1249 εὐκήλῳ δὲ κατείχετο πάντα γαλήνῃ), is more mysterious (1251 τίς χθὼν εὔχεται ἥδε;) and frightening (1245 ἄχος δ' ἕλεν). To capture the image of the Argonauts wandering through the desert, and the

---

291. For a thorough analysis of realism and poetry in the Libyan episode, see Vian (1996) 57-64.

292. Fusillo (1985) 252 is right to observe that there is a distance between the chronotope of the *Argonautica* and that of the novel, because the former has a defined framework of time and space, whereas in the latter both parameters are vague and abstract. On the definition of 'adventure-time' and 'alien world', the dominant chronotope of Greek novel, see Bakhtin (1981) 86-110.

293. According to Praz (1970) 210-213, the notion of 'exotic Aestheticism' has basically two features: it focuses on ancient periods and alien countries, and their curiosities, and it is filtered through imagination; in this sense, the author creates his own, mirage chronotope, 'his' Ancient Greece, 'his' Renaissance, 'his' Orient etc. On the importance of exotic geography in Apollonius' narrative, see Beye (1982) 100-119, Williams (1991) and Clare (2002) 33-83.

294. Clare (2002) 151; see also pp. 150-159, where the Libyan episode is contextualized into the storm/shipwreck narratives of the *Odyssey*. On a comparison between the Odyssean Lotus-Eaters and Apollonius' Libyan adventure, see Knight (1995) 125-127. Williams (1991) 163-173 describes the desert as an "inverted landscape".

sense of their impending doom, Apollonius uses one of the most awe-inspiring similes in the entire epic (1280-1285)[295]. *As when men roam through a city like lifeless ghosts, awaiting the destruction of war or plague or a terrible storm which swamps the vast lands where cattle work; without warning the cult statues sweat with blood and phantom groans are heard in the shrines...* This Gothic picture, full of horror and blood, is soon followed by the coming of the night, whose darkness (ἐρεμνὴ ἕσπερος) foreshadows death (1289-1296)[296].

Typically, Apollonius gives a clear indication as to when dawn breaks and when night comes for each narrated day of the Argonaut voyage–except for the ones spent in the Libyan desert[297]. After the first night of despair, dawn comes again at the point when the Argo resumes the sea voyage and sets sail for Greece (1622-1623 αὐτὰρ ἐς ἠῶ/ λαίφεσι πεπταμένοις). However, the flow of time is not interrupted during the interim period which comprises no less than 17 days of *fabula*-time[298]. How should this anomaly in the handling of time be construed? During the first, dark night, the Argonauts, as they lie separated from each other, seem to enter the realm of sleep; in being lamented by Medea's female followers, that of death (1289-1304)[299]. It should come as no surprise then that in this dream-like atmosphere, real time, measured by reference to the alternation of day and night, freezes. In a way, the sleeping Argonauts are trapped in a different dimension of time and space; this 'unending' night in the vast desert cannot be understood in terms of reality but of imagination[300]. The Libyan narrative may only be seen through the lens of this fantastic chronotope which brings imagination into play and where optical illusions, mirages and hallucinations assume a central role[301].

295. The nightmare scene with the presence of the divine portents again evokes the Theoklymenos passage from *Odyssey* Book 20 (Vian [1996] 190 on v. 1284).

296. Elliger (1975) 312-314 stresses the uncanny tone in the description of Syrtis.

297. Another exception is the lack of indication of dawn and night during the sojourn of the Argonauts on Lemnos (1.650-918).

298. According to the calculations of Vian (1996) 12-13, days 19-20 and 33-35 after the visit to Kirke are part of the *story*-time and have action, whereas days 21 to 32 belong to the 'tempi morti' of the voyage, since the 12 days of the transportation of the Argo constitute no more than a stock number of fairytale narratives.

299. As a rule the Argonauts sleep in groups; their separation here is an equivalent of death (Vian [1996] 190 on v. 1292).

300. The indication of noon (1312 ἔνδιον ἦμαρ ἔην, 1505 μεσημβρινὸν ἦμαρ) during the Libyan episode is no exception to this general rule: it should be construed as a time which conditions divine epiphanies, see below pp. 127-128.

301. Visualization through imagination is an ancient problem, dating from Plato and Aristotle, and has been variously exploited by philosophers, scientists and authors, see Warner (2006) 121-129.

The desert, as also the open sea, can activate the imagination of those travelling across it through the games played by darkness and light. This natural phenomenon is dramatized by Apollonius, who situates the Argonauts within this theatre of mirages. Bizarre apparitions and dramatic disappearances become the main pattern of the Libyan episode, as the gods, or so it is said, conjure up images in the Argonauts' minds; consequently, vision and visualization are key notions around which the episode is structured[302]. The first epiphany is that of the Libyan heroines, who, in inhabiting the desert since the era of gods, when Athena leapt from Zeus' head in full armour (1309-1311), owe their appearance to a dislocation in time, a *time travel*, which is a recurrent theme of fairytale and fantasy. Their visionary status is accentuated by their rendering as noonday demons (1312 ἔνδιον ἦμαρ ἔην)[303], but foremost by being viewed by just one percipient, Jason (1316-1317 αὐτόν δέ μιν ἀμφαδὸν οἶον/ μειλιχίοις ἐπέεσσιν ἀτυζόμενον προσέειπον 'but they remained visible to him alone and addressed the panicked man with kindly words')[304]. Their disappearance is equally mysterious and abrupt (1330 ἄφαντοι, ἵν' ἔσταθεν), as they are covered by a cloud or mist (1361-1362 τις ἀχλὺς/ ἠὲ νέφος μεσσηγὺ φαεινομένας ἐκάλυψεν 'some mist or cloud suddenly concealed them from my sight'). Images of clouds and mist pertain to the divine from Homer and beyond, and are a clear sign that the heroines are no more than an illusion of the desert[305]. Less ethereal is the second apparition, the huge horse that emerges from the sea and flies like the wind into the desert (1364-1368)[306]. That the passage has a supernatural undertone is further reinforced by the temporary interruption of the story by the narrator

---

302. Buxton (2009) 121-125 interprets the Libyan episode as "a play of invisibility".

303. The motif of the *meridianus demon* is explored by fantasy as also by Romantic writers, but has its roots in Hellenistic poetry: see Vian (1996) 126 n. 3 for the parallels from Callimachus and Theocritus and Papanghelis (1989) for the elaboration of the motif by Ovid.

304. Vian (1996) 191-192 on v. 1314 brilliantly points out that the visit of the Libyan heroines is a variation of the typical scene of dream in Homer. Jason's narration of the encounter later on (1349-1362) is also rendered as a dream narrative, cf. Vian (1996) 193 on v. 1349.

305. Warner (2006) 83-93 fully explores the divine, supernatural meaning of the cloud in ancient literature, in the Judaeo-Christian tradition and in Renaissance painting. Her concluding observation aptly describes the mood captured by Apollonius' rendering of the Libyan heroines (p. 93): "Clouds formed the furniture of heaven and the enveloping mists of divine splendour, on the one hand; on the other, ethereal fire has provided a medium for divine manifestations. But the heavens and their mantling clouds have also acted as ethereal screens, or, in an image that anticipated later media, as 'airy films' on which spirit visions appear, as in the case of many signs of divine work, and the unusual mirage known as *fata morgana*".

306. Sea portents are always sent by Poseidon, cf. the equally supernatural scene in Euripides *Hippolytus* (1205-1217) where the wave of the sea is transformed into a huge bull.

(1381-1392 Μουσάων ὅδε μῦθος etc.): the account of the monstrous portent and the subsequent carrying of the Argo across the desert for 12 days
and 12 nights may only be given by a divine 'source'.

Then thirst leads the Argonauts to another site of mirages, the garden
of Atlas[307]. Once again apparition and disappearance suggest a shift in
time. Apollonius visualizes simultaneously two *tableaux*, one before and
one after the arrival of Herakles at the site: *the garden of yesterday* where
Ladon still kept watch over the golden apples and *the garden of today*
where the dragon lies mortally wounded by the arrows of Herakles. The
image of the creature in the liminal state between life and death, of a
corpse with its wounds open, strikes the viewer as an uncanny spectacle
which at the same time fills him with fascination (1400-1405)[308]. *Now,
however, the snake had been destroyed by Herakles, and it lay against the
trunk of the apple tree; only the tip of its tail still moved freely, as it
sprawled lifeless from its head to the end of its dark spine. The arrows
had left the angry poison of the Lernaean Hydra in its blood, and flies
withered on the rotting wounds.* Landscape is also in a state of flux. Not
only does Herakles make a spring gush forth from a rock in the middle
of the desert (1441-1459), but, in an even more impressive way, the
Hesperides are in a process of constant metamorphosis, as they are transformed from lamenting maidens into earth and thence into trees with
human voice–a marvel exceedingly great for the beholders (1408-1431)[309].
Now, the phantom of Herakles perceived across the desert by the supernatural vision of Lynkeus carries the notion of the mirage to extremes
(1476-1480). *As for Herakles, Lynkeus alone at that time thought that he
saw him far away across the vast land, as a man sees or imagines he sees
the moon through a mist at the beginning of a new month.* The snapshot
summarizes all the features pertaining to the illusionary aesthetics of the
Libyan adventure: supernaturalism, games of light and shade, divine mist,
the eye of the imagination, and time travel into the future.

Death forces the Argonauts to face reality again. Though the narrative
becomes temporarily 'realistic' when the death of Mopsos by a snake

307. The rich mythological and literary subtext of the scene is thoroughly discussed
by Vian (1996) 195-196 on v. 1399.
308. The antithesis between experiencing something repulsive and the joy stemming
from its contemplation is pointed out by Aristotle (*Poet.* 1448b), see above pp. 19-20. The
anatomy of the dead body becomes a fascinating spectacle for modern-day phantasmago-
rias, the most characteristic of which is the capturing of corpses in waxworks, see Warner
(2006) 31-44.
309. The trees do not evoke the African landscape but rather a typical *locus amoenus*,
see Vian (1996) 197 on v. 1428. On personified trees as stock characters of fairytale and
fantasy, see *EF* s.v. "Trees".

during the midday heat is described, the visualization of Mopsos' corpse exhibits nevertheless the same analogy of the fantastic and the uncanny as the Ladon death scene. The Argonauts gather around the rapidly decaying corpse as marvelling spectators (1527-1531). *His comrades and the heroic son of Aison gathered around him, struck dumb by his terrible fate. For no time at all was his body to lie exposed to the sun, for at once the poison began to rot his flesh within and the hair on his body grew moist and fell away*[310]. Time animates the snapshot, since here, as in the rest of the Libyan scenes, the extraordinary transformation of the corpse occurs at maximum speed–literally *at once*. The play with visibility and invisibility reaches its climax when Triton appears first as a young man, and then *in his true form* (1537-1622). In combining the divine form with the features of a monster, Triton becomes a grotesque spectacle (1610-1614). *From the top of his belly, and all around his back and his waist, his body was exactly like the glorious form of the blessed gods, but beneath his flanks spread in two directions the long, forked tail of a sea-monster.* It may be argued, then, that the Libyan episode displays the whole range of dark effects: the fantastic, the horrific, the uncanny and ultimately the grotesque; and the recurrent reaction of the Argonauts *qua* viewers is astonishment[311].

Sea and desert are antithetical conditions in the *Argonautica*; and whereas the sea provides the stock setting for a quest plot to unfold, the desert represents the extreme manifestation of Otherness in the Argonaut adventure. When the Argonauts re-enter the Mediterranean, a shift in thematics and tone is expected. But wonder and dream, vision and visuality continue to dominate the epic up to its finale. The confrontation with Talos is resolved through hypnotism, a motif uncommon for Greek poetry, which became very popular with Romantic aesthetics (1665-1672)[312]. Medea–a forerunner of the 'Jekyll and Hyde' complex in this respect–

310. The scene may have a scientific basis, since there is a certain type of snake whose venom causes not just death but also decay of the body (Vian [1996] 200-201 on v. 1531); however, in this passage Apollonius rather than evoking scientific data exploits the uncanny effect of this medical symptom.

311. The term is introduced to describe the result of the aesthetics of metamorphosis upon the viewer by Buxton (2009).

312. The Romantic parallel with this side of Medea could be Svengali, the villainous hypnotist of the novel *Trilby* (1894) by George du Maurier; his ability to hypnotize the young heroine and transform her into a great singer became archetypal for many authors of the *Fin de siècle*. It should be noted that this novel owes its huge success to the cultural context of late 19th century, when mesmerism and hypnotism, suggesting the interconnectedness between sleep and death, held a great fascination for audiences (Warner [2006] 209-212). A similar dark effect is produced by the hypnosis/death of Talos in the *Argonautica*; on this rare motif in Greek literature, see above pp. 66-67.

puts on the evil side of her personality (θεμένη δὲ κακὸν νόον)³¹³ and summons the Keres to perform mesmerism: under the effect of her spell, which is described as an emission of dark phantoms (ἀίδηλα δείκηλα) towards her victim³¹⁴, Talos is manipulated into death. Then, upon sailing the Aegean, the Argonauts enter the most dark and deadly night, the one which men call *katoulas*. The event marks a dramatic climax to the aesthetics of darkness as it offers a thorough description, almost a definition, of the 'total blackness' of Chaos and Hades (1694-1698)³¹⁵. A dazzling light reveals Anaphe, an island which is visible only to the Argonauts, the subjective recipients of divine marvels (τοῖσι φαάνθη νῆσος ἰδεῖν). An allegorical interpretation of the episode suggests the overcoming of the dark powers lurking in the Argonauts' quest and the triumph of light upon their return³¹⁶. This optimistic twist in the plot is heightened by the next scene, the dream of Euphemos (1733-1739)³¹⁷. *He dreamed that the divine clod was in his arms at his breast and was nourished by little drops of milk, and from the clod, small though it was, came a woman looking like a young virgin. Overcome by irresistible desire he made love to her, but lamented as though he had bedded his own daughter whom he had nursed with his own milk.* The virgin is identified as Kalliste, the island of Thera, from which Cyrene will be settled in the future. Still, despite the prospect of the new land, the reader is aware of the coming tragedy of the Minyans; although light prevails against the forces of evil, Medea the witch will triumph in the end. Along the road from Pagasai to Colchis and back, the Argonauts come across sites of fantasy and sites of horror, literary and imaginary places, liminal spaces inhabited by gods, monsters and corpses. Within this context, the dream of Euphemos, where the visionary merges with sexual desire and the hope of a Newfoundland is symbolically represented as incest, turns into a nightmare, and thus comes as a dark coda to the *Argonautica*.

---

313. According to Vian (1996) 141 n. 2 the phrase suggests that Medea has a 'double' personality and at this point assumes her other self.

314. Vian translates the phrase as 'hallucinations malignes', Seaton as 'baneful phantoms' and Hunter as 'dark phantoms': I think ἀίδηλος is deliberately left ambiguous here to denote either 'annihilating, destroying' or 'unseen, obscure'. The procedure evokes the atomic theory of Democritus on the effluence of the atoms to the senses and the impressions created by this emission (Vian [1996] 206 on v. 1672).

315. On how this passage connects to the aesthetics of darkness, see above pp. 10-11.

316. The 'from shadow into light' story pattern underlies many plot types, and especially the quest, see Booker (2004) 215-228.

317. The model is Penelope's dream in *Od.* 19.536-540 (Kessels [1982] 164-166).

II. LYCOPHRON *ALEXANDRA*

THE DARK TRAGEDY

II.1. Alexandra and her demons

> Time with his retinue of ages fled
> Backwards, nor checked his flight until I saw
> Our dim ancestral Past in vision clear;
> Saw multitudes of men, and, here and there,
> A single Briton clothed in wolf-skin vest,
> With shield and stone-axe, stride across the wold;
> The voice of spears was heard, the rattling spear
> Shaken by arms of mighty bone, in strength,
> Long mouldered, of barbaric majesty.
> I called on Darkness—but before the word
> Was uttered, midnight darkness seemed to take
> All objects from my sight; and lo! again
> The Desert visible by dismal flames;
> It is the sacrificial altar, fed
> With living men—how deep the groans! the voice
> Of those that crowd the giant wicker thrills
> The monumental hillocks, and the pomp
> Is for both worlds, the living and the dead.

William Wordsworth *The Prelude* 13.318-335 (1850 version)

Towards the conclusion of William Wordsworth's autobiographical poem *The Prelude*, the poet has a vision of an ancient battle and an archaic sacrifice, both taking place on the Salisbury Plain. Affected by this visionary experience, distant in time ('our dim ancestral Past') and manner ('of barbaric majesty'), he summons darkness; through the power of the word, the poet transcends the limits imposed by the natural world and the historical moment, and becomes a viewer of the collective memory of Britain's past. Clearly this is a passage about the ability of the poet to exceed temporal and spatial thresholds and envision events beyond the reach of man by means of poetic imagination. To thus render poetry as a spiritual, transcendental experience communicates a sense of the sublime to the reader. Still, the sublime of the abovementioned vision resides not so much within its poetological symbolism as within its visualization by the narrating 'I'[1]. Lycophron's Alexandra (as I will thence call the Hellenistic adaptation of Kassandra) resembles the Wordswor-

---

1. The sublime effect caused by Wordsworth's apocalyptic view of poetry and the power of the word is explored by Weiskel (1976) 167-204, esp. 186-195; cf. Shaw (2006) 99-104 who appositely speaks of Wordsworth's "staging of the sublime".

thian persona in more ways than one. Defying the constraints of nature
and time, Alexandra has visions of both future and past; the enigmatic
word is used as a vehicle for her voyage into time; not only does she
visualize the narrated events as occurring before her very eyes but moreover she is psychologically affected by them; her revelatory speech
evokes the sublime, which for Lycophron and the Romantics alike is
more of a feeling than an abstract idea.

The *Alexandra* is a dramatized recitation of a vision about the Trojan
War where the role of the narrator is assigned to one of its characters,
the prophetess Alexandra. The entire war is filtered through Alexandra's discourse, and, as a consequence, it is seen through her female/
Trojan perspective. As a narrator Alexandra offers a dark remake of
the Trojan myth; as a character she visualizes her personal and family
tragedy, and reacts with horror to it. The double function of Alexandra
permeates the generic identity of the poem, its narrative style and
inherent ideology. These parameters will be addressed, also in comparison to the whole range of Romantic aesthetics, from the Gothic to
the Dark Fantastic and thence to its epigonal movement of Aestheticism, so as to shed light on Lycophron's extraordinary literary achievement[2].

The fact that Alexandra's vision informs the core of Lycophron's
enigmatic poem begs the question about the nature of this visionary experience and, by extension, of its literary undertones. The archetype, Kassandra, may be classified as a μάντις 'seer' along with Kalchas, Teiresias, Melampous, and, on a historical level, Pythia, who either exercised
divination or made oracular prophecies. However, Kassandra is unique
in that she embodies the dark association of prophecy and madness, of
symbolism and sensationalism so characteristic of primitive cultures, and
in this respect the closest literary parallel is Theoklymenos from the
Odyssey[3]. Other features, such as the spontaneous delivery of the prophetic message, the sudden burst of the visionary discourse, and the preservation of the identity–it is not the god who speaks through Kassandra
but she delivers the prophecies in her own voice–evoke the rhetoric of

2. Greek text is taken from Hurst/Kolde (2008); the translation is based on Mair
(1921) with modifications and some alterations following Mooney (1988). The numerous
commentaries on the *Alexandra* are indispensable for the interpretation of this enigmatic
poem; in my analysis I have extensively used Holzinger (1895), Mooney (1988), Fusillo/
Hurst/Paduano (1991), Gigante Lanzara (2000), Hurst/Paidi (2004), Lambin (2005),
Hurst/Kolde (2008) and Chauvin/Cusset (2008).

3. For the comparison between Theoklymenos and Kassandra as *the* examples of
ancient prophetic madness and the psychological state of the seer's possession by the god,
see Dodds (1951) 70-82.

the Sibyl[4]. Lycophron's heroine epitomizes the typical traits of Kassandra, as known from the epic, lyric and tragic tradition; some of these traits are nevertheless given an added emphasis or an unexpected twist[5]. Alexandra is profiled as an ecstatic seer (28 ἡ δ᾽ ἔνθεον σχάσασα βακχεῖον στόμα), who pours forth her confused and uncontrolled cries (5 ἄσπετον χέασα παμμιγῆ βοὴν) that are both enigmatic (10-11 δυσφάτους αἰνιγμάτων/ οἴμας τυλίσσων) and dark (7 Σφιγγὸς κελαινῆς, 12 τὰν σκότωι)[6]. Yet the key to her rendering as an uncanny figure is that she becomes something of a hybrid creature, a blending of monsters and manic women–the Sphinx, the Mainads, the Sirens, the Bacchants and the Sibyl–towards the end of the poem (1461-1466).

That said, Lycophron insists on the human side of Alexandra. Thus, although she is endowed with the gift of prophecy by the god Apollo, a possible indication of the heroine's sanctity, her revelations do not have primarily religious connotations nor should her discourse be construed within an apocalyptic context[7]. And in contrast with visionary fantasies and religious allegories, where the prophetic message is, as a rule, conveyed through dreams, Alexandra expresses her prophecies while awake. The visual perception of what lies beyond on part of Alexandra is therefore comparable with the talent of *precognition* or *second sight*, consisting of brief, unexpected glimpses of future events; precognition is not provoked by an external stimulus but has its roots in an emotional or mental disturbance of the self. To credit Alexandra with the talent of precognition has significant implications for the interpretation of Lycophron's poem. First, it suggests that she suffers from a mental illness, a kind of mania or hysteria, and in this respect her speech may be likened to a Romantic mad scene; second, precognition evokes the supernatural dimension of reality, brings to the fore the mixing of superstition and strangeness, of the fantastic and the uncanny that informs 19th century

---

4. See Lightfoot (2007) 8-14 who draws an interesting parallel between the Sibyl and Kassandra on the basis of both their ecstatic inspiration and the retaining of an autonomous voice. That Kassandra is more akin to the Sibyl than to Pythia is convincingly argued by Mazzoldi (2001) 99-107.

5. Kassandra in Greek and Roman literature is fully explored by Neblung (1997); on Lycophron's Kassandra-Alexandra as a seer, see esp. pp. 76-80. Kassandra with her double identity as a virgin and a prophetess, from Homer until the Hellenistic era, is studied by Mazzoldi (2001).

6. Κελαινός here may suggest the riddles or the cruelty of the Sphinx, but also refer vaguely to the notion of horror or mania, as in other passages of the *Alexandra*, see Holzinger (1895) 166 on v. 7 and Mooney (1988) 2 on v. 7.

7. Differently West (2000) 160-164 who argues that Lycophron was influenced by Near Eastern visionary apocalyptic literature and used this particular literary form to emphasize the political message of Alexandra's prophecy.

horror literature[8]; third, in being condemned to live with disbelief (what the psychologists call 'the Kassandra complex'), Alexandra is isolated from, and persecuted by, her social environment, and thus she resembles a Gothic heroine.

Before elaborating further on these points, attention should be drawn on a fourth implication, the one associated with the literary and metapoetic qualities of this dramatized vision. Alexandra as a *dramatis persona* has a vision of the fate awaiting her, her family and her people, and the Greeks, in the aftermath of the Trojan War. The starting point for the Trojan catastrophe is the critical moment when Paris sets sail for Greece (16-27); situated on the 'Hill of Delusion' (29 Ἄτης ἀπ᾽ ἄκρων λόφων), Alexandra 'views' the departure of the Trojan fleet with the bodily eye but 'sees' all the events of past, present and future with the imaginative eye[9]. This is a sublime experience, not unlike the one described by Wordsworth who, in viewing the Salisbury Plain, sees battles and sacrifices of old unfolding in front of his very eyes. Alexandra suggests visionary poetics, since her inspirer, Apollo is the patron saint of all kinds of transcendence; her *logorrheia* is an indication of both prophetic and poetic madness[10]. In being set at dawn (16-17 Ἠὼς μὲν αἰπὺν ἄρτι Φηγίου πάγον/ κραιπνοῖς ὑπερποτᾶτο Πηγάσου πτεροῖς... 'Dawn was just soaring over the steep crag of Phegion on the swift wings of Pegasos...'), Alexandra's vision has a clear metapoetic ring. The morning not only marks the beginning of a day of action in epic but moreover implies the Aristotelian rule that a perfect tragedy should not exceed 'a single revolution of the sun' (*Poet.* 1449b12-13 ἡ μὲν [sc. τραγῳδία] ὅτι μάλιστα πειρᾶται ὑπὸ μίαν περίοδον ἡλίου εἶναι ἢ μικρὸν ἐξαλλάττειν)[11]. Modelled on Kassandra from Aeschylus' *Agamemnon*, Lycophron's heroine is more than a tragic character: *qua* narrator she reconstructs the (already written) tragedies about the Greeks and the Trojans through her own voice—her poetic (:creative) role

8. For the dominant role of superstition (literally evoking the lat. *superstitio* 'to stand paralyzed with fear over a person or object'), in the sense of the hesitation experienced when someone is faced with any form of Otherness, in the formation of the Romantic fantastic, see Siebers (1984) 19-56.

9. Cf. *Il.* 1.70 where Kalchas is said to possess the same ability: ὃς ᾔδη τά τ᾽ ἐόντα τά τ᾽ ἐσσόμενα πρό τ᾽ ἐόντα.

10. Lycophron, however, invests his Alexandra with Dionysiac madness too, cf. for instance 28 ἡ δ᾽ ἔνθεον σχάσασα βακχεῖον στόμα. On the view expressed in Plato *Phaedrus* 244a-245a that religious, ritual and poetic madness are given to men by divine gift (e.g. 244a.6-8 νῦν δὲ τὰ μέγιστα τῶν ἀγαθῶν ἡμῖν γίγνεται διὰ μανίας, θείᾳ μέντοι δόσει διδομένης), see Dodds (1951) 64-101 in his analysis of the "The Blessings of Madness".

11. Cusset (2002-2003) 140 and Hurst/Kolde (2008) 92 on v. 16.

is suggested by the metaliterary terms ὄπα (6), γῆρυν (7), μέλος (1463) and ἔπη (1466)[12].

The transcendental character of Romantic lyricism (as exemplified by the case of William Wordsworth) is a first point of contact between visionary poetics and the *Alexandra*. The question is, does the *Alexandra* capture, at least partly, the visionary moment as expressed by the Romantic poets? The distinguishing features of the genuine *visionary moment* are the following: it begins with a loss of sight; it gives access to a reality beyond the reach of common language; it is static, in that it makes action slow down or come to a standstill; it suggests a contact with eternal or sacred time; it transforms the character of the subject, by causing the self to expand beyond its being; and it presupposes a direct encounter between the subject and the numinous, it is an experience resembling an epiphany or an incarnation[13]. Most of these features are incorporated into Alexandra the character, the narrator, and also the mirrored image of the poet. From the very beginning, emphasis is placed on Alexandra's imaginative eye–the constant repetition of λεύσσω 'I see' is indicative not of physical but of spiritual sight. The making of a personal, idiosyncratic language for the speech of Alexandra strikes us as a typical feature of the visionary experience–to prophesy is to talk incoherently and enigmatically (e.g. 10-11 δυσφάτους αἰνιγμάτων/ οἴμας τυλίσσων, 14 λοξῶν ἐπῶν, 1466 ἑλικτὰ κωτίλλουσα δυσ-φράστως ἔπη)[14]. Pause of action is neatly captured by the symbolic *stasis* of the heroine on the 'Hill of Delusion'–which extends until the end of the poem, when Alexandra eventually withdraws to her prison (1461 τόσσ' ἠγόρευε καὶ παλίσσυτος ποσὶν/ ἔβαινεν εἰρκτῆς ἐντός 'so much she spake, and then rushed back into her prison'). Being at once diachronic and achronic, Alexandra's vision offers a panorama of myth and history, where not only past, present and future but also the inner connections linking the various events to each other may be viewed simultaneously. Transcendence is a liminal state between two structures, in this case the reality experienced by the Trojans as reflected on the dramatized frame and the mystic world of Apollo; Alexandra is both the virgin princess and the inspired prophetess of the god, thus

---

12. Ἐκμιμουμένη 'imitating (the speech of the dark Sphinx)' in v. 7 has also a meta-poetic undertone–it suggests *mimesis*, see Kossaifi (2009) 147-149.

13. The features are pointed out by Clayton (1987) 4-9 on the basis of Wordsworth's poetics.

14. Clayton (1987) 6 notes interesting parallels from Plato describing the language of the Delphic oracle and the Sibyl and from the Bible, e.g. when the Apostles, controlled by the Holy Spirit, are made to speak various languages on the Day of Pentecost.

expanding the self from this into the other world–she is at once a 'quiet maiden' (ἥσυχος κόρη) and a Mainad (ἔνθεον βακχεῖον στόμα)[15]. As for her encounter with the divine, it is staged as an incarnation and an epiphany of Apollo, the latter being evident in the scene of the unfulfilled marriage between the maiden and the god (1454-1457). In sum: Alexandra may be seen–at least partly–as the *persona* of a poet who has a transcendental experience[16].

But Alexandra is not the only avatar representing the poet in the *Alexandra*, and her discourse, delivered in direct speech, occupies the diegetic level of the narration. The higher level of narration is staged as a messenger speech, also in *oratio recta*, reported by a servant–the guard of Alexandra–to king Priam, who correspond to the 'extradiegetic narrator' and his dramatized 'addressee' respectively[17]. It is critical to note that the 'guard-narrator' should be differentiated from the 'Alexandra-narrator': whereas the latter suggests irrationalism, in pouring forth a "confused and inarticulated" discourse, the former delivers an "articulated and rational" *logos*, which purports to be true, comprehensive and linear (1 λέξω τὰ πάντα νητρεκῶς ἃ μ' ἱστορεῖς/ ἀρχῆς ἀπ' ἄκρης 'all I will tell truly that you ask from the utter beginning')[18]. The guard and Alexandra, who also mirror different concepts of the poet-author, share conflicting views of reality. In his world, truthfulness, wholeness and order are still possible–on a metapoetic level this is probably the world of epic poetry (8 τῶν ἄσσα θυμῶι καὶ διὰ μνήμης ἔχω... 'what in heart and memory I hold...')[19]; Alexandra's reality, like her speech, is distorted, enigmatic and uncanny–she therefore incorporates the irrational, dark modes of tragedy, and its epigonal genres, Romantic drama and the Gothic novel.

This two-level narrative, which suggests the hybrid quality of the *Alexandra*, its liminal state between tragedy and epic, has attracted meticulous

15. Kassandra is typically characterized as a Mainad in tragedy, see Eur. *Hek.* 121, 676 and *Tr.* 170, 341 etc.

16. The obvious predecessor of Alexandra here is Hesiod, the poet-prophet (*Th.* 31-32 ἐνέπνευσαν δέ μοι αὐδὴν/ θέσπιν, ἵνα κλείοιμι τά τ' ἐσσόμενα πρό τ' ἐόντα).

17. The mimetic framework and its allusions to Aeschylus' *Agamemnon* and *Prometheus Bound* are discussed by Looijenga (2009).

18. On these first-person voices merging in the *Alexandra* and the *mise en abyme* effect created in relation to the implied author, see Fusillo (1984) 500-506 and Cusset (2009).

19. In arranging the cries of Alexandra into ordered *logos*, the guard resembles 'Homer' who arranges the stories of Odysseus into the *Apologoi*: on this basis, Alexandra as a narrator is comparable to Odysseus, see Cusset (2009) 134-138. On the creative role of the memory of the guard, and on poetry as ἀνάμνησις, see Kossaifi (2009) 149-150.

attention by scholars[20]. As I intend to show, certain forms which the drama and the novel have assumed during the Romantic period may shed new light on the peculiar crossing of genres introduced by Lycophron[21].

From a generic viewpoint, the *Alexandra* poses the vexed question of how it relates to dramatic poetry, and tragedy in particular. Lycophron was a tragedian and a member of the tragic Pleiad, and he chose to compose his poem in iambic trimeters[22]. Formally the *Alexandra* is a messenger speech, which constitutes one of the component parts of tragedy. But, strictly speaking, it is not a 'drama' in the Aristotelian concept of the word, since it has no action or plot. As has been succinctly said, this is "a tragedy without tragedy"; its tragic quality should only be assessed on the basis of its intertextual relations with Aeschylus and Euripides, and of the "true tragic posture" of its heroine[23]. The peculiarity of Lycophron's generic experiment lies within the expanding of "the dramatic form on an epic scale"[24]. Hence the *Alexandra* has been likened to a *monodrama*, a work consisting of a single role and performed by a soloist[25]. If it were actually intended for some kind of staging, this would be aimed at enhancing the dramatic illusion of Alexandra's speech[26]. It is an interesting innovation on part of Lycophron that the messenger's report is not delivered in third but in first person voice,

20. Especially Fusillo (1984) who provides the most comprehensive analysis of the fusion between epic narrative and dramatic discourse in the *Alexandra*; cf. on the same issue Fountoulakis (1998).

21. It is worth noting that Hellenistic and Romantic genre theory and practice share striking similarities: the blurring of boundaries between genres, the emergence of the fragment as an autonomous literary unit and the introduction of modes and moods alongside traditional generic categories are the most significant of these (for a full discussion, see Rajan [2000]). All of these innovations may equally apply to the genre of the *Alexandra*: the crossing of epic and drama, the 'fragmentary' monologue, detached from any dramatic context, and the combination of the visionary mode with the sublime, the sensational and the dark mood aptly describe Lycophron's poem.

22. The notorious 'Lycophron question' will not be addressed here (for a short overview, see Fantuzzi/Hunter [2004] 437-439): it is tacitly accepted that, for the most part, the *Alexandra* should be attributed to Lycophron of Chalkis, the 3rd century tragedian, who was active in Ptolemaic Alexandria.

23. Cusset (2002-2003) 137-142 and more recently Sens (2010).

24. Fantuzzi/Hunter (2004) 440.

25. Tzetzes defines the *Alexandra* as "a monody intended for solo performance" (*Versus de poematum generibus poem*. 135-138 γίνωσκε κυρίως δὲ τὴν μονῳδίαν,/ ὅταν μόνος λέγῃ τις ἐν θρηνῳδίαις,/ κατὰ δὲ παράχρησιν, ἂν λέγῃ μόνος,/ ὥσπερ Λυκόφρων εἰς 'Αλεξάνδραν γράφει), cf. Berra (2009) 273.

26. That the *Alexandra* was more than a mere *Lese-* or *Rezitationsdrama* is pointed out by Fountoulakis (1998). Cameron (1995) 81 suggests that a possible context for the live performance of the *Alexandra* was the "symposiastic riddle tradition": this cannot be excluded, it should, however, be noted that the *Alexandra* is a multi-layered and complex work, much more than a mere *jeu d'esprit*.

which, in theatrical terms, means that the actor playing the messenger would also appear as 'Alexandra' onstage. Moreover, the obscure style of the play in combination with the dramatic visualization of the prophecy would produce an overwhelming, expressionist sensation rather than convey a genuine tragic emotion[27]. The "appropriate use of theatrical intonation and gesticulation"[28] completes the picture of how such a play could have been presented on scene.

At this point, it is worth considering the affinities of the *Alexandra* with dramatic poetry from a different angle: the innovations in genre and performance of drama as introduced by Romantic playwrights. To begin from the latter, theatrical productions during the Romantic era explored new modes of sensational experience for the public, such as the use of special effects or the disguise of a female actor in order to perform a masculine role and vice versa, and were largely based on 'star turns', i.e. on the performance of impressive scenes by solo actors. These are exactly the features that, as said, would be appropriate for the staging of the *Alexandra* as a monodrama[29]. Nevertheless, this scenario is purely hypothetical, and scholars have not yet resolved the issue of whether the *Alexandra* was also written for recitation or reading. Another striking parallel is that most Romantic dramas were not performed onstage but were originally conceived as 'closet dramas'; it is a likely possibility that the *Alexandra*, like the closet dramas, was also intended for silent reading or recitation in small groups[30]. Emphasis on the reading process of drama rather than its theatrical representation coincides with the Romantics' critique of Neoclassical rules concerning tragedy, and their experimentation with new forms beyond the accepted classification scheme of genres. Within this context, Shelley characterizes his *Prometheus Unbound* as a 'lyrical drama' and Byron coins the

27. Fantuzzi/Hunter (2004) 443 remark that the *Alexandra*, in contrast with a typical messenger speech, fails to produce the effect of ἐνάργεια: "The *Alexandra* explores the inevitably problematic theatricality of Kassandra's visions...it shows us how, for the 'clear-sighted' prophet, action takes place merely inside the envisioning and creative mind".

28. Fountoulakis (1998) 295.

29. Fantuzzi/Hunter (2004) 439 link the *Alexandra* with the Hellenistic practice of performing 'star turns', such as messenger speeches, rather than entire tragedies, and also with the rhapsodic recitation of epic. On the pursuit of novelty by Romantic playwrights and the so-called 'star turns', see Pascoe (2005).

30. West (2000) 155 asserts that the *Alexandra* was "surely designed for a reflective and erudite readership" and not "live performance which have made excessive demands on the audience's concentration and the performer's stamina"; nevertheless, she does not exclude the possibility that some passages were initially read aloud to a select group, perhaps in that "animated or impassioned recitation adapted for the subject that Wordsworth prescribed for his own poetry".

term 'mental theatre' to describe his dramatic poems. These terms reflect the re-orientation of drama towards the inner life of a character–its lyric subjectivity–and an increasing interest in the mechanism of human consciousness: such mental dramas, so the Romantics claimed, had a more intense effect when approached through reading[31]. The *Alexandra*, rendered as a dual-voiced monologue, evokes this 'mental theatre', in that it attempts to capture Alexandra's consciousness as she reviews the Trojan War from its beginnings to its aftermath. It is critical to note that another subgenre of 19th century drama, the *monologue*, evolved from the very same concept of the mental theatre[32]. The form was invented by Robert Browning (an author considered to be 'unreadable' by his contemporaries) and had certain salient features–its strongly rhetorical and artificial language, a narrative situation involving apart from the central character a silent listener, and the coexistence of empathy and detachment required from the reader–which also apply, *mutatis mutandis*, to the *Alexandra*[33].

Despite the theatrical qualities of this monologue and the 'dramatic frame' involving the messenger and his silent listener, king Priam, the *Alexandra* also evokes the epic mode. Whereas in drama the temporal level of the narrated events coincides with that of the perception of these events by the spectator (or the reader), in epic all events are transmitted, and often commented, by the narrator and are thus situated on a different temporal level than that of the enunciation[34]. Alexandra does not represent actions but is a narrator who gives an account of other actions; the messenger is also a narrator–not of actions but of Alexandra's narration of actions: exactly as a 'Chinese box' complex[35]. It may be argued that Lycophron with the *Alexandra* introduces the *framed narrative*, where various diegetic levels are embedded into each other. It is an interesting coincidence that this form was extensively exploited by 19th century authors, especially in mystery or horror novels and short stories, for its dramatic potential. In this narrative situation an extradiegetic narrator

31. On the term 'mental theatre', see Richardson (1988) 1-19.

32. Everett (1991) and *NPEPP* s.v. "Monologue".

33. Interestingly enough, Harold Bloom (in Hobby [2009] xv-xviii) views Browning's 'obsessed monologues', with their dark and nightmare atmosphere, as paradigms of what he calls the *Romantic grotesque*–a term suitable for the description of the *Alexandra* too.

34. For this distinction between drama and epic, with related bibliography, see Fusillo (1984) 498 with n. 6. The dimension of time in tragedy as seen by Aristotle is explored by Jakob (1997).

35. Lowe (2004) 308 distinguishes four levels of narration in the *Alexandra*: a primary ('Lycophron' addresses the Ptolemaic reader), a secondary (the guard addresses Priam), a tertiary (Alexandra prophesies) and a quaternary (Apollo inspires Alexandra). On the polyphony of the 'I' in the *Alexandra*, see Kossaifi (2009) 153-154.

assumes a role as listener/transcriber/reader of the intradiegetic narration, which as a rule is delivered in the first person and may comprise an oral narration, diaries, letters and the like[36].

The voices of the narrators are multiplied, and, as a consequence, the reliability of the various 'tellers' is questioned; a second implication is that the framed narrative is not only recontextualized by the framing narrative but also interacts dynamically with it. The *Alexandra*, which is designed as a framed narrative, brings these qualities to the fore. On the one hand, the guard functions as an 'editor' of Alexandra's words, by re-arranging them in linear and logical order: "since the guard claims, improbably, that he can repeat the exact form of Alexandra's ravings, the poet raises, through the use of this frame, the question of accuracy and interpretation in prophecy and, one suspects, in poetry as well"[37]. The distance between the 'editor' and Alexandra is maintained beyond the end of the poem (1461-1463)–*so much she spake, and then rushed back into her prison, but in her heart she wailed her latest Siren song*. Alexandra's silence does not mark the end of her prophecy which continues "as an interior monologue" when she retreats into silence[38]; by extension, the reliability of Apollo, the inspirer of the prophecy, is also doubted, since Alexandra's knowledge of the future is, in many cases, partial and elliptical[39]. On the other hand, frame and framed narrative juxtapose the sanity of the messenger and the ecstatic trance, the madness, of Alexandra. In effect, in reproducing and consuming the delirium of Alexandra, all the narrators–and the addressees who apart from the king include the Trojans

36. Classic examples include Mary Shelley's *Frankenstein* (captain Robert Walton transcribes in his journal the oral narration of Victor Frankenstein who quotes the story of the Creature), Emily Brontë's *Wuthering Heights* (a secondary character, Mr. Lockwood, reconstructs the story of Heathcliff and Catherine Earnshaw by reading Catherine's journal and listening to Nelly Dean's story of the Earnshaw family) and Henry James' *The Turn of the Screw* (an unnamed narrator listens to a male friend reading a manuscript written by a governess narrating her unusual ghost experience). On this narrative device, see especially Newman (1986).

37. Gutzwiller (2007) 124. Cf. Fantuzzi/Hunter (2004) 441 who observe that "the opening and closing frame foregrounds the role of the narrating messenger in such a way as to give self-conscious prominence to the figure of the poet...as for the truth of the messenger's account, the conventional assertion of v.1 (νητρεκῶς) resonates ironically against the inevitable truth of Kassandra's prophecies, and also the inevitable disbelief with which they are greeted".

38. Lowe (2004) 309-310.

39. The idea that "Kassandra's second sight is restricted to what the god cares to reveal" and that "it is not his purpose to save her unnecessary anxiety" is ingeniously suggested by West (1984) 149 n. 105, on the basis that e.g. Alexandra is not informed by Apollo that her rape by Ajax will be prevented by divine intervention.

and the messenger himself–participate in this delirium. The *Alexandra* focuses attention on how delicate the dividing line between sanity and insanity is, and on how contagious the latter may prove to be[40]. Alexandra has actually been locked away, because her madness causes anxiety to the people of Troy. King Priam is himself worried about the hidden truth behind the princess' madness–hence his demand to be informed of each and every word uttered by Alexandra (1 λέξω τὰ πάντα νητρεκῶς ἅ μ' ἱστορεῖς 'all I will tell truly *that you ask*', 1469-1470 ἐπεὶ μ' ἔταξας...πάντα φράζειν κἀναπεμπάζειν λόγον 'since *you did charge me* to come as a messenger to report all to you and truly recount her words'). The threat stemming from Alexandra's madness spills over into the narrative frame: its miasmic effect makes the messenger's closing wish resound with a grim sense of foreboding–*may God turn her prophecies to fairer issue*.

Alexandra represents her own point of view on the narrated stories which is nevertheless unreliable in the eyes of Priam; this subjectivity is a source of *pathos*, of narrator's emotional involvent in his own story. In this respect the *pathos* of the *Alexandra* is not just a theatrical effect but is generated by the very nature of the framed narrative–the same effect is produced by the involvement of the first-person narrator in his story in the novels of Romanticism. Overcome by the horror of her visions, Alexandra has sudden bursts of intense emotion, evoking the lyric mode of the lament–αἰαῖ, τάλαινα (31), στένω, στένω σε δισσὰ καὶ τριπλᾶ (69), στένω σε, πάτρα (72), ἐκεῖνο σ' ὦ τάλαινα καρδία κακόν (258), ἐγὼ δὲ πένθος οὐχὶ μεῖον οἴσομαι (302), οἴμοι δυσαίων (314), ἐγὼ δὲ τλήμων (348), ὦ μῆτερ, ὦ δύσμητερ (1174)...[41] Emotive discourse is, of course, part and parcel of the tragic depiction of Kassandra. In Aeschylus' *Agamemnon*, the heroine breaks her silence with the horrendous exclamation ὀτοτοτοτοῖ πόποι δᾶ, and continues by being emotionally affected by the visions of her imminent death. However, the Aeschylean vision has an obvious dramatic point: after the instant fulfillment of Kassandra's prophecy (the death of Agamemnon and her own) the chorus awaits the next phase, the murder of Klytaimestra by Orestes, thus anticipating the rest of the

---

40. On reading and writing madness as a central preoccupation of the Gothic, see Brewster (2000).

41. Lowe (2004) aptly compares Alexandra's monologue to a *threnos*, that is modelled on the laments of Briseis, Hekabe, Helen and Andromache. However, the archetype is once more offered by Aeschylus' *Agamemnon*, where the initial dialogue of Kassandra and the chorus (1072-1177) is rendered as a powerful lyric passage (Schein [1982] 13-14).

trilogy[42]. The effect achieved by Lycophron is substantially different, since he places the vision too early in the story (and within the idyllic setting of Paris' departure for Greece)–much earlier than possible for her addressees to understand it; this is a vain vision, perceived as pure madness, one that will be accomplished beyond the limits of the poem. Therefore, Alexandra's precognition leaves the *dramatis personae* in a state of indeterminacy and hesitation, like that achieved by a contact with any supernatural experience. Lycophron's Alexandra is more than a tragic heroine. In inhabiting the liminal space between reality and transcendence, between prophecy and madness, between the supernatural and the uncanny, she is isolated, locked in an internal struggle against her own demons[43].

But how does Alexandra narrate? In Aeschylus' *Agamemnon* (and in a great part of apocalyptic literature), the prophetic narration has two distinctive features: the 'multi-temporal' conception of reality, and its rendering as a stream of disconnected images[44]. Although the prophecy is designed as a large-scale *prolepsis*, a narration oriented towards the future, the structure of Alexandra's discourse is not linear but is characterized by the crossing of all temporal levels, reflected in the use of the whole range of tenses[45]. The prophetic eye captures episodes from the entire spectrum of mythical time and extends into the historical 'present' of the author, i.e. the Ptolemaic era[46]. As a consequence, the narrative is made up of snapshots, or, rather, of expressionist sketches–not paintings, in the sense that Alexandra's visions are extremely brief and enlarge on a single detail rather than provide an elaborate illustration of an entire episode. So, instead of aiming at creating ἐνάργεια, like the typical

42. As Knox (1979) 47-52 observes, Kassandra's knowledge may be useless for the characters but is eventually realized by the chorus. Schein (1982) 12 describes the visions of Kassandra and her emotional response as a transcendental experience, beyond the limits of humanity, which elicits the sympathy of the audience.

43. Therefore, West (1984) is right in defending the *pathos* of the *Alexandra* on the basis of some highly emotive passages such as the laments for Hektor and Troilos, the description of the rape of Alexandra and the horrifying story about the tribute of the Lokrian maidens.

44. See e.g. Knox (1979) 42-55 and Schein (1982); on these features in the narration of Lycophron's *Alexandra*, see Fusillo (1984) 507-516.

45. The crossing of temporal levels is critically analyzed by Fusillo (1984) 507-513. Mazzoldi (2001) 267-269 offers a detailed chart illustrating how the various temporal levels pertaining to each of Alexandra's micro-narratives are interwoven in Lycophron's poem.

46. Herein lies the political significance of the *Alexandra* (for a thorough discussion, see West [1984]): however, I do not agree with those arguing that Alexandra's prophecies are political comments primarily aimed at a Ptolemaic audience and therefore do not have a genuine dramatic function *per se* (thus Mazzoldi [2001] 254-257).

ekphrases in rhetoric and poetry, these visions owe their powerful effect to the so-called *presentification*, "the making present of the invisible" according to the definition of Jean-Pierre Vernant[47], or the *presentiality*, a convention of theatrical writing which suggests that the events are actually reviewed and relived in the present by the dramatic character[48]. The centrality of mental vision, that is of the internalization of images comprising not just the visible but primarily the invisible (a ghost-seeing as materialized in dreams or hallucinations), renders Alexandra's prophetic discourse a kind of *phantasmagoria*, which is defined as "a shifting series or succession of phantasms or imaginary figures, as seen in a dream or fevered condition, as called up by the imagination, or as created by literary description"[49]. Lycophron turns his readers into spectators of a phantasmagoria by conjuring up–via Alexandra–dark images of passion, violence, death and destruction.

Even if it is difficult to claim that this Alexandra has been so vividly portrayed so as to acquire, like many Romantic characters, a life of her own, one that extends beyond the limits of Lycophron's poem, she is in many ways a fascinating heroine. Not only because Lycophron works Alexandra's biography into her prophecy, but moreover because her femininity forms one of the focal points of the poem. Some of the typical traits associated with the female, especially in Gothic novels, seem to be also present here: the victimization of the female by the male, the obsession with sexual abuse, the focusing on dark psychology, the omnipresent threat of death, the visionary horrors, the encounter with the Other. So now I will turn my attention to this Gothic-like viewing of the female, as introduced by Lycophron, a key aspect of the *Alexandra* which has been so far neglected.

Alexandra is imprisoned, both literary and metaphorically[50]. The adaptation of Kassandra's story to the thematics of imprisonment–she is a prisoner of Priam and a victim of family hubris–is a major contribution to the Romantic reorientation of this well-known myth. It is not certain

47. Quoted by Hardie (2002) 22-23, who opposes the term to the mere *representation*, the basis of *mimesis* in art according to Plato.

48. For this aspect of the narration of Alexandra, termed as *presentizzazione*, see Fusillo (1984) 513-516.

49. The definition is provided by the *OED*; for an illuminating analysis of these aspects of the *phantasmagoria*, see Thomas (2008) 170-171.

50. Lambin (2005) 252-260 makes an excellent point by explaining Alexandra's imprisonment (as well as other instances of imprisonment and confinement in the poem, such as the digestion of Herakles by a sea monster or the swallowing of Laodike by the earth) on the basis of psychoanalysis.

whether this is entirely Lycophron's invention or whether the Hellenistic poet builds on an earlier source, probably the *Cypria*, the *Little Iliad* or *The Sack of Troy*[51]. But it was Lycophron who turned the imprisonment into a focal dramatic theme by placing it in key sections of the *Alexandra*. The location of the incarceration is twice called εἰρκτή 'prison' (351, 1462) and has also a φύλαξ 'guard' (1469); Alexandra gives her own account of it in vv. 348-351:

> ἐγὼ δὲ τλήμων ἡ γάμους ἀρνουμένη
> ἐν παρθενῶνος λαΐνου τυκίσμασιν
> ἄνις τεράμνων εἰς ἀνώροφον στέγην
> εἰρκτῆς ἁλιβδύσασα λυγαίας δέμας

> And I, unhappy, who refused wedlock, within the building of my stony maiden chamber without ceiling, hiding my body in the unroofed tenement of my dark prison...

According to the scholia Priam had built a stone chamber without windows in the form of a pyramid so that Alexandra might be kept in solitary confinement (Sch. Lyc. 350 ὁ γὰρ Πρίαμος λίθινον οἶκον πυραμοειδῆ ἐποίησε καὶ ἐνέβαλεν αὐτὴν)[52]. Darkness reigns in this odd prison, which is not only characterized as λυγαία 'shadowy, murky' but moreover is likened to the deep sea, since ἁλιβδύσασα δέμας may be literally translated as 'she plunged her body into the bottom of the sea' (cf. Sch. Lyc. 351 ἁλυβδῆσαι κυρίως τὸ ἐν ἁλὶ δῦσαι ἤγουν ἐν θαλάσσῃ βυθισθῆναι). Yet the narrator subtly identifies this claustrophobic space with the princess' maiden chamber. The use of the word παρθενών sets the tone for the continuation of the passage, in which the attempted rapes of Alexandra by Apollo and Ajax are narrated (352-363). This παρθενών-like prison highlights the tension between Alexandra's obsession with virginity and her subordination to male dominance. The submission of the maiden to the different personifications of male power, which include not only Priam (the father and king) and Ajax (the villain) but also Apollo himself (the god), is thus symbolically represented by the setting. Given the parallelism between Hellenistic poetry and the Gothic, Alexandra's

51. According to a largely speculative hypothesis put forward by Holzinger (1895) on v. 349; for the opinions expressed on this controversial question, see Neblung (1997) 76 n. 19 and Mazzoldi (2001) 246.

52. The epic poet Triphiodoros, obviously following Lycophron's version of the story, dramatizes the imprisonment of Kassandra by Priam in his *Sack of Troy* (358-443); the differences in Triphiodoros are a) the transposition of the prophetic burst of the Trojan princess from the beginning to the end of the war, i.e. to the moment when the Wooden Horse is accepted into Troy, and b) the escape of Kassandra from the prison by breaking the bars of the door (359-360 διαρρήξασα δ' ὀχῆας/ ἔδραμεν).

prison evokes locations of darkness in Gothic fiction, usually a castle or a locked room, which is "the locus of torment, punishment, mystery, corruption and insanity"[53]. In other words, in emphasizing the prison setting, Lycophron anticipates the association of the dark side of human psychology with the topography of the *edifice*.

A closer look at Alexandra's story reveals that her imprisonment is also a metaphor, that the edifice in which she is locked is more than a dark chamber. It has been argued that in Gothic fiction, "the haunted house is a building, but it can equally well be a lineage, a title, a family"[54]. Lycophron's Alexandra resembles the Gothic female which is trapped in the past of her lineage–in this respect the Trojan family assumes the role of the *haunted house*. Indeed Alexandra bears the burden of ancestral guilt, dating from the founding of Troy on the Hill of Delusion (29). In a series of flashbacks Alexandra laments the fall of her city which is attributed to sins of her own family. Laomedon defrauds Apollo and Poseidon of their reward, after having completed the building of the Trojan walls (521-525). The first sack of the city by Herakles (31-33) is also caused by the hubristic behaviour of Laomedon. Alexandra's fragmented narration focuses on the hideous sea-monster (34 Τρίτωνος κάρχαρος κύων) which Herakles slays: however, the hero is eventually deceived about his reward by Laomedon (34-37, cf. 523 κοιράνωι ψευδωμότηι 'the perjured king')[55]. The second fall of Ilion has a complex background, involving more male members of the Priamid family. First Priam who, advised by Prylis to kill his male offspring and the mother, puts to death his illegitimate son Mounippos and his mother Killa, instead of Paris and Hekabe. This murder, whose victims include a newborn baby and a woman in childbed (224-228, 319-322), bears the mark of a family curse. Then Paris who, in being involved in two disastrous love stories with Oenone (57-60) and Helen (86-89), incarnates the curse which befalls Troy. The past of the accursed family resides within a series of sites, most prominent of which are the tombs of Dardanos (72-73) and Ilos, where Killa and Mounippos were

53. Cavallaro (2002) 27. The prison as a symbol of Gothic aesthetics is thematized in a series of 16 etchings by Giovanni Battista Piranesi (1720-1778), the so-called 'Imaginary Prisons' (*Carceri d' Invenzione*). Unlike Piranesi, Lycophron does not fully exploit the potential of the prison as a nightmarish location; nevertheless, the association of the prison with dark aesthetics is Lycophron's original achievement.

54. Aguirre (1990) 95.

55. The sea-monster is always an ill omen for Troy. For instance, the arrival of Dardanos at the Troad, which is preceded by a biblical deluge on Samothrace and during which whales, dolphins and seals have intercourse with men (81-85), is interpreted as an anomaly of nature anticipating the abduction of Helen by Paris (see Hurst/Kolde [2008] 108-109).

killed and from which Laodike commits suicide (316-322), but also the walls of Laomedon which are not destined to endure the attack of the Greeks (521-525). The most remarkable feature of this 'Gothic' family drama is its internalization by Alexandra. The heroine re-enacts her family tragedy (in which she herself is one of the main protagonists) within her mind. Thus, the original sin committed by the forefathers, the mythical founders Dardanos and Ilos and the scroundel Laomedon, and the close kin, Priam and Paris, haunts her nightmarish vision.

There is nevertheless a dark side in Alexandra's haunted mind. Alexandra's horror is not only oriented towards 'the Other' as represented by the villains of the family and the evil Greeks[56]. Otherness also resides within her own psyche, in her femicidal fears, her obsession with virginity and horror of rape[57]. The darkness inherent in Alexandra's mind and soul is centred around her abhorrence of sexuality[58], which reaches its climax when she rejects the sexual advances of Apollo (352-356):

ἡ τὸν Θοραῖον Πτῷον Ὠρίτην θεὸν
λίπτοντ' ἀλέκτρων ἐκβαλοῦσα δεμνίων,
ὡς δὴ κορείαν ἄφθιτον πεπαμένη
πρὸς γῆρας ἄκρον, Παλλάδος ζηλώμασι
τῆς μισονύμφου

I who drove from my maiden bed the god Thoraios, Lord of Ptoön, Ruler of the Seasons, as one who had taken eternal maidenhood for my portion to uttermost old age, in imitation of her who abhors marriage, Pallas...

The setting and the identity of the rejected lover are crucial to the understanding of the passage. Apollo's attempt to seduce the maiden occurs in what constitutes the core of the θάλαμος–the bed; the god, motivated by desire, as denoted by λίπτοντα, is eventually driven away from the undefiled bed by Alexandra herself (ἀλέκτρων ἐκβαλοῦσα δεμνίων). The scene, if visualized, bears a striking similarity with the *incubus* legend, a literary and artistic theme with religious connotations. According

56. A key feature of Alexandra's interpretation of the Trojan War is its double motivation both by the sinners of the Trojan family *and* the Greeks. Wavering between the supernatural (the family curse) and the real explanation (the harsh realities of war), Alexandra's prophecy expresses an ambiguity, an uncertainty, a blurring of boundaries between rational and irrational, which is inherent in the 'discourse of haunting': on the rhetoric of haunting, see Cavallaro (2002) 65-74.

57. An enlightening approach to the 'dark psyche' of the Gothic is offered by Cavallaro (2002) 48-58.

58. A faint echo of this peculiar sexuality may be found in a late variation of the Kassandra myth, according to which her appearance was an amalgam of feminine and masculine traits: on the ambivalence of Kassandra's sexual identity, see Moreau (1989) 156-158 and Mazzoldi (2001) 30 n. 13.

to this legend a male demon pursues sexual intercourse with a sleeping woman during the night; the scene, visualized as a nightmare, is set in the maiden's bedchamber[59]. Alexandra's struggle against the ἵμερος of Apollo has therefore religious repercussions; in addition to being a virgin, Alexandra also commits a cardinal sin against the god, a hubris, by denying him intercourse[60]–and this is the reason for her punishment (1457): λέκτρων στερηθεὶς ὧν ἐκάλχαινεν τυχεῖν '[because Apollo was] robbed of my bridal bed which he sought to win'[61].

It should be stressed that Alexandra's fixation with virginity is a theme emphasized–perhaps even invented–by the Hellenistic poets, especially Callimachus and Lycophron[62]. Within the context of Archaic literature the encounter with Ajax in the temple of Athena has no sexual undertones and is regarded, by epic, dramatic and lyric poets alike, as a clear case of sacrilege against a supplicant, whereas, in the Hellenistic reworking of the myth, Alexandra is raped by Ajax, a hubris which results in the yearly tribute of the Lokrian maidens to Troy[63]. Through a metaphor combining eroticism and military aggressiveness, Alexandra likens herself to a dove which falls prey to a vulture (357-358 τῆμος βιαίως φάσσα πρὸς τόργου λέχος / γαμφαῖσιν ἅρπαις οἰνὰς ἑλκυσθήσομαι 'in that day, as a dove, to the eyrie of the vulture, in frenzy shall be haled violently in crooked talons')[64]. The atmosphere becomes darker, as Alexandra's troubled mind focuses on an uncanny detail (361-362):

ἣ δ' εἰς τέραμνα δουρατογλύφου στέγης
γλήνας ἄνω στρέψασα χώσεται στρατῷ

And she [Athena] unto the panels of the beam-carved roof shall turn up her eyes and be angry with the host...

---

59. The intensity of this supernatural scene is captured by the early Romantic painter Henry Fuseli in his 1781 painting "The Nightmare". It is tempting to argue that Lycophron intended to suggest a similar image of his Alexandra who, as a dark Romantic heroine *avant la lettre*, is a victim of sexual assault by a supernatural force in her own, dark bedroom. For an analysis of this scene as a depiction of the dark *psyche* of the Gothic, see Cavallaro (2002) 48-49.

60. Intercourse with a god does not violate the status of virginity, but, on the contrary, it consecrates it (Mazzoldi [2001] 16-19).

61. The story of Apollo's failed attempt to rape Kassandra has already been narrated by Aeschylus (*Ag.* 1202-1213). That the punishment of disbelief is a curse isolating Kassandra from her social and family environment is argued by Mazzoldi (2001) 107-112.

62. On the literary sources on Kassandra/Alexandra παρθένος, see Mazzoldi (2001) 27-30.

63. The episode of Ajax is thoroughly discussed by Mazzoldi (2001) 31-61; on the sacrifice of the Lokrian maidens, see Mari (2009) 406-415.

64. Hurst/Kolde (2008) on 357-360.

The eyes, or to be more accurate the eyeballs, that are turned towards the ceiling belong to Athena's statue, the Palladion. According to a fabulous account–the Sch. Lyc. 361 and 363 note that the story is said μυθικῶς as opposed both to ἀλληγορικῶς and to ἀληθῶς–, this statue had fallen from heaven when Ilion was founded as a favourable sign sent by Zeus (cf. 363-364). Alexandra fancies that the Palladion comes alive only to be able to avert its gaze from her rape, which impersonates a protective demon towards the μισόνυμφος maiden.

The tragedy of the female culminates when Alexandra is joined in marriage with Agamemnon against her will, an unfortunate consequence of slavery, which ends with her brutal murdering by Klytaimestra (1108-1119). The murder will take place in a domestic setting, the bath, where Agamemnon will be previously murdered. Yet it is the body of Alexandra that occuppies the centre of this imaginary stage: the corpse, covered with blood, will lie beside the bathtub, hit cruelly by a sword on her back (1112 ῥήξει πλατὺν τένοντα καὶ μετάφρενον 'she will cleave my broad neck-sinew and my back'). Overcome with emotions of jealousy[65], Klytaimestra exults over the mutilated body of her victim (1113-1115):

καὶ πᾶν λακίζουσ᾽ ἐν φοναῖς ψυχρὸν δέμας
δράκαινα διψὰς κἀπιβᾶσ᾽ ἐπ᾽ αὐχένος
πλήσει γέμοντα θυμὸν ἀγρίας χολῆς

And, sand-viper as she is, will rend all my cold body in blood and set her foot on my neck and glut her laden soul of bitter bile...

Once Alexandra visualizes the moment of her own death, by placing the female body at the core of a horror scene, the prophetic vision becomes a nightmare scenario involving the self. Thus, the unattainable ideal of virginity results, in all three cases of Alexandra's would-be lovers, namely Apollo, Ajax and Agamemnon, into the doom of disbelief, rape and death.

However, the implications exceed the limits of the self, and extend to the family, the city of Troy, the Greeks and the future generations. Once virginity is denied to Alexandra, she becomes a plague for the Greeks (365-366): ἑνὸς δὲ λώβης ἀντί, μυρίων τέκνων/ Ἑλλὰς στενάξει πᾶσα τοὺς κενοὺς τάφους 'and for the sin of one man all Hellas shall mourn the empty tombs of ten thousand children'. Her dark marriage becomes a synonym of Hades, as she confesses in verses 411-412 οὑμὸς

---

65. Through δύσζηλος ἀστέμβακτα τιμωρουμένη 'taking relentless vengeance in evil jealousy' (1117) Lycophron subtly alludes to sexual passion as the reason behind Klytaimestra's vengeance, a 'Romantic' explanation introduced into the myth of the Atreids by Euripides (El. 1030-1038); cf. Hurst/Kolde (2008) on 1117.

ἔσται κἀχερουσίαν πάρα / ῥηγμῖνα δαρὸν ἐστεναγμένος γάμος 'even by the shore of Acheron my bridal shall long be mourned'. Once deified, Alexandra becomes the symbol of perverse femininity. Her worshippers, young maidens who seek to escape marriage, acquire the form of terrifying Erinyes and witches (1136-1138), whereas those who wish to get married will either be stoned to death or condemned to serve in the temple of Athena throughout their entire lifetime (1141-1173). Alexandra is no more a victim but an avenger, as her deviant sexuality marks the beginning of the vicious circle of violence and death[66].

Lycophron foregrounds subjectiveness, the 'I' and the 'not-I', in situating Otherness within his heroine's mind. Unlike Aeschylus who in the *Agamemnon* renders Kassandra the mouthpiece of Apollo, Lycophron eschews the direct reference to the god as the immediate inspirer by projecting his heroine's inner fears upon her prophetic speech. Alexandra's madness reflects the crisis of her inner self, 'the distorted and the distorting mind' in view of the tragic events of the future[67]. The alienation of the self from the self is stressed by the use of the highly 'alienating' language used by Lycophron. Lycophron suggests a transition from the marvellous to the uncanny, implying a turning point which finds its analogy in the Gothic[68]:

> The demonic ceased to be a supernatural category and developed into a much more equivocal notion, suggesting that alienation, metamorphosis, doubling, transformation of the subject, were expressions of unconscious desire, and were not 'accounted for' as reflections or manifestations of supernatural or magical interventions.

Alexandra is not just shown to act under the authority of a supernatural power when she prophesies: she is split between the dark influence of Apollo, the mourning for family and homeland, and her inner obsessions and delusions. She views myth and history through her unconscious, her female identity and Trojan ideology, her death and sex drive. Although she confronts many ghosts –Priam, Apollo, Ajax, Agamemnon, the Trojan

66. For a brilliant analysis of Alexandra in comparison to other feminine figures of the poem from the viewpoint of her disturbed sexuality, see Mari (2009) 437-440. According to this analysis women in the *Alexandra* fall roughly into the following categories: the adulteress (Helen, Klytaimestra, Meda, Penelope), the devourer of men, the nymphomaniac, those who have a clandestine affair (Helen, Killa, Laodike) and the unfortunate lover (Oenone).

67. This is a distinctive characteristic of Gothic horror, as pointed out by Jackson (1981) 24: "From Gothic fiction onwards, there is a gradual transition from the marvellous to the uncanny–the history of the survival of Gothic horror is one of progressive internalization and recognition of fears as generated by the self".

68. Jackson (1981) 62.

ancestors, the Greeks–, the reader eventually becomes aware that Gothic Otherness resides, after all, within her own psyche. Lycophron suggests this by internalizing her drama at the closing of the poem–*so much she spake, and then sped back and went within her prison, but in her heart she wailed her latest Siren song, like some Mimallon of Claros or babbler of Melancraera, Neso's daughter, or Phician monster, mouthing darkly her perplexed words*.

This is what I have called the 'demons' of Alexandra.

II.2. Visions of darkness

> To an anomalous species of terror I found him a bounden slave. "I shall perish," said he, "I must perish in this deplorable folly. Thus, thus, and not otherwise, shall I be lost. I dread the events of the future, not in themselves, but in their results. I shudder at the thought of any, even the most trivial, incident, which may operate upon this intolerable agitation of soul. I have, indeed, no abhorrence of danger, except in its absolute effect–in terror. In this unnerved–in this pitiable condition–I feel that the period will sooner or later arrive when I must abandon life and reason together, in some struggle with the grim phantasm, FEAR."

> Edgar Allan Poe *The Fall of the House of Usher* (1840)

Roderick Usher in Poe's short story *The Fall of the House of Usher* is tormented, psychologically and physically, by a mysterious family evil. Haunted by 'the grim phantasm' of fear, he sees past, present and future through the lens of his troubled mind. Thus, and despite any objective perception of reality, he anticipates the degeneration of his family and its eventual *fall*–which metaphysically coincides with the collapse of the house, the Gothic edifice in Poe's story. Lycophron casts his heroine, Alexandra, in the same Gothic mould; Alexandra's pathos is, like Usher's, the result of fear for the imminent end. Dominated by premonitions, Alexandra is doomed to watch, through her mind's eye, a series of successive *falls*–of the House of Priam, of Troy, of the Greek heroes. The recurrent theme of these falls, *violent death*, "homicide or suicide that dismembers and tortures permeates through the interwoven stories of men like a destructive hurricane, and triumphs in the squalor of the buried-unburied, in the horror of skulls, in the emptiness of shadows"[69]. *Blood* spills over into the narrative, once the *human body* becomes the theatre of violence. The primal cause of all violence seems to be *sexual passion*, the all-consuming, carnal desire that determines the fate of women and underlies the actions of men. Lust, treason and domestic crime cause *families* to disintegrate, and thence its members are condemned to eternal *strife* and endless *wandering*. Humanity, as seen through Alexandra's negative perspective, is hopeless and degenerate, a victim of *moral decay*: "the man that emerges from the world of the *Alexandra* is the paradigm of the antihero, contentious, obdurate and treacherous, who has lost, alongside the shine of the epic hero, the inner profundity of the tragic protagonist."[70]

---

69. Gigante Lanzara (2000) 24.
70. Gigante Lanzara (2000) 22.

An atmosphere of horror, which originates from tragedy[71], dominates the monologue of Alexandra. Alexandra, as a narrator in a state of ecstatic trance, is overcome by the flow of oncoming images; she sometimes "evokes the eerie sense that she is addressing herself to her own vision and a series of figures seen within it"[72]. So, despite the fact that the macro-narrative of the Trojan War forms the underlying structure of the *Alexandra*, and also that the messenger re-arranges the speech in linear order, Lycophron communicates the idea that Alexandra follows the mechanism of free association in her monologue. Long stories are condensed into micro-narratives, which are in turn perceived in a succession of expressionist images, the agents of the actions remain enigmatically anonymous, the language used is ambiguous and obscure, and there is a rapid, associative transition from one narrative to the next–not much unlike the stream-of-consciousness device used by modern novelists[73]. In more ways than one the reader is urged to enter Alexandra's mind and explore her subconscious in that her speech resembles "the associative discourse that is the object of psychoanalysis"[74].

What I wish to demonstrate is that Alexandra offers dark versions of well-known stories. Given that Alexandra resembles a Gothic heroine, in her fear and despair, her insanity and isolation, in one word: her encounter with the Other, it is easy to explain why darkness looms large in her monologue[75]. In highlighting the thematics of darkness, I will show that these stories convey a sense of the eerie and the uncanny which sometimes verges on the grotesque. To this aim, I will review under this dark perspective the micro-narratives of Alexandra's monologue by focusing on their plots, settings and characters.

The first part of the monologue, until verse 364, is dedicated to the misfortunes of Troy and the Priamids. Past and future sacks of Troy involve evil males, who, to some extent, fall into the category of the damned Romantic hero–the *homme fatal*. Its origins may be traced back

71. See e.g. Cusset (2002-2003) and Hurst/Kolde (2008) xxv-xxxvi. There is however a tendency to trace some thematic and stylistic choices made by Lycophron back to comedy; for a list of 30 fairytale motifs with a comic undertone, see Holzinger (1895) 32. Hurst (2009) points out some 'sparks of light' as obvious exceptions in the dark and obscure mood of the *Alexandra*.

72. This enhances the ghost-like effect of her vision, see Lowe (2004) 311.

73. As Fusillo (1984) 509 rightly points out "the macro-narrative is continually interrupted by other lines of the story, which are interconnected with each other through a net of free association, implicit in the enigmatic character of the oracular style and particularly bold due to the animosity and *pathos* of the speaking character."

74. Fusillo/Hurst/Paduano (1991) 48.

75. Gigante Lanzara (2000) 21-24 labels the uniqueness of Alexandra's narration *poetics of excess*.

to Milton's Satan, who is a mixture of beauty and evil, someone ardent and sorrowful, "the perfect type of masculine beauty" according to Baudelaire[76]. The *homme fatal* is a rebel, an outcast or an exile, a scroundel and an adventurer, who takes pleasure in exercising violence, a figure of mysterious origin and unearthly grandeur, bearing the guilt of an old crime, a victim of his own (sexual) passion, with a predisposition towards melancholy or despair, an antihero who possesses dark qualities instead of heroic virtue[77]. Undoubtedly this parallelism has its limitations. First of all, Lycophron does not depict fully-fledged characters but offers minimal portrayals of traditional mythical figures; as a consequence, there is neither psychological depth nor coherence in the brief sketches of his 'characters'. On the other hand, it is almost impossible to find exact analogies between the so-called Byronic hero of Romanticism[78] and the Lycophronian hero of Hellenism, given the different historical, ideological and cultural context that defines these periods and its authors. Still, Lycophron's villains have a Romantic, sometimes a Decadent flavour, as they are both antiheroic and untragic but violent and excessive in their passions, and in a way melancholic, like their 19th century counterparts.

The first villain is Herakles, both a lion and a semi-god, who, by being conceived during a three-night lovemaking (33 τριεσπέρου λέοντος)[79], is bizarre by birth. Herakles represents the archaic form of violence, as his battles against the beasts suggest. The sea monster sent by Poseidon to destroy Troy and the princess Hesione unexpectedly devours the hero himself. The battle takes place in a grotesque setting, the jaws of the leviathan, where Herakles, *a living carver of the monster's liver, being burnt by steam of cauldron on a flameless hearth, shed to ground the bristles of his head* (33-37)[80]. The murdering of another legendary monster, the

---

76. Charles Baudelaire, *Journaux intimes* X: " I do not claim that Joy cannot associate with Beauty, but I say that Joy is one of the most vulgar ornaments, while Melancholy is such an illustrious companion that I can scarcely conceive a type of Beauty without Evil. Obsessed by these ideas, it would be difficult not to conclude that the most perfect type of manly beauty is Satan–in the manner of Milton."

77. For a full analysis of what may be called the Romantic 'metamorphoses of Satan', whose famous examples include, among others, the protagonists of Byron's works, Schedoni of Ann Radcliffe's *The Italian*, Matthew Lewis' *The Monk*, Frollo from Victor Hugo's *The Hunchback of Notre Dame*, Heathcliff from Emily Bronte's *Wuthering Heights*, Dorian Gray and the Phantom of the Opera, see Praz (1970) 55-94.

78. The Byronic hero is exemplified by the life and writings of Lord Byron, on which see Praz (1970) 63-83.

79. The alternative interpretation of τριέσπερος offered by Tzetzes is even darker: Herakles owes this attribute to his three days sojourn in the monster's mouth, which are likened to evenings due to the lack of light (Sch. Lyc. 33).

80. Gigante Lanzara (2000) 191-192 on vv. 31-34 speaks of the "fantastic realism" of the description and the "grotesque effect" of the setting.

Sicilian Skylla–*the savage bitch, the bull-slaying lioness*–, ends as a true horror tale, once her father *restores her again to life by burning her flesh with brands* (47-48)[81]. "Impious violence" and "extreme brutality"[82] characterize the evil acts of Herakles against the members of his family– *the slayer of his children, the one who smote his second mother invulnerable with grievous shaft upon the breast and who in the midst of the racecourse seized in his arms the body of his father in the form of a wrestler* (38-42). His own death strikes an uncanny note, since he, the undead, is slain by a dead man *with swordless guile* (50-51)[83].

After the portrayal of Herakles as a primitive and brutal murderer, the scope of the narration broadens so as to encompass the Romantic theme *par excellence*, love. Love, in its dark associations with eroticism, betrayal and death defines the next fatal man of Troy, Paris. In many respects Lycophron's Paris personifies the dark Romantic hero (86-109): driven by mad passion, he abandons the quiet life of the *boukolos*, he becomes an adventurer and a hunter of women (cf. 109 αἴθων ἐπακτὴρ καγχαλῶν ἀγρεύματι 'a fierce hunter exulting in his capture'). Like a Decadent figure, he is arrogant and immoral with sudden bursts of anger but at the same time a victim of his lust and a man of sorrow (128-143). Lycophron recounts his love affairs with Helen and Oenone, by introducing two themes that came to be considered the cornerstones of Romantic love, namely *dream* and *suicide*[84]–these two stories are narrated by Alexandra in reverse order. The love story of Paris and Oenone stands out as a typical paradigm of Romantic sensibility[85]. Paris betrays his wife, Oenone, for Helen; Oenone, overcome by jealousy, sends her son against Troy; despite being a healer, she refuses to help Paris when he falls wounded by the arrows of Philoktetes (57-64). The end of the story, which concludes with the spectacular suicide of Oenone, *who from the lofty towers casts herself in headlong whirl upon the new slain corpse, and pierced by eager longing for the dead breathes forth her soul on his*

---

81. It should be noted that the return of the Skylla from the dead, her resurrection, is a variation first attested in Lycophron (perhaps his own invention?): see Hurst/Kolde (2008) 100 on v. 45.

82. Hurst/Kolde (2008) 98 on v. 37.

83. A "paradox" story according to Fusillo/Hurst/Paduano (1991) 159 on vv. 50-51; cf. Gigante Lanzara (2000) 195 on vv. 50-51 who describes the story as a "mocking joke".

84. MacAlister (1996) passim on the duo 'dream-suicide' which became the typical subject matter of the Greek novel too.

85. Its novelistic qualities and dark tonality were recognized by Hellenistic and Roman authors who, alongside Lycophron, include Nicander, Parthenius and Ovid: see Sistakou (2008a) 105 and n. 159. The tragic love story of Oenone has also inspired a 19th century Romantic poet, Alfred Tennyson ("Oenone" from *Poems*, 1833).

quivering body (65-68), renders this love story a true example of Romantic tragedy.

Romanticism takes on a darker hue in the narration about Paris and Helen. Paris' liaison with Helen never acquires a realistic dimension as the actual act of lovemaking is a mere hallucination. Paris' ejaculation–suggested by ἐκχέας πόθον 'you poured out your lust' in v. 110 and the metaphor ψαλάξεις εἰς κενὸν νευρᾶς κτύπον 'you shall twang upon your lyre in vain' in v. 139–is the result of a fantasy, *as he shall not see tomorrow's aftermath of love, fondling in empty arms a chill embrace and a dreamland bed*[86]. In this case, the 'villain' is Proteus, *he to whom laughter and tears are alike abhorred*, in putting an *eidolon* in the place of Helen. Paris' doubt as to the real nature of his beloved, his perception of her ghost as animate, his illusonary intercourse capture the essence of the uncanny[87]. When the Trojan prince finally returns to his burnt up fatherland, he weeps with despair (or perhaps terror?) at the sight of Helen's *eidolon* in his arms (141-142 κλαίων δὲ πάτραν τὴν πρὶν ἠθαλωμένην / ἵξῃ χεροῖν εἴδωλον ἠγκαλισμένος)[88]. In a nutshell: the site is Gothic, the mood Romantic, the effect uncanny[89].

The third conqueror of Troy is the most fierce and enigmatic of all, an equal to Schiller's "majestic monster", a Hellenistic forerunner of the Byronic hero–Achilles. Although the literary portrayals of Achilles are numerous and varied from Homer to lyric and tragedy and beyond, none of them denies his heroic stature and grandeur; his depiction either as an effeminate or as an antiheroic and dark figure is probably a Hellenistic achievement[90]. Lycophron contributes much to the image of a passionate

---

86. On the morbid connotations of ψυχρὸν παραγκάλισμα, an allusion to Sophocles' *Antigone* 650, see Hurst/Kolde (2008) 114 on v. 113.

87. On this basic feature of the uncanny, cf. e.g. Jentsch' definition (*On the Psychology of the Uncanny* 1906): "Among all the psychical uncertainties that can become a cause for the uncanny feeling to arise, there is one in particular that is able to develop a fairly regular, powerful and very general effect: namely, doubt as to whether an apparently living being really is animate and, conversely, doubt as to whether a lifeless object may not in fact be animate".

88. On the desperate eroticism of Paris' cold bed, see Gigante Lanzara (2000) 207 on 112-114.

89. It is almost impossible not to recall here the love affair between Nathanael and the doll Olympia from E.T.A. Hoffmann's *Der Sandmann* (1816), the archetypal narrative of the uncanny according to Jentsch and Freud (see above p. 45 n. 148). This is how Hoffmann depicts the uncanny effect of their embrace–not much unlike the description of Lycophron: "Nathanael bent down to Olympia's mouth; icy lips met his burning ones. Just as when, touching her cold hand, he had felt a shudder seize him, the legend of the dead bride flushed suddenly through his mind. But Olympia drew him close to her, and the kiss seemed to warm her lips to life."

90. On the Hellenistic view of Achilles, see Sistakou (2008a) 158-176.

and evil Achilles, who anticipates legendary characters of Romantic literature. His introduction by Alexandra as a *dramatis persona* is striking
in its emphasis upon lovesickness and melancholy. Achilles, the fifth
suitor of Helen, each night lies near sleep and falls into erotic reveries–
*tossing in dreams upon his restless couch her phantom beauty shall
make him waste away* (171-173). The dream renders Achilles the prototype of the Romantic lover[91]. Moreover, the phrase ἐν δὲ δεμνίοις
ἐστροβημένον suggests an illusionary sexual intercourse[92], and it is the
second case within a few verses that making love with Helen's *eidolon*
enhances the uncanny mood of the narrative.

After a digression on the hero's unusual birth and bringing up[93],
Lycophron picks up the thread of his narrative about the sorrows of young
Achilles in love. This is one of the few instances that Lycophron elaborates on an emotion–depression as a result of sexual frustration[94]. The
object of Achilles' desire is now Iphigenia. Emphasis is placed on the
geographical and temporal distance that divides the two lovers. Achilles
gives himself over to despair and melancholy, since *lamenting he shall
pace the Scythian land for some five years yearning for his love* (200-
201). Obsessed by his sexual desire (190 ποθῶν δάμαρτα, 201 ἱμείρων
λέχους), Achilles sails in vain across the sea (186-187 *for Iphigenia her
husband shall search within the Salmydesian Sea*) to dwell on a rocky
island (188-190 *he shall dwell for a long time in the white-crested rock
by the outflowing of the marshy waters of the Celtic stream*). Achilles'
love quest reaches its climax in the next verses (192-194): *and the deep*

    91. This type of dream scene is the hallmark of Romantic sensibility. A salient paral-
lel can be found in Goethe's *The Sorrows of Young Werther* (1787) [from the epistle of
August 21, Book I]: "In vain do I stretch out my arms towards her when I awaken in the
morning from my weary slumbers. In vain do I seek for her at night in my bed, when
some innocent dream has happily deceived me, and placed her near me in the fields, when
I have seized her hand and covered it with countless kisses. And when I feel for her in the
half confusion of sleep, with the happy sense that she is near, tears flow from my
oppressed heart; and, bereft of all comfort, I weep over my future woes" [Transl. R.D.
Boylan].
    92. Tzetzes' comment illustrates the point (Sch. Lyc. 171): τουτέστι ποιήσει αὐτὸν
ἐν ὀνείροις φάντασμα αὐτῆς βλέποντα κινεῖσθαι καὶ ταλαιπωρεῖσθαι ὥσπερ
συνουσιάζοντα αὐτῇ.
    93. The likening of Achilles to the monster Typhon produces a horrifying effect, cf.
Gigante Lanzara (2000) 220 on vv. 177-179. Lycophron also alludes to the version
according to which Thetis had attempted to render Achilles immortal by burning him in
fire (177-179 *the Pelasgian Typhon, out of seven sons consumed in the flame alone escaping the fiery ashes*), a fantasy story fully narrated by Apollonius *Arg.* 4.866-879 (see
Sistakou [2000] 95-97).
    94. The depressive type of lovesickness, as opposed to the manic type, is rare in
ancient literature (its earliest example is Theocritus), being rather a cliché of Medieval and
modern literature as Toohey (2004) 59-103 convincingly argues.

lonely course upon the beach within the wash of the waves shall bear the name of the bridegroom, who mourns his fate and his empty seafaring and her that vanished and was changed to an old witch... The image of the lovesick hero who in floods of tears takes his long and lonely course by the sea within a desolate landscape unites Romantic sensitivity with a sublime feeling of nature[95]. Isolation and the overwhelming feelings of futility and loss–implied by the idea of the κενὴ ναυκληρία and the image of the ἄφαντος Iphigenia–highlight the melancholy state he is in; the passage of time–the five years spent in Scythia in search of Iphigenia–adds up to the creation of the same effect. Yet the Romantic mood becomes darker, and sublimity conveys a sense of horror, once the focus shifts from the infatuated lover to the beloved. Iphigenia has been transformed into a Γραῖα, probably a synonym for 'Witch'. Her bizarre metamorphosis into an old woman adds an uncanny twist to Achilles' romance. Being a lady of darkness, an equal to Hekate, Iphigenia allows blood to flood into the narrative (196-199): *beside the sacrificial vessels and the lustral water and the bowl of Hades bubbling from the depths with flame, which the dark lady blows who cooks the flesh of dead men in her pot.* Carnal violence becomes a spectacle, and the gory scene (the first of many more to come) evokes modern-day splatter movies[96].

Achilles, a lover and a villain, is an ambiguous figure, attractive and repulsive at the same time. Even before arriving at the Troad, on the island of Tenedos, the fatal man experiences the sensation of violent killing in the murdering of Kyknos and his sons. *And now two children are slain together with their father who is smitten on the collar-bone with the*

---

95. The contact of man with wild nature–the rocks, the mountains, the vast sea, the desert–is a source of sublimity for the wandering, lonely man. The idea (along with the image of he Creator) is fully developed by Romanticism; cf. e.g. a famous example from Goethe's *The Sorrows of Young Werther* (from the epistle of August 18, Book I): "From the inaccessible mountains, across the desert which no mortal foot has trod, far as the confines of the unknown ocean, breathes the spirit of the eternal Creator; and every atom to which he has given existence finds favour in his sight. Ah, how often at that time has the flight of a bird, soaring above my head, inspired me with the desire of being transported to the shores of the immeasurable waters, there to quaff the pleasures of life from the foaming goblet of the Infinite, and to partake, if but for a moment even, with the confined powers of my soul, the beatitude of that Creator who accomplishes all things in himself, and through himself!" [Transl. R.D. Boylan]. On solitude, the sublime and the aesthetics of individuation in Romantic thought and art, see Ferguson (1992).

96. The portrayal of Iphigenia as καρατόμος (quite different from Iphigenia the victim in Euripides) reflects, in the view of Mari (2009) 435-437, Lycophron's taste for the *grand guignol* and its black humour. On the macabre and grotesque undertones of the scene, see Fusillo/Hurst/Paduano (1991) 178 on vv. 195-199 and Gigante Lanzara (2000) 225-226 on vv. 195-199.

hard millstone, an omen of good beginning (232-233)[97]. His next victim is Mnemon, 'The Reminder', who fails to warn Achilles against killing the son of Apollo and is therefore cruelly executed–*and he, erred in forgetfulness, shall die upon his face, his breast pierced by the sword* (240-242). This minor figure is one of the darkest inventions of Lycophron, since he personifies Achilles' memory, and his death symbolically suggests the killing of the hero's conscience[98]. Thus alienated from his self, Achilles becomes the Evil One for the Trojans[99]. In a vision of horror, during which Alexandra views the destruction of Troy, character and setting interact with each other to produce a pathetic and sublime effect (243-257)[100]. *And now Myrina groans the sea-shores... And now Ares, the dancer, fires the land, with his conch leading the chant of blood... And all the land lies ravaged before my eyes... And in my ears seems a voice of lamentation from the tower tops reaching to the windless seats of air, with groaning women and rending of robes, awaiting sorrow upon sorrow*[101]. Achilles presents himself as a supernatural creature–upon going ashore he causes the underground streams of the Troad to gush forth!–, a diabolical figure, likened successively to a fiery wolf, to the dancing Ares[102] and to a black, carnivorous falcon. His total amorality is made evident when, after *bloodying Hektor's body with talon and beak* and *staining the land with gore*, he becomes a 'Trafficker of

97. The meaning of the phrase is ironic, since the murder of Kyknos and his children functions as a "macabre prelude" to the murder of Protesilaos (Hurst/Kolde [2008] 135-136 on vv. 232-235).

98. Cf. Sistakou (2008a) 148.

99. Although the context is different, some parallels between the majestic, albeit horrifying, Achilles and Milton's Satan, a figure bursting with heroic energy, may be drawn; for this portrayal of Milton's Satan, see Praz (1970) 55-59.

100. The pathetic element (*pathos*) may be brilliantly combined with the sublime, especially in scenes of epic grandeur like the ones pertaining to the theomachies of Homer, according to Longinus (8.2-9.15). For detailed readings of the scene in the same direction, see esp. Gigante Lanzara (2000) 235-243 and Hurst/Kolde (2008) 136-143.

101. This scene of the apocalypse may also be read against the background of Milton's portrayal of Hell (*Paradise Lost* 1.56-67): "Round he [e.g. Satan] throws his baleful eyes/ that witnessed huge affliction and dismay/ mixed with obdurate pride and steadfast hate/ at once as far as angels ken he views/ the dismal situation waste and wild,/ a dungeon horrible, on all sides round/ as one great furnace flamed, yet from those flames/ no light, but rather darkness visible/ served only to discover sights of woe,/ regions of sorrow, doleful shades, where peace/ and rest can never dwell, hope never comes/ that comes to all."

102. Despite the fact that Ares is probably used here as a metonymy for war (Hurst/Kolde [2008] 137 on v. 249), it cannot be excluded that it also suggests the frenzy of Achilles on the battlefield; it is no coincidence that his son, Neoptolemos, was the inventor of the πυρρίχη, the dance of war. Cf. Fusillo/Hurst/Paduano (1991) 185 on vv. 249-250.

Corpses', and exchanges the body of Hektor for solid gold (269-272)[103]. The narrative takes an unexpected turn, once in this infernal situation Achilles falls victim to his own violence: at the end, the dead hero is contained in a golden urn, an image that gives an uncanny, almost grotesque, finale to Achilles' dark story.

The nightmare of Alexandra, rendered as pathetic discourse, culminates with the visualization of the bloodshed of her family. The narration focuses on the strange background leading each family member to death, sometimes providing also an uncanny *tableau* of the actual dying moment. For the death of the youngest Priamid, Troilos, Alexandra employs *topoi*, mostly associated with homoereotic contexts in Hellenistic literature. Troilos, assuming the role of god Eros, shoots his arrows into Achilles' heart and catches him in his nets. These metaphors are soon inversed, and the reader is eventually made aware that the most powerful blows are not that of love but of death (309-313)[104]. *You did smite with fiery charm of shafts the fierce dragon and seize for a little loveless while in unescapable noose him that was smitten, thyself unwounded by your victim: with severed neck you shall splash over your father's altar-tomb with blood.* Lycophron masterly directs the reader's expectations from the wounds of eros to the fatal blow of the sword, and the final snapshot of the beheaded corpse of Troilos is gothicized by being set against the background of a tomb dripping with blood[105].

Two daughters of Priam face an equally horrible, albeit obscure, death. Laodike is mysteriously swallowed by a chasm of the earth upon the sack of Troy by the Greeks (316-322). *One the earth that gave her birth opening wide shall swallow utterly in yawning depths, as she sees the approaching feet of lamentable doom, there where her ancestor's grove is, and where the groundling heifer of secret bridal lies in one tomb with her whelp, ere ever it drew the sweet milk and ere she cleansed her with fresh water from the soilure of childbed.* If the passage is read in the light of λεύσσουσαν 'as she sees' or, perhaps better, 'in order to be able to

---

103. This is the first of the three instances where Achilles is deliberately marked as an antihero; the second is his disguise as a young virgin and the third his fear of facing Hektor (Hurst/Kolde [2008] 141-142). On Lycophron's negative portrayal of Achilles, see Sistakou (2008a) 164-167.

104. Gigante Lanzara (2000) 244-245 on vv. 307-313 describes the scene in terms of its murky passion, morbidity and grotesque wordplay; cf. Hurst/Kolde (2008) 145 on vv. 309-312.

105. Although commentators agree that τύμβος πατρός in v. 313 denotes the altar of Apollo (e.g. Hurst/Kolde [2008] 145 on v. 313), I think that the use of this noun here is deliberately chosen so as to reflect the Gothic effect of the scene. This is the first of many tomb-settings to come (e.g. vv. 335, 401); for a similar effect, see v. 613.

see' in v. 318, then the whole scene evokes the dark theme of live burial. Laodike is already under ground while watching the Greeks devastating Troy, whereas it is not suggested that she is actually dead[106]–on the contrary, when Alexandra alludes for the second time to Laodike's tragic end, it is expressly said that *she was alive when she descended to Hades* (497 ἡ ζῶσ᾽ ἐς ῞Αιδην ἵξεται καταιβάτις)[107]. Yet it is the setting that evokes chilling Gothic narratives, since the earth opens unexpectedly into a deep gorge only to bring an ancestral curse into light and to reveal a deadly family secret[108]. The site is ancient and dark, consisting of tombs set within the woods: the one belongs to Laodike's ancestor, Ilos or Laomedon[109]; the other to the murdered mistress of Priam and her newborn baby. Laodike is thus swallowed by the same soil that covers the family's murky past, responding, in a way, to the call of her ancestors[110].

Unlike the story of Laodike, which is of Hellenistic origin, Polyxena is celebrated in Attic tragedy for becoming the bride of the dead Achilles. The scene of Polyxena's death is inspired by the tragic *topos* of marriage as a sacrificial rite (323 ὠμὰ νυμφεῖα and γαμηλίους θυηλάς)[111]. However, Lycophron takes a step further by projecting another famous marriage to death, the sacrifice of Iphigenia, on the ritual murdering of Polyxena; within this context, the entire scene of slaughtering, introduced by the ambiguous ἥν (326), may refer either to the death of Polyxena and/or

106. The exact nature of Laodike's death is all the more incomprehensive, because she is grotesquely likened to a tree which returns to the soil that nurtured it (316-317 τὴν μὲν αὐτόπρεμνον [lit. root and branch] ἡ τοκὰς κόνις/ χανοῦσα κευθμῷ χείσεται διασφάγος).

107. For an interpretation of the scene, see Gigante Lanzara (2000) 280 on vv. 497-498.

108. I totally agree with Gigante Lanzara (2000) 247 on vv. 319-321 who speaks of a "morbid, pathetic and horrific" scene whose dark setting indicates that death lurks behind the apparently innocent family ties of the Priamids.

109. Although recent commentators agree, following Holzinger (1895) 216 on v. 319, that the ἅλμα πάππου (319) does not necessarily imply Laomedon, I think that the evocation of the hubristic king, the cause of a family curse, would be far more suitable here than a reference to the mythical founder of Troy.

110. There is a some resemblance between this scene and the closing of Edgar Allan Poe's *The Fall of the House of Usher* (1839), where the young family members are doomed to be buried under their accursed house–they are literally swallowed by a deep fissure on the edifice that opens wide: "While I gazed, this fissure rapidly widened–there came a fierce breath of the whirlwind–the entire orb of the satellite burst at once upon my sight–my brain reeled as I saw the mighty walls rushing asunder–there was a long tumultuous shouting sound like the voice of a thousand waters–and the deep and dank tarn at my feet closed sullenly and silently over the fragments of the *House of Usher*."

111. Seaford (1987) is essential for the understanding of tragic marriage as a ritual of death. For further discussion of sacrificial violence, and its affinities with tragic imagery and discourse, see below pp. 163 and 190.

to that of Iphigenia[112]. The connection between the stories of Achilles' two dead brides is even more complex than this, because the executioner of Polyxena, Neoptolemos, is modelled upon Iphigenia's 'double' –not the victimized maiden but the dark priestess of Tauris (323-329). *And thee to cruel bridal and marriage sacrifice the sullen lion, child of Iphis, shall lead, imitating his dark mother's lustrations; over the deep pail the dread butcherly dragon shall cut thy throat, as it were a garlanded heifer, and slay thee with the thrice-descended sword of Kandaon, shedding for the wolves the blood of the first oath-sacrifice.* Somewhere between the splatter and the Gothic, the scene records a ritual murder which is performed with an object bearing the mark of its antiquity and mysterious origin, the sword of Kandaon. During the last phase of this process, the victim's blood is collected into a cauldron for the wolves to taste it. In other words: the wolves-Acheans thirst after the blood of the butchered Polyxena, an image suggesting that the analogy with modern-day werewolves stories is almost appropriate here[113].

The extreme violence exercised against the Priamids culminates with the killing of Hekabe and Priam. Building on the rich subtext of Greek tragedy and the epic tradition, Lycophron captures the moment of their agonizing death in two expressionist sketches. Hekabe, before being transformed into a dog of Hekate, is visualized as wearing a garb made of stones (333 κύπασσις χερμάδων), an image conveying the strange impression of the lapidation of the aged queen; whereas Priam, lying dead on the 'tomb of Agamemnon', beautifies the monument with his greyish lock of hair (336 κρηπῖδα πηγῷ νέρθε καλλυνεῖ πλόκῳ). In these passages the uncanny effect of 'beauty in death' takes the place of gory descriptions.

The body, strangely attractive even in death, becomes thence the theatre of violence, not of killing but of rape, in the last episode of the fall of the Priamids. It is Alexandra's own body (δέμας) that will suffer the consequences of the Greek hubris as personified by Ajax the Lokrian.

The next section, the *Nostoi* (365-1225), is dedicated to the returns of the Greeks. Despite its associative structure and obscure antiquarianism,

112. Hurst/Kolde (2008) 147 on v. 326. The correspondences between the sacrifice of Polyxena and that of Iphigenia are highlighted by Ciampa (2004).

113. The dark effect of the wolves licking and vomitting the blood of their victims is a simile used in the *Iliad* (16.156-159) to denote the Myrmidons, and Lycophron is definitely alluding to it here (Hurst/Kolde [2008] 148 on v. 329). It should be noted though that the comparison of the warriors, and in particular of the Achaeans, with blood-hungry predators occurs often in the *Iliad*, see Neal (2006) 23-27. On the symbol of the wolf, see also below pp. 178-179.

recurrent ideas, story patterns and common settings function as connective threads throughout this section. Alexandra raped by Ajax–this is the central axis around which the agitated speech of the Trojan heroine will hence evolve. This 'love that is no love' is an uncanny passion sent from the Erinyes (403-407). Therefore, the villain is punished, as his erotic excess, his carnal desire for Alexandra, has only one natural consequence–death (387-402). The hubris of Ajax triggers the fall of the Greeks and their *oikoi*, whose account is framed by some of the most dark pages of the *Alexandra*. First, the shipwrecks of the Greeks off Euboea near the Capherean rocks, whose dramatic description matches the tragic subtext of Aeschylus' *Persians* (373-386), as well as the 'grotesque' narration of the drowning of Ajax near the Gyrean Rocks (387-402)[114]. Then, the pathetic *tomb discourse* of verses 365-416, developed into one of the megathemes as the poem progresses[115]. Finally, the incorporation of a plethora of dark motifs–futile wanderings, bloody strife, fatal women and agonizing deaths of the returning heroes–into the genre of *ktisis*-poetry[116]. These stories develop against the backdrop of the entire Mediterranean region, and incorporate many features from folkore and travellers' tales into their narratives; nevertheless, the *house*, both as a setting and as a metaphor pertaining to the family, plays a key role in many of them.

Already verse 415-416 οἱ δ᾽ ἐπὶ ξένης ξένοι/ παῶν ἔρημοι δεξιώσονται τάφους 'while others, strangers in a strange land, bereft of relatives, shall receive their graves' anticipates a basic motif of the stories to come, the family in decay. The 'associative logic' underlying Alexandra's discourse, the psychology behind the words, is manifest in a series of narratives, beginning with the one about Phoenix (421-423). *He of all men was most hated by his father, who pierced the lamps of his eyes and made him blind, when he entered the dove's bastard bed*: in this case, lust–as suggested by the metaphor of the dove–[117]triggers the hatred of the father towards the son and is compensated by physical violence. Fratricide is another dark facet of the decaying family, as the paradigm of Eteokles and Polyneikes some verses later clearly indicates (437-438). *The maiden*

114. On the tragic and epic models of the shipwreck description, among which two lost tragedies on Nauplios by Sophocles (?) and Lycophron himself, see Gigante Lanzara (2000) 258 on vv. 377-378 and Hurst/Kolde (2008) 156 on vv. 381-386. Comic discourse is used in these scenes of death to produce a grotesque effect, see e.g. Gigante Lanzara (2000) 259-263.

115. For an analysis of the *tomb discourse* in the *Alexandra*, see below pp. 188-190.

116. The fullest account of this section from the viewpoint of *ktisis*-poetry is offered by Gigante Lanzara (2003).

117. Cf. Sch. Lyc. 87 τρήρωνα δὲ αὐτὴν [i.e. Helen] λέγει διὰ τὸ λαγνόν.

daughters of Night armed them that were the brothers of their own father
for the lust of doom dealt by mutual hands: sons and brothers of their
father, the Theban princes fall dead because of the dark intervention of
the Erinyes. The rage of the father and the theme of fratricide are interwoven in the extensive narrative about Teukros (447-469). Teukros is a
tragic hero who is falsely accused by his father Telamon for the death of
his brother Ajax and is therefore driven into exile. Alexandra implicitly
attributes the curse following him to the mere fact that he is the son of
Telamon and Hesione, thus suggesting that the reason behind his evil fate
is his monstrous Greek-Trojan breed[118]. Another story about degenerate
family affairs that end up in bloodshed is that of the Dioskouroi (544-
568). The conflict between Kastor and Pollux and their cousins, Idas and
Lynkeus, over the Leukippids acquires the dimension of a massacre. *And*
first in words they shall tear each other with their teeth... One with his
spear of cornel-wood shall slay one of the pair... The other in turn with
his lance shall pierce the side of the ox and bring him to the ground...
And bronze spear and thunderbolts together shall crush the bulls...[119] The
setting is domestic at the very beginning, a house where a wedding feast
takes place; then, the duel is transferred outdoors, and a fatal strike causes
the tomb of Aphareus to shake (559 ἄγαλμα πήλας τῶν Ἀμυκλαίων
τάφων); Heaven and Hades provide the background to the grand finale
of the bloody combat, whose protagonists are condemned to be eternally
undead (566 ἀφθίτους τε καὶ φθιτούς).

Family strife ending in violence is a leitmotif that resonates throughout the section of the *Nostoi* and culminates, as I will demonstrate below,
with the Fall of the House of the Atreids. Yet another thread holding
these numerous micro-narratives together is the element of the fantastic.
Some stories such as the violent death by a monster (470-478, 486-493)
or the encounter of the Greeks with Anios and his miraculous daughters
(569-583) bring the marvellous to the fore. On the other hand, the returns
of the Greeks offer ample opportunity to Lycophron not only to explore
the fairytale dimension of the *nostos* but also to recast it in darker tones.
Having originated from folklore and fairytale and designed as exotic
travel fantasies, these narratives, by definition, abound with supernaturalism. But in Lycophron the supernatural is not just a literary motif

118. Gigante Lanzara (2003) 16-17 aptly describes Teukros as the prototype of the
Lycophronean hero–a bastard, the ruin of his race, who bears the burden of a family
tragedy and is unjustly driven away from his fatherland.

119. The mortal duel between the Dioskouroi and the Apharids is narrated in a lengthy
digression, based on Archaic models, primarily Pindar, on which see Gigante Lanzara
(2000) 288-294.

inherited from the epic tradition; the dark side of mythology is aestheti-
cized, it becomes an aesthetic category in itself[120]. In what follows, I will
discuss how various forms of the supernatural create an atmosphere of
darkness in the *Nostoi* section of the *Alexandra*.

A striking example of supernaturalism is the story of Diomedes' wan-
derings (592-632)[121]. In contrast to the version known from the *Odyssey*,
Lycophron's Diomedes is less fortunate, because his return to homeland
Argos is prevented by a family plot. Just like Klytaimestra, his wife
Aigialeia plans to slaughter the hero who seeks refuge in the temple of
Hera. Doomed to wander ceaselessly in the West, Diomedes' comrades
are consequently transformed into seabirds. This metamorphosis introduces the grotesque into the narrative, all the more so because the com-
rades-birds retain their human habits along with their bird-like appearance. But the tone becomes uncanny when Diomedes takes the form of
a colossal statue situated at the entrance of the port of Daunia (625-629):
*with pillars which no man shall boast to have moved even a little by his
might, for as on wings they shall come back again, traversing with track-
less steps the terraces.* The 'hero-as-statue' with its supernatural features
has the power to render the curse put by Diomedes on the newfoundland
–*he shall cast an effectual curse upon the fields, that they may never
send up the opulent corn-ear of Demeter*–both terrifying and eternal[122].

The fantastic takes new directions in the subsequent return narratives.
The condensed version of the *Odyssey* forms the core of the *Nostoi* section, a choice that has been justly seen as a tribute to the Homeric epic
(648-819)[123]. A plethora of Odyssean episodes is incorporated into Alexandra's monologue, although here, as anywhere else in this prophetic
speech, the narration follows the 'associative' logic[124]. As expected,
emphasis is placed upon the fantastic and horrific settings of the voyage
narrative, with the *Nekyia*, in its dark remake, forming an essential part of
it. The beginning of the narration finds Odysseus and his men among the

120. The association between the aesthetics of the fantastic and Romanticism is
explored by Siebers (1984) 19-56.
121. On the unusual version followed by Lycophron, see Gigante Lanzara (2000) 297-
303.
122. Future attempts to break the curse will end in the live burial of the Aetolians, see
vv. 1056-1066.
123. Schade (1999) is the essential guide to Lycophron's *Odyssey*.
124. For example Schade (1999) 39-40 structures Lycophron's *Odyssee* according to
geographical criteria (by distinguishing those parts that pertain to the 'Italian' i.e. Western
adventures of the hero from the rest). I think that an attempt to re-arrange the facts chronologically (especially by placing the *Apologoi* section before the episode of Kalypso and
Nausikaa, and by ordering the death of Odysseus after the killing of the suitors) is also
visible in Lycophron.

Lotophagoi and the Skylla, then in the cave of Polyphemos and with the Laistrygonians. Soon it becomes clear that the Odyssean bestiary (668-675) serves as a prelude to the Underworld scene that will follow immediately afterwards. *What Charybdis shall not eat of his dead? What half-maiden Fury-hound? What barren nightingale, slayer of the Centaurs, Aetolian or Curetid, shall not with her varied melody tempt them to waste away through fasting from food? What beast-moulding dragoness shall he not behold, mixing drugs with meal, and beast-shaped doom?*

Charybdis, Skylla, the Sirens and Kirke, all impersonate the dark powers of the female as the harbinger of doom. Charybdis is the woman who devours the male–and Skylla too[125]; the image of the banquet, suggested both by δαιταλωμένους (654) and δαίσεται (668), highlights the perversion of their action. Skylla is a hybrid creature, μιξόθηρος (650) and μιξοπάρθενος (669), a beast and a virgin in the same body. The transformation of the Skylla from a genuine mythological monster, as in the Homeric text, into a teratoid woman, is, if not totally Lycophron's innovation, definitely a choice in line with the emerging Aestheticism of his era[126]. The female is also dangerous in her ability to appeal to the senses. This is the case of the Sirens who despite their strange deformity–they appear to be a degenerate species of the nightingale, cf. 663 ἁρπυιογούνων ἀηδόνων–cause men to melt down their flesh (σάρκας) under the spell of their song. Kirke takes the portrayal of the 'woman-as-beast' a step further: being herself depicted as a dragoness, the bizarre and murderous serpentine woman, she is also an expert in producing strange mutants (θηρόπλαστος) and causing death by metamorphosis (κῆρα κνωπόμορφον)[127].

The centrepiece of this little *Odyssey*, however, is the story about the death of the Sirens (712-737). This is the oldest account of such an event–their death is not recorded in the *Odyssey* nor hinted at in Apollonius' *Argonautica*–, and Lycophron certainly draws on local traditions of Southern Italy for this aitiological digression[128]. And although folklore

125. Provided that ὠμόσιτα δαιταλωμένους 'devoured raw' (654) can only allude to the episode of Skylla (Hurst/Kolde [2008] 193 on v. 654).

126. Schade (1999) 59-61 on v. 650 clearly supports this argument.

127. The Kirke passage owes its grotesque effect to the combination of tragic imagery (for the metaphor of the serpent Lycophron draws upon the *Oresteia*, cf. Klytaimestra as δράκαινα in v. 1114) with vocabulary drawn from comedy and also science; see Schade (1999) 80-82 on vv. 673-675 and Gigante Lanzara (2000) 312-313 on vv. 673-675.

128. Probably Timaios, cf. Schade (1999) 124-126. The only reference to the death of the Sirens, but as a consequence of the passage of the Argonauts and not of Odysseus, may be found in the late antiquity poem attributed to Orpheus, the *Argonautica* (1287-1290).

(exemplified by the establishment of the torch race in honour of Parthenope) plays a major role in the formation of the episode, it is the very
dark aesthetics of this story that has primarily attracted Lycophron as
literary material. The Sirens are the archetype of the *femme fatale*, and
as such represent *the* deadly threat against men. Is it then possible, as
Lycophron claims, that the roles between male and female are reversed,
and that these bloodthirsty predators might become themselves the victims of their seductive charms? Odysseus will be the cause of their
death, indirectly though, since it is the Sirens that will commit suicide
(714-716): *self-hurled from the cliff's top they dive with their wings into
the Tyrrhenian sea, where the bitter thread spun by the Fates shall draw
them*[129]. Even though the text is not clear about the motivation of the
suicide, melancholy as a result of the Sirens' defeat seems to be the most
plausible reason behind their self-destruction[130].

Lycophron's Sirens are less of a mythological monster than the ones
found in the *Odyssey*. Each of them acquires a name (a striking exception within a poem famous for the namelessness of its characters!),
a body and a tomb; each of them succumbs to the ultimate form of
female passion–suicide. Female death, the predecessor of the Romantic
theme of the death of the beautiful woman, is at the centre of attention.
Three snapshots, involving the body within a water setting, capture the
aesthetic moment of these deaths. Parthenope's corpse is washed up on
the beach near the river Glanis; Leukosia is cast near the mouth of the
rivers Is and Laris, to haunt forever the rock that bears her name; the
third one, Ligeia (this is the first mention of a name that will thence
become a hallmark of Aestheticism)[131], is almost breathing, half alive,
when she comes ashore at Terina[132]. There, at the site of their tombs,

129. Αὐτοκτόνοις may also mean 'killing each other', but it is not plausible within
this context: the problem is discussed in detail by Schade (1999) 127 on v. 714.

130. Sadness as the motive for the suicide of the Sirens can be traced in the text that
actually imitates the Lycophronian passage, the Orphic *Argonautica* (1287-1288) δεινὰ
δ' ἀνεστονάχησαν, ἐπεὶ πότμος ἤϊε λυγρός/ μοιριδίου θανάτοιο. There is, however,
a significant parallel, the suicide of the Sphinx once Oedipus solves the riddle.

131. The name Ligeia is also attested by [Aristot.] *Mir.* 839a.33; in previous literature
it is only used as an attribute of the Sirens (Hes. fr. 150.33 M.-W. Σειρήνων τε λίγε]ι[α]γ
[ὄπ]α κλύον, cf. A.R. *Arg.* 4.892-893 ἔνθα λίγειαι/ Σειρῆνες). As a name of a
sea-nymph *Ligea* occurs once in Virgil *G.* 4.336. Milton restores Ligea as a Siren (*Comus*
880 'and fair Ligea's golden comb...'); Edgar Allan Poe probably had Milton's verse in
mind when he wrote the short story *Ligeia* on the death of a beautiful and mysterious
woman.

132. Κλύδωνα χελλύσσουσα in v. 727 conveys the image of a swimmer spitting out
sea water (Sch. Lyc. 727 χελλύσσουσα· καὶ γὰρ οἱ νηχόμενοι τοῖς χείλεσιν ὠθοῦσι
τὸ ὕδωρ); Schade (1999) 136 on v. 727 thinks rather of a dead body from whose mouth
sea water flows.

they will be venerated as goddesses. Thus idolized, the Hellenistic Sirens become the symbols of femininity, mystery and death[133].

Once Odysseus' *nostos* reaches its climax in Ithaca, and Alexandra recounts the dark end of the hero (a result of his poisonous family relations with Kirke, the fatal woman, and Telegonos), the focus turns to the exotic journeying of Menelaos in quest for Helen (820-876). The search for the adulterous wife, a phantom (φάσμα) as rumour has it–*yearning for the winged phantom that fled to the sky*–, takes him to the ends of the earth[134]. From Troy to Cilicia, from Cyprus to Phoenicia and Aithiopia, from Egypt to Italy and Sicily, Menelaos finds himself in a universe of marvel, metamorphosis and grotesqueness, and acquires the function of a spectator within it[135]. Somewhere between the identifiable real world and a land of fable, Menelaos views supernatural creatures, such as Typhon and Proteus, and observes mythological sites. He sees the old lady who, upon betraying Aphrodite's hiding place, is turned into stone (826 γραῦν μαρμαρουμένην); the city where Myrrha, overcome with desire for her father, is transformed into a tree (828-830); then the tomb of Adonis who is killed by a wild boar sent by the Muses (831-833); and the place where Perseus, willing to liberate Andromeda, is swallowed by a terrible sea monster and cuts its entrails *from within* (834-841)–an obvious parallel to the gory story of Herakles, Hesione and the leviathan narrated earlier by Alexandra.

Yet it is Medusa, the avatar of Romantic darkness, that forms the core of Menelaos' fantastic travelogue (842-846). *The harvester who delivered the stony-eyed weasel, whose children sprang from her neck, of her pains in birth of horse and man. Fashioning men as statues from top to toe he shall envelop them in stone–he that stole the lamp of his three wandering guides.* Medusa is evoked here in her theriomorphic essence. She is the monster with the paralyzing gaze (843 μαρμαρῶπις); also a peculiar type of γαλῆ, able to give birth from her neck to such demonic

133. The Sirens, as well as the mermaids and the ondines of European folkore, become a favourite subject matter of Romantic and Decadence aesthetics; on 'The Torrid Wail of the Sirens' see Dijkstra (1986) 258-271.

134. It is not clear whether Lycophron, in using φάσμα instead of εἴδωλον (as Euripides does), emphasizes the spectral form of Helen as a ghost, coming from the realm of fantasy or the dead, thus reinforcing the idea that she is a product of a bad dream or a deadly vision: this is the usual meaning of φάσμα in tragedy (Aesch. *Ag.* 274; Soph. *El.* 644; Eur. *Alk.* 1127, *IT* 42). It should be noted that in two other passages (vv. 142 and 173), Lycophron uses εἴδωλον for Helen within a sexual context. On the Stesichorean version of Helen's *eidolon* followed by Lycophron here, see Holzinger (1895) 289-290 on v. 822.

135. An impression conveyed by the repetition of (ἐπό)ψεται (825, 828, 834, 847); the fact that from verse 852 on it is replaced by ἥξει probably marks a transition to the less 'fantastic' part of Menelaos' journey.

creatures as Chrysaor and Pegasos, who may only be liberated from the pains of childbirth through her butchering by the sickle. But the truly mysterious figure of the passage is Perseus, the bloody harvester who stars in a dark tale. He first steals the single eye of the three Old Women, the Γραῖαι, to force them tell him how he would kill Medusa. Once he succeeds in his heroic enterprise, Perseus becomes himself the 'eye' of the Medusa. The uncanny gift of a vision which fossilizes the beholder, the petrifying eye, is transferred from the female monster to her male slaughterer. Perseus appears to be obsessed with the idea of dominance through taking control over the vision of others. He is the Medusa incarnate, prolonging in this manner her horror for an eternity[136].

Demons and monsters found on the way can be easily multiplied; uncanny situations, strange apparitions, even metamorphosis tales have their share in this strange world, somewhere between the imaginary and the historical[137]. There is also much drama, family drama, unfolding before Alexandra's startled eyes. Odysseus will be murdered by his son Telegonos (795-798) and Idomeneus' entire family will be slaughtered by the very same man to whom he had entrusted it, the villainous Leukos (1214-1225). Yet it is the wifes that represent the most dire threat against the Greek heroes. The coda of the *Nostoi* section is introduced by reference to Nauplios, the leader who persuades the women to plot against their returning husbands (1093-1095): *with such craft shall the hedgehog ruin their homes and mislead the housekeeping hens embittered against the cocks*[138]. Indeed, Greek females–as opposed to Trojan women–are lustful, treacherous and murderous. This is a traditional way to view Helen but quite original as regards the archetype of female faith, Penelope. In an even

---

136. Perseus' monstrous ability to turn men into statues (845 ἀγαλματώσας) is seen as an advantage, though in a much lighter vein, by the misanthrope Knemon in Menander's *Dyscolus* (153-159). –From another viewpoint, to steal the vision of others is considered the ultimate symbol of the uncanny by Sigmund Freud in his essay *The Uncanny*. Could the uncanny hero *par excellence*, the Sandman (and his double, the repulsive Coppelius/Coppola, who steals and sells human eyes) from E.T.A. Hoffmann's short story provide a parallel for the interpretation of Lycophron's weird Perseus figure? On the analysis of this work by Freud, cf. above p. 45.

137. It is striking that two metamorphosis stories are narrated consecutively towards the end of Alexandra's prophecy: the grotesque story of Erysichthon and his daughter Mestra (1391-1396) and the comic one of Midas whom Apollo punished by giving him donkey ears (1401-1403). These are preceded by the fairytale narration about the foundation of Miletos by Neleus (for the two apparitions encountered by Neleus, see vv. 1379-1387).

138. That the adultery of the Greek women was planned by Nauplios is also attested by Tzetzes (Sch. Lyc. 386): [Ναύπλιος] παραπλέων λοιπὸν τὰς χώρας τὰς Ἑλληνίδας παρεσκεύασε τὰς τῶν Ἑλλήνων γυναῖκας μοιχευθῆναι, Κλυταιμνήστραν τὴν τοῦ Ἀγαμέμνονος Αἰγίσθῳ, Αἰγιάλειαν τὴν Διομήδους Σθενέλῳ, Μήδαν δὲ τὴν Ἰδομενέως Λεύκῳ.

more extreme manner than polygamous Helen (πεντάλεκτρος), Penelope is straightforwardly portrayed as a whore (βασσάρα) engaged in sexual orgies in the palace of Odysseus (771-773): *that whore, primly coquetting, will make empty his halls, on feasts out-pouring the poor wretch's wealth*[139]. Diomedes' wife, Aigialeia, driven by lust, will set up an ambush to kill Diomedes–but her plans will be cancelled at the end due to divine intervention (610-614). Idomeneus' wife too, Meda, will be seduced by Leukos, and then murdered by him along with her children (1220-1223).

Situated at the heart of the house all these women embody, in their perversity, the decay and eventual death of the *oikos*. This is perfectly exemplified by the archetypal narrative about the Fall of the House of the Atreids (1099-1122). In this miniature of Aeschylus' *Agamemnon*, Lycophron zooms in on the scene of Agamemnon's and Kassandra's assassination by Klytaimestra[140]. The crime takes place in the bathroom–to be more accurate: in the bath–which, along with the bedroom, is the emblem of domestic intimacy[141]. The human body, humiliated, violated and mutilated, is the focal point within this setting. Trapped by a net (or perhaps a χιτών without openings for the hands and neck)[142], Agamemnon is a creature agonizing in its death throes[143]. *One at the bath while he seeks for the difficult exits of the mesh about his neck, entangled in a net, shall search with blind hands the fringed stitching.* No more a bull as in Aeschylus, Lycophron's Agamemnon is likened to a lamb brutally slaughtered: he is struck by the axe in the middle of the skull and his brains splatter all over the tripods and the basin of the blazing bathroom. *And diving under the hot covering of the bath he shall sprinkle with his brains tripod and basin, when he is smitten in the midst of the skull with the well-sharpened axe.* But the sorrowful ghost of the king wanders for a while, before descending to Hades, letting his melancholic gaze to wander for one last time around the sad home. *His piteous ghost shall wing its way to Taenarus, having looked on the bitter housekeeping of the lioness.*

139. Cf. Sch. Lyc. 772 καὶ Δοῦρις δὲ ἐν τῷ περὶ Ἀγαθοκλέους μάχλον φησὶ τὴν Πηνελόπην καὶ συνελθοῦσαν πᾶσι τοῖς μνηστῆρσι γεννῆσαι τὸν τραγοσκελῆ Πᾶνα. See Schade (1999) 174-176 on vv. 771-773.
140. For a detailed analysis of the scene in the light of tragedy, see Durbec (2006b); cf. Neblung (1997) 84-86.
141. Lycophron follows here Aeschylus' version, whereas Homer has the murder of Agamemnon taking place during a banquet with Aigisthos (*Od.* 4.534-535). The horror of the scene is further heightened by the fact that this is an unheroic death, not occurring on the battlefield but within a domestic environment (Durbec [2006b] 7).
142. Sch. Lyc. 1099 ἐπειδὴ δέδωκεν αὐτῷ ἡ Κλυταιμνήστρα χιτῶνα ἔξοδον μὴ ἔχοντα οὔτε τῶν χειρῶν οὔτε τοῦ τραχήλου.
143. Lycophron eschews mentioning the simile of the fish as Aeschylus does (1382-1383): ἄπειρον ἀμφίβληστρον, ὥσπερ ἰχθύων,/ περιστιχίζω.

Without any narrative pause the scene of murder repeats itself, yet darker than before. The *grand guignol* effect is heightened by more naturalistic horror. In a bathroom full of blood and gore, Alexandra will not be only murdered but also dismembered by Klytaimestra. A frozen corpse covered with blood (ἐν φοναῖς ψυχρὸν δέμας) is first cut into pieces (συντεθραυσμένη) and then butchered (πᾶν λακίζουσα) with anatomical accuracy (ῥήξει πλατὺν τένοντα καὶ μετάφρενον)[144]. Now, the ghost of Alexandra is not just melancholic; in a crisis of horror, this restless phantom, on its flight to Hades, calls upon Agamemnon. *And calling on my master and husband, who hears no more, I shall follow his track on wings of the wind.* It is not only Alexandra that undergoes this uncanny transformation. The murderess, initially called a lioness (a metaphor in accordance with the animal imagery of the passage)[145], has now become a bloodthirsty female serpent, a δράκαινα διψάς and an ἔχιδνα[146].

As violence escalates and the family drama of the Atreids reaches its climax, light is shed upon the motives behind this dark story. Klytaimestra's reason is darkened by her morbid passion, the frenzy of jealousy. Thereupon, she is visualized triumphing over the cold corpse of her supposed rival. *A sand-viper as she is, will rend all my cold body in blood and set her foot on my neck and glut her laden soul of bitter bile, taking relentless vengeance on me in evil jealousy, as if I were a stolen bride and not a spear-won prize.* The House of the Atreids dies ingloriously, by the bloody sword of Orestes, succumbing to its own family curse (1122 κακὸν μίασμ' ἔμφυλον ἀλθαίνων κακῷ 'with evil healing the evil pollution of his race')[147]. But the Erinyes will never be satisfied: metamorphosed into worshippers of the deified Alexandra, they will forever thirst for revenge (1137-1140).

This is the moment when Alexandra, having visualized her gory death, the mutilation of her corpse, her agonizing ghost, and her return for eternal revenge, has seen the blackest vision of all.

---

144. On the rhetoric of the passage, which in some ways evokes the dismemberment of Pentheus in the *Bacchae*, see Durbec (2006b) 11-12.

145. For the "parable of the lion in the house", alluding to Agamemnon and Klytaimestra in the *Agamemnon*, see Knox (1979) 27-38.

146. Nicander offers a detailed description of this deadly serpent (*Ther.* 124-127 and 334-342). Cf. Gigante Lanzara (2000) 386-387 on vv. 1114-1115.

147. The hereditary curse of the Atreids can be dated back to Atreus and Thyestes (Hurst/Kolde [2008] 271 on v. 1122).

II.3. The discourse of darkness

I am come of a race noted for vigor of fancy and ardor of passion. Men have called me mad; but the question is not yet settled, whether madness is or is not the loftiest intelligence–whether much that is glorious–whether all that is profound–does not spring from disease of thought–from moods of mind exalted at the expense of the general intellect. They who dream by day are cognizant of many things which escape those who dream only by night. In their grey visions they obtain glimpses of eternity, and thrill, in awakening, to find that they have been upon the verge of the great secret. In snatches, they learn something of the wisdom which is of good, and more of the mere knowledge which is of evil. They penetrate, however, rudderless or compassless into the vast ocean of the 'light ineffable', and again, like the adventures of the Nubian geographer, 'agressi sunt mare tenebrarum, quid in eo esset exploraturi.'

Edgar Allan Poe *Eleonora* (1842)

The narrator in Poe's short story *Eleonora* offers a fine portrayal of a man who has visions of what lies beyond reality: although others consider him mad, he is aware that he is endowed with the loftiest intelligence; combining imagination and passion, the visionary glimpses into enternity; to him great secrets are revealed–albeit in snatches and fragments. But the most extraordinary feature in this portrayal is the ability of the visionary to explore darkness and eventually bring evil into light. This dark twist of the man of vision holds the key to the interpretation of Alexandra as a prophetess of evil in Lycophron's poem. In effect, being established as a σκοτεινὸν ποίημα since antiquity, the *Alexandra* has always puzzled its readers with its darkness or, to be exact in stylistic terms, with its obscurity[148]. Darkness is programmatically announced in the frame, since king Priam and the servant are invited to address Alexandra's enigmas through the obscure paths of riddle which are wrapped in darkness (12 τὰν σκότῳ). It is impressive that the metaphor of the enigmatic speech as a dense network of paths through which it is very difficult to find your way (10-11 δυσφάτους αἰνιγμάτων οἴμας), and which may prove to be a dead end (14 λοξῶν ἐς διεξόδους ἐπῶν), in other words: the metaphor of the

---

148. The expression derives from the *Suda* (s.v. Λυκόφρων). Berra (2009) offers a thorough survey of ancient testimonies (and modern views) about the nature, content and style of the *obscuritas lycophronea*. On obscurity as a stylistic device in the *Alexandra*, see especially Ciani (1973). Another poet who has a reputation for being obscure is Pindar, on whose darkness see Hamilton (2003).

labyrinth, is typical of Gothic darkness[149]. Narrators and narratees lose their way in the labyrinth of dark words and dark stories; Alexandra is trapped in the maze of her riddling utterance which is continued in eternity (1466 ἑλικτὰ κωτίλλουσα δυσφράστως ἔπη, cf. Sch. Lyc. ad loc. ἑλικτὰ τὰ συνεστραμμένα καὶ σκοτεινὰ διὰ τοὺς χρησμούς). Thus visualized, darkness asserts itself throughout the 1474 verses of Alexandra's nightmare narration. After having detected the dark content of the prophecies in the previous chapter, I will now explore darkness from both a verbal and a conceptual aspect. Before closing my discussion of the *Alexandra* as a dark tragedy, I will finally focus on the *tomb discourse*, the emblem of Gothic darkness, which resonates throughout the entire poem.

To narrate in *riddles*–this is the most distinctive trope which boosts darkness in the *Alexandra*. The word αἴνιγμα figures prominently as a technical term already in verse 10, whereas opening and closure clearly mark Alexandra as the new Sphinx (vv. 7, 1465)[150]. Theoretically, the riddle may be construed as an intellectual pun (usually assuming the form of a deceptive question and a 'right' answer to it), based on grammatical and lexical ambiguity, whose sophistication aims at highlighting the contradictions of language and cognition[151]. The strategies employed by Lycophron include the literary devices of the riddle, among others the extensive use of metaphor, wordplay and the paradox, while the multiple layers of diction and *recherché* vocabulary contribute to the effect of 'masked expression'[152]; all this amounts to an extreme condensation of information within the nexus of riddles and puzzles which paraphrase the myth of the Trojan war. Undoubtedly Lycophron exploits the dynamics of enigmatic discourse, and the reader is constantly asked to decipher the narrative enigmas of the *Alexandra* by recourse to arcane knowledge (εὐμαθὴς τρίβος in verse 11 is a metatextual comment addressed to the reader rather than the characters of the poem). It is worth asking, though, whether the only 'mystery' in the *Alexandra* is of intellectual nature and moreover

149. The word λαβύρινθος obliquely refers to the *Alexandra* of Lycophron in *AP*. 9.191.1-3 οὐκ ἂν ἐν ἡμετέροισι πολυγνάμπτοις λαβυρίνθοις/ ῥηιδίως προμόλοις ἐς φάος, αἴ κε τύχης·/ τοίους γὰρ Πριαμὶς Κασάνδρη φοίβασε μύθους.
150. On the metatextual allusions of the messenger in prologue and epilogue, which, by extension, function as 'reading instructions', see the illuminating article by Looijenga (2009).
151. *NPEPP* s.v. "Riddle".
152. The Alexandrians had a penchant for enigmatic expression, see Hurst/Kolde (2008) xxv-xxxvi.

whether its 'solution' concerns solely the learned reader[153]. In other words, does the *Alexandra* create an atmosphere of suspense and hesitation also for the *dramatis personae*? Moreover, does it convey a sense of horror and, if so, by what means?

Alexandra's prophecy is at the same time a revelation of the future–a transcendental experience as analyzed in the first chapter–and a concealment of truth. The paradox is that whereas the heroine professes to tell the truth (1456 θεσφάτων πρόμαντιν ἀψευδῆ φρόνιν, 1458 θήσει δ᾽ ἀληθῆ), and so does the servant (1 λέξω τὰ πάντα νητρεκῶς, 1471 ἐτητύμως), the very same stories narrated are covered by the mist of falsehood due to the intervention of Apollo (1455 ψευδηγόροις φήμαισιν ἐγχρίσας ἔπη); by consequence both the servant and king Priam remain in ignorance about the hidden 'message' of the prophecy. Yet as characters they are overwhelmed by the dark utterances of Alexandra. The angst of the king for the future of Troy is suggested by his decision to imprison the domestic Sibyl, and the ambiguous closure of the servant's report–*may God turn her prophecies to fairer issue*–reflects the agony experienced. However, this is the second time that Priam is misled by the wrong reading of a prophecy. Lycophron subtly evokes the same story pattern that underlies the entire *Alexandra* in vv. 224-228, when Priam misinterprets the dream of Hekabe: *would that my father had not spurned the nightly terrors of the oracle of Aisakos and that for the sake of my fatherland he had made away with Hekabe and Paris in one doom, ashing their bodies with Lemnian fire. So had not such a flood of woes overwhelmed the land.* The prophetic dream in the past, as the prophecy of darkness in the present, couples the mystery of the enigma with a sense of horror (cf. 225 χρησμῶν νυκτίφοιτα δείματα).

One way of producing suspense is by withholding narrative information. Among the various techniques employed to this aim, the systematic elimination of proper names, which normally function as identity markers in any kind of text, is the cornerstone of Lycophronian suspense[154]. By erasing the names of the characters of the most celebrated Greek myth, Lycophron ironically juxtaposes the anticipation of a known story with the obscurity of a prophetic speech-act. Nameless characters, gradually

153. Cusset (2001d) 71 accurately describes the effect of this obscurity on the reader: "In reading the *Alexandra*, the reader is constantly in an unstable position as regards comprehension: he hesitates incessantly and cannot stop contemplating. He alternates between the shadow of the mystery to come and the light of the *fait accompli*, between the obscure and true knowledge of the prophecy and the clear albeit multiple significance of poetry."

154. On the features and function of the naming strategies of the *Alexandra*, see Sistakou (2009b).

identified by reference to their attributes, and foremost their actions and sufferings, mark a transition from epic certainty into Gothic hesitation. Moreover, namelessness is dramatically significant for the depiction of Alexandra's psyche. Like other Gothic heroines, Alexandra experiences an inner conflict between reason and madness and a confrontation with forms of Otherness around her. Alienation and instability, ignorance and uncertainty cause the subject to dissolve and eventually to be dragged into the abyss of the unnameable. The dark effect of this procedure has been aptly described as *Gothic sublime*, whose basic features are summarized as follows[155]:

> The Gothic sublime is, in many ways, the voice from the crypt that questions the power of reason...and destabilizes the centrality of the ego...It is the voice that wishes to write the narrative of the gap, the infinitesimal lapse, in which reason for the moment gives way to chaos as the mind embraces the full terror of the sublime. The Gothic narrative is to be located at that indeterminate moment of the near-abyss where the subject says, I am my own abyss, and is faced with a horrifying image of its own lack of totality.

Lycophron's bizarre naming strategies definitely enhance this effect[156].

"*Who*, and *what* are you?" is a question with which the addressees of the *Alexandra* are constantly faced because it reflects not only the obscure identity of the characters but primarily the ontological mystery surrounding them. Lycophron responds to this question by making extensive use of metonymy[157]. Animal vocabulary functions as a substitute for anthroponyms to such an extent that the *Alexandra* has been justly likened to an "imaginary menagerie"[158]. All sorts of animals— wild and domestic, birds and reptiles—are included in this strange menagerie; all characters acquire different animal identities, and the same animal metonymy may attach to more than one character[159].

---

155. Mishra (1994) 38.

156. For a definition of the Gothic sublime, and its juxtaposition with Burke's Romantic conception of the sublime as an aesthetic category, see Morris (1985) and Mishra (1994) 19-43; more recently Smith (2000) 11-37 for a study of the Gothic sublime, especially as viewed through the lens of psychoanalysis.

157. By *metonymy* (and by making a subtle distinction from *metaphor*) I wish to imply not only the rhetorical trope but also the association of this figure of speech with psychoanalysis, and in particular the operation of the unconscious termed by Freud as 'displacement'. On this definition of metonymy, that found its most complex formulation in Lacan, see e.g. Ruegg (1979).

158. By Cusset (2001d) 64 who gives a fascinating account of the animal metaphors and their poetic function in the *Alexandra*.

159. Cusset (2001d) speaks of a constant evolution of the animal metaphors and their complementary use when designating the same character.

Herakles is a lion (33), Helen a dove and a hound (87), Paris a wolf
(102), Achilles a wolf (246) and an eagle (260), Neoptolemos a lion
(324), Alexandra a dove (357), Ajax a vulture (358), Aigialeia a bitch
(612), Penelope a fox (771), Klytaimestra a viper (1114)...[160] Animal
metonymies (and not merely similes as found in the Homeric epics)
within the context of Kassandra's prophetic vision are first found in
Aeschylus' *Agamemnon*–for example when the love triangle of
Klytaimestra, Aigisthos and Agamemnon is described by Kassandra as
δίπους λέαινα συγκοιμωμένη λύκῳ,/ λέοντος εὐγενοῦς ἀπουσίᾳ
(*Ag.* 1258-1259)[161]. And although we should not underestimate the
influence of this model text upon the discourse of the *Alexandra*, its
employment by Lycophron on a larger scale aims at creating a far more
dramatic effect than it has in Aeschylus.

Since metonymy, as a linguistic trope seen from a psychoanalytic perspective, stems from the unconscious, it may be inferred that Alexandra's bestiary voices her deepest emotions and thoughts about the
Trojan War and its dark protagonists. In other words, Lycophron conveys
the impression that the 'masked expression' used by Alexandra gushes
forth directly from her unconscious. Thus, in making Alexandra substitute common names (i.e. words denoting animals) for proper names,
Lycophron does not merely point to the 'ego' of the speaking subject. He
also brings the dark part of Alexandra's personality, the 'id', to the fore.
And since the material is known and familiar (the *dramatis personae* of
the Trojan War myth), it is only its formulation (the metonymic discourse) that renders it unknown and unfamiliar. This brings my analysis
once more to the notion of the *uncanny* in the *Alexandra*. It is tempting
to view the duality namelessness/animal metonymy under the perspective of the uncanny[162]:

> The uncanny is a crisis of the proper: it entails a disturbance of what is
> proper (from the Latin *proprius*: 'own'), a disturbance of the very idea of
> personal or private property including the properness of proper names,
> one's so-called 'own' name, but also the proper names of others, of places,
> institutions and events. It is a crisis of the natural, touching upon everything
> that one might have thought was 'part of nature': one's own nature, human
> nature, the nature of reality and the world.

160. For a systematic classification of Lycophron's animals, see Lambin (2005) 236-
241.
161. On intertextuality as the poetic reason behind Lycophron's penchant for the animal metonymies, see the arguments provided by Cusset (2001d) 63-65, on the basis of his
view of the *Alexandra* as a "hypertrophic reworking of Kassandra's prophecy in the
Agamemnon".
162. Royle (2003) 1.

To question the nature and properties of the subject by eliminating its name–this may be a key to approaching the uncanny discourse of the *Alexandra*.

In this metonymic system the uncanny assumes its most intense expression in the recurring image of the wolf[163]. It is no coincidence that ancient scholarship has attempted to explain Λυκόφρων (which Hesychius glosses as δεινόφρων) as a speaking name capturing not only the mysterious obscurity of the *Alexandra* but in particular the obsession with the wolf as an image of darkness within the poem[164]. Alexandra has visions of wolves-Achaeans coming against her family and homeland. They thirst for the blood of Polyxena (329) and sack her city (525). Achilles is *the fiery wolf who shall leap the swift leap of his Pelasgian foot upon the last beach and cause the clear spring to gush from the sand, opening fountains that hitherto were hidden* (245-248): after this miraculous entry, the entire Troad surrenders to war and destruction. Wolves are lustful and evil, as in the case of Paris (102, 147) and Theseus (147) who abduct and rape Helen[165]. The Dioskouroi are also called 'wolves of Attica' (504) because they kidnap Aethra in revenge for the abduction of Helen: according to Tzetzes' rendering of the periphrasis they are οἱ τῶν Ἀθηναίων ἅρπαγες καὶ πορθηταὶ (Sch. Lyc. 504). Military and sexual violence, the most prominent paradigms of male dominion, are always exercised by wolves, the Phoenicians (1293) and the Argonauts (1309), to whom women and lands are an easy prey. There is even a passing allusion to the myth of Lykaon, the mythical king of Arcadia, who is the first paradigm of the werewolf in ancient literature (in v. 481 where the Arcadians are described as λυκαινόμορφοι Νυκτίμου κρεανόμοι 'the wolf-shaped devourers of the flesh of Nyktimos')[166]. Wildness, rapacity, voracity, bloodthirstiness, and meta-

163. As also of the related image of the dog: the *Alexandra* constantly fluctuates "entre chien et loup", as Cusset (2001d) convincingly argues.

164. According to a comment preserved by Tzetzes (Sch. Lyc. Γένος Λυκόφρονος) ὡς καὶ τὸ διὰ τί λέγεται Λυκόφρων; διὰ τὸ αἰνιγματωδῶς καὶ πανούργως λέγειν· καὶ γὰρ οἱ λύκοι πανοῦργοι, on which see Berra (2009) 288-289; cf. Cusset (2001d) 62-63 on Lycophron as a pseudonym.

165. The wolf is a gendered symbol throughout the *Alexandra*, which stresses the predatory nature of the male: see Gigante Lanzara (2000) 204 on vv. 102-103.

166. Cf. Ov. *Met.* 1.163-239. A quite different story about a werewolf is the legacy according to which the demon/ghost of Hero in Temesa which was cast out by Euthymos of Lokroi had also the form of the wolf (as vividly described by Pausanias 6.6.11 δαίμων ὅντινα ἐξέβαλεν ὁ Εὔθυμος, χρόαν τε δεινῶς μέλας καὶ τὸ εἶδος ἅπαν ἐς τὰ μάλιστα φοβερός, λύκου δὲ ἀμπίσχετο δέρμα ἐσθῆτα). Interestingly enough the story of Heros was part of Callimachus *Aitia* (fr. 98-99 Pf.). On the tradition of the werewolves in ancient literature, see Buxton (1987) 67-74 and Ogden (2009) 175-178.

phorically wickedness, craftiness, perversity, violence and lust, typify the
symbol of the wolf, which gives a concrete form to instincts, drives and
impulses from the unconscious[167]. If the wolf represents the 'return of
the repressed', an object of fear and desire at the same time for the
speaking subject, then the discourse of Alexandra embodies the essence
of Gothic aesthetics[168].

Other Gothic concepts, the *abject* and the *grotesque*, may also serve
as keys for the interpretation of animal metonymies in the *Alexandra*[169].
The abject may be defined as anything ambiguous, in-between and composite, an entity with a disturbed identity, any phenomenon simultaneously repulsive and fascinating that resists human understanding[170]. The
deformed discourse of Lycophron not only marks a return from the
human to the animalistic state of being (a state evoking the abject) but
moreover demonstates that the boundaries between taxonomies may
easily be breached. This feature can be illustrated in the long sequence
concerning the successive abductions of women, the primal cause of violence between Europe and Asia (1291-1321): the Phoenicians are first
called sailor hounds (ναῦται κύνες) and then wolves (φορτηγοί λύκοι)
who carry off a bride (κόρην) with the eyes of an cow (βοῶπιν) and the
looks of a maiden bull (ταυροπάρθενον); reacting to this, the Cretan
boars (Κουρῆτες κάπροι) abduct a heifer (πόριν) and carry her of with
a ship that has the form of a bull (ἐν ταυρομόρφῳ) to become a bride
of a general (δάμαρτα στρατηλάτῃ); subsequently an army of thieves
(κλῶπα στρατόν) was sent to involve in a battle with mice (σμίνθοισι
δηρίσοντας) and then a pack of wolves (Ἄτρακας λύκους), the Argonauts, carried off the crow (κεραῗδα), the killer of her brother and children, with the help of a garullous jay (λάληθρον κίσσαν), the Argo...
The shifting between categories and identities becomes more obvious in

167. The evidence from Greek literature about all these negative features of the wolf
is collected by Buxton (1987) 60-67; Buxton (p. 75) attributes the fascination of folklore
and popular literature with wolves and werewolves to the fact that they call into question
the boundaries between human and bestial nature.

168. Although the wolf is a typical symbol of literature (e.g. the wolf, along with the
lion and the leopard, symbolizes sin in Dante's *Inferno* following the negative connotations of animal imagery in the Bible, whereas there are more than 50 occurrences of the
wolf metonymy/metaphor in Shakespeare), some of its manifestations are especially relevant to the Gothic and the uncanny: its centrality in fairytale fantasies like the Little Red
Riding Hood; the adaptation of the symbol in Angela Carter's short story "The Company
of Wolves"; the Gothic legacy of the werewolf; Count Dracula appearing in the form of
the wolf in Bram Stocker's novel *Dracula* (esp. ch. 8-11). In the field of psychoanalysis,
the famous case of the Wolf-Man, who was treated by Freud for his notorious wolf nightmares.

169. On these concepts, see Hurley (2007).

170. For the definition of the abject I follow Kristeva (1982).

the paradigm of Paris who becomes successively a firebrand with wings, a sailor, a wolf and a hunter in his quest for Helen, a dove, a hound and a heifer (86-109). In this large-scale masquerade (if one is allowed to use the metaphor for the entire *Alexandra*) the dramatic characters display the same qualities with the creatures they are costumed as.

Until now we have observed how this bizarre bestiary relates to the uncanny, which in turn enhances the effect of darkness. All the same, some of the uncanny admixtures of different species in the alienated world–or rather the alienated language–of Alexandra communicate a sense of comic and not horror to the reader, are whimsical rather than terrifying: this happens when the discourse of darkness verges on the grotesque[171]. An illuminating example is the exploitation of fish imagery. Since a substantial part of the Trojan myth legacy is a sea voyage narrative, it is only natural that the realm of the sea contributes to the imagery and symbolism used by Alexandra[172]. But in most cases the 'rhetoric of the sea' surprises with its exaggeration and paradoxality.

Sea and fish imagery creates a particularly grotesque atmosphere in the opening scene of the *Nostoi* section. The returning heroes are ship-wrecked as a consequence of Ajax' hubris: the scene resonates with the groans of the dead (an impressive paradox!) who are rendered as *tunnies with the suture of their heads split upon the frying pan whom the down-rushing thunderbolt shall taste as they perish in the murk of the night* (377-383)[173]. To visualize this dense metaphor Tzetzes gives the following explanation: the Greeks are called 'tuna' and the flat rocks 'frying pans' upon which the heads of the victims are crushed so as to acquire deep furrows (Sch. Lyc. 381 ἠλοκισμένων δὲ ἠυλακισμένων, διεφθαρμένων ὥστε δοκεῖν αὐτοὺς αὔλακας ἔχειν κατακοπέντας ὑπὸ τῶν πετρῶν). "Lycophron's grim joke seems to be that the torn bodies are thrown on the rocks as sliced tunnies are thrown in a frying pan, and then the lightning tastes the bodies as a dish that has been

---

171. Hurst (2009) calls 'sparks of light' (*étincelles dans l'ombre*) the tendency of Lycophron–who is an expert in Greek comedy–to lighten up the atmosphere of darkness and sadness in the *Alexandra* by using expressions that communicate a luminous impression of life; cf. Kolde (2009) who discusses parody and irony in the *Alexandra* and also the brief overview of the grotesque in Lycophron by Gigante Lanzara (2000) 37-38.

172. Sea in the *Alexandra* is intimately connected with the myth of the great flood. In effect, the flood, in the case of both Dardanos and Ajax, symbolizes the end of the old order and the birth of a new world: on the point see the brilliant article by Durbec (forthcoming).

173. The tuna metaphor is modelled upon Aesch. *Pers.* 424, yet with an obvious tone of parody in Lycophron, see Gigante Lanzara (2000) on vv. 381-383. The alimentary emphasis derives from comedy (Hurst/Kolde [2008] on vv. 381-383).

cooked"[174]. The grotesquerie of this death is taken to extremes by the detail that the heads of the dead are heavy with wine (384 καρηβαρεῦν-τας ἐκ μέθης)–a strange addition which however conforms with the notion that an uncanny feast takes place here.

Among the shipwrecked Greeks Ajax has a prominent role as a multiformed being, a grotesque entity. Lycophron reworks the scene of Ajax' drowning from the *Odyssey* (4.500-510) by introducing imagery from the realm of the sea[175]. The epic hero is caricatured by acquiring successively the form of the most diverse creatures (387-400): the halcyon, the sea bream, the cuckoo, the dolphin, and, in its deadly state, the fish which is pickled in brime. In a manner similar to the previous passage where the Greeks are rendered as tuna fish, the comedians' exaggeration of voracity and their penchant for edibles and foodstuff is invoked here too. The sliding from the tragedy of Ajax' violent death into the comic representation of the very event heightens the grotesque and bizarre impression of this narratire. At the beginning the reader is struck by the strangeness of the bird and fish transformations of Ajax, which are realized within a familiar yet alienated world. Made of contradictions this out-of-this-world world is full of paradox: the halcyon is a diver (δύπτης), the sea bream is a light-armed soldier (this is the common connotation of γυμνήτης which is normally a military term), then this strange creature becomes a cuckoo in the company of whales. By the end of the scene Ajax is both human, a cold corpse cast ashore, and a dead dolphin (the dual nature is implied by the enjambment in vv. 396-397 ψυχρὸν δ᾽ ἐπ᾽ ἀκταῖς ἐκβεβρασμένον νέκυν/ δελφῖνος). This hybridity is retained until the closure of the scene by the ambiguous word τάριχος denoting both a dead body preserved by embalming, a mummy, and, on the comic side, a fish preserved by pickling. Ajax thus depicted is not simply unheroic neither, as one may suppose, merely ridiculous but a genuine uncanny figure[176].

Before closing the discussion of animal metonymies in the *Alexandra*, it is worth attempting a broader interpretation of Lycophron's bestiary. Despite the fact that this bestiary draws upon real-world experience, and therefore it is not exotic or fantastic in its origin, and although Lycophron primarily exploits its visual potential, since the animal is used as

174. Mooney (1988) on v. 382.
175. An in-depth reading of the Ajax passage is offered by Gigante Lanzara (2000) 260-263.
176. Fish and bird metonymies are also used to denote the shipwrecked Odysseus (749-765) and the bizarre death of the returning hero caused by the sting of a poisonous fish (789-796) with a similarly uncanny effect.

an extremely powerful image of metaphor/metonymy, the symbolism of this thematic choice merits further consideration. Lycophron takes a major step into the reification of animal metonymies by suggesting a substantial, albeit not literal, metamorphosis of his characters into animals, once they possess abhuman bodies. If we argue that the body, as an entity inspiring awe and horror, is central to the understanding of Alexandra's dark discourse, then these abhuman bodies, involved as they are in all kinds of violence, signify a return into primitive forms of being, into animalistic disarray. Seen from a Gothic perspective (in conjunction with aesthetic and philosophical notions of late 19th century Aestheticism), this abhumanness is an indication of *degeneration*[177]:

> Degeneration was evolution reversed and compressed. Like evolution theory, degenerationism concerned itself with the long-term effects of heredity within the life-span of a species, and with biological variations from type that affected not only the individual, but the generations to follow... While the evolution from animal to human, from savage to modern, had taken place gradually, over an unthinkable span of time, degeneration was rapid and fatal. A family line could suffer extinction in four generations, hardly more than a human lifetime; and a culture, too, could sicken and die almost as quickly.

In more ways than one, Alexandra's narrative documents the ruination of the human subject, its material and psychological mutation into something abhuman (the wolf is the ultimate symbol in this respect), and eventually the decay of families, people and cultures. Barbarism and animalism are the two sides of the same coin, that is of the human degeneration as emphasized by Lycophron and European Decadence alike.

The uncanny side of animal metonymy brings us once more to the initial question: by what means does Alexandra's dark discourse create a horror effect? I have argued that as a dramatic heroine Alexandra is overwhelmed by horror, once immersed in the sea of her riddling stories. The prophetic mode marks, by definition, a transition into territories of non-rationality, thus allowing fears and desires to emerge from the unconscious in the form of dark visions. Within this context, the Trojan myth is distorted, the *dramatis personae* deformed, the language obscured. I have also pointed to the fact that the transcendental character of the prophetic speech-act is only a superficial impression. Beneath the surface, transcendence as expressed by Alexandra is not oriented towards what lies beyond human perception but deep within the human psyche. Therefore,

---

177. Hurley (1996) 66, see also the entire chapter dedicated to entropic bodies (pp. 65-88).

instances of sublimity should not be construed as manifestations of Romantic visionarism but of the Gothic sublime proper[178].

Hypotheses about the performativity of the *Alexandra* explain other features of the poem: its *presentiality*, its affinity with *phantasmagoria*, its penchant for the naturalistic horror of the *grand guignol*. To demonstrate how the latter type of horror is achieved, I will now turn my attention to the representation and articulation of the sufferings of the body, including lust and violence[179].

Sexuality is a source of violence everywhere in the *Alexandra*. It is the driving force behind history, as seen in the section where the longstanding conflict between Europe and Asia is attributed to the abduction of women–Io, Europa, Medea, Helen. The core of the prophecy proper is the rape of Alexandra and its aftermath for the Greeks; death and destruction are seen as its catastrophic results. Imagery reflects this broader thematic scheme. In this savage world the image of the wolf warriors corresponds to the one of the dog-like and serpentine women; while the former abduct, rape and sacrifice innocent doves and heifers, the latter become whores and murderers. Alexandra's dark discourse abounds with terms such as λέκτρον, λέχος, δέμνιον and γάμος–always within negative contexts[180]. Erotic frenzy (οἶστρος) nearly turns Aigialeia into a slaughterer of Diomedes, into a second Klytaimestra: she is a shameless and lustful bitch thirsty for bed (612-613 θρασεῖα θουρὰς οἰστρήσῃ κύων πρὸς λέκτρα). Desire is fatal, causing an agonizing death to the lover who dies entangled within the nets of passion. Ajax drowns as a consequence of his dark desire (405-407):

ἥ μιν παλεύσει δυσλύτοις οἴστρου βρόχοις
ἔρωτας οὐκ ἔρωτας, ἀλλ' Ἐρινύων
πικρὰν ἀποψήλασα κηρουλκὸν πάγην.

Aphrodite shall entrap him in the unescapable meshes of desire, in a love that is no love but springing for him the bitter death-drawing snare of the Erinyes.

---

178. According to what Morris (1985) calls "the Gothic revision of the sublime".

179. A very important study of the semantic elements denoting a) marriage and family relations, b) murder and destruction and c) pain and lament, and the role of tragedy in the formation of this vocabulary in the *Alexandra*, is offered by Cusset (2002-2003).

180. Some outstanding examples are: the use of πεντάλεκτρος and αἰνόλεκτρος for Helen (143, 820) and ἀθεσμόλεκτρος for Ajax (1143); the juxtaposition of λέκτρα and τύμβος in v. 613; the emphatic periphrasis for the brothel νυμφεῖα κηλωστά in v. 1387; the bed as a setting of violence (60, 353, 357, 1222); λέχος characterized νόθον and λαθραῖον (423, 1223); γάμος specified as ἐστεναγμένος or δυσσεβής (412, 1151) etc. For a complete listing of the related vocabulary, also in relation to tragedy, see Cusset (2002-2003) 143-145.

Marriage equals a ritual of death in the case of Polyxena whose uncanny wedding is described by the periphrases ὠμὰ νυμφεῖα and γαμήλιοι θυηλαί (323). Sexuality can be perverse or horrifying for those involved in uncanny love acts. This is the strange case of Egesta who mates with the dog-faced river Krimisos (961-963):

> ὧν δὴ μίαν Κριμισός, ἰνδαλθεὶς κυνί,
> ἔζευξε λέκτροις ποταμός· ἡ δὲ δαίμονι
> τῷ θηρομίκτῳ σκύλακα γενναῖον τεκνοῖ

> ...Of these one the river Krimisos, in the likeness of a dog, took to be his bride: and she to the half-beast god bears a noble whelp...

This story highlights once more the grotesque, in the sense of the strange mixing of the genres (ἰνδαλθεὶς κυνί, δαίμονι θηρομίκτῳ), adapted to an erotic context (ἔζευξε λέκτροις, lit. 'joined in bed')[181]. Love is morbid in another dark tale told by Alexandra; the characters implied here are the Amazon Penthesilea and Achilles (999-1001):

> ἧς ἐκπνεούσης λοῖσθον ὀφθαλμὸς τυπεὶς
> πιθηκομόρφῳ πότμον Αἰτωλῷ φθόρῳ
> τεύξει τράφηκι φοινίῳ τετμημένῳ

> ...Slave of that maiden whose eye, smitten as she breathes her last, shall bring doom to the ape-formed Aetolian pest, wounded by the bloody shaft...

The passage highlights a borderline case of the 'love and death' complex: Penthesilea inspires sexual passion to Achilles at her dying moment. But whereas the morbid desire felt by Achilles is not expressly mentioned here[182], attention is focused on the horrifying mutilation of the eye of her corpse and on the fatal wounding of Thersites by the blood-dripping spear of Achilles. Viewing the corpse as an object of desire receives added emphasis in the episode of Paris and Oenone. The idea is fully articulated within two highly effective verses (67-68):

181. The monstrosity of the marriage between Aigesta and Krimisos, and the birth of the grotesque σκύλαξ γενναῖος, is pointed out by Hurst/Kolde (2008) on v. 963.

182. The love story between Achilles and Penthesilea was an episode of the cyclic *Aethiopis*. Whether or not Achilles committed an act of necrophilia on the corpse of Penthesilea was a matter of dispute in antiquity. This dark variation is attested by Tzetzes (Sch. Lyc. on v. 999): οἱ μὴ εἰδότες φασὶν Ἀχιλέα ἀνελόντα Πενθεσίλειαν μετὰ θάνατον αὐτῆς ἐρασθῆναι, ἧς τοὺς ὀφθαλμοὺς ὁ Θερσίτης λαθὼν ἐξώρυξεν. ὁ δὲ Ἀχιλεὺς ὀργισθεὶς ἀνεῖλεν αὐτὸν κατὰ τοῦτον μὲν πλήξας δόρατι, κατ' ἐμὲ δὲ καὶ τοὺς λοιποὺς κονδύλῳ ἤτοι γρόνθῳ μηδὲ διὰ τὸ ἐξορύξαι τοὺς ὀφθαλμοὺς ἀλλ' ὅτι αἰσχροὺς λόγους κατ' Ἀχιλέως ἀπέρριπτεν ὡς δῆθεν ἐρῶντος συγγενέσθαι νεκρᾷ τῇ Πενθεσιλείᾳ.

πόθῳ δὲ τοῦ θανόντος ἠγκιστρωμένη
ψυχὴν περισπαίροντι φυσήσει νεκρῷ.

Caught by the hook of desire for the dead she shall breathe forth her soul
on his quivering body.

Spasms of love (visualized as spasms experienced by a fish which gets
caught by a hook)[183] alternate with spasms of death (περισπαίροντι)–
this 'love and death' snapshot being the ultimate example of morbid
Aestheticism.

If perverse passion plays a key role in the *Alexandra*, it is carnal violence around which the entire poem revolves. Lycophron is almost
obsessed with the detailed representation of the human body at the moment
of extreme suffering, agony, torture, wounding, mutilation, and eventually
death[184]. The discourse of Alexandra is imbued with blood and gore[185].
The recherché vocabulary of the poem records various types of fatal blows
as well as of weapons and other lethal instruments. Injuries may be
inflicted not only by use of knives, swords or stones, but also of teeth
(215), jaws (33, 215) and nails (266). Men thirsty for blood (1171 χεῖρα
διψῶσαν φόνου) use every weapon or object that can cause brutal death–
stone (πέτρον), sword (φάσγανον κελαινόν), axe (ταυροκτόνον στερ-
ρὰν κύβηλιν) or branch (Φαλακραῖον κλάδον). In the manner of wild
animals, men may die entangled in a net just like Agamemnon (1101,1375).
Not only carnage and mass murder resonate with images of extreme violence (like in the duel between the Dioskouroi and the Apharids in 544-
566). Emphasis is placed upon the individual, whose body is consumed by
violence and eventually dehumanized. Hekabe who after being stoned to
death turns into a dog is a vivid example of such a dehumanization.

183. The metaphor is neatly captured by Tzetzes (Sch. Lyc. 67): ἠγκιστρωμένη·
κατεχομένη, ἀπὸ τῆς μεταφορᾶς τῶν ἰχθύων τῶν κατεχομένων ὑπὸ τοῦ ἀγκίστρου.
Hurst/Kolde (2008) on v. 67 suggest that the image of Paris who dies pierced by the
arrows of Herakles is evoked here.
184. A description of the key role of death in the Gothic novel bears a striking similarity to the function of death in the *Alexandra*, if one is allowed to read the latter in the light
of the former (Morris [1985] 308): "Death in the Gothic novel is not conceived in linear
relation to life, as the terminus of a long or short journey. It interrupts the hero on his
wedding day; it intrudes upon the timeless chapels of religion; it mixes corpses with marriage beds and scenes of rape. Life in Gothic fiction never frees itself from the presence
or threat of death. The sublime is always waiting beyond the next turn of the staircase."
185. Αἷμα and its derivatives occur 12 times in the *Alexandra*, an impressive frequency if we consider Lycophron's obsession with hapax words: αἷμα (684, 1356, 1397),
αἵματα (804, 1249), αἱμάσσω (266, 297, 313, 760, 992), αἱματηρός (250), ἀναίμακτος
(988). Similar lists may be compiled with φόνος (11 occurrences), φοίνιος 'bloody or
blood-red' (3 occurrences plus one of φοινίσσω), σφαγή and its derivatives (10 occurrences) etc. For a review of the vocabulary of murder and destruction in the *Alexandra*,
see Cusset (2002-2003) 148-151.

Another example of the human body being tortured and alienated is found in the story of Setaia, the captive Trojan woman who is crucified and then left to be torn apart by vultures (1075-1080):

Σήταια τλῆμον, σοὶ δὲ πρὸς πέτραις μόρος
μίμνει δυσαίων, ἔνθα γυιούχοις πέδαις
οἴκτιστα χαλκείησιν ὠργυιωμένη
θανῇ, πυρὶ φλέξασα δεσποτῶν στόλον,
ἔκβλητον αἰάζουσα Κράθιδος πέλας
τόργοισιν αἰώρημα φοινίοις δέμας.

Poor Setaia! an unhappy fate awaits you upon the rocks, where, most piti-fully outstretched with brazen fetters on your limbs, you shall die, because you did burn the fleet of your masters: bewailing near Crathis your body cast out and hung up for gory vultures to devour.

The visualization of the crucified body of Setaia is achieved by two hapax words, coined to capture the dramatic moment, γυιούχοις 'fettering the limbs' and ὠργυιωμένη 'bound with outstretched arms', and the rare word αἰώρημα 'that which hovers'; yet the most powerful expression sug-gesting the alienation from one's body is ἔκβλητον δέμας[186]. Naturalistic horror is intensified when the body is severely butchered: this is the fate of Alexandra whose body is cut into pieces beside the bath of Agame-mnon. Or of Telemachus who is slaughtered by his own sister Cassiphone with his neck cut into furrows (810 σφαγαῖς ἀδελφῆς ἠλοκισμένος δέρην). Similar descriptions verge on cannibalism when the cut off mem-ber of the victim is ultimately devoured, as when Demeter eats the shoul-der of Pelops (154-155): ἄσαρκα μιστύλασ' ἐτύμβευσεν φάρῳ,/ τὸν ὠλενίτην χόνδρον ἐνδατουμένη 'cut fleshless with her jaws and buried in her throat, devouring the gristle of his shoulder'[187]. Cannibalism is implied in the frequent use of the metaphor of dinner in the *Alexandra*[188], as also in tales about monsters who devour their victims. As when the daughters of Phoinodamas are destined to be given as a κελαινός δόρπος 'black dinner' to the sea monster which is sent against Troy, but at the end they are fed as meat to carnivorous beasts (955 τηλοῦ προθεῖναι θηρσὶν ὠμησταῖς βοράν). *Grand guignol* snapshots include the mutual massacre between Meleager and the boar, when the latter takes bloody vengeance on his murderer's body (491-493):

186. Cf. Gigante Lanzara (2000) on vv. 1075-1078 and 1079-1080.
187. The latter example is more of a caricature according to Gigante Lanzara (2000) on v. 154-155.
188. Dinner, and food in general, is a common metaphor within contexts of death: δόρπος (471, cf. 954 κητοδόρπος), δαίς (137), δαιτρός/δαιτρεύω (35, 160), γεύομαι (383), παιδοβρώς/παιδόβρωτος (347, 1199), κρατοβρώς (1066) etc.

ὁ δ' αὐτὸς ἀργῷ πᾶς φαληριῶν λύθρῳ
στόρθυγξ, δεδουπὼς τὸν κτανόντ' ἠμύνατο
πλήξας ἀφύκτως ἄκρον ὀρχηστοῦ σφυρόν.

That same tusk, that with white gore foamed, when he had fallen took vengeance on his slayer, smiting with unescapable blow the dancer's ankle-bone.

Passages with a taste for morbidity and gore may be easily multiplied in the *Alexandra*. Therefore it is not possible to draw up an exhaustive list of all its manifestations here. What I hope has become evident from the aforementioned paradigms is the crucial role of corporeality in Lycophron's aesthetics, of a concept of the body in its mutilated, fragmented form, in its hybrid and bestial nature, and ultimately of the alienation of the body from the subject–this is yet another way of communicating the idea of abhumanism in the *Alexandra*[189].

Before completing the analysis of what constitutes darkness in the discourse of the *Alexandra*, there remains one more factor to be considered, namely dark settings. As has been hitherto observed, the edifice, exemplified by Alexandra's chamber, provides a Gothic setting for the dramatized frame of the poem. Yet the numerous visions of darkness are set against various backgrounds, locations of catastrophe and horror, upon which I will now turn my attention.

Since the visions of Alexandra are rendered as nightmares, it is inevitable that the same quality pervades the imaginary cosmoi they are set in. Apocalyptic settings form a distinct category. The arrival of Achilles the Evil One in the Troad has a devastating effect upon land and men alike, as if a supernatural force sets the entire cosmos on fire (243-257, cf. 290-297 where, conversely, it is Hektor who sets the Greek ships on fire). This is the concluding in a series of visualizations of the burning Troy that inform the background to the pathetic prophecy of Alexandra–αἰαῖ, τάλαινα θηλαμὼν κεκαυμένη (31) and λεύσσω σε, τλῆμον, δεύτερον πυρουμένην (52)[190]. Scenes of the apocalypse take place during the shipwreck of the returning Greeks (373-386), in the paradoxical natural phenomena accompanying the godsent flood of Samothrace (79-

---

189. Most illuminating for this dimension of the body, and a valuable source of inspiration for my analysis of the *Alexandra*, is the study of Gothic bodies by Hurley (1996).

190. Fire is a recurrent image of catastrophe in the *Alexandra*, whose most striking example is the metonymic use of γρυνός for Paris (86, 1362). According to Tzetzes this metonymy recalls the dream of Hekabe in which she gave birth to a firebrand (Sch. Lyc. 86): γρυνὸν τὸν Ἀλέξανδρον αὐτὸν διὰ τὸ ὄναρ, ὃ εἶδεν Ἑκάβη, ὅτι δαλὸν ἔτεκε καιόμενον, ὅστις κατέφλεξε πᾶσαν τὴν πόλιν καὶ τὴν ἐν Ἴδῃ ὕλην.

85) and especially in the extravagant description of the retreating army of Xerxes towards Asia (1421-1434)[191].

Another major category of settings pertains to *lands of fable*, within which fairytale stories, such as the Argonautic expedition and the wanderings of Odysseus, unfold. Among these fabulous landscapes special reference should be made to the representation of the Underworld in Lycophron's *Nekyia* (681-711). The landscape where the passage to the Underworld is situated resembles a murky plain (ἐρεμνὸν εἰς ἀλήπεδον φθιτῶν); there dwells the seer of the dead (νεκρόμαντις) and it is there that a ritual offering of hot blood to the souls of the deceased takes place (ψυχαῖσι θερμὸν αἷμα προσράνας); to the terrifying waving of the sword (νερτέροις φόβον) the ghosts respond with a thin voice (πεμφίδων ὄπα λεπτήν). Thereupon follows a detailed mapping of the topographies leading to the entrance into the Underworld, among others the celebrated waters of Acheron, Pyriphlegethon, Lethe, Aornos, Kokytos and Styx. Within a handful of verses, darkness is evoked several times–681 ἐρεμνὸν ἀλήπεδον, 687 ἀμαυρᾶς μάστακος, 705 χεῦμα λαβρωθὲν σκότῳ, 706 Στυγὸς κελαινῆς. The tomb of Baios, who was the steersman of Odysseus, and the omnipresence of Pluto and Persephone, further develop the hell atmosphere of the passage. By thus juxtaposing the vague description of a landscape full of desolation and stillness with the legendary toponyms of Hades, Lycophron evokes the theme *par excellence* of his poem, namely death[192].

If the *Alexandra* shares, *mutatis mutandis*, some of its significant features with Gothic narratives of the modern era, among which the prominence of the theme of death, it is only natural that the tomb, as a setting and a concept, dominates throughout this dark monologue. Tomb and entombement are so extensively treated that these themes inform an almost independent discourse within the poem, which I have called the *tomb discourse*[193]. The *tomb discourse* is introduced after the turning point of the poem's plot, namely the rape of Alexandra, and continues

191. Images of grandeur and fall alternate against a background of Asiatic hyperbole, as observed by Hurst/Paidi (2004) on vv. 1421-1434. The Xerxes episode is an admixture of Herodotean description and tragic diction, see Gigante Lanzara (2000) on vv. 1421-1434.

192. It is noteworthy that Schade (1999) 86 uses the term 'Gothic atmosphere' to suggest the dark tonality of the *Nekyia* section. For a thorough commentary of this section, which draws upon the *Odyssey* as well as Aeschylus' *Psychagogoi* and numerous ancient prose writers including Plato and Timaios, see Schade (1999) 86-123, cf. Gigante Lanzara (2000) 314-320.

193. Τάφος occurs 18 times, τύμβος and its derivatives 10 times in the *Alexandra*, a fair number if one considers Lycophron's penchant for hapax words.

until the end of the *Nostoi* section. In a way, the entire *Nostoi* section is staged against the backdrop of a huge cemetery, in which both Greeks and Trojans have their place; what will be explored here is the bizarre typology of this cemetery.

As a consequence of the catastrophic shipwreck of the Greeks, the sea turns into a phantom graveyard, a vast cenotaph (365-416). *And for the sin of one man all Hellas shall mourn the empty tombs of ten thousand children—not in receptacles of bones, but perched on rocks, nor hiding in urns the embalmed last ashes from the fire, as is the ritual of the dead, but a piteous name and legends on empty cairns, bathed with the burning tears of parents and of children and mourning of wives.* The scene, evoking epic and tragic subtexts, as also the rich tradition of Hellenistic epitaphs for those who are lost in the sea, is sublime in its *pathos* and panoramic perspective[194]. A little later it becomes strikingly dark, when the sighs and moans of the dead mingle with the tumult of the tempest (ὅσων στεναγμῶν ἐκβεβρασμένων νεκρῶν...), and when the macabre vision of the fragmented corpses is seen in the light of a thunderbolt (καταιβάτης σκηπτὸς κατ᾽ ὄρφνην)[195]. Immediately follows the grotesque mummification of Ajax who gets buried among the seaweed (τάριχον ἐν μνίοις δὲ καὶ βρύοις σαθρὸν κρύψει) and the eerie entombment of the devoured men into the bellies of sea monsters (ἐν σπλάγχνοισι τυμβευθήσεται). By visualizing these highly original tombs Lycophron wavers between the grotesque and the horrifying.

After this expressionist prelude, monumental tombs come into view, since the wandering Greeks die far from their fatherland; thus entombment becomes a theme of the broader *ktisis discourse*. A prominent example of a peculiar entombment is that of Mopsos and Amphilochos, whose tombs are set apart from each other so as to eternally recall their mutual loathing (444-446)[196]:

Μάγαρσος ἁγνῶν ἠρίων σταθήσεται,
ὡς μὴ βλέπωσι, μηδὲ νερτέρων ἕδρας
δύντες, φόνῳ λουσθέντας ἀλλήλων τάφους.

Magarsos shall stand between their holy cairns, so that even when they have gone down to the habitations of the dead, they may not behold each other's tombs, bathed in blood.

194. See especially Durbec (2009).
195. In staging the tempest during the night Lycophron diverges from the Homeric descriptions of tempests and evokes tragedy, especially Aeschylus' *Agamemnon* (Durbec [2009] 133).
196. The scene is modelled upon the tragic pattern of Eteokles and Polyneikes, see Gigante Lanzara (2000) on vv. 439-442.

Alternating with stories of wanderings and foundations are stories of deaths and burials. Numerous are found in the little *Odyssey*, and include those of Odysseus' crew (648-665), the Sirens (712-736) and Odysseus himself (799-814).

Some tombs explore the boundaries between life and death. In Lycophron the tomb is not an end but a location suggesting continuity, a passage into afterlife. Within this context, the dead Odysseus is a crowned prophet in Hades (799 μάντιν δὲ νεκρὸν Εὐρυτὰν στέψει λεώς...) and Podaleirios is mutated into a ghost healer from the tomb (1050-1055). Sometimes the tomb may inspire sympathy, especially if it concerns the miserable victims of the Trojan War. The rock, where the crucified body of Setaia is exposed, is a location of perennial torture. Other tombs are built on foreign soil for the maidens which are sacrificed in remembrance of Alexandra' rape (1155-1158). *And they, aliens in an alien land, shall have without funeral rites a tomb, a sorry tomb in wavewashed sands, when Hephaestus burns with unfruitful plants the limbs of her that perishes from Traron's peaks, and tosses her ashes into the sea.*

As the monologue of Alexandra advances towards its conclusion, two more tombs merit special attention–those of Hekabe and Hektor (1174-1213). The former is a pseudo-tomb, a ψευδήριον, a monument which owes its existence to the ghostly apparition of Hekabe, a tomb owed to dreams (ψευδήριον σεμνὸν ἐξ ὀνειράτων)[197]. But Hekabe proves to be undead and unburied, since her ghost, a double of Hekate, terrorizes the mortals every night with her loud howls (1176-1177 Βριμὼ Τρίμορφος θήσεταί σ' ἐπωπίδα/ κλαγγαῖσι ταρμύσσουσαν ἐννύχοις βροτούς). The other tomb belongs to Hektor who is destined to rest eternally as a true hero in a location called *The Isles of the Blessed* (1204-1205 νήσοις δὲ μακάρων ἐγκατοικήσεις μέγας/ ἥρως)[198]. The juxtaposition of these tombs strikes a subtle balance between horror and grandeur, unique within the pathetic extravagance of this curious poem. Perhaps because Hektor is the only character that allows a tiny sparkle of light into the Gothic gloom of Alexandra's visions.

---

197. The ghost story behind Hekabe's tomb is told by Tzetzes (Sch. Lyc. 1030): ὁ Ὀδυσσεὺς δειματούμενος καθ' ὕπνους ἱδρύσατο ἱερὸν Ἑκάτης ἀφ' ἑαυτοῦ τὴν ἄκραν καλέσας Ὀδύσσειαν· ἀνέστησε δὲ καὶ κενοτάφιον ἐκεῖσε.

198. Sch. Lyc. 1204 οὐχ ὡς ἄλλοι τὰς Μακάρων νήσους ἐν τῷ Ὠκεανῷ λέγει ὁ Λυκόφρων εἶναι, ἀλλ' ἐν Θήβαις.

III. NICANDER *THERIACA* AND *ALEXIPHARMACA*

The Dark Didactic

III.1. The sensation of science

> After having made a few preparatory experiments, he concluded with a panegyric upon modern chemistry, the terms of which I shall never forget: "The ancient teachers of this science," said he, "promised impossibilities, and performed nothing. The modern masters promise very little; they know that metals cannot be transmuted, and that the elixir of life is a chimera. But these philosophers, whose hands seem only made to dabble in dirt, and their eyes to pore over the microscope or crucible, have indeed performed miracles. They penetrate into the recesses of nature, and show how she works in her hiding places. They ascend into the heavens: they have discovered how the blood circulates, and the nature of the air we breathe. They have acquired new and almost unlimited powers; they can command the thunders of heaven, mimic the earthquake, and even mock the invisible world with its own shadows."
>
> Mary Shelley *Frankenstein* Ch. 3 (1818)

Science is the ultimate sensation of Romantic aesthetics[1]. Construed either as an empirical way of sensing nature or an intellectual challenge of being re-united with it, science holds a fascination both for the German Idealists and the British Romantics of the late 18th and the early 19th century. Based on the organic conception of nature as a whole, an entity far superior to the mere summation of its components, and displaying a predilection for sentiment over rationalism, Romantic science strongly opposes the mechanistic model underlying scientific theories of the Enlightenment. According to the Romantics there are hidden powers within the natural world, mysteries beyond human understanding; thus, emotional involvement with, and spiritual connection to the living nature, genuine respect for natural phenomena rather than the ambition of bringing them under human control through reason, can only warrant the harmonious co-existence of man with the natural world. This should be the aim of any scientific enterprise as expressed by Schelling's *Naturphilosophie* and thence reflected in Goethe's emphasis upon insight as a scientific method, the introduction of a metaphysical dimension into the discipline of biology by Lamarck, the reshaping of chemistry by the British Romantic thinker Humphry Davy and so on. Intellectuals of the 18th and 19th centuries, passionate about

1. The fascination with science during the Romantic era is fully explored by Holmes (2008).

nature, become natural philosophers, physicians, biologists, botanists, chemists, even explorers and collectors of botanical and zoological specimens. Soon their new vision of the natural world finds its way into poetry, and its profound impact is felt in the works of Wordsworth, Coleridge, Shelley, Byron and Keats[2]. Science provides poetry with naturalistic accuracy and a love for detail in the description of the natural environment, whereas, conversely, scientists often borrow metaphors and imagery from poetry to express complex theories. Two paradigms for the latter tendency are of some relevance here. The first is the case of William Bartram, an American naturalist and explorer, whose prose work *Travels* (1791), a treatise which has exerted formative influence on Romantic poetics, combines lyricism with objectivity, vividness with scientific lore, imagery with the careful observation of nature. The other is that of Erasmus Darwin, a scientist, physician, natural philosopher and poet, who writes his treatises on botany in verse (*The Botanic Garden* [1791]) and whose prose work *Zoonomia* (1794) has had a deep impact on poets of Romanticism. During the same period influential writers question the limits of science: the classical example is the demonic scientist Victor Frankenstein, playing the role of the 'Modern Prometheus' in Mary Shelley's novel. This character becomes the prototype for the mad scientist, the negative of the Romantic 'Man of Science', a dark figure of 19th century literature which warns about the dangers arising from the attempt of man to overpower nature beyond ethic standards.

The approach to nature through science and its subsequent poeticization occupy a pivotal role in the search for analogies between Romantic and Hellenistic aesthetics. Alexandria and other metropolises of the Hellenistic era experience a great boom in science. Under the overwhelming influence of Aristotle and his school, and through the patronage of powerful monarchs, sciences flourish in all areas of knowledge–astronomy, geography, biology, mechanics, mathematics, optics, medicine, psychology[3]. Nature and natural phenomena, on the other hand, strongly appeal to intellectuals, scholars, scientists and

2. The idea that the Romantic poets were anti-scientific is a widespread theory of Romantic criticism, which is questioned today (see e.g. Goellnicht [1984] 3-11). The interconnections between science and poetry during the 18th and 19th centuries are outlined by Nichols (2005). For a vivid account of the Romantics' penchant for science, see Holmes (2008) 305-336.

3. For a thorough discussion of the exact sciences in Alexandria, see the brilliant introduction by Fraser (1972) 1.336-446 and Argoud/Guillaumin (1998). A valuable sourcebook on Hellenistic science from Theophrastus until the 3rd century AD is Irby-Massie/Keyser (2002).

poets alike, identities which often coincide in the same person during the Hellenistic era; Eratosthenes of Cyrene, Aratus of Soloi and Nicander of Colophon are the best known examples of the scientist who purports to be a poet, and vice versa. Once science interacts with poetry, a new sense of nature develops. Theocritus is well known for building his imaginary *eutopia* upon material drawn from botany and zoology, whereas Callimachus and Apollonius focus on the cultural aspects of nature which provide a new foil for myth. It is impressive that the descriptions of natural phenomena or physical and psychological conditions by Hellenistic poets are scientifically accurate to the highest degree, and yet they are effectively integrated into the dramatic action of their poems. Sometimes science is seen through a literary prism, when for example intellectuals show a penchant for paradoxography, the collection of natural curiosities and other pseudo-scientific researches. It is more than obvious that the boundaries between scientific and literary discourse are blurred during the Hellenistic era, a phenomenon which finds its historical parallel in the 19th century[4].

Against the background of these preliminary (and inevitably vague) remarks about the affinities between Hellenistic and Romantic aesthetics, I will now turn to the case under discussion: Nicander. The testimonies about the life of Nicander of Colophon are ambiguous to such an extent that his identity, chronology and works are a matter of an ongoing debate between scholars[5]. Some testimonies consider Nicander to be a contemporary of the first generation of Hellenistic poets during the reign of Ptolemy Philadelphus, whereas others assign him to a date near the beginning or even the end of the second century BC. It is not sure whether there existed one or two Nicanders or if the works that have come down to us under this name belong to the same author. According to the biographical tradition he was a physician and a poet, and from this viewpoint he is constantly compared to the astronomer and poet Aratus[6].

---

4. On nature and science as a source of inspiration for Hellenistic poetry, see the articles collected in Harder/Regtuit/Wakker (2009).

5. An introduction to the problem is offered by Gow/Scholfield (1997) 3-8, but is discussed anew by Magnelli (2006a) and (2010) 211-213.

6. Hence the paradoxical anecdote that fictitiously unites the two men (*Vita Arati* 8.25-9.1): οἱ δὲ λέγοντες Νίκανδρον τὸν Κολοφώνιον μετὰ ᾽Αράτου ᾽Αντιγόνῳ συγκεχρονικέναι, καὶ ῎Αρατον μὴ εἶναι ἐπιστήμονα τῶν οὐρανίων μήτε Νίκανδρον τῶν ἰατρικῶν (λέγουσι γὰρ ὡς ἄρα ὁ ᾽Αντίγονος ᾽Αράτῳ μὲν ὄντι ἰατρῷ ἐπέταξε τὰ Φαινόμενα γράψαι, Νικάνδρῳ δὲ ἀστρολόγῳ ὑπάρχοντι τὰ Θηριακὰ καὶ τὰ ᾽Αλεξιφάρμακα, ὅθεν καὶ ἑκάτερον αὐτῶν ἐσφάλθαι κατολισθαίνοντα ἐπὶ τὰ ἴδια τῆς τέχνης) ψεύδονται.

Even if this reference is a metaphor for Nicander's poetics in terms of a fictitious biography, nevertheless it programmatically announces the strange amalgam of poetry and science for which he became famous[7]. The 'Nicandrean question' apart, my focus here are the two, fully preserved, extant poems which are attributed to Nicander, namely the *Theriaca* and the *Alexipharmaca*; whether these poems are composed by the same Nicander or the one is an imitation of the other is irrelevant to the present study, once both hypotheses presuppose the similarities between them[8]. Written with a taste for stylistic hyperbole and ascribed to the scholarly tradition of the 'Homericizing' poetry of the era (in the sphragis of the *Theriaca* the poet calls himself Ὁμήρειος Νίκανδρος), the *Theriaca* and the *Alexipharmaca* demonstrate how scientific knowledge, in this case zoology and botany, may be turned into highly virtuoso verse. The central premise of this chapter is that these two poems (their poetic value apart) mark the point at which scientific lore is transformed into *sensational* discourse–the latter in its literal notion of a language pertaining to the senses and a poetry perceived as a sensuous experience[9]. Some features of these poems, such as the subject matter and the focus upon sensory perception, occasionally take on darker hues. This is the darkness of Nicandrean aesthetics, which I will attempt to explore by recourse to Romanticism[10].

The first question to be addressed concerns the affinity of Nicander's work to the tradition of didactic poetry. Once knowledge becomes the subject matter of poetry, and mythological narrative (or μῦθος in the sense of plot) is not seen as an integral part of it, the didactic genre comes into being. This genre is as old as Hesiod, best exemplified by

7. A striking parallel to the 'poet-physician' in the Romantic era is Keats, as Goellnicht (1984) persuasively argues. Although Keats, a medic himself, never wrote a poem on a scientific subject-matter and overtly saw poetry and science as quite diverse occupations, he introduced ideas, images and methods from various branches of science (botany, chemistry, anatomy, medicine) into his poems.

8. If they were indeed composed by one and the same person, then they were designed to constitute a diptych, and the two poems were meant to be read consecutively (Magnelli [2006b]).

9. I have borrowed the notion of 'sensation' and 'language of the sense' from Romantic aesthetics: for an analysis of the terms, see Jackson (2008) 1-20.

10. Greek text and commentary are based on Jacques (2002) and (2007), translations are taken from Gow/Scholfield (1997). Effe (1977) 56-65 analyzes Nicander's poems as a category of didactic poetry that relies upon the 'formal aestheticization' of the material and therefore belongs to the formal or ornamental type of the genre. For a short but illuminating overview of Nicander's poetics, see Toohey (1996) 61-73 and Hatzimichali (2009). A thorough introduction to Nicander, as well as a detailed literary commentary to the *Theriaca*, is offered by Overduin (2010).

the instruction on agriculture in the *Works and Days*, but is intensified and codified as a distinct mode during the Hellenistic period[11]. But in contrast to the Archaic notion according to which verse is a form equally appropriate to articulate myth, philosophy and science, by the era of Aristotle prose is acknowledged as the ideal vehicle for philosophical and scientific reflection. Therefore, when Hellenistic poets render scientific matter as poetry, they are fully aware of the artificiality of their experiment[12]. Thus, the didactic model formed by Hesiod in the *Works and Days* is, by the time of Aratus and Nicander, crystallized into a literary scenario comprising the narrator/teacher, the addressee/pupil and the subject matter which derives from any field of scientific or technical knowledge. Nicander closely follows this scenario in the proem of the *Theriaca* (1-7):

> Ῥεῖά κέ τοι μορφάς τε σίνη τ᾽ ὀλοφώια θηρῶν
> ἀπροϊδῆ τύψαντα λύσιν θ᾽ ἑτεραλκέα κήδευς,
> φίλ᾽ Ἑρμησιάναξ, πολέων κυδίστατε παῶν,
> ἔμπεδα φωνήσαιμι· σὲ δ᾽ ἂν πολύεργος ἀροτρεύς
> βουκαῖός τ᾽ ἀλέγοι καὶ ὁροιτύπος, εὖτε καθ᾽ ὕλην
> ἢ καὶ ἀροτρεύοντι βάλῃ ἔπι λοιγὸν ὀδόντα,
> τοῖα περιφρασθέντος ἀλεξητήρια νούσων.

> Easily, dear Hermesianax, most honoured of my many kinsmen, and in due order will I expound the forms of savage creatures and their deadly injuries which smite one unforeseen, and the countering remedy for the harm. And the toiling ploughman, the herdsman, and the woodcutter, whenever in forest or at the plough one of them fastens its deadly fang upon him, shall respect you for your learning in such means for averting sickness.

This is a key passage to the understanding of Nicandrean poetics. The first-person speaker sets out with the intention of imparting knowledge to Hermesianax, his addressee, with the phrase ῥεῖα κε φωνήσαιμι; this phrase parallels the opening of the *Alexipharmaca* where the speaker likewise states that he will present his subject matter *easily* (*Alex.* 4-5 ῥεῖα κε αὐδήσαιμι). It has been rightly pointed out that this proem

---

11. Didactic poetry is a hotly debated issue among classicists. Effe (1977) offers a comprehensive study of ancient didactic poetry, with an appended list of previous bibliography on the theoretical aspects of didactic and the authors involved (pp. 253-262). Recent approaches include the volume *Epic Lessons* by Toohey (1996) and *Musa Docta*, a collection of papers by Cusset (2006a); from an intercultural aspect, the collective volume *Calliope's Classroom* by Harder/MacDonald/Reinink (2007). Essential for the typology of the didactic poem is Fakas (2001); cf. for an interesting analysis of the didactic plot Fowler (2000).

12. On this point, see Effe (1977) 22-26; Overduin (2010) 26-30 further elaborates on the artificial imitation of Hesiodic didactic by the Hellenistic poets.

highlights the authority of the speaker *qua* scientist as opposed to the authority of the Muses (as in Hesiod and Callimachus' *Aitia*) or Zeus (as in Aratus' *Phainomena*), thus promoting the idea of individuality versus that of divine inspiration[13]. The vocabulary is meticulously selected so as to emphasize that nature, in its empirical and scientific dimension, is the primary focus of the poem. Words like ἔμπεδα or περιφράζομαι, and the terms ἀλεξητήρια νούσων, μορφάς τε σίνη τε θηρῶν and λύσις point to the latter, whereas the practical experiences of everyday people implied in vv. 4-7 situate the poem within an empirical frame. Yet the subtle shadings of other words, of ὀλοφώιος 'destructive, deadly' and λοιγός 'pestilent, deadly', in evoking dark passages from Homer and other works of high poetry, suggest that Nicander asserts himself not as a mere versifier but as a poet of the grand style[14].

This programmatic claim takes a surprising twist in the subsequent verses. Despite being initially placed within a 'natural' frame of reference, the poem soon reveals an undercurrent of 'supernaturalism'. In one of the rare passages where Nicander uses mythology to explain scientific data, the origin of spiders, snakes and other reptiles is attributed to the blood of the Titans and dated back to the war of Zeus against Kronos and his offspring (8-12):

> ἀλλ' ἤτοι κακοεργὰ φαλάγγια, σὺν καὶ ἀνιγρούς
> ἑρπηστὰς ἐχιάς τε καὶ ἄχθεα μυρία γαίης
> Τιτήνων ἐνέπουσιν ἀφ' αἵματος, εἰ ἐτεόν περ
> Ἀσκραῖος μυχάτοιο Μελισσήεντος ἐπ' ὄχθαις
> Ἡσίοδος κατέλεξε παρ' ὕδασι Περμησσοῖο.

Now I would have you know, men say that noxious spiders, together with the grievious reptiles and vipers and the earth's countless burdens, are of the Titan's blood–if indeed he spoke the truth, Ascraean Hesiod on the steeps of secluded Melisseeis by the waters of Permessos.

---

13. This interpretation of ῥεῖα is first pointed out by Fakas (2001) 63 n. 190, and further elaborated by Magnelli (2006a) 196-197 and (2010) 220-221. Clauss (1991) 162-169 argues that by ῥεῖα Nicander claims for himself the status of Zeus by alluding to the association of easiness and Zeus in the proem of the *Works and Days* (vv. 1-10); he also suggests, less convincingly, that ῥεῖα is a wordplay on the goddess Rhea.

14. Some impressive examples include the phrases ὀλοφώια δήνεα Κίρκης (*Od.* 10.289), ὁ γέρων ὀλοφώια εἰδώς (said of Proteus' cunning, *Od.* 4.460), ὀλοφώιον ἔργον (for the work of the Erinyes, A.R. *Arg.* 4.476), λύκων τ' ὀλοφώιον ἔθνος (Theocr. 25.185). Λοιγός instead of the right form of the epithet λοίγιος is used here to recall the noun λοιγός 'ruin, havoc, destruction', a powerful word of heroic poetry (in the *Iliad* usually in the formulaic expression ἀεικέα λοιγόν, cf. Aesch. *Ch.* 402 βοᾷ γὰρ λοιγὸς Ἐρινὺν, 'Hes.' *Aspis* 240, Pi. *N.* 9.37).

Nicander is divided between his faith in science–*if indeed Hesiod spoke the truth*–and his religious background[15]. Moreover, by evoking the dread and danger of the Titanomachy as dramatized in the *Theogony*, these verses create, from the very beginning of the *Theriaca*, an atmosphere of the sublime for the reader[16]. The continuation of the passage is even more awe-inspiring, since the 'teacher' visualizes another mythological episode involving dark passion (13-18). *And it was the Titan's daughter who sent forth the blighting Scorpion with sharpened sting, when she compassed an evil end for Boeotian Orion, and attacked him after he had laid violent hands upon the immaculate raiment of the goddess. Thereupon the Scorpion, which had lurked unobserved beneath a small stone, struck him in the ankle of his strong foot.* Orion's drama has everything, from latent eroticism to the desire for revenge, from danger to death and destruction, while the setting focuses on the threat lurking under every stone where the scorpion waits in ambush. The narrator has an eye for sensuous detail, such as the sharpened sting (τεθηγμένον ἐκ κέντροιο) which strikes the strong ankle (στιβαροῖο κατὰ σφυρὸν ἤλασεν ἴχνευς) of Orion; sensory awareness is exploited by the recherché epithet χαλαζήεις 'causing cold sweat as when one is struck by hail' which captures the physical symptom of the scorpion's poisonous attack[17]. Eventually it becomes evident that the episode is set within an aitiological frame, since it provides the mythological explanation for the star Orion (19-20). *But Orion's wondrous sign is set conspicuous, fixed there amid the constellations, as of one hunting, dazzling to behold.* Hence the passage is seen as a tribute to the other didactic poet of the era, Aratus. But whereas Aratus' account of the Orion episode in the *Phainomena* (vv. 634-646) is rather sophisticated and stylized in its rendering, Nicander subtly differentiates himself from the tradition, and

15. Religious conscience is not accidentally attributed to Nicander: Jacques (2002) lviii-lx argues that religious superstition (along with pseudo-science) lurks under the scientific veneer of Nicander's poems; Touwaide (1991) 91-96 remarks that mythological narratives and allusions add religious depth to Nicander's natural and medical philosophy. Cf. fr. 31 G.-S. from the *Ophiaca* where the absence of serpents from the region of Clarus, i.e. a natural *paradoxon*, is attributed to the divine intervention of Apollo.

16. It is worth noting that Hesiod is not considered the source of this story by the Sch. Nic. *Ther.* 12a ἰστέον δὲ ὅτι ψεύδεται ὁ Νίκανδρος ἐνταῦθα· οὐδαμοῦ γὰρ τοῦτο εἶπεν ἐν τοῖς πραττομένοις· περὶ γοῦν τῆς τῶν δακνόντων θηρίων γενέσεως, ὅτι ἐστὶν ἐκ τῶν Τιτάνων τοῦ αἵματος, παρὰ μὲν τῷ Ἡσιόδῳ οὐκ ἔστιν εὑρεῖν; instead we are informed that the story is told by Akousilaos. This means that Nicander wants to evoke high poetry rather than ensure 'scholarly' precision; he also presupposes that a similar genealogy for the serpents as recorded in Aesch. *Suppl.* 264-267 is known to his readers. On the sources, see Jacques (2002) 77-78 n. 2.

17. According to the Sch. Nic. *Ther.* 13a εἰσὶ γὰρ σκορπίοι χαλαζήεντες διὰ τὸ τοὺς δεδηγμένους ὑπ' αὐτῶν ἱδροῦν, ὡς ὑπὸ χαλάζης ἢ ὑετοῦ βεβρεγμένους.

highlights, through sensation and visualization, the amazing and horrifying dimension of nature as observed by the man of science[18].

What this 'double proem' conveys is a sense that the natural and the
supernatural struggle with each other in Nicandrean aesthetics. On the one
hand, Nicander fosters critical thinking and favours empiricism–even if it
is merely a pose since his knowledge is mediated through written treatises
rather than practical experience–as the proper means to understand the
surrounding world; on the other, he is not cold-hearted in his attempt to
explore and understand nature; as I will demonstrate below, appeal to the
senses is equally, if not more, important for him than the intellectual
approach to his subject matter. In thus re-interpreting the didactic mode,
Nicander may, *mutatis mutandis*, be compared to the celebrated Romantic
physician and poet, Erasmus Darwin. This is how the latter describes his
authorial intention in the advertisement of his 1791 collection of scientific
poems published under the title *The Botanic Garden*:

> The general design of the following sheets is to enlist Imagination under the
> banner of Science; and to lead her votaries from the looser analogies, which
> dress out the imagery of poetry, to the stricter ones, which form the rati-
> ocination of philosophy. While their particular design is to induce the
> ingenious to cultivate the knowledge of Botany, by introducing them to the
> vestibule of that delightful science, and recommending to their attention the
> immortal works of the celebrated Swedish Naturalist, Linnaeus.

If we read Nicander's proem in the light of the abovementioned 'Preface', we can trace significant points of contact: that imagination (and
anything it stands for such as myth, poeticization and so on) can revivify
science; that analogies underlying poetry enhance the comprehension of
logical structures (these include imagery, visualization and the like); that
the ultimate purpose of such poetic endeavour is the literary rendering of
technical handbooks pertaining to natural science.

By what standards is the dual identity of Erasmus Darwin, and his
overwhelming influence over Romantic poetics[19], relevant to the case

---

18. Probably Nicander, if it is chronologically possible, wrote under the influence of
another dark Hellenistic poet, Euphorion, who recounts that Orion attempted to rape Artemis and was therefore struck by the scorpion (fr. 101 CA). Ps.-Eratosthenes attributes the
story to Hesiod as well (see Overduin [2010] 191-192 on v. 16).

19. The link between Romantic writing and the works of Erasmus Darwin is well
documented in the case of Wordsworth, Shelley and Blake (see Nichols [2005]). Yet the
most outstanding case is that of Mary Shelley who, in the opening of the 1818 'Preface'
to *Frankenstein*, strives to give some credibility to her story by paying hommage to his
scientific writings: "The event on which this fiction is founded has been supposed, by Dr.
Darwin, and some of the physiological writers of Germany, as not of impossible occurrence. I shall not be supposed as according the remotest degree of serious faith to such an
imagination; yet, in assuming it as the basis of a work of fancy, I have not considered
myself as merely weaving a series of supernatural terrors".

under discussion, Nicander of Colophon? To rephrase the question, is there an analogous proportion of science to poetry in Nicandrean aesthetics? There are many reasons that argue for a genuine scientific spirit in his oeuvre. The titles of his extant and lost poems attest to a fascination with all branches of natural science–medicine (Προγνωστικά), toxicology (Ἀλεξιφάρμακα), zoology (Θηριακά, Ὀφιακά, Κυνηγετικά?), entomology (Μελισσουργικά), botany (Ἀλεξιφάρμακα and a poem on φυτῶν ἰδιότητες), hydrography (in his poem on ποταμῶν τῶν περὶ Αἰτωλίαν) and agriculture (Γεωργικά). Specialized treatises on the poisons of the snakes and other poisons underlie the writing of the *Theriaca* and the *Alexipharmaca*, whereas it is attested that the *Prognostica* were based on Hippocratic writings; Nicander, in turn, becomes a source for later iological studies[20]. Passages such as the second proem of the *Theriaca* emphasize the beneficiary role of the scientist for mankind (493-496):

τῶν μὲν ἐγὼ θρόνα πάντα καὶ ἀλθεστήρια νούσων
φύλλα τε ῥιζοτόμον τε διείσομαι ἀνδράσιν ὥρην,
πάντα διαμπερέως καὶ ἀπηλεγές, οἷσιν ἀρήγων
ἀλθήσῃ νούσοιο κατασπέρχουσαν ἀνίην.

Now all the simples and remedies for these ills, the herbs and the time to cut their roots, I will expound to mankind thoroughly and in straightforward fashion,–herbs by whose aid a man may heal the urgent pain of sickness.

Scientificity is announced by the terms διαμπερέως 'through and through' and ἀπηλεγές 'straightforwardly' (cf. Sch. Nic. *Ther.* 495 διαμπερέως· ἀκριβῶς, συντόμως and ἀπηλεγές· ἀληθῶς, προφανῶς); authority by ἐγώ διείσομαι and the collective addressee ἀνδράσιν. On the whole, Nicander's scientific exactitude should not be called into question, as it is also evident in the use of abstract nouns, scientific nomenclature, technical terminology and vocabulary pertaining to human anatomy[21].

There is no doubt that Nicander is neither ignorant of, nor indifferent to, scientific concepts, data and taxonomies, and the related

---

20. For an in-depth analysis of the affinities between Nicander and natural scientists, both before and after his era, see Touwaide (1991) and especially Jacques (2002) xx-lxv; on the reception of Nicander by scientists, see Hatzimichali (2009) 20-25.

21. The stylistic correspondences between Nicander and the *Corpus Hippocrateum* are discussed by de Stefani (2006), see also Oikonomakos (1999); for a study of the anatomic vocabulary of Nicander, see Jacques (2007) xxxiv-xxxvii. The fusion of poetic and scientific vocabulary is treated by Crugnola (1961). Some general thoughts on the scientific spirit, e.g. as regards matters of generic classifications of the snakes, and related expressions in Nicander in Gow/Scholfield (1997) 18-25.

literature[22]. However, he explicitly identifies himself as a poet at the closure of his two poems; he wants to be remembered by his audience (καὶ εἰσέτι Νικάνδροιο μνῆστιν ἔχοις) not as a naturalist but as a poet in the tradition of Homer (*Ther.* 957 Ὁμήρειος, *Alex.* 629 ὑμνοπόλος)[23]. Still, Nicander's attachment to Homeric diction and the *glossai* does not suffice to explain this claim. Despite the rigidity of his subject matter, Nicander employs various means to achieve a high degree of literariness–impressive vocabulary, vivid imagery, mythological digression[24]. But above all he seems to be exploring the boundaries between the object (be it nature or the technical material *per se*) and the subjective viewpoint imposed upon it. This is the point where scientific empiricism becomes an aesthetic experience through the mediation of the senses: *sensation* thus defined is the basis for understanding Nicandrean and Romantic aesthetics alike[25].

This is how Wordsworth views sensation as a means of bringing poetry into the heart of science (*Lyrical Ballads* 'Preface'):

> The Poet will sleep then no more than at present; he will be ready to follow the steps of the Man of Science, not only in those general indirect effects, but he will be at his side, carrying sensation into the midst of the objects of the science itself. The remotest discoveries of the Chemist, the Botanist, or Mineralogist, will be as proper objects of the Poet's art as any upon which it can be employed, if the time should ever come when these things shall be familiar to us, and the relations under which they are contemplated by the followers of these respective sciences shall be manifestly and palpably material to us as enjoying and suffering beings.

Obviously Nicander does not share the idealistic enthusiasm of Wordsworth nor his emotional intensity; it is true that Nicander is rather detached, playful, even ironic in his literary experiment[26]. Even

22. Therefore views assuming that Nicander is only concerned with linguistic experimentation and aesthetic formalism at the expense of accuracy are in my opinion one-sided and fail to capture the essence of Nicandrean poetics: these views are especially supported by Effe (1977) 56-65 and Toohey (1996) 61-73.

23. According to Touwaide (1991) the Homeric model is one of the two principal parameters of Nicander's poetics, the other one being scientific literature.

24. On the poetic strategies employed by Nicander to render his tedious material attractive to the reader, see Spatafora (2005) and Overduin (2010) 97-124; cf. Cusset (2006b) who compares poetical imagery in Aratus and Nicander.

25. For a detailed analysis of the intellectual interrelations between literature and science, with special emphasis upon the sensory experience as a vital component of Romantic aesthetics, see Jackson (2008).

26. Here are two comments on Nicander's distancing from his material by Toohey (1996): "[Nicander's detachment] seems almost to lead to a prurient interest in human suffering" (p. 72); and "this detachment above all manifests itself in his enthusiasm for language, but also in his concomitant lack of enthusiasm for content" (p. 73).

so, sensation is omnipresent in his work. Among the senses invoked, Nicander shows a predilection for sight, taste and smell, sometimes hearing; kinesthesis, temperature and pain, as well as the stimulation of sensory receptors situated within the body (throat, stomach, brain, arteries and the like) carry Nicandrean sensation to extremes. The narrator alternates between distance from, and engagement in, sensory stimulations and their affect on body and mind; at the beginning of each of the medical cases treated he assumes the role of a cold-hearted observer but soon conveys the feeling that he is sensing the symptoms *from within* the suffering body. Here is an example that illustates the point (*Ther.* 334-339): *Again, the form of the dipsas will always resemble that of a small viper; yet death will come quicker to those whom this grim snake assails. Its thin tail, darkish throughout, grows blacker from the end forward. From its bite the heart is inflamed utterly, and in the fever the dry lips shrivel with parching thirst*[27] ...

Sense and sensation are of primary importance to Nicandrean aesthetics, and a strategy typically employed through which it is communicated to the reader is visualization. Nicander is almost obsessed with visual detail, not unlike the natural scientist who is equally interested in macro- and micro-analysis of his living specimens. There exists a remarkable philological anecdote, according to which the first manuscript of Nicander's poems was adorned with illustrations (of scorpions? of serpents? of plants? of mythological scenes?) probably created by the poet himself[28]. Or at least this is how the phrase of Tertullian (*Antidote for the Scorpion's Sting* 1) *Nicander scribit et pingit* 'Nicander writes and draws' has been interpreted; it cannot be excluded however that Tertullian is metaphorically emphasizing here the ability of Nicander to visualize what he is describing in his poems.

In any case: on the one hand, visual precision is a concomitant of science; on the other, visualization is an artistic and rhetorical device aiming at the creation of ἐνάργεια. The abundance of descriptive epithets accounts

27. Toohey (1996) 65 observes on these verses: "[The first aspect of] the passage is that it is macabre, wilfully so. The second is the voyeuristic nature of this sequence. These lines convey a bizarre gratification in the observation of situations involving extreme human suffering. The description within this passage is vivid, graphic, clearly intrigued by the situation which it depicts, but it is firmly detached. Nicander exhibits little concern for the unfortunate victim of the dipsas' attentions".

28. The hypothesis in Gow/Scholfield (1997) 9 n. 2; cf. Gutzwiller (2007) who argues that "it is entirely credible that painted drawings originally accompanied the poetic text, since prose treatises of the period were often illustrated". The traces of the ancient illustrations are to be found in the miniatures of the Medieval manuscript Parisinus Suppl. 247; for a description of these miniatures, see Gow/Scholfield (1997) 222-223 and Jacques (2007) cxxiii-cxxvi.

for both, and so does the unique variety of colour vocabulary found especially in the *Theriaca*[29]. An impressive example is the classification of the
scorpion into seven species according to its colour (*Ther.* 769-804): the
λευκός, the πυρσός, the ζοφόεις, the greenish (χλοάων) and the livid
(ἐμπέλιος), the honey-like (μελίχλωρος) and the red-white (φλογὶ
εἴκελα γυῖα...πτερὰ λευκά)[30]. Often visualization conjures up images
that evoke sensory stimulations and communicate sensations to the reader.
When for example the asp (ἀσπίς in Greek with its double meaning 'shield'
and 'snake) in its thickness is likened to a spear, the reader is invited to
mentally relive the actual experience of the hunter carrying a thick weapon
amidst wild beasts (*Ther.* 169-171): *the asp's thickness is seen to be that
which a spear-maker fashions for a hunting-spear for fighting bulls and
deep-voiced lions.* Or when the exact shading of the Egyptian asp's brown
colour brings back memories of the Nilotic landscape (174-176): *often,
when it grows dark with Aethiop soil, a smoky brown like the sludge which
the many-mouthed Nile in flood pours into the sea, as it dashes against the
waves.* Sensation here stirs the imagination, the *phantasia* of the reader, an
effect occasionally pursued by Nicandrean descriptions[31].

Appeal to the senses, visualization, and, a novel element, *animation*
further attest to the fact that Nicander may be considered the Hellenistic
equivalent of the Romantic Dr. Darwin, naturalist and author of *The
Botanic Garden.* This is how the latter understands the poetic rendering
of botany in the 'Proem' to the second book of his collection, *The Loves
of the Plants*:

> Gentle Reader!
> Lo, here a Camera Obscura is presented to thy view, in which are lights
> and shades dancing on a whited canvas, and magnified into apparent
> life!—if thou art perfectly at leisure for such trivial amusement, walk in,
> and view the wonders of my Enchanted Garden. Whereas P. Ovidius Naso,
> a great Necromancer in the famous Court of Augustus Caesar, did by art
> poetic transmute Men, Women, and even Gods and Goddesses, into Trees
> and Flowers; I have undertaken by similar art to restore some of them to
> their original animality, after having remained prisoners so long in their
> respective vegetable mansions; and have here exhibited them before thee.

---

29. According to Papadopoulou (2009), who offers a comprehensive guide to colour
terminology in Nicander, the function of colour descriptors in Nicander's poems is twofold: first they serve to classify the species and describe the symptoms of venom poisoning
and second they allude to literary texts of high prestige such as the Homeric epics.

30. See Jacques (2002) 210-212 n. 85 and Papadopoulou (2009) 116-117 for a comparison of the passage with scientific writings.

31. The literary representation of the sensation and its communication to the reader
evokes 'the poetics of suggestion', which form a basic tendency of Romanticism (for a
thorough analysis, see Jackson [2008] 23-44).

Vividness in depiction allows nature to be mirrored in verse in ways that are unexpected, impressive, almost marvellous–as if viewing the projections of a camera obscura. The limits of naturalistic observation are exceeded by animation. In Darwin this is a notion suggesting a return to a primal stage during which the forces of nature and its objects were animate and alive. The literary metaphor employed to explain the animalistic state of nature is that of the metamorphosis poetry–it was Ovid, says Darwin, that has once transformed men and women into trees and plants, hence the latter should be restored to their original *anima* through poetry.

Metamorphosis, which dramatizes the transmutation of the animate into the inanimate, is a marginal parameter of animation in the *Theriaca* and the *Alexipharmaca*[32]. Only a few metamorphoses stories are haphazardly arranged within these quasi-scientific poems. When for example the flower hyacinthus is characterized πολύθρηνος 'mournful' the epithet establishes a link with the mythological background of Hyacinthus, the young lover of Apollo (*Ther.* 902-906)[33]: *the mournful hyacinth, over whom Phoebus wept, since without willing it, hard by the river of Amyclae he slew with a blow the boy Hyacinthus in the bloom of youth; for the iron mass rebounding from a rock smote upon his temple and crushed the sheath beneath it.* The story involves the Romantic thematics of 'love and death' which acquires a touch of morbidity, as when the anatomical detail of Hyacinthus' crushed skull is highlighted[34]. The eternal lament of the pine tree recalls another mythical event, evolving around an unusually horrifying theme: the flaying of Marsyas while still alive by Apollo (300-304): *the pine which makes moan on the spot*

32. It remains an open question whether Nicander was specifically interested in the natural implications of the process of transformation in the *Heteroioumena*; Forbes Irving (1990) 24-32 is rather reluctant to accept such a possibility and argues that cult was the main focus of the poem, despite the fact that the *Heteroioumena* systematically dealt with metamorphoses of humans into stones, trees, birds and animals. On the contrary, the obscure Boios in his *Ornithogonia* and of course Ovid in the *Metamorphoses* place particular emphasis on the continuity of human traits into the new forms of the plants or animals into which a man or a woman is transformed.

33. Cf. Nic. *Georg.* fr. 74.31-32 G.-S. ὑακίνθῳ αἰαστῇ likewise conveying the idea of animation. Elsewhere (Sch. Nic. *Ther.* 585a) the commentator attributes another poem about Hyacinthus to Nicander (or was this metamorphosis story treated in the *Heteroioumena*?). The story deals with two Hellenistic favourites, aesthetic death and ritual mourning, and was also treated in a lost aitiological epyllion on the genesis of flowers written by Euphorion (see Sistakou [2008a] 130-131). On a literary reading of the Hyacinthus digression, see Overduin (2010) 513-516 on vv. 902-906.

34. Cf. Sch. Nic. *Ther.* 903 σόλος ἀφαλλόμενος ἐνέπεσε κόρσῃ, τουτέστι τῇ κεφαλῇ. κάλυμμα δὲ τὸν περὶ τὸ κρανίον ὑμένα. Overduin (2010) 516 on v. 906 remarks that "the adjective gives a medical touch to the description, as it apparently distinguishes between different layers of cerebral membrane".

where Phoebus stripped the skin from the limbs of Marsyas; and the tree, lamenting in the glens his farfamed fate, alone utters her passionate plaint unceasingly. A story of excess with grotesque undertones is reflected on the natural paradox of the crying tree. The growing of the plant persea from the sword-axe of Perseus is a story on the cusp of paradoxography (*Alex.* 99-105). According to this recondite piece of natural history the persea sprouts up from a piece of steel, and, in an even more miraculous way, it appears spontaneously at the very spot where the scabbard chape of Perseus' falchion initially fell (101-102 ῥεῖα Μυκηναίῃσιν ἐνηέξησεν ἀρούραις...μύκης ὅθι κάππεσεν ἅρπης). Moreover, like the story of Hyacinthus, the narration about Perseus cutting off the head of Medusa with a falchion (101 αὐχέν' ἀποτμήξας ἅρπῃ γονόεντα Μεδούσης) is a hallmark of Hellenistic morbidity and Romantic darkness.

Occasionally the reader catches a glimpse of a primeval past, set within a mythological universe in which gods and heroes converse freely with plants and animals; this is the point where the natural frame of reference converges with supernaturalism. Once upon a time Apollo who cherished the tamarisk bestowed upon it the gift of prophecy. The anecdote explains the bizarre claim that this plant is since regarded with respect among men as a seer (*Ther.* 613 μάντιν ἐνὶ ζωοῖσι γεράσμιον 'an honoured prophet among mortals'). It is also said that once the lily quarrelled with Aphrodite over the brightness of the white colour, and as a punishment the goddess gave it an obscene figure (*Alex.* 407-409): *wherefore in the midst of its petals Aphrodite attached a thing of shame to vex it, making to grow there the shocking yard of an ass*[35]. In the abovementioned examples it is personification that creates the animating effect[36]. Another device, aitiology, may dramatically animate natural history too. Indeed, curious details of the serpents' anatomy are twice attributed to mythological episodes in the *Theriaca*, both of which are probably Nicander's own invention. These episodes highlight the supernatural to the detriment of scientificity. *If the tale be true* (εἰ ἔτυμον) and *the tale is current* (ἐρέει φάτις) are markers that question the veracity of tales which are however considered complementary to scientific reasoning proper[37]. Why does the haimorrhoos move haltingly like the lame

35. This aitiological story which verges on the grotesque is also recounted in Nicander's *Georgica* (fr. 74.25-30 G.-S.). For other sources, see Jacques (2007) 178-179 n. 43.
36. All the cases of personification in the *Theriaca* are discussed by Overduin (2010) 97-99.
37. On the veracity of myths, as conveyed through aitiology, as a basic question of Hellenistic poetics, see Overduin (2010) 104-106.

(χωλεύουσι)? Helen the Direful–so the story goes–punished this snake when it attacked and killed her steersman, Kanobos, by breaking its spine (316-317): *therefore Helen crushed the middle of its trailing shape, breaking the ligatures of the back about the spine, so that the backbone started from its body.* A similar tale is narrated in connection to a dark story involving Demeter the Vengeful and the gecko, a small lizard that had previously been a boy (484-486): *of him the tale is current how the Sorrowing Demeter did him injury when she marred the limbs of him as a boy by the well Callichorum.* Another metamorphosis that illustrates a natural *paradoxon*[38].

With an almost mythopoetic enthusiasm Nicander depicts nature as a cosmos inhabited by the most amazing creatures and plants, conceived as living organisms which possess their own *anima*. Nicander's take on the animated nature corresponds thus to the Romantic notion of nature not as a mechanical system but as a living organism; it comprises attitudes, such as the return to animalism or a heightened sense of affect, that also point towards Romantic science. Two questions should be posed within this interpretative frame: first, is there an ideology behind Nicander's depiction of nature, and second, which place does man occupy within this natural cosmos? A passage that illuminates both questions is found at the beginning of the *Theriaca* (57-79). The focus is turned on ordinary people, towards which the entire poem is programmatically oriented. The scenario is quite plain: night falls and the man of toil must sleep in the open; to ensure that he will not be attacked by the poisonous creatures lurking everywhere, he must collect various odorous herbs to prevent them from approaching. Within this narrative frame a catalogue of 15 different herbs is introduced, some of which are personified. The man, "an intruder rather than a protagonist" in the natural landscape[39], is surrounded by living, semi-humanized plants. The mint with the long hair (χαιτήεσσα) delights (ἀγαλλομένη) for being watered by the river; another plant, the λύγος, has an odour that causes horror to snakes (ῥίγιστον ὄδωδεν); creeping thyme grazes on the soil like an animal (νοτερὴν ἐπιβόσκεται αἶαν) for it loves life (φιλόζωος); less favourable to man are the horrid hypericum (σκύρα τ' ἐχθρά) that harms the

38. The metamorphosis of Askalabos into a lizard was treated by Nicander in the *Heteroioumena* (cf. Anton. Liberalis *Met.* 24), on which see Jacques (2002) 143-144 n. 50/1 and Overduin (2010) 539-541 Appendix II. The story of Helen and the haimorrhoos is also set against the background of metamorphosis poetry: not only Kanobos is catasterized after his death but from the tears shed by Helen grows the plant heleneion–probably recounted in the *Heteroioumena* too, see Gow/Scholfield (1997) 176 on v. 316.

39. On the limited, almost ornamental role of man within nature in the *Theriaca*, see Overduin (2010) 99.

herdsmen (σίνατο) and the sulphurwort that chases away the monstrous snakes with its stench (θηρί' ἀποσσεύει τε καὶ ἀντιόωντα διώκει).

In this and similar passages Nicander depicts a magical landscape, an enchanted garden, not substantially different from the Romantic ideal of the 'enlivened' nature. It is full of wonder in its huge variety of animal and plant species in all their colourful and mystical manifestations[40]. It bears the signs of a past during which the gods commanded its creatures at will. It is sometimes idyllic in its floral beauty and the allure of its hidden forces[41]. Yet man's coexistence with nature is not harmonious–as ideally presupposed by the Romantics. Far from being a serene, 'Golden Age' scenery, Nicander's nature is a danger zone. In terms of low and everyday realism, it represents an actual threat against men of toil, travellers, herdsmen, innocent children–even if designed as an autonomous and self-sufficient system, where harm and remedy, poison and antidote exist side-by-side[42]. For nature in Nicander is not a place of light but of darkness[43].

But is Nicander conveying his credo about nature and science (in a fashion akin to the philosophical rendering of astronomy in Aratus' *Phainomena*) through the medium of didactic poetry or does the strong taste for morbidity and the quest for sensationalism overpower the scientific content of his poems? It is difficult to decide whether Nicander imposes the view of the physician on his poetic oeuvre or vice versa. However, the dark aesthetics that pervade his poetry mark a divergence from the style of scientific literature of the era, thus rendering the latter hypothesis much more credible[44].

40. Gow/Scholfield (1997) 228-237 append an exhaustive catalogue of flora, fauna, animal, minerals, substances etc. in Nicander which is revealing in its variety and quantity. Cf. the table compiled by Overduin (2010) 536-538 in which all the animate and inanimate species mentioned in the *Theriaca* are listed.

41. Spatafora (2005) 232-240 analyzes the motif of floral beauty as a reminiscence of the *locus amoenus* in Nicander; a somewhat different approach is found in Overduin (2010) when he remarks e.g. that (p. 104) "in most descriptions of nature Nicander seems to have consciously pictured an anti-bucolic world, subverting the image of the *locus amoenus*".

42. See Jacques (2002) lxxxiv-lxxxvi and Overduin (2010) 103-104.

43. The worldview proposed by Nicander is a passive one. As Toohey (1996) 70 observes: "The world for Nicander imposes itself. One watches this world, almost as if it were a book. This world, despite all of these hopeless remedies, is a universe which one is helpless to influence (one does not so much watch it helplessly, as one is watched)." On how Nicander depicts earth as a hostile and threatening place, see Spatafora (2005) 248-256. Differently Clauss (2006) who argues that for Nicander knowledge is the key to rediscovering Eden.

44. Two facts may further corroborate this claim: a) the 'dry' style that is attested for the naturalistic treatises of Theophrastus, Erasistratus, Apollodorus and others, on which see the illuminating collections of fragments in Jacques (2002) 269-309; b) the deep impact of Nicander's aesthetics on poets, such as Virgil, Lucan and Nonnus, on which see Jacques (2002) cxvi-cxxiii and Overduin (2010) 126-128.

It is a *communis opinio* among scholars that the *Theriaca* and the *Alexipharmaca* exhibit an overwhelming fascination with the macabre[45]. Not only does the subject matter, poisonous serpents and plants and death from poison, offer ample opportunity for the macabre to unfold. Macabre is not just a theme but a prevailing mood, a filter through which naturalism is viewed and re-interpreted. The animated nature is everywhere intertwined with death: the words θάνατος, πότμος, αἶσα, κῆρα and Ἀιδωνεύς occur over 30 times in both poems. But since death lurks all over the savage nature, which is depicted as a hostile place full of serpents, a feeling of terror affects the reader. The most common adjective to denote a serpent is σμερδαλέος, a strong epic epithet describing mythical monsters like Skylla and Hekate. Recurrent images such as the serpent with the blood-red gaze or the one which flickers its tongue, and crypto-mythological allusions to the Hesiodean Typhon, heighten the *pathos* in the *Theriaca* at times[46]. On the other hand, the *Alexipharmaca* displays a voyeuristic pleasure in viewing human bodies in all kinds of extreme suffering–bodies that are teetering on the edge of death. Within this context the dual function of the plant as an antidote and a fateful poison, by suggesting that a landscape full of death exists alongside the *locus amoenus*, stimulates the dark imagination of the reader.

Romantic scientists bring "the beauty and terror" of nature to the fore[47]. The physician and poet Nicander, though acknowledging the two faces of nature and admiring its miraculous aspects, privileges its darker dimensions. This is the point at which the sensation of science verges on sensationalism. The dark aesthetics of the *Theriaca* and the *Alexipharmaca*, as seen through the prism of the poisonous serpents and plants, and of the humans with the suffering bodies, will be explored in the following chapters.

---

45. To such an extent that Toohey (1996) 62 compares their tonality to the sensationalism usually reserved for tabloid newspapers and Spatafora (2005) speaks of an "impressionistic style" that aims at the emotional involvement of the reader.

46. On the vocabulary of terror in Nicander, see Spatafora (2005) 241-248.

47. Cf. Holmes (2008) who epitomizes the Romantic concept of science in the title of his book as follows: *The Age of Wonder. How the Romantic Generation Discovered the Beauty and Terror of Science.*

III.2. Venomous creatures, monstrous plants

> Nothing could exceed the intentness with which this scientific gardener
> examined every shrub which grew in his path; it seemed as if he was look-
> ing into their inmost nature, making observations in regard to their creative
> essence, and discovering why one leaf grew in this shape, and another in
> that, and wherefore such and such flowers differed among themselves in
> hue and perfume. Nevertheless, in spite of the deep intelligence on his part,
> there was no approach to intimacy between himself and these vegetable
> existences. On the contrary, he avoided their actual touch, or the direct
> inhaling of their odors, with a caution that impressed Giovanni most disa-
> greeably; for the man's demeanor was that of one walking among malig-
> nant influences, such as savage beasts, or deadly snakes, or evil spirits,
> which, should he allow them one moment of license, would wreak upon him
> some terrible fatality.

> Nathaniel Hawthorne *Rappaccini's Daughter* (1844)

This excerpt by Nathaniel Hawthorne seems to explore the boundaries of
Dark Romanticism. The protagonist, the medical researcher Dr. Rappaccini, cultivates a secret garden filled with poisonous plants; as a scientist
he carefully examines each exotic species, yet as an individual he is horrified by the evil forces, imagined as beasts or snakes, that reside within
these deadly plants. Dr. Rappaccini could incorporate the man of science
walking in the Nicandrean landscape, or, to be more accurate, the persona of the narrator/teacher who is mystified by the wonderful and terrifying knowledge about poisons. As already argued, the *Theriaca* and
the *Alexipharmaca* have the form of a natural science handbook; nevertheless, beneath the scientific surface lurks an aesthetic project rather
than a technical treatise[48]. Nicander belongs to a distinct tradition which
exhibits a penchant for making poetry out of the most unsuitable material. Leaving myth, fiction and fantasy aside, the Hellenistic taste for
poeticizing anything, from *glossai* to name catalogues, from literary
exempla to curiosities and *paradoxa*, may explain the various facets of
Nicander's literary experimentation with his scientific scenario. But what
does this scenario comprise? Contrary to the programmatic statement of
the titles and proems, Nicander's *Theriaca* and *Alexipharmaca* extend
across multiple disciplines. Toxicology (*iologica* on poisons and antidotes), zoology (especially *ophiologica* which emphasize the natural features of serpents), the branch of botany studying medical herbalism,

---

48. According to the famous aphorism by Gow/Scholfield (1997) 18 "the victim of
snakebite or poison who turned to Nicander for first aid would be in sorry plight".

medicine (pathology and pharmacology), sub-scientific branches of knowledge like paradoxography and some practical advice on agriculture for farmers (*georgica*) constitute the complex material of these poems[49]. The most diverse sources from Aristotle and Theophrastus to Apollodorus and Erasistratus, and a variety of perspectives (scientific, psychological, literary) are moulded to the generic form of didactic epic, thus reinforcing the idea that Nicander is exploiting the aesthetic potential of science here.

Should both poems be considered complementary to each other, i.e. should they have been composed to form a diptych, then their titles must have had a special symbolism[50]. Whereas the first poem concerns monstrous creatures and their poisons, the second proposes precautions and remedies against them–does this imply that the moral outlook of Nicander's composition is, on the whole, optimistic[51]? Could be, although the macabre mood of the poems suggests quite the opposite. The title of the first poem is revealing in this sense. Θηριακά is an ambiguous title, corresponding to the broad sense of a study, treatise or writing 'concerning venomous beasts' and/or to the technical meaning ἡ θηριακή [sc. ἀντίδοτος] 'the antidote against a poisonous bite' (*LSJ* s.v. θηριακός)[52]. It is beyond doubt though that Nicander wanted the noun θήρ 'wild beast or fabulous monster' to resonate as a key theme of his poem; therefore θηρῶν is placed in the very first verse to denote the subject matter of his epic. Which is dark, as it recalls the gloomy age following the fall of the Titans from whose blood the serpents came into being. The cosmogonic origin of the θηρία is an aition explaining their violent nature, the one which inspires terror to men in the postlapsarian era[53]. Darkness of subject

49. The exact correspondences between technical literature and Nicander are explored by Touwaide (1991).

50. For the poems as a "theriological diptych", fitting within one papyrus roll just like the *Alexandra* or *Argonautica* Book 4, see Magnelli (2010) 217-220.

51. A positive account of Nicander's worldview is owed to Clauss (2006) whose core argument is summarized as follows (p. 162): "The *Theriaca* effectively counters the postlapsarian gloom of the Hesiodic poem with a sustained and spirited account of how knowledge makes life easy, even in the face of the deadly creatures that came into being after the fall of the Titans". Likewise Magnelli (2010) 221-223.

52. On the obscurity of this elliptic title, see Overduin (2010) 174. The distinction between the two made by Ps.-Dioscorides in the preface of his iological treatise is obviously an imitation of Nicander (*De iis* Praef. 9-12): ὁ μὲν [sc. λόγος] περὶ τῶν ἰοβόλων προαγορεύεται θηριακός· ὁ δὲ περὶ τῶν θανασίμων ἀλεξιφάρμακος, ὃν τάξαντες δὴ προδείξομεν τὰ εἰωθότα παρακολουθεῖν· τά τε δυνάμενα βοηθεῖν πρὸς ἕκαστον αὐτῶν.

53. As Clauss (1991) 176 remarks "the θηρία came into being as a result of violence done against the race of the Titans...all such creatures were created during the violent end of the age of Kronos and Rhea".

matter is further emphasized by the affective vocabulary at the beginning of the *Theriaca*: after σίνη ὀλοφώια θηρῶν 'the deadly injuries of savage creatures' of the preface, κακοεργὰ φαλάγγια 'noxious spiders', ἀνιγροὶ ἑρπησταί 'grievious reptiles' and ἄχθεα μυρία γαίης 'the earth's countless burdens' are periphrases implying terror. Real serpents qualify as monsters–θηρία, κνώδαλα, τέρα–everywhere in the *Theriaca*[54].

The terror of the serpent is an archetypal image aiming at the sublime. This is how Edmund Burke describes its effect (*A Philosophical Enquiry into the Origin of Our Ideas of the Sublime and Beautiful* 2.2):

> No passion so effectually robs the mind of all its powers of acting and reasoning as *fear*. For fear being an apprehension of pain or death, it operates in a manner that resembles actual pain. Whatever therefore is terrible, with regard to sight, is sublime too, whether this cause of terror be endued with greatness of dimensions or not; for it is impossible to look on anything as trifling, or contemptible, that may be dangerous. There are many animals, who though far from being large, are yet capable of raising ideas of the sublime, because they are considered as objects of terror. As serpents and poisonous animals of almost all kinds.

So, Nicander's θηρία need not be mythical to inspire terror. 'Real-life' dimension and the anxiety of pain and death aroused by the very image of the poisonous animal suffice to create the sublime. As a consequence, it is explicable why Nicander eschews a highly symbolic bestiary in favour of the various species of serpents found in nature. Theriomorphy is not the product of fantasy, of poetic imagination carried to extremes as when it generates Typhons and Medusas, but of the artistic reworking of natural observation.

Before exploring further the terror before the serpent as a parameter of the sublime, we must first consider the status of the visual in Nicander's poetry. It is noteworthy that the only visual representations in the *Theriaca* and the *Alexipharmaca* are those of the fauna–barely of the flora (the latter seem to have been vividly depicted in the lost *Georgica*). Apart from snakes, the fauna include spiders, scorpions, bees, wasps, myriopods, lizards and the like. Creatures belonging to the microcosm of nature hold a fascination for Hellenistic poets and artists. Their visualization in text (and, alternatively, in images of painters and sculptors) is

---

54. Θήρ, used almost as a synonym for the serpent, is mentioned in critical passages of the *Theriaca* such as the 'Theogony' proem and the fable about the dipsas and the ass (where the phrases 351 οὐλοὸς θήρ and 357 οὐλομένη θήρ); cf. fr. 32.3 G.-S. where the Libyan desert is called θηροτρόφος. Κνώδαλον, a word with epic and tragic resonances, as in the verse Αἰγύπτοιο τά τε τρέφει οὐλοὸς αἶα/ κνώδαλα (759-760). The asps are called τέρα in the highly emotive verse ἐχθρῶν που τέρα κεῖνα καρήασιν ἐμπελάσειε (186).

attributed to the deep influence of science on the formation of Hellenistic aesthetics. An obsession with detail is thus explained as "an interest in the particular" and "a scientific, almost clinical interest in specificity", a style of "exaggerated realism", or what André Hurst has termed, in reference to Apollonius, "the vérifiable"[55]. Nicander excels at exactly this type of visualization[56].

Within this context, Nicander illustrates his creatures meticulously, by creating images that, more or less, follow a specific pattern. The serpent is introduced by its name, then the focus is on physical appearance and size. An illuminating example, among many, is the depiction of the haimorrhoos (286-292): *it equals a footprint in length, but as to breadth it dwindles tapering from the fiery head down; at times, it is of sooty hue, or again a reddish brown; it narrows moderately at the neck, and its tail is sharply compressed and stretches flattened from the middle onward; in its forehead beneath its snow-white horns are planted two eyes, of which the irises are somewhat those of locusts.* The passage resembles a biological treatise in its exactitude and rigidity–only until it reaches its denouement: σμερδαλέον δ' ἐπί οἱ λαμυρὸν πέφρικε κάρηνον 'on high rises terrible its devouring head' (293)[57]. If the poetic rendering of the haimorrhoos as a cruel monster evokes the terrible sublime, the much more dramatic description of a little insect, the peculiar κεφαλοκρούστης or κρανοκολάπτης, verges on the grotesque (759-768)[58]. It is introduced as one of monsters of the Egyptian landscape whose *terrible head nods ever in grim fashion* each time *it plants its sting in the top of a man's neck or on his head, and it may easily and on the spot bring the doom of death.* Even if this is a real creature, the incongruity between actual size and exaggerated monstrosity–σμερδαλέον νεύει κάρη αἰὲν ὑποδράξ–has an almost comic undertone[59].

55. The terms in Fowler (1989) 113, who dedicates an entire chapter to the Hellenistic penchant for the creatures, plants and animals, in literature and art (pp. 110-136).

56. Nicander does not primarily draw upon science but on literature to create the detailed images of serpents: for the analysis of some Nicadrean images, see Cusset (2006b) 75-104.

57. The dramatic emphasis on the height reached by the horrifying head of the haimorrhoos aims at creating a sensational effect, since it is not consistent with scientific data: cf. Overduin (2010) 296 on v. 293 who observes that Nicander "uses the standard pose of the threatening snake with its head up high as a stock description...the terrible head can hardly be rising more than 10-15 cm above the ground". On the imitation of this sensational description by Aelian (*N.A.* 15.13), see Jacques (2002) 113-115 n. 27.

58. On the obscure biological identity of this insect, see Jacques (2002) 209-210 n. 84.

59. Cf. Overduin (2010) 470 on v. 765 who notes: "The creature's look, unvarying by nature, is qualified by the poet as αἰέν, giving the impression that the creature's evil nature is showing all the time. The result, a tiny creature with a perennial evil expression, is a comical exaggeration of what the *cranocolaptes* is really supposed to look like".

Apart from the head, the eyes and the tongue are emphatically described as in vv. 227-230 on the appearance of the male viper: *but the eyes in the viper's face turn blood-red when he is angered, and as his forked tongue flickers rapidly, he lashes the end of his tail–wayfarers call him the snaky Cocytus*. Death lurks in the teeth of the serpent, its fangs and jaws, anatomical details which deserve exhaustive treatment. The dragon has three rows of deadly teeth (441-442), the asp has four fangs rooted deeply in its jaws from whence *it belches forth poison unassuageable on a body* (182-185), whereas the female viper bites with her whole mouth and leaves its mark upon the skin where *you can easily observe that the jaws have opened wide about the flesh* (232-234). There are also oddities, like the positioning of the spider's teeth at the centre of its stomach (718) or the herbiverous scorpion with the hard teeth which is depicted as an insatiable eater of grass (782-785)[60]. The physical description is completed with the enumeration of biological features, habits, dwellings of the serpents, and change of behaviour in accordance with the season of the year. Serious attention is devoted to the moving image of the serpent, a prelude to its attack upon men. The image of the haimorrhoos once more offers a dramatic illustration (294-297): *with an oblique and halting movement it ever steers its little body on its brief journeys from the middle of the back like the Cerastes, scraping its belly over the earth, and with its scaly body it makes a slight rustling as though crawling through a heap of straw[61].*

This is only a small sample indicating the fixation of Nicander with accuracy as documented by an acute observer of nature. But whereas the spectator 'sees' the serpent in action, and the narrator 'verbalizes' the image, a new dimension of the visual emerges. The viewer projects his own imagination on the object viewed, in the case of the *Theriaca*, the serpent. The unseen imposes itself on the seen, the invisible on the visible–this is a Romantic answer to mimetic concepts of art as representative of life[62]. To put it differently, Nicander's naturalistic realism is superficial, once psy-

60. The scorpion attacks with its sting not its jaws. Therefore Nicander is "either making serious observational errors, or perhaps he assumes that the round and well-fed paunch of the livid scorpion can only have grown this size by grazing all the time like a cow" (Overduin [2010] 476 on vv. 783-784). A scorpion represented as a cow would also create a grotesque effect. On the scientific inconsistencies of both descriptions, see Jacques (2002) 200 n. 77/3 and 215-216 n. 89.

61. Another noteworthy passage is the one comparing the course of the viper to that of the dipsas with the underlying image of the moving ship (265-270): the same terrifying image of the moving serpent is found in Apollonius *Arg.* 4.1541-1547 in a simile depicting the crooked course of the Argo. For a comparison between the two passages, see Cusset (2006b) 82-84.

62. This Romantic conception of visuality is explored by Thomas (2008) 7-19.

chological impressions, imaginary horrors, conceptual and emotional associations animate the serpentine image[63]. One category comprises the psychological response of the subject, as expressed in the use of a highly affective vocabulary. Οὐλόμενος, ὀλοός, ἐχθρός, λευγαλέος, σμερδαλέος, ἀμείλικτος, βροτολοιγός as recurrent attributes of the serpent reflect the affect of the viewer–not any empirical 'truth' about the nature of the object. When the objective merges with the subjective, the effect is that of darkness (227-229): αὐτὰρ ἐνωπῆς γλήνεα φοινίσσει τεθοωμένος, ὀξὺ δὲ δικρῇ γλώσσῃ λιχμάζων 'the eyes in the viper's face turn blood-red when he is angered, and his forked tongue flickers rapidly...'. Terror before the angered, rattling snake is in the eye of the beholder[64].

Affective language may equally apply to the object itself, for in Nicander the serpent is more than an animate creature: it suggests humanization. The serpent possesses negative human features; thus its poisoning is the result of evil intent[65]. As argued, the *Theriaca* programmatically proclaims the dark side of the serpent in title and proem. The reader senses its moral degradation, since the serpent is portrayed as destructive (ὀλοφώιος), malignant (κάκηθες) and implacable (ἄσπειστος), an evil-doer (κακοεργός) motivated by rage and wrath (κοτέουσα, τεθοωμένος), a blood-thirsty beast (αἵματος ἰσχανόων). Although direct characterizations of this type occur sporadically, humanization, with emphasis on negative emotion, is an undercurrent flowing against scientificity everywhere in the *Theriaca*. A notable example is the sensational description of the attack of the cenchrines (469-477). Unlike other dark passages which unfold during the night, the scene of the attack is set against the background of a sweltering summer noon; it is there that the cenchrines lurks thirsty for blood and patiently awaits for its victims to appear. *Do you not dare, bold though you be, to face him in his fury, for fear he wind about and strangle you as he lashes your body all around with his tail, and gorge your blood after he has broken both your collar-bones.* The

63. The most characteristic instances of the 'emotive' vocabulary of Nicander are collected by Spatafora (2005) 241-243.

64. Intertextuality intensifies imagination here. Φοινίσσω is a tragic word, employed in contexts of blood, slaughter and death (e.g. Eur. *Hec.* 150 φοινισσομένην αἵματι, *Or.* 1285 σφάγια φοινίσσειν); interestingly enough, Ps.-Aristotle in the *Mirabilia* 843b explains the name of the Phoenicians on the basis of φοινίσσω=φονεύω and gives φοινίσσω as a synonym of αἱμάσσω. Λιχμάζω evokes the horrifying descriptions of the hundred snake-like heads of the Typhon from Hesiod's *Theogony* (826) and of the mythical Gorgons from the 'Hesiodic' *Aspis* (235). Τεθοώμενος is attested in a passage by Hermesianax as an attribute of Kerberos (fr. 7.11 CA); cf. Overduin (2010) 277 on v. 228.

65. For an overview of the anthropomorphising depiction of the serpent, see Overduin (2010) 97-98; cf. Overduin (2009) 90-91 on the serpent between human and animal behaviour.

confrontation of human and serpent which occurs, as on the Homeric battlefield, face to face, the entanglement of the victim by the attacking serpent, the aftermath of this fierce battle which consists of an act of blood-
sucking, and above all the madness of the cenchrines increase the *pathos*
of the scene[66]. In several passages like this the physical monstrosity of the
serpent seems to be the mirror of its evil spirit.

Affect and a heightened sense of *pathos* add new depth to Nicandrean
terror. The snake is not a mere image evoking pain and death but living
proof that nature has a dark psyche. Which is manifest in passages evolving around the key theme of *violence*. At times the description of the
serpents as violent entities yields to narratives about their violent impulses
and actions. The mating of the vipers in vv. 128-136 offers an outstanding
example of how natural violence is dramatized in the *Theriaca*. Already
the setting anticipates darkness, when the narrator gives the warning to his
addressse '*beware of meeting at the crossroads the dusky male viper
when he has escaped from her bite and is maddened by the blow of the
smoke-hued female*'. Setting (the crossroad) and occasion (two snakes
mating) have already been mentioned some verses before within a magical context (98-100): *if however you can cast snakes coupled at crossroads, alive and just mating, into a pot, you have a preventive against
deadly disasters*–the mating snakes, caught alive, are the ingredients for
the making of an antidote[67]. After having created an atmosphere of supernatural terror by reference to the ominous image of the crossroad, Nicander proceeds with the narrative digression on the bloody intercourse of the
vipers. The story highlights how the female, blinded by lust, decapitates
her male partner, and in turn the young-born vipers kill their mother to
avenge their father's horrible death. This is one of the natural *mirabilia*
that have early on attracted the attention of authors such as Herodotus and
the paradoxographer Antigonus of Carystus[68]. What perhaps may be seen
as Nicander's contribution is a unique taste for cruel and gory detail in
combination with psychological emphasis. *The lustful female fastens upon
him, tearing him with her foul fang, and cuts off the head of her mate...*

---

66. The Homeric subtext of the scene is dicussed by Overduin (2010) 361-363 on vv.
474-477. In any case, the 'madness' of the cenchrines and its 'unnatural' portrayal is
highlighted by Jacques (2002) 141-143 n. 49.

67. This is one of the passages indicating how superstitious belief in magic found its
way into Nicandrean poetry (Jacques [2002] lix); moreover, the crossroad evokes celebrated Hellenistic passages with a dark content, such as Theocr. 2.36 about the appearance
of Hekate and Call. *H.Dem.* 114 about the fate of Erysichthon as a beggar (Overduin
[2010] 237-238 on v. 128).

68. For a comparative reading of Herodotus 3.109 and the Nicandrean passage, as well
as for the dependence of Aelian on Nicander, see Jacques (2002) 92-93 n. 16.

the young vipers avenge their sire's destruction, since they gnaw their
mother's thin flank and thereby are born motherless...

Intercourse and birth ending in cannibalism are extreme cases of natural violence, which is further explored by similar dark narratives: the
furious chase of the deers after the snakes in their lurking places (141-
144), the attack of the ichneumon on the asp's eggs (190-199) followed
by the fierce struggle between them in the marshes of Egypt (200-208)
and the 'war of hate' between the eagle and the dragon (448-457). Obviously Nicander builds on widespread credos about 'the law of the jun-
gle', an idea explicitly expressed by Hesiod. In distinguishing human
justice from the violence of animals, Hesiod introduces a religious/moral
dimension to the problem (*WD* 276-280): it was Zeus that, while granting men δίκη, had let birds and fish and animals devour each other,
because these creatures were not endowed with any sense of law and
order. Nicander elaborates on this Hesiodic premise, nevertheless not
with a moralizing intent[69]. Such passages in the *Theriaca* exhibit a fascination with natural morbidity. It is exactly at this critical point that intellectual excitement caused by scientific observation and a taste for sensational stories of lust, blood and death converge.

Now, how does this particular type of natural sensationalism connect
to Romantic aesthetics? For the Romantics the individual and the characteristic, as well as the ugly and the exceptional, are much more interesting
categories than the beautiful, the ideal and the harmonious. In many
respects, this is an idea that may equally well apply to Hellenistic aesthetics. Nicander, in poeticizing a bizarre subject matter, the venomous creature, exploits its potential to create a sensational effect. The Romantic
naturalist William Bartram offers again a close parallel to Nicander's fascination with serpents from both a visual and a psychological aspect. Bartram dedicates a great part of his travels (Part II. Ch. X) to an extensive
account and description of serpents, which are not only sensationally
visualized but moreover humanized in regard to their psychology. This is
for example how Bartram depicts the moccasin serpent[70]:

---

69. Yet another passage, the ainos of the dipsas and the ass which presupposes a
Golden Age setting (343-358), has a clear Hesiodic ring and a moral orientation: for a
thorough analysis, see Overduin (2010) 312-325. Jacques (2002) 120-121 n. 33 discusses
the mythical quality of this aitiological story as opposed to 'scientific' explanations of
natural phenomena.

70. This is very 'Nicandrean' in style and colouring. Yet Bartram sometimes questions
the evilness of the serpent as when he declares that "there is another snake...which is a
very beautiful creature, and I believe not of a distructive or vindictive nature" or that "the
green snake is a beautiful innocent creature". On the innocence of certain species of serpents, cf. *Ther.* 488-492.

> The moccasin snake is a large and horrid serpent to all appearance, and there are very terrifying stories related of him by the inhabitants of the Southern states…They have one peculiar quality, which is this, when discovered, and observing their enemy to take notice of them, after throwing themselves in a coil, they gradually raise their upper mandible or jaw until it falls back nearly touching their neck, at the same time slowly vibrating their long purple forked tongue, their crooked poisonous fangs directed right at you, gives the creature a most terrifying appearance…

Seen from this perspective, it is also explicable why Nicander shows a predilection for natural vs. mythical terror. Science becomes aesthetically interesting to such an extent that it functions as a substitute for myth. Within this context, the displacement of the mythical in favour of the 'real', the 'existent', the 'natural' motivates a hybrid form of naturalism, what might be termed the *physica curiosa*[71]. The quest for the *paradoxa* is not a Hellenistic idea, since Greeks have always exhibited a penchant for aberrations or anomalies found in nature. But whereas Aristotle and his School delimit the boundaries between the scientific and the marvellous, Hellenistic authors, in verse or in prose, develop a taste for liminal cases of the natural. Nicander is also attracted by natural phenomena on the cusp of the marvellous, which suggest an experimentation with mythical or protoscientific concepts. I will briefly discuss three instances of the *physica curiosa* within the *Theriaca*: the physically anomalous, the natural marvel and the return of the imaginary[72].

There is nothing irregular in the anatomy of the serpent, nevertheless some of its physical features arouse curiosity that exceeds scientificity. Some of these only suggest the *paradoxon* like the ability of the serpent to be 'rejuvenated' through the renewal of its skin (31-32, 137-138, cf. 343-358 for the *ainos* narrating how the ass gave eternal youth to the dipsas). Or peculiar anatomical traits that are inappropriate to serpents: like the horns of the cerastes (260-261) and the combination of horns with the locust-like eyes on the forehead of the haimorrhoos (291-292). Strange breeds that transgress the boundaries between species form a distinct category of the monstrous, and aim at producing a grotesque effect[73]. Since Nicander seems to be intrigued by real-life beings, there

71. The term is used by Eco (2007) 241-269 to describe how the monster, a mystical symbol during the Middle Ages, returned during the modern era in the form of a 'scientific curiosity'. Cf. the exciting discussion of the 'nature monstrous', primarily in Middle Ages aesthetics, in Williams (1996) 177-215.

72. For an overview of the *paradoxa* in the *Theriaca*, see Overduin (2010) 114-117.

73. Williams (1996) 179-183 points out that theriomorphic combinations between human and animal, or various animal forms, are common in the Middle Ages, which through them explored the possibilities of the grotesque in the animal kingdom.

is hardly a place for theriomorphic curiosities in his poem. Yet in the section dealing with the microcosm of the venomous animals, we sense an undercurrent of monstrosity under the naturalistic surface. Similes obliquely refer to hybridity in the catalogue of the venomous insects (715-804). The grotesque catalogue comprises the spider with the teeth on its belly and another one, black and hairy, the grape- and the star-spider, the wolf- and the wasp-spider, the antlet which though resembling an ant is as poisonous as the spiders, the tiny spiders that are likened to blister-beetles, the monstrous κεφαλοκρούστης which looks like a moth, the scorpion with the jaws and the other one with the wings, the locust-like scorpion...[74] It is in the very same section of the *Theriaca* that a celebrated natural marvel is explored. The paradox belief of the Greeks (and many semi-scientists from antiquity until modern times)[75] that the carcasses of the oxen can give birth to bees, better known as the practice of the *bougonia*, is mentioned in passing in a digression about the nature of the wasps (739-741): *the ravenous wasp which resembles the horse in its high spirit, for horses are the origins of wasps and bulls of bees which are engendered in their rotting carcasses*[76]. The paradoxographical effect is intensified some verses later, when the scorpions are considered to be the offspring of the crabs (788-796)! This grotesquery is carried to extremes by Ovidian metamorphosis epic, which features a long catalogue of similar thaumatic births from dead bodies[77].

After these great *paradoxa* which bridge death with birth in nature, the last category of the *physica curiosa* in Nicander concerns what I have termed 'the return of the imaginary'. This term suggests that although Nicander effaces imaginary elements from his account of natural history, these elements tend to reappear alongside purely scientific data. The mythical aitiology of natural phenomena and the religious colouring of several passages apart, there are yet other mechanisms of supernatural recollection. Liminal species of serpents, beings oscillating

74. Even Gow/Scholfield (1997) 23, who favour a scientific reading of Nicander, admit, in referring to the weird spiders, that "this list must owe something to superstitious terrors".

75. The idea was not alien to Aristotle and Theophrastus as we are informed by the author of the *Geoponica* (15.1.20): Θεόφραστος καὶ Ἀριστοτέλης φασί, τὰ ζῷα οὐ μόνον ἐξ ἀλλήλων γεννᾶσθαι, ἀλλὰ καὶ αὐτόματα γίνεσθαι, καὶ ἀπὸ τῆς γῆς σηπομένης· αὐτῶν δὲ τῶν ζῴων καὶ τῶν φυτῶν μεταβάλλεσθαί τινα εἰς ἕτερα.

76. For the *bougonia* in ancient agriculture and paradoxographical literature, see Overduin (2010) 460-461 on v. 741.

77. *Met.* 15.361-390, cf. Overduin (2010) 477-478 on v. 791. The Ovidian catalogue culminates with an extreme *paradoxon* according to which human bone marrow may give birth to snakes (*Met.* 15.389-390 *sunt qui, cum clauso putrefacta est spina sepulcro,/ mutari credant humanas angue medullas*).

between the living and the conceptual, assert their existence in the *Theriaca*. Among them, the enigmatic amphisbaena, which is reported to be a reptile with two heads (ἀμφικάρηνον), one at each end of its body (372-383)[78]. Later natural scientists accept the existence of the amphisbaena as a natural wonder, yet until the age of Nicander its presence seems to be a matter for poets rather than scientists. Greeks must have been familiar with this fabulous serpent early on: thus, when Aeschylus compares Klytaimestra to the amphisbaena, he immediately makes clear that this snake is a 'realistic' version of the horrendous Skylla (*Ag.* 1233-1234 ἀμφίσβαιναν, ἢ Σκύλλαν τινὰ/ οἰκοῦσαν ἐν πέτραισι). Undoubtedly, the Nicandrean passage is meant to be read in the light of the Aeschylean passage. Thus, the Aeschylean subtext with its fairytale dimension destabilizes the scientific in Nicander[79]. Another legendary serpent is the basilisk, never mentioned by this name in Nicander. The 'King of Snakes' (ἑρπηστῶν βασιλεύς) is treated as a real serpent in the *Theriaca* (396-410), although it is reputed in antiquity to be non-existent. Many authors claim "not to have ever seen an actual basilisk", despite the fact that special treatises were dedicated to its portrayal[80]. What is striking in Nicander's account of the basilisk is the vividness of its colour–in contrast to the greenish, reddish and deep colouring of the common serpents, the basilisk is the only blond (ξανθός) serpent in nature. What is even more extraordinary is that *none of the heavy-coiled monsters of earth abide his hissing but they turn and flee*–a variation on the widespread belief that the basilisk can kill upon casting its glance on any living being[81]. By thus suggesting its illusionary monstrosity, Nicander, albeit not explicitly, triggers an association

78. On the ambiguity of the amphisbaena between the real and the fabulous, see Jacques (2002) 125-126 n. 38. Overduin (2010) 328-329 is undecided whether Nicander thought that the amphisbaena was a real or an imaginary serpent, but he nevertheless stresses that the reference of it here aims at sensationalism rather than accuracy.

79. West (2006) points out a very interesting parallel about the semi-fabulous nature of the amphisbaena in Near Eastern tradition.

80. E.g. Galen *De simplicium medicamentorum temperamentis ac facultatibus* 12.250 βασιλίσκον μὲν γὰρ τὸ θηρίον οὐδὲ εἶδον οὐδέποτε and Paulus Aeg. *Epit. Med.* 5.20 τοῦτο τὸ θηρίον σπανίως μὲν ὑπὸ ὀφθαλμῶν ἀνθρώπων γίνεται. Individual chapters or treatises on the basilisk are attested for Erasistratus (3rd c. BC), Ps.-Dioscorides (1st c. AD), Aetius (1st/2nd c. AD), Paulus Aegineta (7th c. AD) etc. Jacques (2002) 130-132 n. 42 brilliantly discusses the paradox that although the basilisk was considered fabulous, scientific literature abounds with realistic descriptions of this serpent; yet it is difficult to agree with his view that Nicander has erased the marvellous from his description.

81. For example in the sensational account given by Heliodorus (*Aeth.* 3.8.2): καὶ ὄφεων δὲ ὁ καλούμενος βασιλίσκος ὅτι καὶ πνεύματι μόνον καὶ βλέμματι πᾶν ἀφαυαίνει καὶ λυμαίνεται τὸ ὑποπῖπτον ἴσως ἀκήκοας.

with the supernatural[82]. So does the reference to the dragon (δράκων), which despite being a broad term denoting any huge size serpent and not a specific subspecies, evokes at the same time every fairytale serpentine creature. The question is, does Nicander through reference to the dragon allow the reader a glimpse into the realm of legend[83]? Yes, firstly, by associating its bringing-up by God Paieon on Mount Pelion in a narrative beginning with the once-upon-a-time particle ποτε (439-440); secondly, by depicting it as a splendid, luminous, shining creature (ἄγλαυρος) with an incredible triple row of teeth (441-444); and, thirdly, because Nicander as a rule uses the term δράκων within mythological contexts (in vv. 608-609 he refers to Kadmos and Harmonia as δράκοντε, cf. fr. 562 SH on Laokoon and the lethal dragons)[84].

Thus far, I have focused on the ophiological section of the *Theriaca*, and the devices by which Nicander creates an effect of terror. But, despite the fact that the depiction of snakes is considered by scholars the most attractive, and hence most studied, aspect of Nicandrean poetics, this was not meant to be the primary focus of the poem. To corroborate this view, one has to consider the structure of both the *Theriaca* and the *Alexipharmaca*, which roughly falls into three thematic areas alternating with each other. The first concerns poisons and poisoning, the second precautions and antidotes, the third the effects of both on the human body. Whereas the latter will be treated separately in the next chapter, I will now turn my attention to the first two.

Poison holds an irresistible allure for authors dealing with violent human passions, from Greek tragedy down to Shakespeare, and from Romanticism and Decadence to modern-day novel, a fact that hardly needs documentation. To mention only one fascinating example of how the poison has been aesthetically exploited by Romanticism: the short story cited at the beginning of this chapter, "Rappaccini's Daughter", dramatizes an extreme case of a mad scientist, who not only cultivates a garden with poisonous plants ("that Eden of poisonous flowers") but moreover

---

82. On Nicander's depiction of the basilisk under the influence of paradoxography, see Barbara (2006).

83. There is a philological controversy on the matter. Gow/Scholfield (1997) 179 on v. 438 identify the dragon with a species of python thereby rejecting its fabulous dimension, whereas Jacques (2002) 135-138 n. 46/1 tackles the problem of the natural vs. the supernatural element in this passage. Overduin (2010) 344-349 tends to accept the dragon as a legendary creature, and places special emphasis on the literary and intertextual allusions underlying its presentation.

84. It is no coincidence that all cultures and eras, and prominently the Greek tradition, recognized a powerful symbol in the dragon, as Williams (1996) 202-207 demonstrates.

feeds his own beautiful daughter on poison ("her whole nature was so
imbued with them, that she herself had become the deadliest poison in
existence"); eventually, she is transformed into a poisonous entity ("poison was her element of life") and is killed by taking a powerful antidote
("to Beatrice as poison had been life, so the powerful antidote was
death").

Unlike Hawthorne, Nicander does not contextualize the poison within
a dramatic plot; nevertheless, he exploits the sensation stemming from
its mysterious forces in a manner which, if not parallel, is comparable to
Hawthorne's. Of course, Nicander has a scientific point of departure, and
uses iological treatises as his source. But each time a serpent releases its
venom, the context resonates with expressions evoking bane and death.
Ἄτη, an epic and tragic word, is a common alternative for 'venom'.
Moreover, dark epithets are attached to the technical term ἰός such as
γυιοφθόρος, ἀμείλικτος, βαρύς, κακοεργός, μέλας, ὀλοφώιος, ὀξύς,
πικρός and χολοιβόρος, thus promoting the affective along with the
scientific in the account of snake poisons in the *Theriaca*. Toxic plants
and substances are somewhat differently depicted in the *Alexipharmaca*[85]. In contrast to the *Theriaca*, where venoms motivate long zoological digressions, the *Alexipharmaca* lacks this pure naturalistic aspect.
Poisonous plants are hardly ever visualized, but their delineation relies
on other features: name, odour and taste (qualities stimulating senses
other than sight), sometimes colour, occasionally habitat.

Concise though these illustrations may be, they convey a sense of
morbid aestheticism which is inherent in Nicander's monstrous plants[86].
Within this context, it is no coincidence that the aconite is programmatically announced as the monstrous plant *par excellence* in the second
proem of the *Alexipharmaca* (12-15). *You must, to be sure, learn of the
aconite, bitter as gall, deadly in the mouth, which the banks of Acheron
put forth; there is the abyss of the Wise Counsellor whence few escape,
and there the towns of Priolas fell crashing in ruins.* This dark opening
leaves no doubt as to the subject matter around which the poem evolves,

85. Jacques (2007) xxi-xxxi provides a catalogue of the 22 poisons of plants (all of
which are found in iological treatises), their classification, as well as a list of composite
poisons in Nicander.

86. The term is introduced by Praz (1970) 323 to denote the obsession with 'monstrous' botany as demonstrated by the legendary Des Esseintes, the chief character of the
Decadent novel *À rebours* by J.-K. Huysmans. Praz' description may *mutatis mutandis*
apply to the atmosphere of Nicander's poetry: "Enthusiasm for monstrous flowers and
tropical plants, for contorted shapes, in fact for 'Medusean' beauty in its most paradoxical
forms–all this was presented by Huysmans with the minuteness of a Dutch still-life
painter". More striking parallels between the two texts are discussed below pp. 232-233.

namely death. An impression reinforced by the setting of Acheron and Hades which provide the semi-mythical, semi-historical environment for the growing of the aconite[87]. According to the scholiast of the passage the aconite has a strange aitiological background (Sch. Nic. *Alex.* 13b): they say that it sprouted from the vomit of Kerberos, who, when dragged out of Hades by Herakles, became nauseous. This weird episode, albeit not explicitly narrated by Nicander, equalls the dark opening of the *Theriaca* about the birth of the snakes from the blood of the Titans; whereas the latter draws upon Hesiod, the former belongs to the paradoxographical tradition of Theopompus, but both hold a fascination for dark Hellenistic poets like Apollonius and Euphorion[88]. The scientific appendix to the aconite passage enhances the monstrosity of the plant. A plethora of speaking names suggests its killing ability against a variety of natural species. It can kill mice (μυοκτόνος), strangle leopards (παρδαλιαγχές) and murder every female on earth (θηλυφόνος)[89].

Other toxic plants share a scientific as well as a mythological background. The deadly arrow-poison is an extraordinary example of how naturalism merges with mythology. Opening and closure to this section point to an aitiological explanation of the scholarly type (207-248). The τοξικόν is thus called either because it is the poison with which the arrows of barbaric people are soaked or, less probably, because it suggests that, when it strikes, it is as rapidly fatal as an arrow[90]. In a way both explanations may be seen as deriving from the cultural anecdote according to which the nomads of Gerrha and Euphrates poison their arrows with this substance[91]. Yet before closing this account, the narrator adds one superfluous remark on the physical effects of the τοξικόν (246-248): *and the wounds, quite past healing, blacken the flesh, for the stinging poison of the Hydra eats its way in, while the skin, turning putrid with the infection, breaks into open sores...* 'Hydra' establishes a connection to the mythical by evoking the serpentine monster killed by Herakles; moreover, the Hydra, along with the Chimera and other monstrosities, is an emblem of the fantastic for Greeks, a synonym of the

---

87. On the literary and scientific sources for the aconite and its habitat in the Heraclea of Pontus, considered by many to be the entrance to Hades, see Jacques (2007) 61-64 n. 2.

88. Probably Nicander is indebted to Euphorion who included this episode in his poem Ξένιος (fr. 37 CA), see Gow/Scholfield (1997) 190 on v. 13.

89. The synonyms are mentioned by other iologists, like Dioscorides and Pliny: for a thorough account, see Jacques (2007) 68-70 n. 4/1-3.

90. Sch. Nic. *Alex.* 208a and Gow/Scholfield (1997) 194 on v. 208.

91. On the use of the τοξικόν exclusively by barbaric people in war or hunt, see the numerous parallels in Jacques (2007) 132-136 n. 22.

marvellous and the irrational and anything lying beyond the natural[92]. Thus, the clinical description of the body which is poisoned by the τοξικόν visualizes not so much the actual effectiveness of the poison in question but rather the imaginary horrors stemming from the incurable bite of the Hydra[93].

But Nicander takes yet another step towards the mythopoesis of the hydra-tree. While referring to the common symptoms of its powerful poison, he employs a bold metaphor to depict a curious state of the patient (215-216): *often too in his distress he cries aloud even as one whose head, the body's master, has just been cut off with the sword.* The image of the patient screaming as if decapitated by a sword, not attested in medical literature, is obviously inspired by the decapitation of the Hydra by Herakles[94]. This device points to what I have earlier termed 'the return of the imaginary'. In effect, the fantastic disguises itself as scientific. A very similar passage, exploring the same device, is found in the immediately following section on the meadow-saffron, the so-called ἐφήμερον (249-278). It is expressly stated that this poison, which kills in one single day, is thought to have been used–or invented–by Medea: as said, *this is the loathsome fire of Colchian Medea*[95]. Its distinguishing feature is that it causes extreme irritation on the flesh of youngsters (254 ἥ τ' ἔκπαγλα νέην φοινίξατο σάρκα).

92. Thus, Aelian dismisses the Hydra as a fairytale for poets, a story opposed to the natural oddity of the two-headed amphisbeana (*N.A.* 9.23): τὴν μὲν ὕδραν τὴν Λερναίαν τὸν ἆθλον τὸν Ἡράκλειον ᾀδέτωσαν ποιηταὶ καὶ μύθων ἀρχαίων συνθέται, ὧνπερ οὖν καὶ Ἑκαταῖος ὁ λογοποιός ἐστιν· ᾀδέτω δὲ καὶ Ὅμηρος χιμαίρας φύσιν κεφαλὰς ἐχούσης τρεῖς...καὶ ταῦτα μὲν ἔοικεν ἐς τοὺς μύθους ἀποκεκρίσθαι· ἡ δὲ ἀμφίσβαινα ὄφις δικέφαλός ἐστι...

93. Perhaps Nicander has literary depictions of the Hydra in mind, as e.g. the one included in the *Arg.* 4.1400-1405. The myth of the Hydra fires the imagination of the Romantic naturalist Erasmus Darwin who projects its serpentine form upon an actual poisonous tree of Indonesia, the upas (*The Loves of the Plants* 3.237-244): "Fierce in dread silence on the blasted heath/ fell upas sits, the Hydra-tree of death./ Lo! from one root, the envenom'd soil below,/ a thousand vegetative serpents grow;/ in shining rays the scaly monster spreads/ o'er ten square leagues his far-diverging heads;/ or in one trunk entwists his tangled form,/ looks o'er the clouds, and hisses in the storm." There is an extraordinary parallel in the *Theriaca* where the plant called 'the viper's bugloss' is vividly depicted as *putting out its head like that of a viper* (636-642).

94. Jacques (2007) 124-125 n. 19/3c notes that this is a bizarre comparison, found nowhere in iological treatises; on the effect of the image, see Gow/Scholfield (1997) 194 on v. 215. The scholiast argues, rather inconvincingly, that the comparison is owed to a misinterpretation of *Il.* 10.457 (Sch. Nic. *Alex.* 216a): τοῦτο δὲ εἶπε πλανηθεὶς ἐκ τοῦ ποιητοῦ καὶ κακῶς νοήσας τό· «φθεγγομένου δ' ἄρα τοῦ γε κάρη κονίῃσιν ἐμίχθη».

95. Cf. Sch. Nic. *Alex.* 249b δοκεῖ δὲ ἡ Μήδεια τὴν κατασκευὴν αὐτοῦ εὑρηκέναι, διὸ καὶ Κολχικὸν λέγεται. See Jacques (2007) 137-139 n. 23.

What else is this superfluous remark if not a projection of the Medea myth upon clinical medicine[96]?

A Kerberos plant, a Hydra plant, a Medea plant–all three point to monstrosity through projection of imaginary horrors. Myth is one way of poeticizing the monstrous plant; to suggest that the forces of evil lurk beneath the idyllic surface of nature is another. Blood and gore against the backdrop of the *locus amoenus* are dramatized in the uncanny narrative about the encounter between man and leech (495-510). It is striking how the realistic scenario of the thirsty wanderer who drinks from a natural source of water is transformed by Nicander into an idealized, poetic *tableau*. Or, to be more precise, into two *tableaux*. In the first, *a man whose throat is constrained by parching thirst falls on his knees and draws water from the stream like a bull, parting with his hands the delicate, moss-like plants...* In the second, *a man's eyes are shrouded beneath dark night, and without thinking he drinks from a pitcher, tipping it up and pressing his lips to its...* The expectation created is that of a Theocritean landscape. But it is not only the natural landscape that may be read in the light of Theocritus' bucolic poetry. The snapshot evoked is the episode of Hylas from *Idyll* 13, and the man drawing water from the source is modelled upon Hylas himself. The subsequent attack of the leeches, anticipated by this dark *locus amoenus* which is rendered as a pitch-black night, clearly parallels the attack of the water Nymphs against Hylas[97]. *Then, approaching eagerly along with the water there rushes upon him in its desire for food the blood-loving leech, long flaccid and yearning for gore...* Soon it is realized that the water scenery is not idyllic but dark, as its inhabitants, the hideous leeches, long for blood and death (φιλαίματος βδέλλα, ἱμείρουσα φόνοιο)[98]. The

96. Both qualities of the meadow-saffron, its fiery nature (πῦρ) and its deadly effect upon the skin, correspond to the poisonous presents offered by Medea to Glauke, namely the golden coronet which sets the hair of the young princess on fire and the poisoned dress which consumes her flesh (Eur. *Med.* 1185-1203).

97. There are significant verbal echoes between the two passages: λεπτὰ μνιώδεα θρῖα in *Alex.* 497 is probably a variation of περὶ δὲ θρύα πολλὰ πεφύκει of *Id.* 13.40, in both cases the pitcher of water is called κρωσσός, and the way the leeches fasten on the victim's skin (*Alex.* 506 ἀθρόα προσφύονται) parallels how the Nymphs cling to Hylas' hand (*Id.* 13.47 ταὶ δ'ἐν χερὶ πᾶσαι ἔφυσαν). The scene of the man kneeling to drink water like a bull is probably a reminiscence of a similar passage from Apollonius' *Argonautica* (4.1447-1449): (Herakles likened to a beast of the field) αὐτὰρ ὅγ', ἄμφω χεῖρε πέδῳ καὶ στέρνον ἐρείσας,/ ῥωγάδος ἐκ πέτρης πίεν ἄσπετον, ὄφρα βαθεῖαν/ νηδύν, φορβάδι ἶσος ἐπιπροπεσών, ἐκορέσθη. For the same image in Nicander describing the thirst of the victim of the dipsas, see *Ther.* 340-342.

98. Φιλαίματος is a tragic epithet whose most impressive occurrence is found in Aeschylus (*Septem* 45) as an attribute of the personified Phobos. Ἱμείρω is used as a rule within love contexts implying strong desire: for contexts of death cf. Arat. *Phain.* 975 ἐφ' αἵματος ἱμείρωνται and the anonymous *Hymn. Hecat.* 10 αἵματος ἱμείρουσα.

226   THE AESTHETICS OF DARKNESS

experience of horror is almost tangible, when the scenario turns into a horrible nightmare. The lonely man, shrouded in the gloomy night, swallows along with the water the living leech, which sucks the blood directly from the inside of his throat[99]. The details of the attack could not have been more appalling: *the leeches fasten on in numbers and suck the body's blood, settling now at the entrance where the breath always gathers to pour through the narrow pharynx, and sometimes one clings about the mouths of the stomach inflicting pain, and swallows a fresh repast.* Anatomical accuracy does not derive from the detached observation of the scientist but aims at extreme sensationalism. Nicander thus turns a scientific digression into a splatter sequence.

Gradually the narrator reveals that the 'monstrous plant' and the 'deadly substances' are *alive*. In nature virulent poisons are animated and enter the human body following mysterious, unexplored paths. The salamander, the so-called sorcerer's lizard, is the essential ingredient for the making of love potions, obviously very harmful to the lover who drinks from it[100]. Another strange liquid is the blood of the bull: one may only drink it in a moment of madness, probably while attempting to commit suicide[101]. And if these poisons evoke extreme human situations, involving morbid eroticism, black magic or the unhealthy desire to die, what about other weird venoms like the 'draught of the toad' and the 'drink of the seahare'? Not only are these creatures hard to define, since they transgress biological classes (the former is an amphibian, the latter belongs to the gastropods, a type of sea-snails), and thence are mentioned as manifestations of the natural grotesque. More interestingly, where is a man supposed to encounter these creatures, and in what form are they drinkable? Nicander once more points towards superstitious not natural terrors.

To complete his scenario, Nicander counterbalances the terrors of the serpent and the horrors of the plant by offering the hope of healing

99. The night in the Nicandrean passage is portrayed as ζοφερή, an epithet usually employed to denote the darkness of the abyss, see e.g. Hes. *Th.* 814 Τιτῆνες ναίουσι, πέρην χάεος ζοφεροῖο.
100. Jacques (2007) 226 n. 58 draws a parallel between Nicander's φαρμακὶς σαύρη and Theocritus' *Idyll* 2 where Simaitha prepares a deadly love potion by mixing, among other things, a salamander (*Id.* 2.58 σαύραν τοι τρίψασα κακὸν ποτὸν αὔριον οἰσῶ).
101. Yet Nicander is not the first to record death from the bull's blood: Herodotus attests the same for the Egyptian king Psammenitos (3.15 αἷμα ταύρου πιὼν ἀπέθανε παραχρῆμα); this type of suicide must have been very widespread in antiquity, cf. Apoll. Soph. *Lex. Homer.* s.v. ταύριον αἷμα θανάσιμον, ἀπὸ Μίδα καὶ Ἰάσονος· περὶ γὰρ Θεμιστοκλέους οὐ πᾶσι συμφωνεῖται. Many historical personalities committed suicide by the bull's blood, see Gow-Scholfield (1997) 195 on v. 312; for this poison between legend and reality, see Jacques (2007) 153-155 n. 29.

through antidotes. Antidotes play a key role in both his extant epics, and it is worth wondering one more time whether their exhaustive treatment reflects a positive worldview about nature and the role of science therein. The question must remain open but I suspect that the antidote sections, as the ones dealing with the poisons and the suffering bodies, serve aesthetic rather than ideological ends. Writing about antidotes represents, however, a different challenge for Nicandrean poetics. In these particular sections the discourse becomes less and less descriptive; instead, emphasis is placed on recherché names of plants and related technical terminology, thus rendering the word–rare, exotic, unusual–the heart of this discourse[102]. As a consequence, Nicander offers endless lists of phytonyms, whose aesthetic appeal is widely exploited by Hellenistic poets, as well as by their literary counterparts of the 19th and 20th century[103].

There are of course notable differences in the treatment of antidotes in the *Theriaca* and the *Alexipharmaca*. Whereas in the prior epic the antidotes, remedies and precautions are more general and apply to all cases of snake poisoning (they are therefore gathered in distinct sections, vv. 21-114, 493-713, 837-956, of the *Theriaca*), in the latter each venom has its own, one or several, individualized antidote (hence the recurrent structural pattern poison-symptom-antidote in the *Alexipharmaca*)[104]. The lexicographical obsession with names apart, remedies and antidotes are part of a long-standing pharmacological tradition, to which Nicander belongs and which he undoubtedly helped develop further[105]. Nevertheless, certain inconsistencies concerning the preparation of the antidotes, such as the lack of reference to specific dosage, put Nicander's scientific exactitude to the test[106]. Other features, especially those related to supernatural or magic forces, in one word to 'the return of the imaginary', point to the same direction. Assuming once more that the aesthetic effect is dominant in Nicander, I will argue that the antidotes are exploited not for their practical value as first aid for everyday people: it is through

102. On Nicander's experimentation with poetic and scientific vocabulary, and for a full assessment of his rhetoric and diction, see Overduin (2010) 65-88.
103. Jacques (2002) xc-xcii, who is otherwise reluctant to emphasize the poetic aspects of Nicander, admits that the lists of his flowers and herbs evoke the 'superb bouquets' described by Balzac in his novel *Le Lys dans la vallée* (1835), thus acknowledging poetic charm to what he calls "les énumérations balzaciennes de Nicandre".
104. For this important distinction, see Jacques (2007) xxvii-xxxviii.
105. For a thorough study of Nicander's antidotes against the background of ancient pharmacology and botany, see Jacques (2007) xxxvii-lxvii.
106. According to Jacques (2002) lvi-lviii this lack of precision is a common medical practice, since the physician and the pharmacologist are the ones who decide on dosage for each particular case treated.

these antidotes, composed of the most incredible substances, that the reader is allowed to enter into an alluring, albeit dark, laboratory.

This is the laboratory of the alchemist–if we may employ this term to read Nicander[107]. Protochemical procedures and magical practices, and, above all, the art of preparation of matter are omnipresent in both his poems. The section following immediately after the proem of the *Theriaca* displays many of these features (21-114). To be more precise, the reader of the section experiences a gradual increase of the mystical at the expense of the practical. In other words, if the setting and the precautions included in these verses strongly evoke Hesiodic didactic of the kind found in the *Works and Days* (as for example when the narrator adapts his instructions to specific times of the day or different weather conditions or elaborates on everyday scenarios), substances and procedural technicalities described therein belong to the sphere of chemistry. The first means of confronting the harmful doom of the snakes is to transmutate organic and inorganic matter by use of fire (35-56)[108]. Some of the strange ingredients include the horn of the stag, herbs, roots, flowers, nettles, the chemical substances sulphur and bitumen, minerals such as the lignite (the so-called γαγάτης λίθος) or the Thracian stone. The reaction of the latter to fire suggests alchemic procedures. The narrator advises his addressee to *set fire to dry lignite which not even the violence of a fierce flame consumes* or to *ignite in the fire the Thracian stone, which when soaked in water glows, yet quenches its brightness at the least smell of a drop of oil*[109]. Such paraphernalia do not serve any pharmaceutical purpose but reveal an obsession with the mystical potential of chemistry. Thereupon follows the catalogue of the animated herbs with the repulsive odour (57-79). The subsequent instructions involve another procedure, the making of herbal pastes for the anointment of the body as a precaution against snakes (80-97). Soon the catalogue of anointments is enriched with human saliva (*many a time too have noxious creatures fled in terror from the scent of a man's spittle*), even a caterpillar rubbed while still alive (*but if you rub a caterpillar from the garden in a little vinegar, the dewy caterpillar with a green back...*).

107. Hellenistic Alexandria, however, had its own alchemist: Bolos 'the Democritean' from the Egyptian city of Mendes (active either during the 3rd or the 2nd century BC), who refashioned Theophrastus' book on the *History of Plants* into doctrines concerning sympathy and antipathy in nature under the influence of astrology, occultism and magic: see Fraser (1972) 1.439-444.

108. Nicander is describing here simple or complex mixtures of θυμιάματα which repulse snakes through odour, see Jacques (2002) 81-83 n. 7.

109. On the *physica curiosa* related to these stones, see the testimonies collected by Jacques (2002) 83-84 n. 8.

Animate and inanimate, organic and inorganic participate in the making of antidotes, as the next recipe clearly illustrates. And although Nicander draws upon Philinos of Cos, a celebrated anatomist and a pupil of Herophilos, for this particular recipe, a fact that proves his dependence on medical and pharmaceutical treatises[110], the preparation of this complex unguent provides one of the most dark descriptions in the *Theriaca* (98-114). In accordance with the standards of the ancient pharmaceutical handbooks, which featured detailed, long recipes, Nicander proposes the mixing of two mating snakes, a freshly killed stag, a portion of rose-oil, some ordinary oil and wax. Among these ingredients, there are two that derive from living creatures; the first of these, the snakes, must be captured upon the act of intercourse taking place at a crossroad–the potential candidate for such a gruesome finding could only be the mythical prophet Teiresias[111]; the latter is perhaps even more difficult to find, once the marrow of a stag just slaughtered is required for the making of the snake repellent[112]. All the ingredients should be mixed and boiled within a cauldron, but the procedure must be carried out with precision (106-111): *these you must quickly heat in a round, bellying pot until the fleshy portions are softened and come in pieces about the spine; next take a shaped, well-made pestle and pound up these many ingredients in a mixture with the snakes; but cast aside the vertebrae, for in them a venom no less deadly is engendered.* If the passage is read against the recipe of Philinos, the similarities are obvious. Yet there is one significant difference: what Nicander is portraying here by employing grand style and affective language is not the making of a drug. He conveys the image of a witch cooking a magic potion in a huge pot–a scene evoking death rather than therapy[113].

110. For a thorough comparison of Philinos and Nicander on this recipe, see Jacques (2002) 89-90 n. 13.

111. The parallel with Teiresias is brilliantly pointed out by Overduin (2010) 227, who notes, in addition, that the story was probably treated by Nicander himself in the *Heteroioumena* (cf. Anton. Liberalis *Met.* 17.5 Τειρεσίας δὲ γυνὴ μὲν ἐξ ἀνδρός, ὅτι τοὺς ἐν τῇ τριόδῳ μιγνυμένους ὄφεις ἐντυχὼν ἀπέκτεινεν).

112. The adjective employed for the deer, νεοσφαγέος, is a reminiscent of tragedy, see Overduin (2010) 229 on v. 101.

113. Two alluring witch scenes following the same pattern may be quoted here. The one is the description of how Medea prepares a magic potion made of roots, seeds, flowers, stones, frost, the wings of an owl, the entrails of a wolf, the skin of a snake, the liver of a stag and the beak of a crow in order to rejuvenate Aison from Ovid's *Metamorphoses* 7.257-284. The other belongs to the blackest pages of Shakespeare's *Macbeth*, when the three witches boil similarly horrifying ingredients–including frogs, snakes, dogs, lizards, even human organs and limbs–within a charmed pot to summon Hekate (Act IV, Scene 1).

Ingredients that are alive, along with all their dark associations, form one aspect of Nicander's recipes[114]. To reconstruct the methods applied to matter constitutes another. Separating and combining elements, dissolving substances, mixing and boiling material, distilling, straining and draining liquids, powdering herbs, frementing plants, extracting oil–procedures recurrent in Nicander were also exploited by Medieval alchemists. Nicander demonstrates the transmutability of matter by recording how substances may change state under the influence of chemical processes, an idea that brings him all the more closer to alchemistic credos. The evocation of magic and practical applications of chemistry for the preparation of drugs confirm the same view[115].

Plant alchemy, the so-called spagyric, is omnipresent in Nicander, in the endless lists of phytonyms which mix to prepare the most exotic drugs. Yet alchemy is specifically evoked when Nicander treats chemical elements like minerals and metals. Two passages illustrate the point. In the first, which derives from the *Alexipharmaca* (511-520), the mixing of snow or ice with vinegar makes composite drugs, and soil or various forms of salt (salt water, salt rocks, salt flakes) are used as simple antidotes. These were substances preferred by the alchemists, who also experimented with metals. An illuminating passage is found in the *Alexipharmaca* where metals undergo a series of alchemical procedures (49-54). ...*Quenching in vinegar and honey a red-hot lump of metal between the jaws of the fire-tongs, or dross of iron which the flame of the fire has separated within the melting-pot in the furnace; or sometimes just after warming in the fire a lump of gold or silver you should plunge it in turbid draught.* Such a detailed description serves artistic not scientific ends. Against this background, the reader is once more invited to enter a dark laboratory and, as a mystified viewer, to watch iron corroding when immersed in vinegar and honey (known to the Greeks as the ὀξύμελι which causes metals to rust)[116] and

114. For similar weird ingredients, cf. *Ther.* 557-561 the membranes of the brain of a domestic fowl and the lobe of a boar's liver, and vv. 620-624 the frogs boiled with vinegar and the liver or the head of a poisonous snake mixed with wine; *Alex.* 133-138 the head of a hog or lamb or goat or goose, 555-558 the eggs of a tortoise, the flesh of a hog and the limbs of a sea-turtle, and 573-577 the boiled or roasted flesh of a frog and the spleen of the toad. A fine analysis of the animal drugs in Jacques (2007) l-liii.

115. Surprisingly enough, Nicander is mentioned alongside the alchemist Albertus Magnus by Des Esseintes, the protagonist of J.-K. Huysmans' novel *À rebours* (Ch. 13): "A smile flitted over his lips, for suddenly he remembered a quaint comparison old Nicander makes, likening, from the point of view of shape, the pistil of a lily to an ass' genitals, while a passage from Albertus Magnus also occurred to him where that miracle-worker gives a singular formula for discovering by the use of a lettuce whether a girl is still virgin." [Anonymous 1928 transl.].

116. On this process, see Jacques (2007) 74-75 n. 5.

the melting of two of the most important alchemic metals, gold and silver, in a cauldron[117].

It seems that for Nicander the knowledge of matter and the re-enactment of chemical procedures do not possess the spiritual depth normally associated with alchemy. This may be in general true, yet at times philosophical notions and transcendental ideas find their way into Nicander's poetry. An exceptional paradigm is the digression on the four archetypal elements, namely earth, water, air, fire (*Alex.* 171-177). This is the sole non-mythological digression dealing with philosophical issues in both the *Theriaca* and the *Alexipharmaca*. Not only does Nicander draw on Empedocles for the theory of the four elements (perhaps also on Heracleitus for the eternal strife between them, cf. Sch. Nic. *Alex.* 174a) but moreover he employs philosophical terminology–the ἀείζωον πῦρ and the curious neologism ἀχύνετον ὕδωρ[118].

The acquisition of wisdom is also at issue once the ultimate goal of every physician is pursued: the mystical recipe of how to prepare the *panacea*. There are several passages in the *Theriaca*, situated in key positions within the poem, that feature the panacea in its double identity, as an all-healing plant of divine origin and as a bizarre concoction against all poisons. The second proem to the *Theriaca*, where the narrator asserts that the herbalist offers salvation to mankind, introduces the reader into a natural landscape where supernatural forces are at work (496-508). It is in the thick woods, on which poisonous snakes pasture, that the πάνακες or πανάκειον is found. This is a plant with unusual properties (the golden-hued flower and the root situated at the surface of the soil) first discovered on the snowy peak of Pelion by Chiron. Admittedly the plant is previously mentioned in the botanical treatises of Theophrastus, and Nicander is consciously evoking science here[119]. But he also enhances the mythical element by providing not one but all three different aitiologies explaining its connection to the divine: apart from Chiron, Herakles (626-627) and Asklepios (685-686) are said to be the inventors of this miraculous plant[120].

---

117. That Nicander aims at sensationalism by referring to iron and silver is confirmed by Jacques (2007) 74-75 n. 5/3a who notes that Dioscorides, Pliny and Galen ignore the medical usage of these metals.

118. The philosophical parenthesis is poetically developed through mythopoesis and personification, cf. Sch. Nic. *Alex.* 172a ἀτμεύειν <δὲ> <ὅ ἐστι> δουλεύειν, ὑποκεῖσθαι. ὡς μῦθον <γὰρ> λέγει ὅτι ἀνέμοις θάλασσα καὶ πῦρ δουλεύει, καὶ θάλασσα μὲν δεσπόζει νηῶν, πῦρ δὲ ὕλης.

119. For a thorough discussion of the related evidence, see Jacques (2002) 147-150 n. 53.

120. Overduin (2010) 433 on v. 685 maintains that only in the third passage does Nicander think of the actual plant, whereas in the other two cases πανάκειον is a poetic periphrasis and not a technical term. Even if this is accurate, nevertheless all three passages are meant to evoke each other.

The critical passage on the panacea, however, is placed at the end of the *Theriaca* (934-956)[121]. This time the actual name is totally eliminated and replaced by the periphrasis πάσησιν ἀλεξητήριον ἄταις. Not unlike the alchemists who sought to prepare the elixir of life, Nicander is fascinated by the idea of the absolute medicine that would cure all poisonings. He thus proceeds with the detailed description of the ultimate recipe for the most desired drug ever prepared. Processes across the spectrum of alchemy are described, involving preparation of matter (τευξάμενος), mixing (ταράξῃς), mingling (ἄμμιγα), kneading (ἐπι-πλήσσων), pouring juice (χέας), blending (συμφύρσαιο), shaping cakes (καταρτίζοιο κύκλους), weighing (πλάστιγγι ἄχθος ἐρύξας), shaking (ταράξας) and then drinking the recommended dosage (χαδεῖν)! The same variety applies to the instruments and utensils used but foremost to the 26 different ingredients mixed. Yet another instance where science, mysticism, rhetorical hyperbole and a plethora of fascinating names converge to create a sensational effect[122].

The venomous creature, the monstrous plant, the alchemies of the antidote–this is Nicander's dark scenario. Oscillating between the natural and the supernatural, Nicander exploits the sensation of science, its spiritual depth, and the allure of the word. These qualities bring him all the more closer to the quest for Aestheticism. Nicander contemplates nature and senses what lies beyond; but foremost he seems excited by the beauty (and the horror) of the natural species and their sensations–including the wide range of colours and forms, their exotic names and strange qualities. It is nature that inspires deformity, monstrosity and morbidity. Nicander's taste for extravagance is comparable to the obsession with the natural monstrous experienced by literary characters such as Dr. Rappaccini. Or the bizarre Des Esseintes, the prototype of the Decadent aisthete, the protagonist of J.-K. Huysmans' novel *À rebours* (1884). As a collector of monstrous plants ("he wanted natural flowers imitating the false"), Des Esseintes admires the strangest plants ever found ("thinking of nothing but the strange species he had bought, ceaselessly haunted by his memories of superb and extraordinary blooms"). Chapter 8 of the novel comprises long lists of the names and

121. Jacques (2002) lxxiii rightly remarks that the whole antidote section develops towards, and culminates with, the panacea.

122. Overduin (2010) 524 stresses the aesthetic puprose of this last recipe, in remarking that "Nicander seems to have placed this recipe at the end of the poem, to give one last display of his virtuosity, presumed knowledge, and dexterity, fitting thirty odd ingredients in some twenty lines. As a *tour de force* of fitting many names in few verses it is somewhat reminiscent of Hesiod's catalogue of the fifty Nereids in *Th.* 240-264".

qualities of these eccentric plants–varieties displaying all the nuances of colour, others resembling the human flesh, some likened to metals, animated and animal-like, plants that are carnivorous ("those vegetable ghouls"), unscented flowers, all kinds of vegetative grotesqueries. Eventually Des Esseintes exclaims:

> "All the same, these plants are amazing things," he muttered to himself; then he stepped back and embraced in one view the whole collection. Yes, his object was attained; not one of them looked real; cloth, paper, porcelain, metal seemed to have been lent by man to Nature to enable her to create these monstrosities. When she had found herself incapable of copying human workmanship, she had been reduced to mimick the membranes of animals' insides, to borrow the vivid tints of their rotting flesh, the superb horrors of their gangrened skin. [Anonymous 1928 transl.]

Both Des Esseintes and Nicander are viewers. *Qua* fascinated viewers of the extraordinary in nature, they see the world around them as a thrilling, albeit horrifying, 'aesthetic phenomenon'; it is no more the Romantic nature that attracts them but the very Decadent idea of its artificiality. This aesthetic approach is also reflected in the way of viewing the poisoned body to which I will now turn my attention.

III.3. The poisoned body

And several days later–exactly one week after he had left his mountain solitude–Grenouille found himself on a dais in the great hall of the University
of Montpellier and was presented as a scientific sensation of the year to a
crowd of several hundred people. In his lecture, Taillade Espinasse described
him as living proof of the validity of his theory of earth's fluidum letale.
While he stripped Grenouille of his rags piece by piece, he explained the
devastating effect that the corruptive gas had perpetrated on Grenouille's
body. One could see the pustules and scars caused by the corrosive gas;
there on his breast a giant, shiny-red gas cancer; a general disintegration of
the skin; and even clear evidence of fluidal deformation of the bone structure, the visible indications being a club-foot and a hunchback. The internal
organs as well had been damaged by the gas–pancreas, liver, lungs, gall
bladder and intestinal tract–as the analysis of a stool sample (accessible to
the public in a basin at the feet of the exhibit) had proved beyond doubt. In
summary, it could be said that the paralysis of the vital energies caused by
a seven-year contamination with fluidum letale Taillade had progressed so
far that the exhibit–whose external appearance, by the way, already displayed significant molelike traits–could be described as a creature more dis-
posed towards death than life. Nevertheless, the lecturer pledged that within
eight days, using ventilation therapy in combination with a vital diet, he
would restore this doomed creature to the point where the signs of a complete recovery would be self-evident to everyone... [Transl. J.E. Woods]

Patrick Süskind *Perfume: The Story of a Murderer* Ch. 30 (1985)

The body in agony with all its anatomical details has never ceased to fascinate authors and artists from antiquity until our day. Literature, painting,
sculpture, cinematography, in a word: Western culture in all its artistic
manifestations, abound with scenes meticulously visualizing the ravages of
disease, plague, infection, inflammation or poisoning as displayed on the
human body. Seeing the human body on the dissecting table of the physician
produces the kind of 'scientific sensation' that is portrayed in the abovementioned scene from Patrick Süskind's *Perfume* (whose naturalistic horrors
resemble, in many respects, those of Nicander's poetry). Like the victims of
poisoning in Nicander, Grenouille–the main character who has an uncanny
sense of smell–falls victim to an exotic poison, the *fluidum letale*[123]. The

123. This imaginary poison is nevertheless 'scientifically' described by his own inventor in the novel–just like the poisons in Nicander (*Perfume* Ch. 30): "His thesis was that
life could develop only at a certain distance from the earth, since the earth itself constantly
emits a corrupting gas, a so-called *fluidum letale*, which lames vital energies and sooner
or later utterly extinguishes them. All living creatures therefore endeavour to distance
themselves from the earth by growing–that is, they grow away from it and not, for

reader is invited to watch the presentation of the poisoned body by doctor Taillade, and thus become one of the spectators in his amphitheatre; eventually, the triumph of science is announced, as a promise of recovery of Grenouille's suffering body is given. The scenario (poisoning–body in decay–remedy) and the narrative frame (a parallel can be drawn between the doctor and his audience in the modern novel and the narrator/physician addressing the narratee/spectator in Nicander) evoke recurrent patterns found in the *Theriaca* and the *Alexipharmaca*. As poisoning and remedy have already been discussed, it is the representation of the physical body and the dimension of corporeality in Nicander's poetry that will now be examined[124].

The *Theriaca* and the *Alexipharmaca* comprise over fourty different portrayals of the poisoned body, all of which display the extreme realistic style of a clinical examination, literally taking place before the very eyes of the reader. The symptom, marking the transition from a state of health to that of disease, forms the core of these descriptions, as if suddenly a demonic, uncontrollable force takes hold and affects the human body[125]. One of the most extensive descriptions, and the first to be found in the *Theriaca*, concerns the symptoms caused by the biting of the viper (235-257)[126]. The passage may be divided into several subsections according to the symptoms depicted. At the beginning of the bite the wound comes into being (235-243)[127]:

τῆς καὶ ἀπὸ πληγῆς φέρεται λίπει εἴκελος ἰχώρ,
ἄλλοτε δ' αἱματόεις, τοτὲ δ' ἄχροος· ἡ δ' ἐπί οἱ σάρξ
πολλάκι μὲν χλοάουσα βαρεῖ ἀναδέδρομεν οἴδει,
ἄλλοτε φοινίσσουσα, τότ' εἴδεται ἄντα πελιδνή·
ἄλλοτε δ' ὑδατόεν κυέει βάρος, αἱ δὲ χαμηλαί

instance, into it; which is why their most valuable parts are lifted heavenwards..." [Transl. J.E. Woods].

124. The conceptualization of the physical body in Archaic and Classical Greece through the examination of the symptoms caused by disease is thoroughly discussed by Holmes (2010).

125. The symptom symbolizes the estrangement of the subject from its body, and therefore represents the uncanny: a brilliant analysis of the symptom from a semiotic viewpoint is given by Holmes (2010) 9-19.

126. Jacques (2002) 108-109 n. 24/1 points out that all the symptoms listed by Nicander are also found in iological treatises (e.g. in Philoumenos): it is true that Nicander depends on medical writings, yet–and this is a point systematically missed by Jacques–he does not merely repeat but rewrites each source-text to serve his own aesthetic purposes.

127. For another impressive visualization of the wound, see *Ther.* 360-363. A grotesque wound likened to the one caused by a mouse, is associated with the horrifying dragon (446-447): βληχρὸν γὰρ μυὸς οἷα μυληβόρου ἐν χροῒ νύχμα/ εἴδεται αἱμαχθέντος ὑπὸ κραντῆρος ἀραιοῦ.

πομφόλυγες ὡς εἴ τε περὶ φλύκταιναι ἀραιαί
οἷα πυρικμήτοιο χροὸς πλαδόωσιν ὕπερθεν.
σηπεδόνες δέ οἱ ἀμφὶς ἐπίδρομοι, αἱ μὲν ἄτερθεν
αἱ δὲ κατὰ πληγὴν ἰοειδέα λοιγὸν ἱεῖσαι.

And from the wound she makes there oozes a discharge like oil or, it may be, bloody or colourless, while the skin around starts up into a painful lump, often greenish, now crimson, or again of livid aspect. At other times it engenders a mass of fluid, and about the wound small pimples like slight blisters rise flabbily from the skin, which looks scorched. And all around spread ulcers, some at a distance, others by the wound, emitting a dark blue poison.

The centrality of the wound to Nicander's depiction is not coincidental: from an anatomical viewpoint the wound is the opening through which the poison enters into the human body[128]. To visualize the wound Nicander combines two levels of discourse, the scientific (which consists of the technical vocabulary such as πληγή, ἰχώρ, σάρξ, πομφόλυγες, φλύκταιναι and σηπεδόνες)[129] and the literary, including metaphor (ἀναδέδρομεν, πυρικμήτοιο, λοιγός) and an excessive emphasis on colour terminology[130]. If, as argued above, colour is a vital parameter of the visualization of the flora and fauna, the wide-ranging colour palette used to describe the wound creates a highly dramatic effect. Thus asserting its aesthetic autonomy, the wound becomes disgustingly beautiful, an image which is at the same time repulsive and alluring to look at, whereas the deep blue-violet hue of the poison itself (ἰοειδέα λοιγὸν) provides a dark coda to this sensational image[131]. The passage on the viper bite continues in an almost sublime manner (244-246):

πᾶν δ᾽ ἐπί οἱ δριμεῖα δέμας καταβόσκεται ἄτη
ὀξέα πυρπολέουσα· κατ᾽ ἀσφάραγον δέ τε λυγμοί
κίονά τε ξυνιόντες ἐπασσύτεροι κλονέουσιν.

128. According to Jacques (2002) 109 n. 24/2 the passage on the wound responds to a celebrated medical problem: how do vipers and other snakes cause putrefaction through biting, or, in other words, wherein does their destructive power reside (φθοροποιὸς δύναμις)?

129. Among these terms, ἰχώρ evokes the epic word that denotes the juice flowing in the veins of the gods (e.g. *Il.* 5.340), which Nicander uses in its medical sense 'serous or purulent discharge': on this ambiguous word, see Overduin (2010) 281 on v. 235.

130. Papadopoulou (2009) 112 demonstrates that the colours associated with the viper bite in Nicander's passage are far more elaborate and subtly shaded as compared to the ones found in Aetius and Philoumenos.

131. Even if ἰοειδής derives from ἰός 'poison' here, Nicander is at the same time alluding to the somewhat aenigmatic Homeric adjective ἰοειδής in the phrase ἰοειδέα πόντον, clearly suggesting a dark colour (purple since it derives from ἴον 'the flower violet', yet the scholia interpret it as 'black' [Sch. *Il.* 11.298 [ἰοειδέα] μέλανα διὰ τὸ βάθος]).

And over the whole body the piercing bane eats its way with its acute inflammation; and in the throat and about the uvula retchings following fast upon one another convulse the victim.

In the phrase δριμεῖα ἄτη a word of epic-tragic sublimity and an adjective denoting metaphorically physical pain combine to produce a "violent image"[132], further reinforced by πυρπολέουσα 'burning and destroying with fire', a vivid illustration of how the inflammation affects the body. Then the focus shifts to the inside of the body, the throat, which is agitated by retchings following one upon another. Soon the symptoms diffuse across the entire nervous system (247-249):

ἀμφὶ καὶ εἰλίγγοις δέμας ἄχθεται· αἶψα δὲ γυίοις
ἀδρανίη βαρύθουσα καὶ ἰξύι μέρμερος ἵζει,
ἐν δὲ κάρῃ σκοτόεν βάρος ἵσταται

The body is oppressed also with failures of sense in every part, and forthwith in the limbs and loins is seated a burdening, dangerous weakness, and heavy darkness settles in the head...

(Ε)ἴλιγγος, literally 'vertigo, a swimming in the head', is followed by weakness of the limbs until eventually the victim sinks into torpor. The dominant image is that of heaviness (ἄχθεται, βαρύθουσα, ἵζει, βάρος) but it is darkness that gives the passage a climactic ending. After dizziness, the victim is affected by thirst and tremor (249-252):

αὐτὰρ ὁ κάμνων
ἄλλοτε μὲν δίψῃ φάρυγα ξηραίνεται αὔῃ,
πολλάκι δ᾽ ἐξ ὀνύχων ἴσχει κρύος, ἀμφὶ δὲ γυίοις
χειμερίη ζαλόωσα πέριξ βέβριθε χάλαζα.

Meantime the sufferer at one moment has his throat parched with dry thirst, often too he is seized with cold from the finger-tips, while all over his frame an eruption with wintry rage lies heavy upon him.

The imagery is now drawn from the field of meteorology, as the symptoms alternate between drought (ξηραίνεται αὔῃ), the cold of winter (κρύος, χειμερίη) and a shower of hail (χάλαζα). By recourse to colouring and imagery, i.e. by appeal to the senses not the intellect, Nicander distances himself from anatomical accuracy and his description becomes vague and poetic rather than scientific[133]. One can almost sense the afflictions of the poison from within the body of the victim (253-255):

---

132. Overduin (2010) 283 on v. 244.
133. Cf. Overduin (2010) 285 on v. 252: "Nicander seems to be describing symptoms here in terms of images and sensations, rather than naming sorts of wounds".

πολλάκι δ' αὖ χολόεντας ἀπήρυγε νηδύος ὄγκους
ὠχραίνων δέμας ἀμφίς· ὁ δὲ νοτέων περὶ γυίοις
ψυχρότερος νιφετοῖο βολῆς περιχεύεται ἱδρώς.

And again a man often turns yellow all over his body and vomits up the bile
that lies upon his stomach, while a moist sweat, colder than the falling
snow, envelops his limbs.

Vomit, and the concomitant symptoms of paleness and sweat, mark a
progression in narrative time: once the poison has run its course from
inflammation to vertigo and shivering, vomit seems to be its natural
end. Nicander does not provide further information on the subsequent
condition of the victim, especially on the critical matter of his eventual
death[134]; he only dwells upon iconographical detail to intensify the morbid sensation of this static *tableau* (256-257):

χροιὴν δ' ἄλλοτε μὲν μολίβου ζοφοειδέος ἴσχει,
ἄλλοτε δ' ἠερόεσσαν, ὅτ' ἄνθεσιν εἴσατο χαλκοῦ.

In some cases his colour is that of sombre lead, in others his hue is murky,
or again it is like flowers of copper.

The final impression conveyed to the reader *qua* spectator is that of darkness, expressed through reference to three of its shadings, the grey of the
lead, the murky and the mysterious colouring of the copper-flower,
somewhere between deep blue and green[135].

The detailed analysis of just one passage portraying the poisoned body
among numerous others demonstrates how medical and humoral physiology merge with iconography and poetic diction to produce darkness in
Nicander. Disease, pain and severe physical symptoms offer illustrations
of the human body that attract the reader/spectator with their outlandish
beauty[136]. The reason why pain and danger, both of which are associated
with the effects of natural poisoning in Nicander, are a source of passion
is thus explained by Edmund Burke (*A Philosophical Enquiry into the
Origin of Our Ideas of the Sublime and Beautiful* 1.6):

> The ideas of *pain, sickness,* and *death,* fill the mind with strong emotions
> of horror; but *life* and *health,* though they put us in a capacity of being
> affected with pleasure, make no such impression by the simple enjoyment.

134. Doctors explicitly state that death follows the viper bite, see e.g. Philoumenos *De
venenatis animalibus* 17.1-2 τοῖς δὲ ὑπὸ ἔχεως ἢ ἐχίδνης δηχθεῖσιν...ὁ δὲ θάνατος
ἐν ἡμέραις ἑπτά, καὶ ὡς ἐπὶ τὸ πλεῖστον τῇ τρίτῃ. Occasionally, though, Nicander
inserts similar remarks into his narrative, as e.g. in *Alex.* 400-401 ἐν δὲ μονήρει/ ῥηιδίως
ἀκτῖνι βαρὺν κατεναίρεται ἄνδρα.
135. In the view of Gow/Scholfield (1997) 174 on v. 257.
136. Within this context, Toohey (1996) 65 speaks of the 'voyeuristic' quality of
Nicander's descriptions.

The passions therefore which are conversant about the preservation of the individual turn chiefly on *pain* and *danger*, and they are the most powerful of all the passions.

Burke attributes the arousing of passion to the horror that affects the individual when the latter is confronted with threats against his physical and corporeal integrity. Burke's principle may in turn account for the strange pleasure experienced upon viewing the bodies of others as affected by pain and death. This type of pleasure is finely portrayed in an anecdote from Plato's *Republic* (439e-440a):

’Αλλ’, ἦν δ’ ἐγώ, ποτὲ ἀκούσας τι† πιστεύω τούτῳ· ὡς ἄρα Λεόντιος ὁ ’Αγλαΐωνος ἀνιὼν ἐκ Πειραιῶς ὑπὸ τὸ βόρειον τεῖχος ἐκτός, αἰσθόμενος νεκροὺς παρὰ τῷ δημίῳ κειμένους, ἅμα μὲν ἰδεῖν ἐπιθυμοῖ, ἅμα δὲ αὖ δυσχεραίνοι καὶ ἀποτρέποι ἑαυτόν, καὶ τέως μὲν μάχοιτό τε καὶ παρακαλύπτοιτο, κρατούμενος δ’ οὖν ὑπὸ τῆς ἐπιθυμίας, διελκύσας τοὺς ὀφθαλμούς, προσδραμὼν πρὸς τοὺς νεκρούς, «’Ιδοὺ ὑμῖν,» ἔφη, «ὦ κακοδαίμονες, ἐμπλήσθητε τοῦ καλοῦ θεάματος.»

"I rely on a story I once heard," I answered. "It's about Leontius, son of Aglaion, who was on his way up from the Piraeus, under the outer side of the north wall, when he noticed some corpses lying on the ground with the executioner standing by them. He wanted to go and look at them, and yet at the same time held himself back in disgust. For a time he struggled with himself and covered his eyes, but at last his desire got the better of him and he ran up to the corpses, opening his eyes wide and saying to them, 'There you are, curse you–a lovely sight! Have a real good look!' " [Transl. D. Lee]

The moral of the story is that desire, as in the case of Leontius, may prove stronger than reason (440b ὅταν βιάζωνταί τινα παρὰ τὸν λογισμὸν ἐπιθυμίαι). Leontius is driven by a morbid desire, verging on algolagny, to witness a horrifying and repulsive spectacle, namely the dead human body in the aftermath of an execution[137]. It is this desire (ἐπιθυμία), which already in Plato has a pure aesthetic dimension (καλὸν θέαμα), that Nicander's poetry indulges. In poeticizing extreme naturalistic horrors, the iological poems of Nicander oscillate between reality and art, between scientific 'truth' and its representation through mimesis. Within this context, Nicander's penchant for this strange, alluring 'beauty of

137. Algolagny is a notion associated with the Decadent movement, and covers the entire range of sadistic desires (Praz [1970] 437-457). Among them, the desire of viewing executions, quite similar to that attributed to Leontius in the Platonic excerpt, is typical of the sadist (Praz [1970] 438): "I have no doubt that this anecdote [i.e. about George Shelwyn who had a taste for witnessing criminal executions] gave rise to the French legend of the Englishman whose greatest pleasure was to attend executions, a legend which was developed during the Romantic period and received a new stimulus from the Goncourts".

disgust' will be analyzed in its association with four key notions: clinical realism, *pathos*, the grotesque and the abject[138].

By clinical realism I refer to the scientific viewpoint from which the poisoned body is observed. This refers to the accurate portrayal of anatomy, the effect of visceral naturalism, the convention of autopsy as well as the detached stance of the physician/narrator. Indeed, anatomy establishes a link between poetry and medicine. Material deriving from iological treatises, and the related terminology, are incorporated into Nicander's verses to make sure that these are read in the light of scientific discourse. A systematic overview of symptomatology in Nicander demonstrates that the effects of poisoning may be classified as follows: cooling and freezing, development of ulcers, suffocation, putrefaction, overheating and warming, brain failure and eventual derangement of the victim[139]. The list of symptoms associated with specific organs—eyes and ears, tongue and jaws, skin, limbs, bladder, stomach, heart, nervous system—is inexhaustible[140]. And whereas the external manifestations of poisoning, such as wounds, are visible to the naked eye, the affection of the internal organs presuppose the performance of anatomy on a corpse. The symptoms of the aconite bite are observable on human entrails (*Alex.* 19-23): *the top of the belly is gripped with pain—the swelling, open mouth of the lower stomach, which some call the 'heart' of the digestive vessel, others the 'receiver' of the stomach—and the gate is closed immediately upon the beginning of the intestines where a man's food in all its abundance is carried in*. Nicander evokes the mood of an anatomy lesson and the setting of a dissecting table here, once the reader/spectator gains access to the inside of the human body[141]. Vomit and urine are also vividly illustrated, as for example when it is said that *the belly voids the polluted scourings, even as a carver pours off the turbid water in which the meat was washed* (*Alex.* 257-258) or *the urine is stopped and the lowest part of the belly throbs, as when a tympanitic dropsy settles in abundance about the mid navel* (*Alex.* 340-342). Retention of excrement and blockage of air in the bowels are extensively treated in a passage (*Alex.* 284-297) where anatomical illustration (*while the stomach blinds with wanton obstruction the two channels of liquid and solid food, and*

---

138. On the 'beauty of disgust' and the fascination with disease and physical decomposition in Romantic, Decadent and Modern literature from Shelley to Hugo, and from Baudelaire to Kafka, see Eco (2007) 302-309.

139. Jacques (2007) xxxii-xxxiii.

140. For a catalogue, see Jacques (2007) xxxiii-xxxiv.

141. In effect, the symptom offers a glimpse into an unseen reality, i.e. the cluster of things that consitute the physical body (Holmes [2010] 17).

rumbles with the wind it has penned within) blends with impressive poetic similes (the air circulating in the stomach is likened to *the thunder of stormy Olympus or the wicked roaring of the sea as it booms beneath rocky cliffs*)[142]. Numerous passages like these testify to the fact that Nicander insists on an extreme type of realism, which I have termed 'visceral naturalism', enhanced by poetic discourse, thus turning his anatomy lesson into a proper aesthetic event–a visual spectacle in a very real sense.

But how is the impression of the anatomy lesson conveyed to the reader? Nicander masterly adapts the didactic genre to suit his own medical scenario. The second person apostrophe seems to be addressed to another physician or pharmacologist. This is the profession of Protagoras to whom the *Alexipharmaca* is dedicated, whereas Hermesianax, the addressee of the *Theriaca*, still remains an obscure personality but the medical identity may attributed to him too[143]. In accordance with the conventions of didactic, the addressee acquires the role of an apprentice[144]. The authority of the narrator is beyond question (note the programmatic promise that he possesses technical skill on poisons and antidotes or rhetorical apostrophes like the repetitive οἶδα marking the beginning of each new section of the *Theriaca*) and so is his willingness to conduct a masterclass (e.g. ἂν ἴδοις, ἂν μάθοις, ἂν γνοίης, τεκμαίρευ, πιφαύσκεο, φράζεο etc.). During this masterclass the examination of the suffering body proceeds systematically from one symptom to another (also with some respect to chronological ordering, beginning with the wound); the consistent use of present tense for the depiction of symptomatology reinforces the illusion of autopsy; τεκμήρια and σήματα, i.e. visible marks, suggest first-hand observation. Through the form of didactic, the narrator communicates the idea that he is well

142. It is noteworthy that Nicander's use of anatomical vocabulary is not consistent, since the same term may apply to more organs or vice versa: terms used ambiguously include those denoting the stomach, the heart, the belly and the intestine (Jacques [2007] xxxv-xxxvii).

143. On Protagoras the doctor, see Jacques (2007) lxxvi and n. 196. Hermesianax has not been identified with any of Nicander's contemporaries (he is definitely not the poet, Gow/Scholfield [1997] 7), but the context requires a doctor/addressee here, like Nicias to whom Theocritus dedicates his Cyclops on the remedy for love, see Overduin (2010) 39-40.

144. Jacques (2007) lxxvi-lxxvii subtly observes that Nicander alternates freely between the viewpoint of the doctor (second person) and that of the patient (third person). The *Theriaca* offers even more interesting examples illustrating that the second person (i.e. the one referring to the addressee) may either denote the doctor or the patient (e.g. in vv. 876-878 πολλάκι δ᾽ ἢ πέπεριν κόψας νέον ἢ ἀπὸ Μήδων/ κάρδαμον ἐμπίσαιο· σὲ δ᾽ ἂν πολυάνθεα γλήχων/ στρύχνον τ᾽ ἠδὲ σίνηπι κακηπελέοντα σαῶσαι), cf. Jacques (2002) lxx.

acquainted with the anatomical body, a medical expertise and a healer at once. Yet, this body is primarily the object of medicinal knowledge–and experimentation if we take into account the antidotes–a fact that explains the non-empathetic, detached stance of the narrator/physician[145].

Detachment of the narrator, however, does not exclude the affective response of the reader. Once the anatomical body, sensationally visualized, is an enduring and returning image, it becomes the object of the spectator's gaze–as if set at the centre of a theatrical stage. The theatricality in the depiction of the Nicandrean body creates effects similar to those of drama proper[146]. Aristotle's notion of *pathos* is, to some degree, relevant to the point (*Poet.* 1452b)[147]:

πάθος δέ ἐστι πρᾶξις φθαρτικὴ ἢ ὀδυνηρά, οἷον οἵ τε ἐν τῷ φανερῷ
θάνατοι καὶ αἱ περιωδυνίαι καὶ τρώσεις καὶ ὅσα τοιαῦτα.

Suffering is an action that involves destruction or pain (e.g. deaths in full view, extreme agony, woundings and so on). [Transl. M. Heath]

One of the parameters of tragedy causing pity and fear is the representation of death, physical pain or wounding; scenes focusing on corporeal sufferings should take place before the very eyes of the audience, on stage, or may, alternatively, be so vividly depicted through language *as if being placed before the eyes* of the audience[148].

Ἐνάργεια combined with representations of physical *pathos* provides the key to understanding horror in Nicander. A third parameter is exaggeration, as exemplified by the portrayal of the symptoms resulting from the haimorrhois bite (*Ther.* 298-308):

νύχματι δ᾽ ἀρχομένῳ μὲν ἐπιτρέχει ἄχροον οἶδος
κυάνεον, κραδίην δὲ κακὸν περιτέτροφεν ἄλγος·
γαστὴρ δ᾽ ὑδατόεσσα διέσσυτο, νυκτὶ δὲ πρώτῃ
αἷμα διὲκ ῥινῶν τε καὶ αὐχένος ἠδὲ δι᾽ ὤτων
πιδύεται χολόεντι νέον πεφορυγμένον ἰῷ,
οὖρα δὲ φοινίσσοντα παρέδραμεν· αἱ δ᾽ ἐπὶ γυίοις
ὠτειλαὶ ῥήγνυνται ἐπειγόμεναι χροὸς ἄτῃ.

---

145. Toohey (1996) 72-73. Cf. Overduin (2010) 102: "Empathy on account of the poet is not very prominent in Nicander's descriptions, and his general detachment gives us the impression that he is more interested in sensational details than in emotion."

146. Spatafora (2005) 256-257.

147. For a discussion of *pathos* in Aristotle, see Belfiore (1992) 134-141.

148. That dramatic techniques, gestures and vivid rhetoric enhance the emotional affect of pity and fear because evil appears to be 'near' is argued by Aristotle (*Rhet.* 1386b): <καὶ> διὰ τοῦτο καὶ τὰ σημεῖα, οἷον ἐσθῆτάς τε τῶν πεπονθότων καὶ ὅσα τοιαῦτα, καὶ τὰς πράξεις καὶ λόγους καὶ ὅσα ἄλλα τῶν ἐν τῷ πάθει ὄντων, οἷον ἤδη τελευτώντων...ἅπαντα γὰρ ταῦτα διὰ τὸ ἐγγὺς φαίνεσθαι μᾶλλον ποιεῖ τὸν ἔλεον, καὶ ὡς ἀναξίου ὄντος καὶ ἐν ὀφθαλμοῖς φαινομένου τοῦ πάθους.

μήποτέ τοι θήλει' αἱμορροῖς ἰὸν ἐνείη·
τῆς γὰρ ὀδαξαμένης τὰ μὲν ἀθρόα πίμπραται οὖλα
ῥιζόθεν, ἐξ ὀνύχων δὲ κατείβεται ἀσταγὲς αἷμα,
οἱ δὲ φόνῳ μυδόεντες ἀναπλείουσιν ὀδόντες.

But when first it bites, a swelling of dark, unhealthy hue rises, and a sore
pain freezes the heart, and the stomach's content turned to water gushes
out, while on the first night after, blood wells from the nostrils and throat
and ears, freshly infected with the bile-like venom; urine escapes all
bloody; wounds on the limbs break open, hastened by the destruction of the
skin. May no Female Blood-letter ever inject its venom into you! For when
it has bitten, all together the gums swell from the very bottom, and from the
finger-nails the blood drips unstaunchable, while the teeth, clammy with
gore, become loose.

This is one of the very few passages in Nicander's poetry where the narrator becomes indeed empathetic (in his warning μήποτέ τοι θήλει'
αἱμορροῖς ἰὸν ἐνείη which is addressed not to the doctor's apprentice
but to the potential victim of the haimorrhois). *Pathos* is omnipresent in
this 'blood and gore' scene that projects imaginary horrors upon scientific data. Verse 300 marks a critical turning point in the narrative: swelling, heartache and vomit, i.e. physical symptoms of snake bite, give way
to the one and only symptom with nightmarish dimensions, namely
bleeding. That the passage suggests a transition into the realms of fancy
where nightmare and horror reign is reinforced by its temporal marking.
It is night. During this night of agony the victim of the haimorrhois experiences exactly what its name promises: uncontrollable flow of blood all
over his body. Haemorrhage as represented here far exceeds the standards of a medical description. Horror reverberates through the entire
sequence which seems to be taken from a splatter film. Close-ups and
gory details graphically portray the gushing forth of the blood[149]. Yet it
is the mingling of medical realism with otherworldly symptoms that produces a lurid effect: not only the nose and the gums but also the ears and
the finger-nails drip with blood, whereas the skin opens up to make old
wounds bleed again[150].

Nevertheless, it takes more than a bloodshed to create *pathos* in Nicander. Any excess in the depiction of symptoms builds up *pathos* too.

149. An interesting expression is ἀσταγὲς αἷμα explained by the scholiast as follows
(Sch. Nic. *Ther.* 307b): ἀσταγὲς δὲ ἤτοι ἄστακτον, ἢ μὴ στάζον, ἀλλὰ κρουνηδὸν
φερόμενον, οἰονεὶ πολυσταγές. Other words indicating violent flow of blood are
πιδύεται, παρέδραμεν, ἐπειγόμεναι and κατείβεται.

150. Some of these features (special colour effects, extreme close-ups, accumulation
of detail, exaggeration) figure prominently in the aesthetics of 'trash' culture: cf. to the
point the brilliant discussion of Martin (2005) on how to read 'Hesiod's' *Aspis* in the light
of the trash aesthetics of modern cinematography.

Another horror device, alongside hyperbolic visualization, is the simula-
tion of sound effects, as exemplified by the case of the arrow-poison
(*Alex.* 214-223). Infection by this poison causes the victim to scream and
yell chillingly. Metamorphosis into various creatures (sheep, wolf, bull,
dog) is implied by the wide range of the sounds he produces: in the
beginning he bleats (μηκάζει) and babbles (φλύζων); he then cries
aloud (βοάᾳ) as if being beheaded; he shouts (ἐπεμβοάᾳ γλώσσῃ
θρόον) like a priestess of Rhea and barks (ὑλαγμός) like her votaries on
the mountains; eventually he bellows (βρυχανάαται) and howls
(ὠρυδόν)[151]. Confusion of identities is a proof of the victim's derangement, and frenzy is the ultimate failure of the poisoned body.

So are other extreme situations which explore *pathos*, most prominently death. Sometimes a deep sleep is a prelude to death (by drinking
the tears of the poppy, *Alex.* 433-442) or, even more impressively, an
euphemism for it (when a man wastes away into an evil sleep, *Ther.*
738-746). Death by poison acquires a metaphysical dimension when it
follows the noxious drinking of hemlock (*Alex.* 186-194). The blending
of physical with metaphysical is sensed from the very beginning of the
catalogue of symptoms. Darkness of night (νύκτα φέρον σκοτόεσ-
σαν) is a striking metaphor for the failure of the brain; it is suceeded
by rolling of the eyes, tottering and crawling. Death gets all the more
closer and is manifest in the blocking of breath, frozen limbs and con-
traction of the arteries. The passage is given a sublime climax, once it
is solemnly said, in a rhetoric evoking high poetry, that eventually the
victim's soul beholds Hades (ψυχὴ δ᾽ Ἀιδωνέα λεύσσει)–thus bringing to memory Homeric and tragic contexts of death and the netherworld[152].

At the opposite end of the spectrum there is the grotesque. What has
thus far seemed 'realistic' in the depiction of the poisoned body is carried to extremes by emphasis on deformity or the description of unusual
side effects. Moreover, the lack of confines between outer and inner
body (as when the human entrails are foregrounded or when open wounds
display the permeability of the body through the skin) and the exaggeration of bodily needs such as urination, vomiting or defecation, are two
aspects of the grotesque that, as already argued, are amply exemplified

151. "Noise" is an essential feature of trash cinematography, cf. Martin (2005) 158
who remarks "the trashier the movie, the louder it is": this aesthetics explains, in Martin's
view, the frequency of sound words in the *Aspis*.

152. The contrasted image, that of the poisoned man who contemplates the sun during
his agony, is found in verses 275-276 ἐννέα δ᾽ αὐγάς/ ἠελίου μογέων ἐπιόσσεται,
though to a similar *pathos* effect (cf. Spatafora [2005] 258).

in Nicandrean bodies[153]. The *Theriaca* offers extraordinary examples of the degradation of the body due to poisoning, by conjuring up mental images that are weird and comic at the same time. The first passage focuses on total loss of hair as a result of the biting by a sepedon (326-333):

τῆς δ᾽ ἤτοι ὀλοὸν καὶ ἐπώδυνον ἔπλετο ἕλκος
σηπεδόνος, νέμεται δὲ μέλας ὀλοφώιος ἰός
πᾶν δέμας, αὐαλέη δὲ περὶ χροῖ καρφομένη θρίξ
σκίδναται ὡς γήρεια καταψηχθέντος ἀκάνθης·
ἐκ μὲν γὰρ κεφαλῆς τε καὶ ὀφρύος ἀνδρὶ τυπέντι
ῥαίονται, βλεφάρων δὲ μέλαιν᾽ ἐξέφθιτο λάχνη·
ἄψεα δὲ τροχόεντες ἐπιστίζουσι μὲν ἀλφοί,
λευκαί τ᾽ ἀργινόεσσαν ἐπισσεύουσιν ἔφηλιν.

Upon the parched skin everywhere the hair withers and is dispersed like the down of a thistle when it is rubbed. For from the head and the brows of a man who has been bitten the hairs break off and from the eyelids the dark lashes perish, while round spots bespeckle his limbs and leprous eruptions swiftly spread a chalk-like rash.

One may claim of course that this description displays all the features of Nicandrean *pathos*: poetic expression, visualization based on the contrast between the black poison and the gradual 'whitening' of the victim's skin, and rendering of envenomation as a horrible disease (in this case, ἔφηλις 'leprosy'). Yet what is illustrated here is a strangely deformed body–a 'grotesque body'[154]. A prominent feature of the 'grotesque body' is that it is a body "in the act of becoming"[155], and it is noteworthy that Nicandrean bodies are unstable, in a state of flux, as they are being physically transformed under the influence of various poisons. Like the one described here, which is remarkably unnatural during its mutation into a hairless body, into an entity without hair, brows and eyelashes. Indeed, the process of hair loss is likened to the dispersion of the down of the thistle, an image deriving from the realm of plants. Although it is daring to view this image as an indication of the mixture

153. According to the definition of the grotesque by Bakhtin (1984) (p. 317) "this is why the main events in the life of the 'grotesque body', the acts of the bodily drama, take place in this sphere. Eating, drinking, defecation and other elimination (sweating, blowing of the nose, sneezing), as well as copulation, pregnancy, dismemberment, swallowing up by another body–all these acts are performed on the confines of the body and the outer world, or on the confines of the old and new body" and (p. 318) "the grotesque image displays not only the outward but also the inner features of the body: blood, bowels, heart and other organs. The outward and inward features are often merged into one."

154. The term belongs to Bakhtin (1984) 315-323 who discusses the 'grotesque body' (irregular and open to the outer world) by juxtaposing it with both what he calls the 'classical body' (which is stable and self-contained) and the 'naturalist body'.

155. Bakhtin (1984) 317.

246   THE AESTHETICS OF DARKNESS

between human and plant which constitutes an archetypal concept of the
grotesque, it is worth noting that the uncanny, almost comic, mental
image of the bald body with the chalk-white skin conveyed here invokes
grotesqueness all the same[156].

Imagination projects itself on the naturalistic body to create a grotesque effect in several other passages. In evolving around the part of the
body which is prominently subject to exaggeration, the genitals, the following example from the *Theriaca* features the grotesque (721-723):

αὐτίκα δὲ χρώς
μέζεά τ᾽ ἀνδρὸς ἔνερθε τιταίνεται, ἐν δέ τε καυλός
φύρματι μυδαλέος προϊάπτεται

And straightaway his skin and his genitals below grow taut, and his member projects, dripping with foul ooze...

A poison causing erection is a symptom that, although known to the iologists, is grotesque to a high degree[157]. Καυλός 'stalk' is a term transferred from plants to the human body to denote the penis; apart from this,
the unknown nature of the liquid dripping from the penis–is it urine or
semen?–and the image of an actual ejaculation (through προϊάπτεται)
belong to the rhetoric of the phallus, thus placing the passage into the
broader context of the grotesque[158]. Well beyond medical realism and
accuracy, Nicander fantasizes strange manifestations of the poison in the
human body. In a striking passage from the spider section of the *Theriaca*
the vomit expelled from the victim's throat takes the form of a spider's
web (732-733): ἔμετον δ᾽ ἐξήρυγε δειρῆς/ λοιγὸν ἀραχνήεντα 'from
his throat he discharges a deadly vomit like a spider's web'. The metaphor of the spider's web is attested elsewhere (also before Nicander)
in medical contexts, especially in regard to body fluids[159]. However, by

156. Some verses later (340-342), the victim of the dipsas is illustrated as a bull drinking with gaping mouth water from a stream: the image suggests the grotesque mixture of
human and bestial, as Spatafora (2005) 260 rightly observes.
157. The iologists familiar with the symptom (Philoumenos, Aelius) are however later
than Nicander; for the testimonies, see Jacques (2002) 200-201 n. 77/4.
158. Cf. Bakhtin (1984) 317: "The essential role belongs to those parts of the 'grotesque body' in which it outgrows its own self, transgressing its own body, in which it
conceives a new, second body: the bowels and the phallus. These two areas play the
leading role in the grotesque image, and it is precisely for this reason that they are pre-
dominantly subject to positive exaggeration, to hyperbolization".
159. According to the scholia, Nicander, in coining the adjective ἀραχνήεις, is either
suggesting the sticky texture of the vomit or its web-like appearance (Sch. Nic. *Ther.* 733a
ἀραχνώδης ἔμετος γλίσχρος ἐστὶ κατὰ τὴν ἀφήν. ἔχει δ᾽ ὄψιν ἀραχνῶν...ἄλλως·
λοιγὸν ἀραχνήεντα οἷον λεπτόν, ἀράχνη ὅμοιον). Cf. Aristot. *HA* 583a ἀραχνιῶδες
τὸ γάλα ἐν τοῖς μαστοῖς, Hipp. *Coa praesagia* 571 ἀραχνιῶδες οὖρον, Plin. *NH* 29.86
urina similis aranei textis.

thus visualizing the vomit caused by the spider bite Nicander creates a mental image that captures a subtle shading of dark aesthetics, somewhere between the grotesque, the uncanny and the horrifying. The return of the unconscious, in this case the fear of being transformed into the very object of repulsion, becomes the core of the bizarre image of the spider-man[160].

The last act of the 'drama of the body' in Nicander deals with the confines between inside and outside manifestations of the bodily, between substances contained within the body and the wastes discharged from it, as also between the physical and the spiritual. Confines that are blurred as the ultimate manifestation of poisoning. The keyword here is estrangement, alienation, denoting the chasm that divides the subject from its body. A sick body is indeed uncontrollable, liable to demonic forces beyond comprehension, and as a consequence its organs lead their own, independent life; nevertheless, their failure deeply affects the subject[161]. The fact that the body is a precondition for the existence of the subject, yet to a great degree independent from it is a contradiction that may be linked to the abject. As a concept, the abject resides in dark areas marking the blurring of the boundaries between subject and object, inner and outer self[162]. The poisoned body, a living body that foreshadows the corpse, is a physical abject, whose disorderly state is manifest in its wounds and filthy body fluids. As Kristeva remarks in defining the abject[163]:

> These body fluids, this defilement, this shit are what life withstands, hardly and with difficulty, on the part of death. There, I am at the border of my condition as a living being. My body extricates itself, as being alive, from that border. Such wastes drop so that I might live, until, from loss to loss, nothing remains in me and my entire body falls beyond the limit–*cadere*, cadaver.

160. It is tempting to see this Nicandrean image in the light of metamorphosis myths, where human, animal and plant traits mingle to produce a new, hybrid entity. The culmination of this theme is found in the opening lines of Franz Kafka's *Metamorphosis* where the uncanny blends with the grotesque: "One morning, when Gregor Samsa woke from troubled dreams, he found himself transformed in his bed into a horrible vermin. He lay on his armour-like back, and if he lifted his head a little he could see his brown belly, slightly domed and divided by arches into stiff sections..." [Transl. D. Wyllie].
161. Cf. Holmes (2010) 16: "Symptoms are demonic, too, because they are messengers from a foreign world, a world automated by forces that we are unable to control simply by intending or exhorting or supplicating: not only are we incapable of moving our heart in the way we move our legs, but we cannot check our bile as an Iliadic warrior can check his *thumos*".
162. A psychoanalytic concept introduced by Kristeva (1982) 1-31.
163. Kristeva (1982) 3.

248   THE AESTHETICS OF DARKNESS

Whereas liquids are amply exemplified in Nicander's poems, the image of the corpse is found only once in the *Theriaca* in the passage on the basilisk (403-408):

τύμματι δ' ἐπρήσθη φωτὸς δέμας, αἱ δ' ἀπὸ γυίων
σάρκες ἀπορρείουσι πελιδναί τε ζοφεραί τε·
οὐδέ τις οὐδ' οἰωνὸς ὑπὲρ νέκυν ἴχνια τείνας,
αἰγυπιοὶ γῦπές τε κόραξ τ' ὀμβρήρεα κρώζων,
οὐδὲ μὲν ὅσσα τε φῦλα νομάζεται οὔρεσι θηρῶν
δαίνυνται· τοῖόν περ ἀυτμένα δεινὸν ἐφίει.

His bite swells a man's body, and from the limbs the flesh falls away livid and blackening. Nor even will a bird pursuing its track above the corpse, be it eagle or vulture or raven that croaks of rain, nor yet any species of wild beast that pastures upon the hills, feed upon it: such the terrible stench that it sends forth.

In effect, this a preview of the victim's future as a corpse. But already in the previous phase, which documents the affect of the body by the venom, decomposition is visualized as a process towards death. Flesh melts away from the body, while colouring suggests the paleness of the cadaver and the darkness of Hades (σάρκες...πελιδναί τε ζοφεραί τε). For a while the corpse is exposed to the vultures to feed upon it, but soon is rejected even by them due to its horrible stench, thus becoming a new abject[164].

But the poison also affects mind and soul, it penetrates into the deepest realms of the self. Once suffering is internalized, the integrity of the self is severely threatened, and madness emerges. Madness takes various forms: it manifests itself, for example, as a return to infancy, when the victim of the salamander is visualized as crawling on hands and knees (*Alex.* 542-543)[165]. Or as self-harm owed to mental disorder, as when someone poisoned by the chamaeleon-thistle gnaws his tongue with his dogteeth (*Alex.* 283-284). Dementia reaches its peak in two passages of the *Alexipharmaca*, in which the body turns Bacchic[166].

164. Obviously Nicander has *Il.* 1.4-5 in mind (for other parallels, see Overduin [2010] 335 on vv. 405-410). In my opinion, the passage is modelled upon the extensive description of the plague in Thucydides *Histories* which concludes like this (2.50): τὰ γὰρ ὄρνεα καὶ τετράποδα ὅσα ἀνθρώπων ἅπτεται, πολλῶν ἀτάφων γιγνομένων ἢ οὐ προσῄει ἢ γευσάμενα διεφθείρετο.
165. It is noteworthy that there is no parallel for this symptom in medical literature. The grotesque image of the victim as an infant is also found in the passage in which he is urged to suck milk from a woman's breast (*Alex.* 356-357 ἢ ὅγε καὶ θηλῆς ἅτε δὴ βρέφος ἐμπελάοιτο/ ἀρτιγενές, μαστοῦ δὲ ποτὸν μοσχηδὸν ἀμέλγοι).
166. Passages which evoke scenes of religious ecstasy are characteristic of the *Alexipharmaca*, cf. vv. 215-223 for the simile about the priestess of Rhea: on their intense emotional effect on the reader, see Spatafora (2005) 250-262.

In the former case the victim experiences a physical symptom, blurred vision, like the Silenus during a night of intoxication by the drink of Dionysus (30-35). The latter is much more striking, because it results into a strange behavioural disorder–αἰσχρολογία (159-161)[167]:

οἱ μέν τ' ἀφροσύνῃ ἐμπληγέες οἷά τε μάργοι
δήμια λαβράζουσι παραπλῆγές θ' ἅτε Βάκχαι
ὀξὺ μέλος βοόωσιν ἀταρμύκτῳ φρενὸς οἴστρῳ.

The victims are struck with madness and utter wild and vulgar words like lunatics, and like crazy Bacchanals bawl shrill songs of the mind unabashed.

This manic body is liberated from fear and shame; its frenzy (οἶστρος) foreshadows Bacchic horror. The self breaks free from the social and physical constraints imposed by the 'healthy' body once reborn in the orgiastic cult of Dionysus: in a state of ecstasy it becomes the autonomous body *par excellence*.

Nicandrean bodies display a series of un-Classical traits. Irregular, disrupted, and ever-changing, fragmentary rather than complete, these bodies may be read as a palimpsest[168]. The wounds bring the depths of the body into light; anomalies and excrescences, changes in colour and texture, massive discharges of liquids point at failures of bodily workings; primitive fears and instincts claim their presence in imaginary concepts of corporeality; generalized physical disorders cause the unity of body and soul to dissolve. Viewed from this complex perspective, the poisoned body in the *Theriaca* and the *Alexipharmaca* asserts its abhumanness. Such an alienated body becomes a spectacle and a source of delight for the master of the absurd and the uncanny–Franz Kafka in his short story *A Country Doctor* (1919) depicts the wound as a roseate flower:

> On his right side, in the region of the hip, a wound in the size of the palm of one's hand has opened up. Rose coloured, in many different shadings, dark in the depths, brighter on the edges, delicately grained, with uneven patches of blood, open to the light like a mine. That's what it looks like from a distance. Close up a complication is apparent. Who can look at that without whistling softly? Worms, as thick and long as my little finger, themselves rose coloured and also spattered with blood, are wriggling their

167. Despite being attested by later iologists like Dioscorides (see Jacques [2007] 105-106 n. 14/b), this symptom is a paradox stemming from poetic rather than medical imagination.
168. For a definition of the 'body as palimpsest' from a Gothic viewpoint, see Hurley (1996) 90-92.

white bodies with many limbs from their stronghold in the inner of the
wound towards the light. Poor young man, there's no helping you. I have
found out your great wound. You are dying from this flower on your side.
[Transl. I. Johnston]

To thus exploit the aesthetic potential of the wounded body is an extraordinary feat–and Nicander should be credited with its accomplishment
well before Kafka.

HELLENISTIC DARKNESS

An Afterword

Sick Muse

Alas, my poor muse! what ails you this morning? Your sunken eyes run
with night visions, and on your complexion I see by turns madness and
horror, icy and tight-lipped.

Greenish succubus and rose-colored imp, have they emptied over you their
vials of fear and of love? Has a nightmare, with rude despotic fist, dragged
you to the bottom of a fabled marsh of Minturnae?

Would that your bosom, exhaling wholesome odors, could be always har-
boring hard thought, your Christian blood flowing in rhythmic streams

like the metrical beat of ancient syllables, subject by turn to the father of
song, Apollo, and to great Pan, lord of the harvest. [Transl. K. Waldrop]

Charles Baudelaire *The Flowers of Evil* (1857)

Is the Hellenistic Muse sick? Does Baudelaire's *Muse malade*, the goddess of poetry who, disturbed by nightmares and dark visions, breathes
out madness and horror, provide a framework for the understanding of the
aesthetics of darkness? And does the blending of horror and eroticism
inspired by this sick Muse set the tone not only for Romantic and Decadent aesthetics but for Hellenistic poetry as well? To read darkness as a
complex notion involving the fantastic, the Gothic, the grotesque and the
uncanny is the premise upon which this study is based. Hellenistic poets,
especially those treated here, explore the artistic potential of darkness in
ways alien to other contemporary authors–that Callimachus incorporates
the anti-Romantic trends of the era is manifest in his sense of irony and
distance, as also in the absence of sensationalism and *pathos* from his
poetry[1]. Apollonius, on the other hand, is Romantic in the literal meaning
of the word. The voyage of the Argonauts is narrated from the perspective
of a fantasy romance, adapted as it is to the pattern of a quest plot: this
quest is oriented towards a primitive, marvellous world. Colchis, a dark
setting in itself, becomes a Gothic edifice in which the young female finds
herself imprisoned by a tyrannical father–within its confines, visions of

---

1. Bonelli (1979) 5-25 takes a somewhat different view when he claims that Callimachus expresses a new sensibility through erudition, whereas he displays a taste for sensuality in many poems (e.g. in *The Bath of Pallas*). Bonelli attributes this tendency to what
he terms the 'aestheticization' of the epic.

love and death become a liberating force for Medea. In reading the *Argonautica* the audience is invited to enter a land of fable, which is dominated by past myths, monsters and demonic forces, and to sense darkness and horror while traversing this imaginary land. With Lycophron's *Alexandra* the aesthetic experience approaches pure Gothic. The tragic monologue, which re-enacts the prophetic vision of Kassandra/Alexandra, is a claustrophobic form *per se*, where the 'I' and forms of Otherness struggle with each other. Trapped in her own delirium, Alexandra not only reviews the events of the Trojan myth from a dark viewpoint, but also envisions her own destiny and responds with horror to it. Alexandra as an ecstatic narrator recounts stories of Gothic horror, featuring stock characters of Romanticism such as the villain, the 'Byronic hero' and the *femme fatale*. And as if to justify its characterization as a σκοτεινὸν ποίημα, the *Alexandra* is written in a riddling discourse, verging at times on the grotesque, at times on the uncanny. To view the world from within the subject–this is the Romantic contribution of the *Alexandra* to Hellenistic aesthetics. Last but not least, Nicander specializes in another type of darkness, the dark science. By using the form of didactic epic, a plotless genre, Nicander exploits the sensation caused by scientific data. He thus combines various disciplines (zoology, botany, toxicology, medicine) and visualizes scientific phenomena to fascinate the reader. If asked 'what is dark in Nicander?' one may respond 'almost everything from subject matter to style'. To poeticize anything poisonous in nature–serpents, spiders, plants, substances–and to suggest alchemy as the remedy for poison is a dark start in itself. But to put the poisonous body, a body in agony, in display, creates a wide range of effects: 'visceral realism', *pathos*, the grotesque, the abject. Nicander's epics are dominated by the dark atmosphere that allures the reader and the sensational visualization of monstrous creatures, of open wounds, of decaying bodies. Darkness in Nicander sometimes exceeds Romanticism and extends to a morbid, albeit detached, Aestheticism.

But these conclusions have already been drawn, so the question is whether the notion of darkness can be applied to other authors and poems of the Hellenistic and post-Hellenistic era. If we choose to further widen the scope, which ones should be taken into account? First and foremost, metamorphosis poetry[2]. Although transformation myths are found from the very beginnings of Greek literature (the sources include Homer, Hesiod, tragedy and many more), it was in Hellenistic

---

2. For a fascinating study of metamorphosis from antiquity until today in myths of magic and wonder, fairytales and uncanny fictions of our day, see Warner (2002).

times that metamorphosis formed a distinct literary genre. Probably during its earlier stages, the transition into another identity was considered a result of hubristic behaviour or sin, and therefore metamorphosis narratives served moral, religious or philosophical purposes. The aestheticization of metamorphosis is a Hellenistic feat, especially connected with Nicander and Boios[3]. Although we are unaware of the exact content, form and rhetoric of their metamorphosis poems, it seems probable that, whereas Nicander in the *Heteroioumena* tended to stress the paradoxographical and cult aspects of transformation stories, Boios in the *Ornithogonia* was more interested in the fairytale-like, monstrous and grotesque elements inherent in the genre. A hybrid of mythology and aitiology, metamorphosis expresses many facets of the peculiar taste of the era for all forms of Otherness, mystery, and primitivism, human psychology, sentimentality and eroticism, and, above all, for the horrors stemming from alienation (*alienation* is after all an idea reflected in Nicander's title *Heteroioumena* 'Things made alien')[4]. As is so often the case, a Hellenistic tendency finds its fulfillment in Augustan poetry. Therefore, a study of metamorphosis genre can only be comprehensive, if Ovid's *Metamorphoses* is seen as its final outcome: in Ovid's epic the depiction of how the human body transforms into a different identity proves to be an invitation for the reader to immerse himself in the pleasures of the uncanny. Metamorphosis poetry with its emphasis upon uncanny experiences of the subject becomes the ultimate challenge for heroic epic[5], and thus marks the transition from Romantic to Modernistic aesthetics[6].

Another line of enquiry leads to the dark side of love. Love is a recurrent theme in every period of Greek literature, but 'Romantic' love becomes a trend in the poetry of high Hellenism[7]. Callimachus'

3. Forbes Irving (1990) 19-37.
4. The significance of corporeality and its relation to the self for the interpretation of metamorphosis is stressed by Segal (2005).
5. Doubling, the idea of the other self or *alter ego*, that haunts 19th century horror literature is worth exploring within the context of metamorphosis poetry, as Warner (2002) 161-203 brilliantly demonstrates. In the case of doubling, metamorphic change and mutation is internalized, it becomes a matter of consciousness not of mere 'corporeality' or appearance; by extension, it is tempting to consider this aspect of the double, the evil self, as an alternative to the values of heroic epic.
6. Ziolkowski (2005) 74-98 discusses the "modernization of metamorphosis" as a hallmark of 20th century poetics, whose most celebrated paradigm is Franz Kafka's *Metamorphosis*.
7. That Romantic love was not first invented by the Medieval troubadours but by the poets of Hellenistic and Roman times is argued by Rudd (1981). Rohde (1960) along with other 19th century scholars was one of the first to stress the connection.

Aitia which comprises several romances with a happy ending and Theocritus who dramatizes unrequited love in melodramatic narratives are two distinct cases; yet, the *Argonautica* marks the passage from epic and tragic love to modern, novelistic romance. For centuries to come love (of heroes, of women, of ordinary men, of royals) permeates hexametric or elegiac poetry, whereas mythology provides poets with exciting stories of love intrigue. The Hellenistic turn towards the passions and sorrows of love is, not unjustly, seen as the first manifestation of Romantic aesthetics in world literature. Still, the question posed at the beginning of this afterword merits a second thought: is the Hellenistic Muse sick? To rephrase the question: did love as illness emerge as the quintessential theme of Hellenistic poetics? Euripides was perhaps the first poet to develop an exceptionally strong taste for morbid passions, a tendency that never ceased to be in vogue throughout the subsequent centuries. Fourth century was dominated by the sensational love narratives of Antimachus written in a flamboyant style; alongside Antimachus, Philitas and even Hedyle were acknowledged as the forerunners of subjective elegy on similar thematics. What is striking however is that the aesthetics of morbidity culminated during the 3rd and 2nd centuries with Apollonius, Euphorion, Nicander, Lycophron, Moschus, Nicaenetus, to quote some well-known paradigms of Hellenistic darkness[8].

But the picture is not complete before we reach a key case, Parthenius of Nicaea. In what respect is his prose collection of love stories, known under the title *Erotika Pathemata*, a paradigm of the aesthetics of darkness[9]? Since a stylistic analysis is not an option as regards this work, content and story patterns will be briefly discussed instead. Mapping themes and motifs of the *Erotika Pathemata* is not an easy task[10]. Eros in the *Erotika Pathemata* is utterly 'unhealthy'[11]: a quarter of the stories deals with some kind of incest, others involve rape and betrayal, but all

---

8. For a comprehensive survey of Greek love poetry during the last three centuries BC, see Lightfoot (1999) 17-31. For similar points on the interconnectedness of love, death, metamorphosis and magic during this era, see Sistakou (2008a) 121-135.

9. The Romantic 'love and death' complex is introduced as the main theme of the new poetry by the *Erotika Pathemata* (see Papanghelis [1994] 79-82, Lightfoot [1999] passim and Sistakou [2008a] 135-142).

10. Lightfoot (1999) 224-263 discusses the basic motifs; for a systematic exposition of the love motifs and their combination in the *Erotika Pathemata*, see Voisin (2008).

11. The word νόσος/νόσημα appears in several of Parthenius' summaries to suggest incest (5, 13, 17); see for example how the passion of Periander's mother for her son is portrayed in story 17: προϊόντος δὲ τοῦ χρόνου τὸ πάθος ἐπὶ μεῖζον ηὔξετο καὶ κατέχειν τὴν νόσον οὐκ ἔτι οἵα τε ἦν, ἕως ἀποτολμήσασα προσφέρει λόγους τῷ παιδί... On the eroticism of the *Erotika Pathemata*, see Francese (2008).

end with exile, metamorphosis, suicide, murder, or a combination of them. Clearly all these motifs strike a melodramatic note, especially in their accumulation and hyperbole; insistence on carnal desire and the actual moment of the forbidden intercourse, a big dose of sadism, extreme cases of cannibalism point to the sickness of Decadence in addition to the dramatic passions of Romanticism. Among the motifs listed above there is at least one that may be exceptionally associated with darkness, namely incest. Although incest is not Parthenius' own invention–as a literary theme it is as old as the Oedipus myth, whereas Euripides had a reputation among his contemporaries for presenting incestuous love affairs on stage–, he displays an obsession with its aesthetic potential. Romantic and Gothic novels abound with incest, as it is the sickness of this passion that heightens the algolagnic quality of these novels and intensifies the feeling of horror[12]; sensationalism as a result of mingling low genres with high literature was an effect sought by Hellenistic and Romantic poets alike[13].

To add new depth to the reading of Parthenius, and of other Hellenistic writers with a taste for the macabre and the algolagnic, one may only think of similar stories by Edgar Allan Poe or Oscar Wilde. To further justify the parallelism between the Hellenistic era and 19th century culture, one has to point out that the quest for sensual stories involving morbidity, violence and death was a favourite sport of some eccentric intellectuals of European *Fin de siècle*. A strange case of such an intellectual was the French scholar and writer Marcel Schwob (1867-1905), an admirer of Poe, Wilde and Flaubert[14]:

> In his capacity of scholar, Schwob made passionate researches into certain *faisandé* periods and aspects of the past; he, too, like Gourmont, was interested in the Latin of the Decline; he made a study of the slang of the Medieval criminal bands, and of the career of that strange poet of the underworld, François Villon; he disinterred from old texts and archives the figures of vagabonds, eunuchs, brigands, criminals; he had a strong feeling for what Flaubert had called 'la vieille poésie de la corruption et de la venalité', and an adoration for certain historic prostitutes…he felt the charm of the Medieval *fillettes communes*, 'celles qui hantent à l'entour des villes de France, assises sur le pierres des cimetières, pour donner du plaisir à

---

12. Praz (1970) views incest as a vital ingredient of the Romantic tales of terror, and offers paradigms from Byron, Shelley, Flaubert, D'Annunzio and Swinburne among others (see Index s.v. "Incest").

13. Cf. Lightfoot (1999) 243 who observes that "incest stories form one of the intersections between myth and folktale…stories about incest which are lost to us because they circulated in a genre too low to have been preserved". A similar theme (or perhaps a reversal of incest) is cannibalism, found also in Parthenius.

14. As portrayed by Praz (1970) 369-370.

ceux qui passent'; he translated *Moll Flanders*; he investigated grisly, mysterious episodes of the Middle Ages, the Crusade of the Innocents, stories
of lepers, of victims of the plague, of beggars, folklore of a ghastly kind;
and he followed with interest the criminal trials of his own day. The story
of the incest of Annabella and Giovanni in Ford's *'Tis pity she's a Whore*
found in him a fervent admirer.

Perhaps it is too daring to draw a parallel between Parthenius and
Schwob–a first objection would be that the latter focused not only on
morbid eroticism but on morbidity as an aesthetic value *per se*. Yet, both
mark the end (or the culmination) of an era that introduced low human
passions into literature; which had a dislike for moralism and conversely
an attraction to everything 'sick'; that they attempted to dig up stories of
wickedness and evil from a distant past, and refashion them into Decadent literature[15].

The comparison should not be pressed too hard, but all the same it gives
an idea of the potential and limitations of the method adopted in the
present study. To read Hellenistic poetry through the lens of Romanticism, and not vice versa, constitutes a paradox, once it projects terms and
patterns of a posterior historical phase onto literary and artistic phenomena existing previously. Nevertheless, it seems justified within the
broader conception of intertextuality as an exploration of how texts
engage in open and limitless relations with all other texts beyond authorial or historical boundaries. In my view, to take the opposite, a-historical
direction from the present to the past means to re-interpret ancient literature from a new angle or re-read it under a new light. It has not always
been easy to hold to this methodological principle during the analysis of
such distant cultural periods as the Hellenistic era and 19th century literature. Terms as 'Gothic' and, of course, 'Romantic' are problematic
once detached from their historical context. The very reference to writers
such as Percy Shelley or Edgar Allan Poe or works like *Frankenstein* in
a study of Hellenistic poetry could be anathema to many classicists,
given the discontinuity between Hellenistic and Romantic aesthetics, or,
more generally, between ancient and modern literature. What I hope to
have shown, however, is that it is worth attempting a parallelism between
Hellenistic and Romantic aesthetics; so, before closing, I would briefly
like to refer to certain ideological and cultural affinities between the Hellenistic and the Romantic era.

---

15. For a reading of Hellenistic poetry from the perspective of European Decadence,
see Bonelli (1979) and Papanghelis (1994).

The Romantic age was eventful, revolutionary, an era which saw the emergence of new ideologies, upon which the leading figures of literature considered their duty to reflect with their writings. Politics, society and religion underwent dramatic changes during the centuries following the death of Alexander too: the political role of the poet within the new historical context (including the dominion of monarchy, cultural syncretism, and eventually the rise of Rome) was of increasing importance, at least for some of the authors of the era[16]. While the political consciousness found novel ways of expression, philosophical and religious ideologies are much more difficult to detect in the highly diversified corpus of Greek literature during the last centuries before Christ. Yet, as E.R. Dodds has brilliantly shown, a sustained conflict between reason and the forces of the irrational took place during the same period, until the latter eventually prevailed[17]. Whereas in the 4th and 3rd centuries science triumphed over religion, the horizons widened, society became free and open to accept people of different origin and culture, during the subsequent centuries the Greek world experienced a return to religion and cult as also a growing influence of magic, occultism, astrology and Eastern superstition. Dodds attempts to explain what he terms "the Failure of Greek Rationalism" and "the Return of the Irrational" by attributing the phenomena to the fear of the individual when faced with his own social and intellectual freedom. This is what happened to the man of late Hellenism, and, surprisingly enough, to the man of Romanticism as well[18]:

> All these developments [i.e. the Return of the Irrational] are perhaps symptoms, rather than causes in the intellectual climate of the Mediterranean world–something whose nearest historical analogue may be the Romantic reaction against rationalist "natural theology" which set in at the beginning of the nineteenth century and is still a powerful influence today. The adoration of the visible cosmos, and the sense of unity with it which had found expression in early Stoicism, began to be replaced in many minds by a feeling that the physical world–at any rate the part of it below the moon–is under the sway of evil powers, and that what the soul needs is not unity with it but escape from it. The thoughts of men were increasingly preoccupied with techniques of individual salvation, some relying on holy books allegedly discovered in Eastern temples or dictated by the voice of God to some inspired prophet, others seeking a personal revelation by oracle, dream, or waking vision; others again looking for security in ritual, whether

16. Recent scholarship has focused on the political dimension of Apollonius' *Argonautica* (e.g. Mori [2008] esp. 19-51 on the politics of Alexandrian poetry) or the incorporation of contemporary historical events into Lycophron's *Alexandra*, among others.
17. Dodds (1951) 236-269.
18. Dodds (1951) 248.

by initiation in one or more of the now numerous "mysteria" or by employing the services of a private magician. There was a growing demand for
occultism, which is essentially an attempt to capture the Kingdom of
Heaven by material means–it has been well described as "the vulgar form
of transcendentalism".

Dodds' masterful portrayal of the irrational, transcendental elements
dominating individual psychology from the first century BC onwards is
directly comparable to the Romantic reaction against naturalism:
Romantics replaced 18th century optimism and trust in reason with the
belief that evil is the only reality of life and that feeling and imagination are the only means by which man may understand God[19]. Taking
this hypothesis as a point of departure, it is not difficult to see the connection of the irrational with horror and darkness, nor to explain why
this aesthetic trend kept spreading through Hellenistic to Imperial literature and beyond.

Then, there is the intellectual framework. Romantics held controversial views regarding science and nature. Science was a matter of constant
debate between Romantic intellectuals who, on the one hand, were
attracted by scientific progress, whereas, on the other, warned against
excessive scientific investigation to the detriment of emotion or the
human psyche itself[20]. But the "man of science" was the *alter ego* of the
poet, two identities interconnected within the concept of Romantic science. Moreover, Romantic poets moved in the same circles with scientists, were attracted by their experiments (the highly theatrical staging of
the electrochemical experiments of Humphry Davy is a telling example),
and were deeply influenced by them in the formation of their poetics–
just like their Hellenistic, in particular Alexandrian, predecessors. Optics,
botany, physics and medicine, especially the practice of dissection, flourished during both periods. On the other side, pseudo-sciences and the
obsession with paradoxography allowed superstition to blend with the
scientific spirit in Alexandria, and it is not without significance that the
beginnings of alchemy may be traced back to this era[21]:

19. According to the analysis of Dawson as summarized by Dodds (1951) 264 n. 71.
20. Vitalism, a Romantic belief according to which a metaphysical factor determines life beyond physicality, developed as a contrast to mechanistic views put forward by 18th century scientists. The vitalism debate, seen as an attack to the Age of
Reason, was the subject of a notorious event, the so-called 'Immortal Dinner', where
the antagonism between Romantic poetry and science was declared: for this anti-scientific reaction of the Romantics, see Holmes (2008) 305-336. However, as argued
above pp. 193-194, science flourished and developed in all fields of human knowledge
during the 19th century.
21. Fraser (1972) 1.443-444.

It is enough to see how in this province [i.e. of alchemy], as in that of astrology, the first steps towards the occult are a recognizable perversion of current scientific and philosophical doctrine. It seems probable that Bolos' study both of Theophrastus' botanical writings and also of his own predecessors in the field of regular paradoxography, led to this construction of a common theoretical basis for the alleged natural phenomena which formed the traditional subject-matter of such work. This contradictory alliance between the irrational and the rational, which reached its climax three hundred years later in Claudius Ptolemy, is thus visible in the world of second-century Alexandria, where it first emerges as the combined product of declining Greek science and native Egyptian traditions.

Nature, on the other hand, was interpreted according to the emerging sensibility of both eras; the concept of an idyllic nature has deep roots in Romantic aesthetics, being the emotive and subjective response to the purely natural. A lyrical approach to nature is characteristic of Hellenism, and especially of the bucolics of Theocritus; on the other hand, its dark aspects are suggested by Nicander's nightmarish portrayal of the evil lurking everywhere in the natural landscape[22].

The 'Romantic' awakening is evident especially in art and aesthetics, and in the shifting cultural identities of the Hellenistic era and the 19th century respectively. The Romantics' attraction to, and struggle against, 'Classical inheritances' is comparable to the dilemma 'tradition or innovation' for which Hellenistic aesthetics became famous[23]. Human psychology, passion and *pathos*, a love for the remote and the exotic, a focus on the particular rather than the general is richly attested in both aesthetic trends; ugliness was (re)discovered, and, along with it, darkness, horror and the concomitant feeling of the sublime. These are the favourite themes of art, whereas ancient and modern Romantics have a penchant for the colourful, visual detail. The dynamics of visualization, transferred from the spectacle to the rhetoric of the text, is a distinguishing feature of both cultures. All these pertain to pure aesthetic pleasure, which has replaced *katharsis* as the ultimate purpose of

22. Fowler (1980) 23-31 argues that Hellenistic poets developed a lyrical, almost Romantic, sensitivity towards the 'sweetness of nature'. On Nicander's dark perception of nature, see pp. 207-209.

23. Graver (2005) re-evaluates the deep influence of Classical, i.e. ancient, models in literature and art, upon Romantics, and the latter's admiration for antiquity. On the other hand, Dodds (1951) 237 argues that in the Hellenistic age there was "a new freedom for the mind to travel backwards in time and choose at will from the past experience of men those elements which it could best assimilate and exploit. The individual began consciously to *use* the tradition, instead of being used by it. This is most obvious in the Hellenistic poets, whose position in this respect was like that of poets and artists of today".

art[24]. Within this post-Aristotelian context, Hellenistic literature developed into Romantic directions. The individual and the society as a whole had to redifine their relationship with heroism and its values: love and fantasy, passion and horror were seen as alternatives to the thematics of war and its glory[25]. Mood and atmosphere were valued more than the coherent μῦθος; by extension, poetry became sensational rather than philosophical. In my opinion, darkness as an aesthetic choice incorporates a series of features that acquired growing importance for the development of Hellenistic literary taste: the view of the world from within the subject, as exemplified by the monologue of Alexandra; the portrayal of passion, rather than its tragic consequences, as embodied by Apollonius' Medea; the emergence of the fantastic and the supernatural as distortions of reality in the *Argonautica*; the prevalence of the 'spectacular' over the scientific in Nicander.

During a long period of change in taste and culture, from the era of Alexandrian high-Hellenism to Parthenius, poets elaborated on aesthetic experiences. As in the following catalogue of flowers from Nicander's *Georgica*, in which the allure of exotic names rivals the dark mood of a death discourse (fr. 74.55-72 G.-S.)[26]:

ἦ γὰρ καὶ λεπταὶ πτερίδες καὶ παιδὸς ἔρωτες
λεύκη ἰσαιόμενοι, ἐν καὶ κρόκος εἴαρι μύων,
κύπρος τ' ὀσμηρόν τε σισύμβριον ὅσσα τε κοίλοις
ἄσπορα ναιομένοισι τόποις ἀνεθρέψατο λειμών
κάλλεα, βούφθαλμόν τε καὶ εὐῶδες Διὸς ἄνθος,
χάλκας, σὺν δ' ὑάκινθον ἰωνιάδας τε χαμηλάς
ὀρφνοτέρας, ἃς στύξε μετ' ἄνθεσι Περσεφόνεια.
σὺν δὲ καὶ ὑψῆέν τε πανόσμεον, ὅσσα τε τύμβοι
φάσγανα παρθενικαῖς νεοδουπέσιν ἀμφιχέονται,
αὐτάς τ' ἠιθέας ἀνεμωνίδες ἀστράπτουσαι
τηλόθεν ὀξυτέρῃσιν ἐφελκόμεναι χροιῇσι.
πᾶς δέ τις ἢ ἐλένειον ἢ ἀστέρα φωτίζοντα
δρέψας εἰνοδίοισι θεῶν παρακάββαλε σηκοῖς
ἢ αὐτοῖς βρετάεσσιν, ὅτε πρώτιστον ἴδωνται·
πολλάκι θερμία καλά, τοτὲ χρυσανθὲς ἀμέργων
λείριά τε στήλῃσιν ἐπιφθίνοντα καμόντων
καὶ γεραὸν πώγωνα καὶ ἐντραπέας κυκλαμίνους
σαύρην θ' ἢ χθονίου πέφαται στέφος Ἡγεσιλάου.

---

24. Konstan (1991) 26-27 distinguishes three phases in the ancient tradition concerning the audience's involvement with poetry: from the beginnings (including the view of Homer and the Archaic poets) up to Plato, poetry has been regarded as a source of enchantment; Aristotle and the rhetoric tradition emphasize the reader's control over the emotion produced mainly by the characters of tragedy; in the next phase (called the 'romantic tradition' by Konstan) "desire in the text is thought to stimulate desire in the reader or listener".
25. On the reversal of heroic values in Hellenistic poetry, see Sistakou (2008a).
26. For an analysis of the passage, see Gow/Scholfield (1997) 211-213.

Yes, and delicate ferns and the acanthus which resembles the white poplar, and the crocus which closes in the spring, henna too and scented bergamot-mint and all other lovelinesses that unsown a meadow rears in hollow, watered spots, ox-eye and fragrant flower-of-Zeus, chrysanthemums and also hyacinth and low-growing violets, dark, and abhorred of Persephone among flowers. And of their company are the towering all-scent and the cornflags which encircle the graves of virgins lately dead, and sparkling anemones with which their dazzling colours lure living maidens from afar. And everybody plucks elecampane or gleaming blue-daisy and sets it down by the roadside shrines of gods or upon the statues themselves, as soon as he sees them, gathering sometimes, too, fair lupins, or else the gold-flower and lilies that fade upon the tombstones of the dead, and salsify with its great-beard, and modest cyclamens and garden-cress, which men call the garland of the Netherworld Captain.

Before the very eyes of the reader the colourful meadow is turned into a huge cemetery, but the emotion is less strong than the sensuality of the scene–a fleeting moment of flower gathering. Here, the flower, a Romantic symbol *par excellence*, incorporates beauty and death at once. Was Nicander consciously introducing Romanticism or even Decadence with such passages? Probably not. Like previous Hellenistic poets, but in a higher degree, he displayed a penchant for verbal and intellectual sensationalism. Yet as the object becomes the source not of meaning but of pure sensation, as aesthetics prevail over moralism and emotion, Romantic agony gradually yields to Aestheticism, nature to artificiality, and darkness to cold, static paleness[27]. Oscar Wilde brilliantly captures the beauty of darkness in *The Picture of Dorian Gray* (Ch. 11):

> There was a horrible fascination in them all. He saw them at night, and they troubled his imagination in the day. The Renaissance knew of strange manners of poisoning–poisoning by a helmet and a lighted torch, by an embroidered glove and a jewelled fan, by a gilded pomander and by an amber chain. Dorian Gray had been poisoned by a book. There were moments when he looked on evil simply as a mode through which he could realize his conception of the beautiful.

---

27. According to the definition given by Praz (1970) 303: "Delacroix, as a painter, was fiery and dramatic; Gustave Moreau strove to be cold and static. The former painted gestures, the latter attitudes. Although far apart in artistic merit...they are highly representative of the moral atmosphere of the two periods in which they flourished–of Romanticism, with its fury of frenzied action, and of Decadence, with its sterile contemplation. The subject-matter is almost the same–voluptuous, gory exoticism. But Delacroix lives inside his subject, whereas Moreau worships his from the outside, with the result that the first is a painter, the second a decorator". It is tempting, I think, to put Apollonius or Lycophron in the place of Delacroix, and Nicander in that of Moreau.

BIBLIOGRAPHY

ABBREVIATIONS

EF=J. Clute / J. Grant (eds.). 1997. *The Encyclopedia of Fantasy*. London: Orbit.

NPEPP=A. Preminger / T.V.F. Brogan (eds.). 1993. *The New Princeton Encyclopedia of Poetry and Poetics*. Princeton, New Jersey: Princeton University Press.

RENT=D. Herman / M. Jahn / M.-L. Ryan (eds.). 2005. *Routledge Encyclopedia of Narrative Theory*. London–New York: Routledge.

EDITIONS

1. Fragments

B.: A. Bernabé (ed.). 1996. *Poetae epici Graeci. I: Testimonia et fragmenta*. Stuttgart-Leipzig: Teubner.

CA: I.U. Powell (ed.). 1925. *Collectanea Alexandrina. Reliquiae minores poetarum Graecorum aetatis Ptolemaicae 323-146 A.C., epicorum, elegiacorum, lyricorum, ethicorum, cum epimetris et indice nominum*. Oxford: Oxford University Press.

Matthews: see Matthews (1996).

Pf.: see Pfeiffer (1949).

SH: H. Lloyd-Jones / P. Parsons (eds.). 1983. *Supplementum Hellenisticum*. Indices confecit H.-G. Nesselrath. Berlin-New York: De Gruyter.

TrGF: B. Snell / R. Kannicht / S. Radt (eds.). 1971-. *Tragicorum Graecorum fragmenta*. Göttingen: Vandenhoeck & Ruprecht.

2. Texts

Apollonius of Rhodes *Argonautica*: see Vian (1974), (1993) and (1996). Scholia: C. Wendel (ed.). 1935. *Scholia in Apollonium Rhodium vetera*. Berlin: Weidmann.

Aristotle *Poetics*: R. Kassel (ed.). 1965. *Aristotelis de arte poetica liber*. Oxford: Oxford University Press.

'Longinus' *On the Sublime*: D.A. Russell (ed.). 1968. *Libellus de sublimitate Dionysio Longino fere adscriptus*. Oxford: Oxford University Press.

Lycophron *Alexandra*: see Hurst / Kolde (2008). Scholia: E. Scheer (ed.). 1958. *Scholia in Lycophronem*. Berlin: Weidmann.

Nicander: see Jacques (2002) and (2007).

Theocritus: see Gow (1952).

BIBLIOGRAPHY

(A second chronology in brackets refers to the first edition of the book, whereas the first to the edition cited in the present study.)

Abrams, M.H. 1971 [1953]. *The Mirror and the Lamp. Romantic Theory and the Critical Tradition.* Oxford: Oxford University Press.

Aguirre, M. 1990. *The Closed Space: Horror Literature and Western Symbolism.* Manchester: Manchester University Press.

Alcock, S. 1997. "The Heroic Past in a Hellenistic Present". In: P. Cartledge / P. Garnsey / E. Gruen (eds.), *Hellenistic Constructs. Essays in Culture, History, and Historiography.* Berkeley–Los Angeles: University of California Press. Pp. 20-34.

Alsen, E. (ed.). 2000. *The New Romanticism. A Collection of Critical Essays.* New York: Routledge.

Ambühl, A. 2004. "Entertaining Theseus and Heracles: The *Hecale* and the *Victoria Berenices* as a Diptych". In: M.A. Harder / R.F. Regtuit / G.C. Wakker (eds.), *Callimachus II.* Leuven: Peeters. Pp. 23-48.

— 2005. *Kinder und junge Helden. Innovative Aspekte des Umgangs mit der literarischen Tradition by Kallimachos.* Leuven: Peeters.

Argoud, G. / Guillaumin, J.-Y. (eds.). 1998. *Sciences exactes et sciences appliquées à Alexandrie (IIIe siècle av.J.-C.-Ier siècle ap.J.-C.): Actes du colloque international de Saint-Étienne (6-8 Juin 1996).* Saint-Étienne: Publications de l'Université de Saint-Étienne.

Ashfield, A. / de Bolla, P. (eds.). 1996. *The Sublime. A Reader in Eighteenth-Century Aesthetic Theory.* Cambridge: Cambridge University Press.

Asper, M. 1997. *Onomata Allotria. Zur Genese, Struktur und Funktion poetologicher Metaphern bei Kallimachos.* Stuttgart: Franz Steiner.

Attebery, B. 1992. *Strategies of Fantasy.* Bloomington: Indiana University Press.

Auerbach, E. 1953. *Mimesis: The Representation of Reality in Western Literature.* Transl. by W.R. Trask. Princeton, NJ: Princeton University Press.

Bakhtin, M.M. 1981. *The Dialogic Imagination.* Transl. by C. Emerson and M. Holmquist. Texas: University of Texas Press.

— 1984. *Rabelais and His World.* Transl. by H. Iswolsky. Bloomington: Indiana University Press.

Ballabriga, A. 1986. *Le Soleil et le Tartare. L'image mythique du monde en Grèce archaïque.* Paris: Éditions de l'École des Hautes Études en Sciences Sociales.

Barbara, S. 2006. "Le basilic de Nicandre, *Thériaques*, 396-410: caractéristiques et essai d'identification". In: Ch. Cusset (ed.), *Musa Docta. Recherches sur la poésie scientifique dans l'Antiquité.* Saint-Étienne: Presses de l'Université de Saint-Étienne. Pp. 119-153.

Bardel, R. 2005. "Spectral Traces: Ghosts in Tragic Fragments". In: F. McHardy / J. Robson / D. Harvey (eds.), *Lost Dramas in Classical Athens. Greek Tragic Fragments.* Exeter: Exeter Press. Pp. 83-112.

Barkhuizen, J.H. 1979. "The Psychological Characterization of Medea in Apollonius of Rhodes, *Argonautica* 3, 744-824". *AClass* 22, 33-48.

Barlow, S.A. 2008 [1971]. *The Imagery of Euripides.* London: Bristol Classical Press.

Baumbach, M. 2006. "Ambiguität als Stilprinzip: Vorformen literarischer Phantastik in narrativen Texten der Antike". In: M. Baumbach / N. Hömke (eds.). 2006. *Fremde Wirklichkeiten. Literarische Phantastik und antike Literatur*. Heidelberg: C. Winter. Pp. 73-107.

— / Hömke, N. (eds.). 2006. *Fremde Wirklichkeiten. Literarische Phantastik und antike Literatur*. Heidelberg: C. Winter.

Belfiore, E.S. 1992. *Tragic Pleasures. Aristotle on Plot and Emotion*. Princeton, New Jersey: Princeton University Press.

Berkowitz, G. 2004. *Semi-Public Narration in Apollonius'* Argonautica. Leuven: Peeters.

Berra, A. 2009. "*Obscuritas lycophronea*. Les témoignages anciens sur Lycophron". In: Ch. Cusset / É. Prioux (eds.), *Lycophron: éclats d'obscurité*. Saint-Étienne: Publications de l'Université de Saint-Étienne. Pp. 259-318.

Bettenworth, A. 2005. "Odysseus bei Aietes: Primäre und sekundäre Intertexte bei Apollonios Rhodios, *Argonautika* 3.210-421". In: A. Harder / M. Cuypers (eds.), *Beginning from Apollo. Studies in Apollonius Rhodius and the Argonautic Tradition*. Peeters: Leuven. Pp. 1-17.

Beye, C.R. 1982. *Epic and Romance in the* Argonautica *of Apollonius*. Carbondale and Edwardsville: Southern Illinois University Press.

von Blanckenhagen, P.H. 1975. "Der ergänzende Betrachter. Bemerkungen zu einem Aspekt hellenistischer Kunst". In: *Wandlungen: Studien zur antiken und neueren Kunst, Ernst Homann-Wedeking gewidmet*. Waldsassen–Bayern: Stiftland Verlag. Pp. 193-201.

Bomarito, G. (ed.). 2006. *Gothic Literature: A Gale Critical Companion*. Vols. 1-3. Detroit, Mich.: Thomson Gale.

Bonelli, G. 1979. *Decadentismo antico e moderno. Un confronto fra l'estetismo alessandrino e l'esperienza poetica contemporanea*. Torino: G. Giappichelli.

Booker, C. 2004. *The Seven Basic Plots*. London-New York: Continuum.

Botting, F. 2000. "In Gothic Darkly: Heterotopia, History, Culture". In: D. Punter (ed.), *A Companion to the Gothic*. Malden, MA: Blackwell. Pp. 3-14.

Boyle, A.J. 1997. *Tragic Seneca. An Essay in the Theatrical Tradition*. London–New York: Routledge.

Bremer, J.M. 1987. "Full Moon and Marriage in Apollonius' *Argonautica*". *CQ* 37, 423-426.

Brewster, S. 2000. "Seeing Things: Gothic and the Madness of Interpretation". In: D. Punter (ed.), *A Companion to the Gothic*. Malden, MA: Blackwell. Pp. 281-292.

Bruce, J.D. 1913. "Human Automata in Classical Tradition and Mediaeval Romance". *Modern Philology* 10, 511-526.

Burgess, J.S. 2001. *The Tradition of the Trojan War in Homer and the Epic Cycle*. Baltimore–London: The Johns Hopkins University Press.

Buxton, R. 1987. "Wolves and Werewolves in Greek Thought". In: J. Bremmer (ed.), *Interpretations of Greek Mythology*. Kent: Croom Helm. Pp. 60-79.

— 1994. *Imaginary Greece. The Contexts of Mythology*. Cambridge: Cambridge University Press.

— 1998. "The Myth of Talos". In: C. Atherton (ed.), *Monsters and Monstrosity in Greek and Roman Culture*. Bari: Levante (*Nottingham Classical Literature Studies* 6). Pp. 83-112.

— 2009. *Forms of Astonishment. Greek Myths of Metamorphosis*. Oxford: Oxford University Press.

Byre, C.S. 1996. "The Killing of Apsyrtus in Apollonius Rhodius' *Argonautica*". *Phoenix* 50, 3-16.

— 1997. "On the Departure from Pagasae and the Passage of the Planctae in Apollonius' *Argonautica*". *MH* 54, 106-114.

Cajani, G. 2002. "Tra Callimaco e il 'Sublime' ". In: D. Lanza (ed.), *La poetica di Aristotele e la sua storia: atti della giornata internazionale di studio organizzata dal Seminario di Greco in memoria di Viviana Cessi*. Pisa: Edizioni ETS. Pp. 69-79.

Callebat, L. 1998. "Le grotesque dans la littérature latine". In: M. Trédé / P. Hoffmann / C. Auvray-Assayas (eds.), *Le rire des anciens. Actes du colloque international (Université de Rouen, École normale supérieure, 11-13 janvier 1995)*. Paris: Presses de l'Ecole normale supérieure. Pp. 101-111.

Cameron, A. 1995. *Callimachus and His Critics*. Princeton, NJ: Princeton University Press.

Campbell, M. 1994. *A Commentary on Apollonius Rhodius* Argonautica *III 1-471*. Leiden: Brill.

Carrière, J. 1959. "En relisant le chant III des *Argonautiques*". *Euphrosyne* 2, 41-63.

Cavallaro, D. 2002. *The Gothic Vision. Three Centuries of Horror, Terror and Fear*. London-New York: Continuum.

Chauvin, C. / Cusset, C. 2008. *Lycophron* Alexandra. Paris: L'Harmattan.

Ciampa, S. 2004 "Le 'nozze crudeli' di Polissena in Licofrone (*Alex*. 323-329)". *Aevum(ant)* 4, 519-539.

Ciani, M.G. 1973. " 'Scritto con mistero.' Osservazioni sull' oscurità di Licofrone". *GIF* 4, 132-148.

Clare, R.J. 2002. *The Path of the Argo*. Cambridge: Cambridge University Press.

Clauss, J.J. 1993. *The Best of the Argonauts*. Berkeley–Los Angeles: University of California Press.

— 1997. "Conquest of the Mephistophelian Nausicaa. Medea's Role in Apollonius' Redefinition of the Epic Hero". In: J.J. Clauss / S.I. Johnston (eds.), *Medea*. Princeton, NJ: Princeton University Press. Pp. 149-177.

— 2000. "Cosmos without Imperium: The Argonautic Journey through Time". In: M.A. Harder / R.F. Regtuit / G.C. Wakker (eds.), *Apollonius Rhodius*. Leuven: Peeters. Pp. 10-32.

— 2006. "*Theriaca*: Nicander's Poem of the Earth". *SIFC* 4, 160-182.

Clayton, J. 1987. *Romantic Vision and the Novel*. Cambridge: Cambridge University Press.

Cohen J.J. (ed.). 1996. *Monster Theory: Reading Culture*. Minneapolis: University of Minnesota Press.

Conte, G.B. 2007. *The Poetry of Pathos. Studies in Virgilian Epic*. Oxford: Oxford University Press.

Crugnola, A. 1961. "La lingua poetica di Nicandro". *Acme* 14, 119-152.

Currie, B. 2005. *Pindar and the Cult of Heroes*. Oxford: Oxford University Press.

Cusset, Ch. 1998. "Les paysages dans le chant II des *Argonautiques* d'Apollonios de Rhodes". In: C. Mauduit / P. Luccioni (eds.), *Paysages et milieux naturels dans la littérature antique. Actes de la table ronde organisée au Centre d'Études et de recherches sur l'occident romain de l'université Jean Moulin, Lyon 3 (25 septembre 1997)*. Paris: De Boccard. Pp. 97-112.

— 2001a. "Le Jason d'Apollonios de Rhodes. Un personnage romanesque?". In: B. Pouderon / C. Hunzinger / D. Kasprzyk (eds.), *Les personnages du roman grec. Actes du colloque de Tours, 18-20 novembre 1999*. Lyon: Maison de l'Orient Méditerranéen Jean Pouilloux / Paris: De Boccard. Pp. 207-218.

— 2001b. "L'Italie vue d'Alexandrie. Homère revisité par Apollonios de Rhodes". *Lalies* 21, 153-163.

— 2001c. "Apollonios de Rhodes, lecteur de la tragédie classique". In: A. Billault / C. Mauduit (eds.), *Lectures antiques de la tragédie grecque. Actes de la table ronde du 25 novembre 1999*. Lyon–Paris: De Boccard. Pp. 61-76.

— 2001d. "Le bestiaire de Lycophron: Entre chien et loup". *Anthropozoologica* 33/34, 61-72.

— 2002-2003. "Tragic Elements in Lycophron's *Alexandra*". *Hermathena* 173-174, 137-153.

— 2004. "Les Argonautiques d'Apollonios de Rhodes comme itinéraire à travers la sauvagerie. D'Homère à Alexandrie, en passant par Hérodote et Xénophon ou comment l'adresse au lecteur supplée à l'insouciance de Jason". In: M.-C. Charpentier (ed.), *Les espaces du sauvage dans le monde antique*. Besançon: Presses Universitaires de France-Comté. Pp. 31-52.

— (ed.), 2006a. *Musa Docta. Recherches sur la poésie scientifique dans l'Antiquité*. Saint-Étienne: Presses de l'Université de Saint-Étienne.

— 2006b. "Les images dans la poésie scientifique alexandrine: les *Phénomènes* d'Aratos et les *Thériaques* de Nicandre". In: Ch. Cusset (ed.), *Musa Docta. Recherches sur la poésie scientifique dans l'Antiquité*. Saint-Étienne: Presses de l'Université de Saint-Étienne. Pp. 49-104.

— 2009. "L'*Alexandra* dans l'*Alexandra*: du récit spéculaire à l'œuvre potentielle". In: Ch. Cusset / É. Prioux (eds.), *Lycophron: éclats d'obscurité*. Saint-Étienne: Publications de l'Université de Saint-Étienne. Pp. 119-138.

Danek, G. 2009. "Apollonius Rhodius as an (anti-)Homeric Narrator: Time and Space in the *Argonautica*". In: J. Grethlein / A. Rengakos (eds.), *Narratology and Interpretation. The Content of Narrative Form in Ancient Literature*. Berlin–New York: De Gruyter. Pp. 275-291.

de Bolla, P. 1989. *The Discourse of the Sublime. History, Aesthetics and the Subject*. Oxford–New York: Blackwell.

— 2003. *The Education of the Eye: Painting, Landscape, and Architecture in Eighteenth-Century Britain*. Stanford University Press: Stanford, California.

Delage, E. 1930. *La géographie dans les* Argonautiques *d'Apollonios de Rhodes*. Bordeaux: Feret et Fils.

de Paz, A. 2000. "Innovation and Modernity". In: M. Brown (ed.), *The Cambridge History of Literary Criticism. V.5: Romanticism*. Cambridge: Cambridge University Press. Pp. 29-48.

de Stefani, C. 2006. "La poesia didascalica di Nicandro: un modello prosastico?". In: L. Cristante (ed.), *Incontri triestini di filologia classica 2005-2006*. Trieste: Edizioni Universitá di Trieste. Pp. 55-72.

Devereux, G. 1978-1979. "Achilles' 'suicide' in the *Iliad*". *Helios* 6, 3-15.

Dickie, M. 1990. "Talos Bewitched. Magic, Atomic Theory and Paradoxography in Apollonius *Argonautica* 4.1638-88". In: F. Cairns / M. Heath (eds.), *Papers of the Leeds International Latin Seminar* 6. Leeds: Francis Cairns Publications. Pp. 267-296.

Dijkstra, B. 1986. *Idols of Perversity. Fantasies of Feminine Evil in Fin-de-Siècle Culture*. New York–Oxford: Oxford University Press.

Dodds, E.R. 1951. *The Greeks and the Irrational*. Berkeley–Los Angeles: University of California Press.

Doody, M.A. 1977. "Deserts, Ruins and Troubled Waters: Female Dreams in Fiction and the Development of the Gothic Novel". *Genre* 10, 529-572.

Drakakis, J. / Townshend, D. (eds.). 2008. *Gothic Shakespeares*. New York: Routledge.

Dufner, C.M., 1988. *The* Odyssey *in the* Argonautica*: Reminiscence, Revision, Reconstruction*. Diss. Princeton.

Durbec, J. 2006a. "Les avatars d'une formule Indo-Européenne: De la mort des dragons et de quelques autres monstres chez les poètes hellénistiques". *PP* 61, 161-175.

— 2006b. "Lycophron, *Alexandra* 1099-1119: la mort d'Agamemnon et de Cassandre (Étude littéraire de la réécriture des tragiques chez Lycophron II)". *Θεατρογραφίες* 14, 6-14.

— 2008. "Several Deaths in Apollonius Rhodius' *Argonautica*". *Myrtia* 23, 53-73.

— 2009. "Ajax et le naufrage de la flotte grecque: L'*Alexandra* de Lycophron, v. 365-416". *PP* 365, 128-136.

— forthcoming. "L'*Alexandra* de Lycophron entre prophétie et eschatologie indoeuropéenne". In: *Mélanges en l'honneur du Professeur Gilles Dorival*. Aix-en-Provence: Presses Universitaires de Provence.

Dyck, A.R. 1989. "On the Way from Colchis to Corinth: Medea in Book 4 of the *Argonautica*". *Hermes* 117, 455-470.

Easterling, P. 2008. "Theatrical Furies: Thoughts on *Eumenides*". In: M. Revermann / P. Wilson (eds.). *Performance, Iconography, Reception. Studies in Honour of Oliver Taplin*. Oxford: Oxford University Press. Pp. 219-236.

Eco, U. 2007. *On Ugliness*. Transl. by A. McEwen. New York: Rizzoli.

Effe, B. 1977. *Dichtung und Lehre. Untersuchungen zur Typologie des antiken Lehrgedichts*. München: C.H. Beck.

Elliger, W. 1975. *Die Darstellung der Landschaft in der griechischen Dichtung*. Berlin: De Gruyter.

Endsjø, D.Ø. 1997. "Placing the Unplaceable: The Making of Apollonius' Argonautic Geography". *GRBS* 38, 373-385.

Everett, G. 1991. " 'You'll Not Let Me Speak': Engagement and Detachment in Browning's Monologues". *Victorian Literature and Culture* 19, 123-142.

Fakas, Ch. 2001. *Der hellenistische Hesiod. Arats* Phainomena *und die Tradition der antiken Lehrepik*. Wiesbaden: Dr. Ludwig Reichert Verlag.

Fantuzzi, M. 2000. "Theocritus and the Demythologizing of Poetry". In: M. Depew / D. Obbink (eds.), *Matrices of Genre: Authors, Canons, and Society*. Cambridge, Mass.: Harvard University Press. Pp. 131-151.

— / Hunter, R. 2004. *Tradition and Innovation in Hellenistic Poetry*. Cambridge: Cambridge University Press.

BIBLIOGRAPHY 273

— / Papanghelis, Th.D. (eds.). 2006. *Brill's Companion to Greek and Latin Pastoral*. Leiden: Brill.
— 2008. "Which Magic? Apollonius' *Argonautica* and the Different Narrative Roles of Medea as a Sorceress in Love". In: Th.D. Papanghelis / A. Rengakos (eds.), *Brill's Companion to Apollonius Rhodius*. Second, Revised Edition. Leiden: Brill. Pp. 287-310.
Feeney, D.C. 1991. *The Gods in Epic. Poets and Critics of the Classical Tradition*. Oxford: Oxford University Press.
Ferguson, F. 1992. *Solitude and the Sublime. Romanticism and the Aesthetics of Individuation*. New York–London: Routledge.
Finkelberg, M. 1998. *The Birth of Literary Fiction in Ancient Greece*. Oxford: Oxford University Press.
Forbes Irving, P.M.C. 1990. *Metamorphosis in Greek Myths*. Oxford: Oxford University Press.
Fountoulakis, A. 1998. "On the Literary Genre of Lycophron's *Alexandra*". *AAntHung* 38, 291-295.
Fowler, B.H. 1989. *The Hellenistic Aesthetic*. Madison, Wis.: University of Wisconsin Press.
Fowler, D. 2000. "The Didactic Plot". In: M. Depew / D. Obbink (eds.), *Matrices of Genre: Authors, Canons, and Society*. Cambridge, Mass.: Harvard University Press. Pp. 205-217.
Francese, Ch. 2008. "L'érotisme dans les *Erotica Pathémata*". In: A. Zucker (ed.), *Littérature et érotisme dans les* Passions d'amour *de Parthénios de Nicée*. Grenoble: Jérôme Millon. Pp. 163-173.
Fraser, P.M. 1972. *Ptolemaic Alexandria*. Oxford: Clarendon Press.
Fuhrer, T. 1992. *Die Auseinandersetzung mit den Chorlyrikern in den Epinikien des Kallimachos*. Basel–Kassel: F. Reinhardt.
Fuhrmann, M. 1973. *Einführung in die antike Dichtungstheorie*. Darmstadt: Wissenschaftliche Buchgesellschaft.
Fusillo, M. 1984. "L'*Alessandra* di Licofrone: Racconto epico e discorso 'drammatico'". *ASNP* 14.2, 495-525.
— 1985. *Il tempo delle* Argonautiche. *Un analisi del racconto in Apollonio Rodio*. Roma: Edizioni dell' Ateneo.
— / Hurst, A. / Paduano, G. 1991. *Licofrone* Alessandra. Milano: Guerini.
— 1994. "El sueño de Medea". *Revista de Occidente* 158/159, 92-102.
— 2008. "Apollonius Rhodius as 'Inventor' of the Interior Monologue". In: Th.D. Papanghelis / A. Rengakos (eds.), *Brill's Companion to Apollonius Rhodius*. Second, Revised Edition. Leiden: Brill. Pp. 147-166.
Gamer, M. 2004. *Romanticism and the Gothic. Genre, Reception, and Canon Formation*. Cambridge: Cambridge University Press.
Gelzer, T. 1993. "Transformations". In: A.W. Bulloch / E.S. Gruen / A.A. Long / A. Stewart (eds.), *Images and Ideologies. Self-Definition in the Hellenistic World*. Berkeley–Los Angeles: University of California Press. Pp. 130-151.
Gigante Lanzara, V. 1995. "L'impiego del mito e la dimensione del favoloso negli inni di Callimaco". *Maia* 47, 167-174.
— 2000. *Licofrone* Alessandra. Milano: Rizzoli.
— 2003. "Le vie del mare: Eroi e città nei vaticini di Cassandra". *PP* 58, 12-60.

Gill, C. / Wiseman, T.P. (eds.). 1993. *Lies and Fiction in the Ancient World*. Austin: University of Texas Press.

Gleckner, R.F. / Enscoe, G.E. (eds.). 1962. *Romanticism. Points of View*. Englewood Cliffs, N.J.: Prentice Hall.

Glei, R. 2008. "Outlines of Apollonian Scholarship 1955-1999". In: Th.D. Papanghelis / A. Rengakos (eds.), *Brill's Companion to Apollonius Rhodius*. Second, Revised Edition. Leiden: Brill. Pp. 1-28.

Goellnicht, D. 1984. *The Poet-Physician: Keats and Medical Science*. Pittsburgh: University of Pittsburgh Press.

Goldhill, S. 1991. *The Poet's Voice*. Cambridge: Cambridge University Press.

Gow, A.S.F. 1952. *Theocritus:* Vol. 1. *Introduction, Text, and Translation*. Vol. 2. *Commentary, Appendix, Indexes and Plates*. Cambridge: Cambridge University Press.

— / Scholfield, A.F. 1997 [1953]. *Nicander. The Poems and Poetical Fragments*. London: Bristol Classical Press.

Graver, B.E. 2005. "Classical Inheritances". In: N. Roe (ed.), *Romanticism*. Oxford: Oxford University Press. Pp. 38-48.

Green P. 1997a. " 'These Fragments Have I Shored against my Ruins': Apollonios Rhodios and the Social Revalidation of Myth for a New Age". In: P. Cartledge / P. Garnsey / E. Gruen (eds.), *Hellenistic Constructs. Essays in Culture, History, and Historiography*. Berkeley–Los Angeles: University of California Press. Pp. 35-71.

— 1997b. *The Argonautika: The Story of Jason and the Quest for the Golden Fleece*. Berkeley–Los Angeles: University of California Press.

Griffin, A.H.F. 1986. "Erysichthon: Ovid's Giant". *G&R* 33, 55-63.

Griffin, J. 1977. "The Epic Cycle and the Uniqueness of Homer". *JHS* 97, 39-53.

Gutzwiller, K. 1992. "Callimachus' *Lock of Berenice*: Fantasy, Romance, and Propaganda". *AJPh* 113, 359-385.

— 2007. *A Guide to Hellenistic Literature*. Malden, MA: Blackwell.

Halliwell, S. 1998 [1986]. *Aristotle's* Poetics. Chicago: The University of Chicago Press.

— 2002. *The Aesthetics of Mimesis. Ancient Texts and Modern Problems*. Princeton: Princeton University Press.

Halperin, D.M. 1983. *Before Pastoral. Theocritus and the Ancient Tradition of Bucolic Poetry*. New Haven: Yale University Press.

Hamilton, J.T. 2003. *Soliciting Darkness. Pindar, Obscurity, and the Classical Tradition*. Cambridge, MA: Harvard University Press.

Händel, P. 1954. *Beobachtungen zur epischen Technik des Apollonios Rhodios*. München: C.H. Beck.

Harder, M.A. 1988. "Callimachus and the Muses: Some Aspects of Narrative Technique in *Aetia* 1-2". *Prometheus* 14, 1-14.

— 1994. "Travel Descriptions in the *Argonautica* of Apollonius Rhodius". In: Z. von Martels (ed.), *Travel Fact and Travel Fiction. Studies on Fiction, Literary Tradition, Scholarly Discovery and Observation in Travel Writing*. Leiden: Brill. Pp. 16-29.

— 2002. "Intertextuality in Callimachus' *Aetia*". In: *Callimaque*. Vandœuvres–Genève: Fondation Hardt. Pp. 189-223.

— / MacDonald, A.A. / Reinink, G.J. (eds.). 2007. *Calliope's Classroom. Studies in Didactic Poetry from Antiquity to the Renaissance*. Leuven: Peeters.

— / Regtuit, R.F. / Wakker G.C. (eds.). 2009. *Nature and Science in Hellenistic Poetry*. Leuven–Paris–Walpole, MA: Peeters.

Hardie, P. 2002. *Ovid's Poetics of Illusion*. Cambridge: Cambridge University Press.

Harpham, G.G. 2006 [1982]. *On the Grotesque. Strategies of Contradiction in Art and Literature*. Aurora, CO: The Davies Group.

Harrauer, C. 2004. "Gewaltig aber in seiner verderblichen Grausamkeit ist Aietes". *AAntHung* 44, 171-183.

Hassig, D. (ed.). 2000. *The Mark of the Beast*. New York–London: Routledge.

Hatzimichali, M. 2009. "Poetry, Science and Scholarship: The Rise and Fall of Nicander of Colophon". In: M.A. Harder / R.F. Regtuit / G.C. Wakker (eds.). 2009. *Nature and Science in Hellenistic Poetry*. Leuven–Paris–Walpole, MA: Peeters. Pp. 19-40.

Heiland, D. 2004. *Gothic and Gender. An Introduction*. Malden, MA: Blackwell.

Heiserman, A.R. 1977. *The Novel Before the Novel. Essays and Discussions about the Beginnings of Prose Fiction in the West*. Chicago–London: University of Chicago Press.

Henrichs, A. 1993. "Response". In: A.W. Bulloch / E.S. Gruen / A.A. Long / A. Stewart (eds.), *Images and Ideologies. Self-Definition in the Hellenistic World*. Berkeley–Los Angeles: University of California Press. Pp. 171-195.

Hitch, S. 2012. "Hero Cult in Apollonius Rhodius". In: M.A. Harder / R.F. Regtuit / G.C. Wakker (eds.), *Gods and Religion in Hellenistic Poetry*. Leuven: Peeters. Pp. 131-162.

Hobby, B. (ed.). 2009. *The Grotesque*. Edited with an Introduction by Harold Bloom. New York: Bloom's Literary Criticism.

Hogle, J.E. (ed.). 2002. *The Cambridge Companion to Gothic Fiction*. Cambridge: Cambridge University Press.

Holmes, B. 2010. *The Symptom and the Subject. The Emergence of the Physical Body in Ancient Greece*. Princeton–Oxford: Princeton University Press.

Holmes, R. 2008. *The Age of Wonder. How the Romantic Generation Discovered the Beauty and Terror of Science*. London: Harper Press.

Hölscher, U. 1988. *Die Odyssee: Ein Epos zwischen Märchen und Roman*. München: C.H. Beck.

Holzinger, C. von. 1895. *Lycophron's* Alexandra. Leipzig: Teubner.

Horowski, J. 1973. "Le folklore dans les Idylles de Théocrite". *Eos* 61, 187-212.

Hume, K. 1984. *Fantasy and Mimesis. Responses to Reality in Western Literature*. New York–London: Methuen.

Hume, R. 1969. "Gothic Versus Romantic: A Revaluation of the Gothic Novel". *PMLA* 84, 282-290.

Hunter, R.L. 1987. "Medea's Flight: The Fourth Book of the *Argonautica*". *CQ* 37, 129-139.

— 1989. *Apollonius of Rhodes*. Argonautica *Book III*. Cambridge: Cambridge University Press.

— 1993. *The* Argonautica *of Apollonius: Literary Studies*. Cambridge: Cambridge University Press.

— 2005. "The Hesiodic *Catalogue* and Hellenistic Poetry". In: R. Hunter (ed.), *The Hesiodic* Catalogue of Women. *Constructions and Reconstructions*. Cambridge: Cambridge University Press. Pp. 239-265.

— 2008a [1995]. "The Divine and Human Map of the *Argonautica*". Repr. in R. Hunter, *On Coming After. Part 1: Hellenistic Poetry and its Reception.* Berlin: De Gruyter. Pp. 257-277.

— 2008b [2001]. "On Coming After". Repr. in R. Hunter, *On Coming After. Part 1: Hellenistic Poetry and its Reception.* Berlin: De Gruyter. Pp. 8-26.

— 2008c. "The Reputation of Callimachus". In: R. Hunter, *On Coming After. Part 1: Hellenistic Poetry and its Reception.* Berlin: De Gruyter. Pp. 537-558.

— 2009. *Critical Moments in Classical Literature: Studies in the Ancient View of Literature and its Uses.* Cambridge: Cambridge University Press.

Hurley, K. 1996. *The Gothic Body. Sexuality, Materialism, and Degeneration at the* Fin de Siècle. Cambridge: Cambridge University Press.

— 2007. "Abject and Grotesque". In: C. Spooner / E. McEvoy (eds.), *The Routledge Companion to Gothic.* New York: Routledge. Pp. 137-146.

Hurst, A. / Paidi, F. 2004. *Λυκόφρονος* Ἀλεξάνδρα. Athens: Στιγμή.

— / Kolde, A. 2008. *Lycophron* Alexandra. Texte établi, traduit et annoté par A.H. en collaboration avec A. Kolde. Paris: Les belles lettres.

— 2009. "Étincelles dans l' ombre?". In: Ch. Cusset / É. Prioux (eds.), *Lycophron: éclats d'obscurité.* Saint-Étienne: Publications de l'Université de Saint-Étienne. Pp. 195-208.

Hutchinson, G.O. 2003. "The *Aetia*: Callimachus' Poem of Knowledge". *ZPE* 145, 47-59.

Innes, D.C. 1995. "Longinus, Sublimity and the Low Emotions". In: D. Innes / H. Hine / C. Pelling (eds.), *Ethics and Rhetoric.* Oxford: Oxford University Press. Pp. 323-333.

Irby-Massie, G.L. / Keyser, P.T. (eds.). 2002. *Greek Science of the Hellenistic Era: A Sourcebook.* London–New York: Routledge.

Jackson, N. 2008. *Science and Sensation in Romantic Poetry.* Cambridge: Cambridge University Press.

Jackson, R. 1981. *Fantasy: The Literature of Subversion.* London–New York: Routledge.

Jacobs, C. 1985. "On Looking at Shelley's Medusa". *Yale French Studies* 69, 163-179.

Jacques, J.-M. 2002. *Nicandre. Les Thériaques.* Paris: Les belles lettres.

— 2007. *Nicandre. Les Alexipharmaques.* Paris: Les belles lettres.

Jakob, D. 1997. "Aristoteles über die Einheit der Zeit in der Tragödie: zu Poetik 1449b 9-16". In: H.-Ch. Günther / A. Rengakos (eds.), *Beiträge zur antiken Philosophie: Festschrift für Wolfgang Kullmann.* Stuttgart: Franz Steiner. Pp. 245-253.

Janko, R. 1986. "The Shield of Heracles and the Legend of Cycnus". *CQ* 36, 38-59.

Johnston S.I. 1999. *Restless Dead. Encounters between the Living and the Dead in Ancient Greece.* Berkeley–Los Angeles: University of California Press.

Kambylis, A. 1965. *Die Dichterweihe und ihre Symbolik.* Heidelberg: C. Winter.

Kayser, W. 1963. *The Grotesque in Art and Literature.* Transl. by U. Weisstein. Bloomington: Indiana University Press.

Kegel-Brinkgreve, E. 1990. *The Echoing Woods. Bucolic and Pastoral from Theocritus to Wordsworth.* Amsterdam: J.C. Gieben.

Ker, W.P. 1908 [1896]. *Epic and Romance. Essays on Medieval Literature.* London: Macmillan.

Kessels, A.H.M. 1982. "Dreams in Apollonius' *Argonautica*". In: J. den Boeft / A.H.M. Kessels (eds.). *Actus. Studies in Honour of H.L.W. Nelson*. Utrecht: Instituut voor Klassieke Talen. Pp. 155-173.

Klooster, J.J.H. 2007. "Apollonius of Rhodes". In: I.J.F. de Jong / R. Nünlist (eds.), *Time in Ancient Greek Literature*. Leiden: Brill. Pp. 63-80.

Kloss, G. 2006. "Mythos und Realität. Paradoxe Phantastik in antiken Texten". In: M. Baumbach / N. Hömke (eds.). *Fremde Wirklichkeiten. Literarische Phantastik und antike Literatur*. Heidelberg: C. Winter. Pp. 143-159.

Knapp, S. 1985. *Personification and the Sublime: Milton to Coleridge*. Cambridge, Mass.: Harvard University Press.

Knight, V. 1991. "Apollonius, *Argonautica* 4.167-70 and Euripides' *Medea*". *CQ* 41, 248-250.

— 1995. *The Renewal of Epic. Responses to Homer in the Argonautica of Apollonius*. Leiden: Brill.

Knox, B. 1979. *Word and Action: Essays on the Ancient Theater*. Baltimore–London: The Johns Hopkins University Press.

Köhnken, A. 1965. *Apollonios Rhodios und Theokrit. Die Hylas- und Amykosgeschichten beider Dichter und die Frage der Priorität*. Göttingen: Vandenhoeck & Ruprecht.

Kolde, A. 2009. "Parodie et ironie chez Lycophron: un mode de dialogue avec la tradition?". In: Ch. Cusset / É. Prioux (eds.), *Lycophron: éclats d'obscurité*. Saint-Étienne: Publications de l'Université de Saint-Étienne. Pp. 39-57.

Konstan, D. 1991. "The Death of Argus, or What Stories Do: Audience Response in Ancient Fiction and Theory". *Helios* 18, 15-30.

— 1994. *Sexual Symmetry. Love in the Ancient Novel and Related Genres*. Princeton, NJ: Princeton University Press.

— forthcoming. "Propping Up Greek Tragedy: The Right Use of *Opsis*". In: G. Harrison / V. Liapis (eds.), *Performance in Greek and Roman Theatre*. Leiden: Brill.

— forthcoming. "A Senecan Theory of Drama?". In: R. López Gregoris (ed.), *Actas de las Jornadas Internacionales de Teatro Romano*.

Kossaifi, C. 2009. "Poétique messager. Quelques remarques sur l'incipit et l'epilogue de l'*Alexandra* de Lycophron". In: Ch. Cusset / É. Prioux (eds.), *Lycophron: éclats d'obscurité*. Saint-Étienne: Publications de l'Université de Saint-Étienne. Pp. 141-159.

Krevans, N. 1993. "Fighting against Antimachus: The *Lyde* and the *Aetia* Reconsidered". In: M.A. Harder / R.F. Regtuit / G.C. Wakker (eds.), *Callimachus*. Groningen: Egbert Forsten. Pp. 149-160.

Kristeva, J. 1982. *Powers of Horror: An Essay on Abjection*. Transl. by L.S. Roudiez. New York: Columbia University Press.

Kucich, G. 2005. "Romance". In: N. Roe (ed.), *Romanticism*. Oxford: Oxford University Press. Pp. 463-479.

Kullmann, W. 1992. *Homerische Motive: Beiträge zur Entstehung, Eigenart und Wirkung von Ilias und Odyssee*. Stuttgart: Franz Steiner.

Kyriakou, P. 1994. "Empedoclean Echoes in Apollonius Rhodius' *Argonautica*". *Hermes* 122, 309-319.

— 1995. "Katabasis and the Underworld in the *Argonautica* of Apollonius Rhodius". *Philologus* 139, 256-264.

Lambin, G. 2005. *L' Alexandra de Lycophron*. Rennes: Presses Universitaires de Rennes.

Leitao, D.D. 2003. "Adolescent Hair-Growing and Hair-Cutting Rituals in Ancient Greece: A Sociological Approach". In: D.B. Dodd / Ch.A. Faraone (eds.), *Initiation in Ancient Greek Rituals and Narratives. New Critical Perspectives*. London-New York: Routledge. Pp. 109-129.

Levin, D.N. 1971. *Apollonius' Argonautica Re-Examined*. Leiden: Brill.

Lightfoot, J.L. 1999. *Parthenius of Nicaea*. Oxford: Oxford University Press.

— 2007. *The Sibylline Oracles*. With Introduction, Translation and Commentary on the First and Second Books. Oxford: Oxford University Press.

Livrea, E. 1987. "L' episodio libico nel quarto libro delle 'Argonautiche' di Apollonio Rodio". *QAL* 12, 175-190.

Loehr, J. 1996. *Ovids Mehrfacherklärungen in der Tradition aitiologischen Dichtens*. Stuttgart-Leipzig: Teubner.

Looijenga, A.R. 2009. "Unrolling the *Alexandra*: The Allusive Messenger-Speech of Lycophron's Prologue and Epilogue". In: Ch. Cusset / É. Prioux (eds.), *Lycophron: éclats d'obscurité*. Saint-Étienne: Publications de l'Université de Saint-Étienne. Pp. 59-80.

Lowe, N.J. 2004. "Lycophron". In: I.J.F. de Jong / R. Nünlist / A. Bowie (eds.), *Narrators, Narratees, and Narratives in Ancient Greek Literature*. Leiden: Brill. Pp. 307-314.

MacAlister, S. 1996. *Dreams and Suicides. The Greek Novel from Antiquity to the Byzantine Empire*. London–New York: Routledge.

Magnelli, E. 2006a. "Nicander's Chronology. A Literary Approach". In: M.A. Harder / R.F. Regtuit / G.C. Wakker (eds.), *Beyond the Canon*. Leuven: Peeters. Pp. 185-204.

— 2006b. "La chiusa degli *Alexipharmaca* e la struttura dei due poemi iologici di Nicandro". In: Ch. Cusset (ed.), *Musa Docta. Recherches sur la poésie scientifique dans l'Antiquité*. Saint-Étienne: Presses de l'Université de Saint-Étienne. Pp. 105-118.

— 2010. "Nicander". In: J.J. Clauss / M. Cuypers (eds.), *A Companion to Hellenistic Literature*. Malden, MA: Wiley-Blackwell. Pp. 211-223.

Manakidou, F. 1993. *Beschreibung von Kunstwerken in der hellenistischen Dichtung*. Stuttgart: Teubner.

Manieri, A. 1998. *L'immagine poetica nella teoria degli antichi. Phantasia ed enargeia*. Pisa-Roma: Istituti editoriali e poligrafici internazionali.

Mans, M.J. 1984. "The Macabre in Seneca's Tragedies". *AClass* 27, 19-35.

Mari, M. 2009. "Cassandra e le altre: riti di donne nell'*Alessandra* di Licofrone". In: Ch. Cusset / É. Prioux (eds.), *Lycophron: éclats d'obscurité*. Saint-Étienne: Publications de l'Université de Saint-Étienne. Pp. 405-440.

Martin, R. 2005. "Pulp Epic: The *Catalogue* and the *Shield*". In: R. Hunter (ed.), *The Hesiodic Catalogue of Women. Constructions and Reconstructions*. Cambridge: Cambridge University Press. Pp. 153-175.

Matthews, R. 2002. *Fantasy. The Liberation of Imagination*. New York-London: Routledge.

Matthews, V.J. 1996. *Antimachus of Colophon*. Leiden: Brill.

Mazzoldi, S. 2001. *Cassandra, la vergine e l'indovina: identitá di un personaggio da Omero all'Ellenismo*. Pisa: Istituti editoriali e poligrafici internazionali.

McKay, K.J. 1962. *Erysichthon. A Callimachean Comedy*. Leiden: Brill.

McNelis, Ch. 2003. "Mourning Glory: Callimachus' *Hecale* and Heroic Honors". *MD* 50, 155-161.

Meijering, R. 1987. *Literary and Rhetorical Theories in Greek Scholia*. Groningen: E. Forsten.

Mellor, A.K. 2005. "Feminism". In: N. Roe (ed.), *Romanticism*. Oxford: Oxford University Press. Pp. 182-198.

Meuli, K. 1921. *Odyssee und Argonautika. Untersuchungen zur griechischen Sagengeschichte und zum Epos*. Berlin: Weidmann.

Meyer, D. 2008. "Apollonius as a Hellenistic Geographer". In: Th.D. Papanghelis / A. Rengakos (eds.), *Brill's Companion to Apollonius Rhodius*. Second, Revised Edition. Leiden: Brill. Pp. 267-285.

Miles, R. 1993. *Gothic Writing 1750-1820: A Genealogy*. Manchester–New York: Routledge.

Miller, C.R. 2006. *The Invention of Evening. Perception and Time in Romantic Poetry*. Cambridge: Cambridge University Press.

Miller, P.A. 1998. "The Bodily Grotesque in Roman Satire: Images of Sterility". *Arethusa* 31, 257-283.

Mishra, V. 1994. *The Gothic Sublime*. New York: State University of New York Press.

Mitchell, W.J.T. 1994. *Picture Theory*. Chicago: University of Chicago Press.

Modleski, T. 2008. *Loving with a Vengeance. Mass-Produced Fantasies for Women*. Second, Revised Edition. New York: Routledge.

Mooney, G.W. 1988 [1921]. *The* Alexandra *of Lycophron*. New Hampshire: Ayer Company, Publishers.

Moreau, A. 1989. "Les ambivalences de Cassandre". In: A.-F. Laurens (ed.), *Entre hommes et dieux: le convive, le héros, le prophête*. Paris: Les belles lettres. Pp. 145-167.

Mori, A. 2008. *The Politics of Apollonius Rhodius'* Argonautica. Cambridge: Cambridge University Press.

Morris, D.B. 1985. "Gothic Sublimity". *New Literary History* 16, 299-319.

Morrison, A.D. 2007. *The Narrator in Archaic Greek and Hellenistic Poetry*. Cambridge: Cambridge University Press.

Murgatroyd, P. 2007. *Mythical Monsters in Classical Literature*. London: Duckworth.

Nagy, G. 1979. *The Best of the Achaeans. Concepts of the Hero in Archaic Greek Poetry*. Baltimore–London: The Johns Hopkins University Press.

— 1990. *Pindar's Homer. The Lyric Possession of an Epic Past*. Baltimore–London: The Johns Hopkins University Press.

Neal, T. 2006. "Blood and Hunger in the *Iliad*". *CPh* 101, 15-33.

Neblung, D. 1997. *Die Gestalt der Kassandra in der antiken Literatur*. Stuttgart–Leipzig: Teubner.

Nelis, D. 2001. *Vergil's* Aeneid *and the* Argonautica *of Apollonius Rhodius*. Leeds: Francis Cairns Publications.

— 2005. "Apollonius of Rhodes". In: J.M. Foley (ed.), *A Companion to Ancient Epic*. Malden, MA: Blackwell. Pp. 353-363.

Newman, B. 1986. "Narratives of Seduction and the Seductions of Narrative: The Frame Structure of *Frankenstein*". *ELH* 53, 141-163.

Newman, J.K. 2008. "The Golden Fleece. Imperial Dream". In: Th.D. Papan-
    ghelis / A. Rengakos (eds.), *Brill's Companion to Apollonius Rhodius*. Sec-
    ond, Revised Edition. Leiden: Brill. Pp. 413-444.
Nichols, A. 2005. "Roaring Alligators and Burning Tygers: Poetry and Science
    from William Bartram to Charles Darwin". *PAPhS* 149, 304-315.
Oerlemans, O. 2002. *Romanticism and the Materiality of Nature*. Toronto: Uni-
    versity of Toronto Press.
Ogden, D. 2009. *Magic, Witchcraft and Ghosts in the Greek and Roman Worlds*.
    Oxford: Oxford University Press.
Oikonomakos, K. 1999. "Les 'Alexipharmaques' et le 'Corpus hippocratique':
    Nicandre lecteur d'Hippocrate?". *REG* 112, 238-252.
Overduin, F. 2009. "The Fearsome Shrewmouse: Pseudo-Science in Nicander's
    Theriaca?". In: M.A. Harder / R.F. Regtuit / G.C. Wakker (eds.). *Nature
    and Science in Hellenistic Poetry*. Leuven–Paris–Walpole, MA: Peeters.
    Pp. 79-93.
— 2010. *Nicander of Colophon*. Theriaca: *A Literary Commentary*. Dissertation
    Radboud Universiteit, Nijmegen.
Papadopoulou, M. 2009. "Scientific Knowledge and Poetic Skill: Colour Words
    in Nicander's *Theriaca* and *Alexipharmaca*". In: M.A. Harder / R.F. Reg-
    tuit / G.C. Wakker (eds.). *Nature and Science in Hellenistic Poetry*. Leu-
    ven–Paris–Walpole, MA: Peeters. Pp. 95-119.
Papadopoulou, Th. 1997. "The Presentation of the Inner Self: Euripides' *Medea*
    1021-55 and Apollonius Rhodius' *Argonautica* 3, 772-801". *Mnemosyne*
    50, 641-664.
Papanghelis, Th.D. 1989. "About the Hour of Noon: Ovid *Amores* 1.5". *Mne-
    mosyne* 42, 54-61.
— 1994. *Η ποιητική των Ρωμαίων «Νεωτέρων»*. Athens: Μορφωτικό
    Ίδρυμα Εθνικής Τραπέζης.
Parsons, P. 1993. "Identities in Diversity". In: A.W. Bulloch / E.S. Gruen /
    A.A. Long / A. Stewart (eds.), *Images and Ideologies. Self-Definition in
    the Hellenistic World*. Berkeley–Los Angeles: University of California
    Press. Pp. 152-170.
Pascoe, J. 2005. "Romantic Drama". In: N. Roe (ed.), *Romanticism*. Oxford:
    Oxford University Press. Pp. 409-425.
Payne, M. 2007. *Theocritus and the Invention of Fiction*. Cambridge: Cam-
    bridge University Press.
Peckham, M. 1951. "Towards a Theory of Romanticism". *PMLA* 66, 5-23.
Petrovic, I. 2006. "Delusions of Grandeur: Homer, Zeus and the Telchines in
    Callimachus' *Reply* (*Aitia* Fr. 1) and *Iambus* 6". *A&A* 52, 16-41.
Pfeiffer, R. 1949. *Callimachus:* Vol. 1. *Fragmenta*. Oxford.
— 1955. "The Future of Studies in the Field of Hellenistic Poetry". *JHS* 75,
    69-73.
— 1968. *History of Classical Scholarship. From the Beginnings to the End of
    the Hellenistic Age*. Oxford: Oxford University Press.
Phinney, E. 1967. "Narrative Unity in the *Argonautica*, the Medea-Jason
    Romance". *TAPhA* 98, 327-341.
Plantinga, M. 2000. "The Supplication Motif in Apollonius Rhodius' *Argonau-
    tica*". In: M.A. Harder / R.F. Regtuit / G.C. Wakker (eds.), *Apollonius
    Rhodius*. Leuven: Peeters. Pp. 105-128.

Plastira-Valkanou, M. 1999. "Alcmena's Dream in Moschus' *Megara*: An Interpretation in the Light of Ancient ὀνειροκρισία". *Habis* 30, 127-134.

Pollitt, J.J. 1986. *Art in the Hellenistic Age*. Cambridge: Cambridge University Press.

Porter, J.R. 1990. "Tiptoeing through the Corpses: Euripides' *Electra*, Apollonius, and the Bouphonia". *GRBS* 31, 255-280.

Potolsky, M. 2006. *Mimesis*. New York–London: Routledge.

Praz, M. 1970 [1933]. *The Romantic Agony*. Oxford: Oxford University Press.

Prioux, É. 2007. *Regards alexandrins. Histoire et théorie des arts dans l'épigramme Hellénistique*. Leuven: Peeters.

Punter, D. (ed.). 2000. *A Companion to the Gothic*. Malden, MA: Blackwell.

— 2007. "The Uncanny". In: C. Spooner / E. McEvoy (eds.), *The Routledge Companion to Gothic*. New York: Routledge. Pp. 129-136.

Quint, D. 1993. *Epic and Empire. Politics and Generic Form from Virgil to Milton*. Princeton: Princeton University Press.

Rabinowitz, N.S. 1993. *Anxiety Veiled. Euripides and the Traffic in Women*. Ithaca–London: Cornell University Press.

Radke, G. 2007. *Die Kindheit des Mythos. Die Erfindung der Literaturgeschichte in der Antike*. München: C.H. Beck.

Rajan, T. 2000. "Theories of Genre". In: M. Brown (ed.), *The Cambridge History of Literary Criticism. Vol. 5: Romanticism*. Cambridge: Cambridge University Press. Pp. 226-249.

Reinsch-Werner, H. 1976. *Callimachus Hesiodicus. Die Rezeption der hesiodischen Dichtung durch Kallimachos von Kyrene*. Berlin: Nikolaus Mielke Verlag.

Rengakos, A. 1994. *Apollonios Rhodios und die antike Homererklärung*. München: C.H. Beck.

Renger, A.-B. 2006. "Fremde Wirklichkeiten und phantastische Erzählungen als 'Urtendenz der Dichtung selber' (Benjamin): Homers *Odyssee* und moderne (bzw. zeitgenössische) Fantasy". In: M. Baumbach / N. Hömke (eds.), *Fremde Wirklichkeiten. Literarische Phantastik und antike Literatur*. Heidelberg: C. Winter. Pp. 109-142.

Richardson, A. 1988. *A Mental Theater: Poetic Drama and Consciousness in the Romantic Age*. Pennsylvania: The Pennsylvania State University Press.

Richardson, N.J. 2006. "Literary Criticism in the Exegetical Scholia to the *Iliad*: A Sketch". In: A. Laird (ed.), *Ancient Literary Criticism*. Oxford: Oxford University Press. Pp. 176-210.

Roberts, A.M. 2005. "Psychoanalysis". In: N. Roe (ed.), *Romanticism*. Oxford: Oxford University Press. Pp. 219-236.

Roe, N. 2005. "Introduction". In: N. Roe (ed.), *Romanticism*. Oxford: Oxford University Press. Pp. 1-12.

Rohde, E. 1960 [1914]. *Der Griechische Roman und seine Vorläufer*. Darmstadt: Wissenschaftliche Buchgesellschaft.

Ronen, R. 1986. "Space in Fiction". *Poetics Today* 7, 421-438.

Rosenmeyer, Th. 1987. "Euripides' *Hecuba*. Horror Story or Tragedy?". In: *International Meeting of Ancient Greek Drama, Delphi 8-12 April 1984, Delphi 4-25 June 1985*. Athens: European Cultural Center. Pp. 264-270.

Rosokoki, A. 1995. *Die Erigone des Eratosthenes*. Heidelberg: C. Winter.

Rossi, L.E. 2000. "La letteratura alessandrina e il rinnovamento dei generi letterari della tradizione". In: R. Pretagostini (ed.), *La letteratura ellenistica*. Roma: Quasar. Pp. 149-161.

Roth, P. 2004. "Apollonios Rhodios zwischen Homer und Hesiod: Beobachtungen zum Argonautenkatalog". In: M. Janka (ed.), *Enkyklion kepion (Rundgärtchen). Zu Poesie, Historie und Fachliteratur der Antike. Festschrift für Hans Gärtner*. München–Leipzig: K.G. Saur. Pp. 43-54.

Royle, N. 2003. *The Uncanny*. Manchester: Manchester University Press.

Rubio, S. 1992. *Geography and the Representation of Space in the Argonautica of Apollonios of Rhodes*. Diss. San Diego.

Rudd, N. 1981. "Romantic Love in Classical Times?". *Ramus* 10, 140-155.

Ruegg, M. 1979. "Metaphor and Metonymy: The Logic of Structuralist Rhetoric". *Glyph* 6, 141-157.

Russo, J. / Fernandez-Galiano, M. / Heubeck, A. (eds.). 1992. *A Commentary on Homer's* Odyssey. *Vol. 3: Books 17-24*. Oxford: Oxford University Press.

Rynearson, N. 2009. "A Callimachean Case of Lovesickness: Magic, Disease and Desire in *Aetia* frr. 67-75 Pf.". *AJPh* 130, 341-365.

Said, S. 1998. "Tombes épiques d'Homère à Apollonios". In: S. Marchegay / M.-Th. Le Dinahet / J.-F. Salles (eds.). *Nécropoles et pouvoir: idéologies, pratiques et interprétations. Actes du colloque "Théories de la nécropole antique", Lyon 21-25 janvier 1995*. Paris: De Boccard. Pp. 9-20.

Sandner, D. (ed.). 2004. *Fantastic Literature. A Critical Reader*. Westport, Connecticut–London: Praeger Publishers.

Scheer, T.S. 2003. "The Past in a Hellenistic Present: Myth and Local Tradition". In: A. Erskine (ed.), *A Companion to the Hellenistic World*. Malden, MA: Blackwell. Pp. 216-231.

Schein, S. 1982. "The Cassandra Scene in Aeschylus' *Agamemnon*". *G&R* 29, 11-16.

Scherer, B. 2006. *Mythos, Katalog und Prophezeiung. Studien zu den Argonautika des Apollonios Rhodios*. Stuttgart: Franz Steiner.

Scott, G. 1996. "Shelley, Medusa, and the Perils of Ekphrasis". In: F. Burwick / J. Klein (eds.), *The Romantic Imagination: Literature and Art in England and Germany*. Amsterdam–Atlanta: Rodopi. Pp. 315-322.

Seaford, R. 1987. "The Tragic Wedding". *JHS* 107, 106-130.

Segal, Ch. 2005. "Il corpo e l'io nelle *Metamorfosi* di Ovidio". Transl. by L. Koch. In: A. Barchiesi, *Ovidio. Metamorfosi Vol. 1: Libri I-II*. Milano: Fondazione Lorenzo Valla-Arnoldo Mondadori editore. Pp. xv-ci.

Sens, A. 2010. "Hellenistic Tragedy and Lycophron's *Alexandra*". In: J.J. Clauss / M. Cuypers (eds.), *A Companion to Hellenistic Literature*. Malden, MA: Wiley–Blackwell. Pp. 297-316.

Shaw, Ph. 2006. *The Sublime*. London–New York: Routledge.

Siebers, T. 1984. *The Romantic Fantastic*. Ithaca–London: Cornell University Press.

Silk, M. 1974. *Interaction in Poetic Imagery: With Special Reference to Early Greek Poetry*. Cambridge: Cambridge University Press.

— 2004. "Shakespeare and Greek Tragedy: Strange Relationship". In: C. Martindale / A.B. Taylor (eds.), *Shakespeare and the Classics*. Cambridge: Cambridge University Press. Pp. 241-258.

Sistakou, E. 2001. "Παράδοση και νεοτερικότητα στον κατάλογο των Αργοναυτών (Απολλ. Ρόδ. *Αργ.* 1.23-233)". *Hellenica* 51, 231-264.
— 2008a. *Reconstructing the Epic. Cross-Readings of the Trojan Myth in Hellenistic Poetry.* Leuven: Peeters.
— 2008b. "Beyond the *Argonautica*: In Search of Apollonius' *Ktisis* Poems". In: Th.D. Papanghelis / A. Rengakos (eds.), *Brill's Companion to Apollonius Rhodius.* Second, Revised Edition. Leiden: Brill. Pp. 311-340.
— 2009a. "Fragments of an Imaginary Past. Strategies of Mythical Narration in Apollonius' *Argonautica* and Callimachus' *Aitia*". *RFIC* 137, 380-401.
— 2009b. "Breaking the Name Codes in Lycophron's *Alexandra*". In: Ch. Cusset / É. Prioux (eds.), *Lycophron: éclats d'obscurité.* Saint-Étienne: Publications de l'Université de Saint-Étienne. Pp. 237-257.
Smith, A. 2000. *Gothic Radicalism. Literature, Philosophy and Psychoanalysis in the Nineteenth Century.* Hampshire–New York: Macmillan Press & St. Martin's Press.
Spatafora, G. 2005. "Riflessioni sull'arte poetica di Nicandro". *GIF* 57 (2), 231-262.
Spooner, C. / McEvoy, E. (eds.). 2007. *The Routledge Companion to Gothic.* New York: Routledge.
Staley, G.A. 2010. *Seneca and the Idea of Tragedy.* Oxford: Oxford University Press.
Steig, M. 1970. "Defining the Grotesque: An Attempt at Synthesis". *The Journal of Aesthetics and Art Criticism* 29, 253-260.
Stephens, S.A. 2000. "Writing Epic for the Ptolemaic Court". In: M.A. Harder / R.F. Regtuit / G.C. Wakker (eds.), *Apollonius Rhodius.* Leuven: Peeters. Pp. 195-215.
— 2003. *Seeing Double. Intercultural Poetics in Ptolemaic Alexandria.* Berkeley–Los Angeles: University of California Press.
Stevens, D. 2000. *The Gothic Tradition.* Cambridge: Cambridge University Press.
Suerbaum, U. 1997. "Shakespeare und die griechische Tragödie". In: H. Flashar (ed.), *Tragödie: Idee und Transformation.* Stuttgart–Leipzig: Teubner. Pp. 122-139.
Sullivan III, C.W. (ed.). 1997. *The Dark Fantastic. Selected Essays from the Ninth International Conference on the Fantastic in the Arts.* Westport, Connecticut–London: Greenwood Press.
Šwiderek, A. 1952-1953. "La conception de la tradition populaire dans les *Aitia* de Callimaque". *Eos* 46, 49-58.
Taplin, O. 1977. *The Stagecraft of Aeschylus.* Oxford: Oxford University Press.
Thomas, R.R. 2006 [1990]. In: G. Bomarito (ed.), *Gothic Literature: A Gale Critical Companion.* Detroit, Mich.: Thomson Gale. Pp. 1.326-332.
Thomas, S. 2005. "The Fragment". In: N. Roe (ed.), *Romanticism.* Oxford: Oxford University Press. Pp. 502-520.
— 2008. *Romanticism and Visuality. Fragments, History, Spectacle.* London–New York: Routledge.
Thompson, G.R. (ed.). 1974. *The Gothic Imagination: Essays in Dark Romanticism.* Pullman, WA: Washington State University Press.
Thomson, P. 1972. *The Grotesque.* London: Methuen and Co.

Todorov, T. 1975. *The Fantastic: A Structural Approach to a Literary Genre*. Transl. by R. Howard. Ithaca: Cornell University Press.

Toohey, P. 1988. "An (Hesiodic) Danse Macabre. The Shield of Heracles". *ICS* 13, 19-35.

— 1996. *Epic Lessons. An Introduction to Ancient Didactic Poetry*. London-New York: Routledge.

— 2004. *Melancholy, Love, and Time. Boundaries of the Self in Ancient Literature*. Ann Arbor: The University of Michigan Press.

Touwaide, A. 1991. "Nicandre, de la science à la poésie. Contribution à l'exégèse de la poésie médicale grecque". *Aevum* 65, 65-101.

Trott, N. 2005. "Gothic". In: N. Roe (ed.), *Romanticism*. Oxford: Oxford University Press. Pp. 482-501.

Vian, F. (ed.). 1974. *Apollonios de Rhodes*, Argonautiques. *Tome I: Chants I-II*. Texte établi et commenté par F.V. et traduit par É. Delage. Paris: Les belles lettres.

— 1978. "ΙΗΣΩΝ ΑΜΗΧΑΝΕΩΝ". In: E. Livrea / G.A. Privitera (eds.), *Studi in onore di Anthos Ardizzoni*. Roma: Edizioni dell' Ateneo e Bizzarri. Pp. 2.1025-1041.

— 1987. "Poésie et géographie: Les Retours des Argonautes". *CRAI* 131, 249-262.

— (ed.). 1993 [1980]. *Apollonios de Rhodes*, Argonautiques. *Tome II: Chants III*. Texte établi et commenté par F.V. et traduit par É. Delage. Paris: Les belles lettres.

— (ed.). 1996 [1981]. *Apollonios de Rhodes*, Argonautiques. *Tome III: Chants IV*. Texte établi et commenté par F.V. et traduit par É. Delage et F.V. Paris: Les belles lettres.

Voisin, D. 2008. "*Dispositio* et stratégies littéraires dans les *Erotica Pathémata*". In: A. Zucker (ed.), *Littérature et érotisme dans les* Passions d'amour *de Parthénios de Nicée*. Grenoble: Jérôme Millon. Pp. 39-65.

Walde, Ch. 2001. *Antike Traumdeutung und moderne Traumforschung*. Düsseldorf: Artemis & Winkler.

Warner, M. 2002. *Fantastic Metamorphoses, Other Worlds*. Oxford: Oxford University Press.

— 2006. *Phantasmagoria. Spirit Visions, Metaphors, and Media into the Twenty-first Century*. Oxford: Oxford University Press.

Watkins, C. 1995. *How to Kill a Dragon. Aspects of Indo-European Poetics*. Oxford: Oxford University Press.

Webb, R. 1997. "Imagination and the Arousal of the Emotions in Graeco-Roman Rhetoric". In: S.M. Braund / C. Gill (eds.), *The Passions in Roman Thought and Literature*. Cambridge: Cambridge University Press. Pp. 112-127.

Webster, T.B.L. 1964. *Hellenistic Poetry and Art*. London: Methuen & Co.

Weir, D. 1995. *Decadence and the Making of Modernism*. Amherst: University of Massachusetts Press.

Weiskel, Th. 1976. *The Romantic Sublime: Studies in the Structure and Psychology of Transcendence*. Baltimore–London: The Johns Hopkins University Press.

West, M. 2005. "*Odyssey* and *Argonautica*". *CQ* 55, 39-64.

West, S. 1984. "Lycophron Italicised". *JHS* 104, 127-151.

— 2000. "Lycophron's *Alexandra*: 'Hindsight as Foresight Makes No Sense'?".
  In: M. Depew / D. Obbink (eds.), *Matrices of Genre. Authors, Canons, and
  Society*. Cambridge, Mass.–London: Harvard University Press. Pp. 153-
  166.
— 2006. "The Amphisbaena's Antecedents". *CQ* 56, 290-291.
Wheatcroft, J.H. 2000. "Classical Ideology in the Medieval Bestiary". In:
  D. Hassig (ed.), *The Mark of the Beast*. New York–London: Routledge.
  Pp. 141-154.
Wilk, S.R. 2000. *Medusa. Solving the Mystery of the Gorgon*. Oxford: Oxford
  University Press.
Williams, A. 1995. *Art of Darkness. A Poetics of Gothic*. Chicago: The Univer-
  sity of Chicago Press.
Williams, D. 1996. *Deformed Discourse. The Function of the Monster in Medi-
  aeval Thought and Literature*. Exeter: University of Exeter Press.
Williams, F. 1993. "Callimachus and the Supranormal". In: M.A. Harder /
  R.F. Regtuit / G.C. Wakker (eds.), *Callimachus*. Groningen: Egbert For-
  sten. Pp. 217-225.
Williams, M.F. 1991. *Landscape in the* Argonautica *of Apollonius Rhodius*.
  Frankfurt am Main: Peter Lang.
Wimmel, W. 1960. *Kallimachos in Rom: Die Nachfolge seines apologetischen
  Dichtens in der Augusteerzeit*. Wiesbaden: Franz Steiner.
Wolfe, G.R. 1986. *Critical Terms for Science Fiction and Fantasy: A Glossary
  and Guide to Scholarship*. Westport, Connecticut: Greenwood Press.
Wright, T. 2006 [1865]. *A History of Caricature and Grotesque in Literature
  and Art*. New York: Elibron Classics.
Zanker, G. 1981. "*Enargeia* in the Ancient Criticism of Poetry". *RhM* 124, 297-
  311.
— 1987. *Realism in Alexandrian Poetry: A Literature and its Audience*. London–Sydney: Croom Helm.
— 1996. "Pictorial Description as a Supplement for Narrative". *AJPh* 117, 411-
  423.
— 2004. *Modes of Viewing in Hellenistic Poetry and Art*. Madison: The University of Wisconsin Press.
Ziolkowski, Th. 2005. *Ovid and the Moderns*. Ithaca–London: Cornell University Press.

INDEX LOCORUM

Valerius Flaccus
 Arg. 4.423:70 n.69

Virgil
 Aen. 3.251:70 n.69

Vitruvius
 De Architectura 7.5.3-4:40

GENERAL INDEX

abject, the 45, 179-180, 247-249
Acherousia 109-110
Achilles 46, 65, 88, 157-161, 184, 187
Addison, Joseph 31
Aeschylus 39-40, 143-144, 151, 164, 171, 177, 220
Aestheticism 232-233, 263—*see also* Decadence
Agamemnon 150, 171-172
Aietes 77, 82-84, 116, 121
Aigialeia 171, 183
Aikin, John 37
Aitia-Prologue 7, 9, 13—*see also* Callimachus
aition/aitiology 57, 70, 113, 121, 167, 199, 206, 211
Ajax 146, 149-150, 164, 181
alchemy 228-232
Alexandra 133-190—*see also* Kassandra
Alexandra 48-49, 133-190, 254—*see also* Lycophron
Alexipharmaca 196-197, 209, 210, 222-226, 227, 230-231, 235, 240-241—*see also* Nicander
Alkestis 47
alter ego 45, 63
amphisbaena 220
Amykos 66
animal metonymy 176-182
animals unknown to science 124
animation 204-209
antidotes 226-233
Antigone 45-47
Antimachus 13
Apollo 109, 136, 137-138, 146, 149, 206
Apollonius Rhodius 6, 10, 17, 195, 253—*see also Argonautica*
Apsyrtos 82, 96
Aratus 16, 195, 199-200, 208
Argonautica 10, 48, 53-130, 253-254—*see also* Apollonius Rhodius

Argonauts 57, 58, 60, 62-63, 65-66, 68-70, 73-77, 83, 92, 96, 115-116, 121, 125, 129-130
Ariadne 93, 97
Aristophanes 39
Aristotle 16, 19-20, 22-23, 38, 136, 242
Asclepiades of Myrleia 35
Aspis 43-44
associative discourse 154, 166
automaton 45, 67
Bakhtin, Michail 41, 102
Barbauld, Anna Laetitia 37
Bartram, William 194, 217-218
basilisk 220
Baudelaire, Charles 155, 253
bestiary 167, 176-182, 212
blood 123, 153, 161, 163, 172, 225-226, 243
body 153, 163, 168-169, 171-172, 182, 183-187, 203, 209, 234-250
Boios 255
bougonia 219
Browning, Robert 141
Burke, Edmund 18-19, 37, 212, 238-239
Byron, Lord 140
Byronic hero 155, 157
Callimachus 6, 8-15, 16-17, 34-35, 195, 253
cannibalism 186, 216-217
Carroll, Lewis 61
catasterism 11-12
cenchrines 215-216
Chalkiope 82, 92, 116
chronotope 102, 125-126
Clashing Rocks 55-56, 74—*see also* Symplegades
Classical 5, 20-21, 31, 80, 261
clinical realism 240-242
Clute, John 33
Colchis 77, 114-116

PRINTED ON PERMANENT PAPER • IMPRIME SUR PAPIER PERMANENT • GEDRUKT OP DUURZAAM PAPIER - ISO 9706

N.V. PEETERS S.A., WAROTSTRAAT 50, B-3020 HERENT